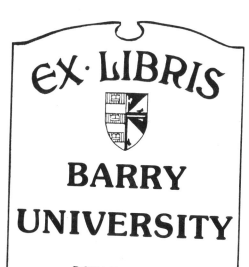

Disgrace at Gettysburg

The Arrest and Court-Martial of Brigadier General Thomas A. Rowley, USA

JOHN F. KRUMWIEDE

McFarland & Company, Inc., Publishers
Jefferson, North Carolina, and London

LIBRARY OF CONGRESS CATALOGUING-IN-PUBLICATION DATA

Krumwiede, John F.
    Disgrace at Gettysburg : the arrest and court-martial of
Brigadier General Thomas A. Rowley, USA / John F.
Krumwiede
        p.   cm.
    Includes bibliographical references and index.

    ISBN-13: 978-0-7864-2309-5
    softcover : 50# alkaline paper ∞

    1. Rowley, Thomas Algeo, 1808–1892.   2. Generals —
United States — Biography.   3. United States. Army —
Biography.   4. Rowley, Thomas Algeo, 1808–1892 — Trials,
litigation, etc.   5. Trials (Military offenses) — United States.
6. Gettysburg, Battle of, Gettysburg, Pa., 1863.   7. United
States — History — Civil War, 1861–1865 — Campaigns.   I.
Title.
E467.1.R78K78   2006
973.7'3092 — dc22
                                                        2005031457
British Library cataloguing data are available

On the cover: Brig. Gen. Thomas Rowley (Courtesy of the U.S.
Army Military History Institute)

Manufactured in the United States of America

*McFarland & Company, Inc., Publishers
    Box 611, Jefferson, North Carolina 28640
    www.mcfarlandpub.com*

For Franklin and Helen Krumwiede,
who created my interest in the Civil War

Acknowledgments

I wish to express my appreciation to Richard E. Matthews, Gary Augustine, and James L. McLean Jr., who took the time to review this manuscript at various stages of its development. Any errors or mistakes that remain are solely my responsibility.

William Phillis generously shared the diaries, photos, and articles pertaining to his great-great-grandfather, Col. John Patterson, and the 102nd Pennsylvania. The Wyoming Historical and Genealogical Society made available Edmund Dana's papers and diary. The only source that exceeds the Dana Collection in importance is the National Archives, where over a century ago unknown War Department clerks organized the Rowley files.

Michael Dreese introduced me to George McFarland and answered many questions concerning the colonel and his 151st Pennsylvania. Brenda B. Kepley, NARA, and Kenneth E. Thompson, Portland, helped close the Camp Berry gap. Robert E. Mulligan Jr. investigated the G. K. Warren Papers, New York State Archives, and Jennifer Ambrose the George Meade Papers, Historical Society of Pennsylvania.

Dr. Richard J. Sommers, David H. Keough, and Rich Baker helped me navigate the Military History Institute's stacks, corridors, and hidden rooms that no longer exist. Howard Madaus answered my question, "What happened to the First Brigade's flag at Gettysburg?"

Carol Krogan, Vernon County Museum, Wisconsin, Andi Wittwer, Sawyer County Historical Society, and Dolores A. Beaudette, Chippewa Falls, Wisconsin, supplied essential information on Rufus Dawes and Clayton Rogers.

Commendations are due Lynn Lepley, the Rev. Tim Perkins, Bob McGowan and his wife plus Clarence McAllister for putting the 102nd Pennsylvania online and making available information that I would not have seen otherwise. John J. Slonaker, Pennsylvania State Archives, guided me in locating James K. Moorhead's papers and searching the J. Horace McFarland Collection.

Not only did John Heiser prepare the book's maps, but he also filled my endless requests for vertical files at the GNMP library.

A full copy of Washington P. Shooter's Gettysburg letter was secured through the efforts of Dan Corsello, Charleston, South Carolina, CWRT, and Dorothy McIntyre. Faye Smith, librarian, Venango County Historical Society, tolerated my numerous questions about Alfred B. McCalmont and the 142nd Pennsylvania. Mike Russert made available his copy of Vincent Flanagan's dissertation on G. K. Warren. Dr. Gerald P. Sherwin gave me an alternative and Al Gambone Darius Couch. Clark B. Hall, Zann Miner, and Virginia B. Morton provided information on Culpeper during the Civil War. The Civil War Research Seminar presented by Wayne E. Motts continues to be a valuable tool.

My last chapter cites several books and articles, some of which have a different opinion concerning Thomas Rowley on July 1, 1863. These differences do not diminish their literary standing and usefulness to the author.

Table of Contents

Acknowledgments vii

Preface xi

  1. Pittsburgh, Pennsylvania 1

  2. The War Begins 6

  3. The Peninsula Campaign 16

  4. Second Bull Run, Antietam, and Fredericksburg 33

  5. First Corps Brigadier 45

  6. The Gettysburg Campaign 59

  7. Camp Berry, Maine 103

  8. The Culpeper Court-Martial 108

  9. The Defendant Reacts 137

10. Jubal Early's Invasions of Pennsylvania 152

11. Aftermath 169

Conclusion 186

Appendix I. Commands of Thomas A. Rowley 195

Appendix II. Court-Martial Participants 197

Appendix III. Thomas A. Rowley's Defense Statement 198

Appendix IV. "Transfer from Jail to Pleasanter Quarters": 201
   Colonel Edmund Dana, Prisoner of War

Chapter Notes 211

Bibliography 229

Index 239

Preface

GETTYSBURG, 2:00 PM, JULY 1, 1863: Northwest of Gettysburg, Maj. Gen. Abner Doubleday's First Corps line ran from Fairfield Road on the left to Mummasburg Road on the right, a distance of about a mile and a half. Federal infantry from Brig. Gen. James Wadsworth's, John Robinson's, and Thomas Rowley's divisions had stopped the advance of Lt. Gen. Ambrose P. Hill's Third Corps and Maj. Gen. Robert Rodes's division from Lt. Gen. Richard Ewell's Second Corps. Since noon, the Confederates' inability to coordinate attacks had provided Doubleday with opportunities to shift units and stop Rodes's isolated assaults on his right. After resting in line of battle for over an hour, Maj. Gen. Henry Heth and Dorsey Pender received Robert E. Lee's orders to attack Doubleday's center and left.

Heth advanced first and drove Col. Chapman Biddle's, Roy Stone's, and Brig. Gen. Solomon Meredith's brigades back to Seminary Ridge. From here, the Federals watched Pender's men advance through Heth's lines and start up the slope. Thirty minutes later, the First Corps began a withdrawal to Cemetery Hill. They had fought well for over six hours. With nothing left in reserve and no reinforcements in sight, pulling back was the only viable choice. Morale remained high until they reached Baltimore Street, the primary north-south escape route through Gettysburg. Here, the ensuing chaos and confusion had the impact of a slap to the face.

From the north, Maj. Gen. Oliver Howard's Eleventh Corps and part of the First Corps pushed south down Baltimore. Like a river at flood stage, they collided with the balance of the First Corps retreating eastward on High Street. Complete deadlock took hold for several minutes. No plans existed for the inevitable retreat to Cemetery Hill. Now, no one came forward and took command. To some, the resulting tangle of men, horses, and wagons was a worse experience than the earlier fighting. Patience and tolerance, already in short supply, soon disappeared. Tempers flared and accusations, later regretted, flew back and forth. Finally, the congestion broke and the disorderly retreat resumed. Over 3,600 Federals were captured that day, most of them within Gettysburg.[1]

On Cemetery Hill, general officers tried to organize a defensive line to stop Lee's advance. Under pressure from Maj. Gen. Winfield Scott Hancock, Doubleday positioned Meredith's Iron Brigade on the western slope of nearby Culp's Hill. James Wadsworth sent his aide, Lt. Clayton Rogers, to find and bring up Lt. Col. Rufus Dawes and the Sixth Wisconsin. Sometime between 5:00 and 5:30 p.m., they made contact and rode together up the hill. Nearing the crest, Rogers and Dawes saw the disorganized remnants of what had been two Federal corps, now a confused rabble of exhausted and demoralized men. Some movement on the left caught their attention. Two officers were engaged in a heated discussion. One of them, a general, "had become insane ... raving ... storming ... giving wild orders." Rogers, the First Division's provost, concluded that the brigadier was drunk and placed him under arrest. The prisoner, Brig. Gen. Thomas A. Rowley, surrendered his sword. Dawes escorted him to the rear.[2]

How did a brigadier general find himself in such an untenable position, and what happened after the arrest? Answers to these and other questions follow, but first: Who was Thomas Rowley? On July 1, 1863, he was the victim of a command structure that failed. Like many that day, Rowley confronted challenges that exceeded his physical stamina and military skills. Ten months later, an army court-martial, lacking impartiality and marching to its own drum, found him guilty. Two experienced lawyers, Abraham Lincoln and Edwin Stanton, overturned the verdict. His military career essentially over, Rowley was not the court-martial's only casualty. Of those directly or indirectly involved with the April 1864 trial, the victims far outnumbered the survivors.

The written and oral defense testimony from 11 qualified and competent army officers justifies this book. They cannot be dismissed as merely "friends and aides [who] staunchly swore to his [Rowley's] sobriety."[3] Their testimony is used to reconstruct the events of July 1, 1863. Initially, I intended to focus on Gettysburg and the subsequent court-martial. In some instances, this effort lifted the fog of war, but in other cases the fog remained settled in place. Clearly, an objective evaluation would require appropriate attention to events before July 1863 and after April 1864. I gave priority to finding the personal letters and diaries of men who served with and under General Rowley. As was the case for my earlier work on James S. Wadsworth, everything has been included, warts and all. I have largely restricted my personal judgment to the closing analysis. As will be seen, the ensuing tragedy extended far beyond Thomas Rowley.

An 1864 court-martial was very different from those portrayed today in motion pictures and on television. For a better understanding of what happened at Gettysburg and Culpeper, I have inserted information concerning Civil War rules, regulations, and procedures where appropriate.

1. Pittsburgh, Pennsylvania

No more gentlemanly and noble hearted man goes with the volunteers.—The Pittsburgh Commercial Journal[1]

Confusion existed from the very beginning. Newspaper obituaries and local histories reported his year of birth from 1807 to 1809. Rolls of the Washington Infantry and letters to the War Department, however, moved it up to 1816–1818. In any case, Thomas A. Rowley was born in Pittsburgh, Pennsylvania, the son of George Rowley, a veteran of the War of 1812 and grandson of William Rowley, who fought in both the Revolutionary and 1812 conflicts. Another source states that he was merely the son of Irish immigrants. Educated in public or common schools, Thomas began working as a store clerk, then apprenticed to cabinetmaker John Mollwain.[2]

In 1839, Rowley joined the Jackson Independent Blues, a volunteer militia unit that traced its history back to 1792. He probably entered local politics the same year. After serving two terms as clerk of courts for Allegheny County, Rowley was elected Sixth Ward alderman in 1846, no doubt supported by fellow militia members.[3]

Newspaper reporting of events near the Rio Grande River that year inflamed public opinion. Many in Congress began clamoring for war with Mexico and President Polk agreed. Mustered into Federal service December 16, 1846, the Blues became Company A, First Regiment Pennsylvania Volunteers. Three companies from Philadelphia reached Pittsburgh "via the Canal" (Pennsylvania) and joined the seven raised locally. With the regiment now at full strength, it was time to leave for Mexico. Second Lt. Rowley married Mary Ann Cust shortly before his departure. Pittsburgh's *Commercial Journal* said good-bye to the groom:

> No officer goes from this city more worthy of respect than Lieutenant Rowley of the Blues. He has resigned the position of Alderman of the Sixth ward. No more gentlemanly and noble hearted man goes with the volunteers. He is deservedly popular among all classes.[4]

On December 22, 10 companies, accompanied by artillery, marched to Pittsburgh's Market Street wharf. The Jackson Blues boarded the steamer

Allequippa at 1:00 p.m. Five steamboats pulled away at 9:00 a.m. the next day and moved down river. The crowd gave three cheers and a band played "Auld Lang Syne." The regiment reached New Orleans on December 31 and on New Year's Day camped outside the city.[5]

In early January 1847, the First Pennsylvania Regiment boarded three sailing ships and departed Louisiana. They disembarked January 28 on the Isle of Lobos, about 120 miles from Vera Cruz. The men encamped and watched as General Winfield Scott assembled his army. Now an official war correspondent, Rowley sent letters to the Pittsburgh newspapers. On Lobos, he observed:

> The Colonel of a South Carolina regiment had an alarm sounded during the night beating up his men, with the object of testing their promptness. It took them half an hour to line up whereas the First Pennsylvania was ready and lined up in ten minutes.[6]

Twenty-five days later, the army started moving toward Vera Cruz, Mexico. With some embellishment, Rowley described the regiment's status.

> Our regiment being the best drilled and finest looking will have the right of the brigade and will act with the regulars. There are 8,000 men here and we are bound to take Vera Cruz. We have drilled like everything. We have become like regulars in all things and we can fight as well as they.... Our regiment is the brag regiment and old Scott says he will give us a chance to distinguish or extinguish ourselves.

Scott's advance units went ashore March 8.[7]

Outside Vera Cruz, Company A came under fire for the first time. Pushing forward, the First Pennsylvania and a Tennessee regiment captured an old castle and a hill overlooking the city. Rowley summed up the fighting for the *Pittsburgh Chronicle.*

> Landed without opposition on 9th of March. On 10th left beach and marched over sand hills rising 200 feet above the sea level. Had a small brush with the enemy and at 3 o'clock came to the ruins of an old convent. About 200 Mexicans were posted there. The Tennesseeans and the Blues were about one-half mile in advance of the Regiment. We attacked them and drove them off at the first fire. When the Regiment came up the Colonel said: "Boys, you have done it up brown. We will give them another turn." We then marched down the railroad to within one and a half miles of Vera Cruz, where they gave two more volleys and ran. The Tennesseeans came up and with them our Regiment took possession of a hill commanding the city. Four hundred Mexicans fired continually as we climbed the almost perpendicular ascent.

Four spent balls struck Rowley that afternoon but "only one gave any pain."[8]

Heavy artillery was brought up to the hill's crest. Manned by sailors, the guns began bombarding Mexican fortifications. After four days, the city surrendered and at noon on March 29 the American flag flew over Vera Cruz. Scott now moved his army into the interior, its goal Mexico City. During April, Thomas Rowley resigned his commission and left the service because of a "severe disease" afflicting one foot.[9]

Returning to Pittsburgh on May 16, 1847, he spent the summer recuperating. In early September, Rowley received a commission to recruit a local militia company for immediate service. He succeeded and the new unit became part of Colonel George Hughes's Maryland and District of Columbia regiment. Mustered into Federal service October 4 as Company H, they left Pittsburgh on November 10 on the steamer *Diadem*. Their ship ran into a severe storm while sailing across the gulf and almost sank. Landing at Vera Cruz on December 11, Rowley's Rough and Ready Guards marched to Jalapa the next day and joined the regiment at National Bridge. Here they spent the remainder of the war fighting guerrillas and garrisoning the town.[10]

Hughes's regiment left Mexico in June 1848 and arrived in Pittsburgh on July 10. Honorably mustered out of Federal service a week later, Rowley rejoined his wife, Mary Ann, only to share her grief. Two of their daughters had recently died, victims most likely of the frequent epidemics that swept through Pittsburgh. In January 1855, four Blues officers and other local citizens organized the Washington Infantry of Pittsburgh, a new volunteer militia company. Veterans from the Jackson Blues and Company H enrolled. The members were inspected and mustered into service April 14, 1855. Initially commissioned first lieutenant, Thomas Rowley received a promotion to captain August 2, 1858. Standing just over five and one-half feet tall, the new captain weighed close to 200 pounds. The unit's history observed that its three first officers "were solid men, their aggregate weight being about 700 pounds." Rowley also worked part time for the city as a private contractor, paving streets and hauling fill. Remaining active in politics throughout the 1850s, he served as deputy clerk of courts and now a Republican, supported Lincoln's bid for the presidency.[11]

In December 1860, James Buchanan's secretary of war, John B. Floyd, ordered the guns and ammunition removed from the local Allegheny Arsenal and sent south. Rumors spread throughout Pittsburgh that a shipment of muskets had already left for Texas. Local citizens decided to take matters into their own hands. Rowley's militia unit set up a cannon on the Ohio River's north shore at Glass House Riffle and threatened to sink any steamboat carrying armaments. In spite of this threat, guns continued to be assembled on a wharf for shipment by barge. Captain Rowley assembled the Washington Infantry one February evening. After loading muskets, the company marched to the wharf and surrounded the cannon, which remained in the city.[12]

Since 1856, the Washington Infantry had been called out several times to quell riots threatened in the mining district. A more rewarding assignment came in January 1861. Abraham Lincoln would visit Pittsburgh on February 14 and 15. Departing Springfield, Illinois, the morning of February 11, the newly elected president began a "triumphal tour to the seat of the national government." By Valentine's Day, seven states had seceded from the Union. Many citizens, North and South, felt that war was imminent. Stirred to high levels of patriotism, northerners wanted to see their new leader. To accommodate as many as possible, Lincoln followed a circuitous route to the capital. The presidential train arrived in Indianapolis at 5:00 p.m. the first day. After breakfasting with Governor Morton and visiting the state capital, Lincoln departed at 11:00 a.m., reaching Cincinnati by midafternoon. At 9:00 p.m., the train headed north for Columbus where Governor Denniston hosted a formal dinner for the president-elect. Lincoln set out for Pittsburgh at 8:00 a.m. the next day, making several stops along the way.[13]

Reception plans called for local dignitaries to meet the train at the Federal Street railroad station in Allegheny City and escort the president, his wife, and three sons to the Monongahela House, a Pittsburgh hotel. Residents decorated their homes with flags. That afternoon, most factories shut down and stores closed. The special Pittsburgh, Fort Wayne & Chicago train was scheduled to arrive in Allegheny City at 5:20 p.m. Local militia units, commanded by Brig. Gen. James S. Negley, began forming about 4:00 p.m. An hour later, several carriages followed by the Pennsylvania Dragoons, Jackson Independent Blues, and Rowley's Washington Infantry left for the station. Rain seemed imminent so they placed Lincoln's carriage beneath the platform's roof with soldiers on either side.[14]

The locomotive of a westbound freight broke an axle near Freedom, Pennsylvania, a small town on the Ohio River 25 miles west of Pittsburgh. The accident stopped all rail traffic for almost three hours. At first, spectators in Allegheny City and Pittsburgh ignored rumors of a delay, but by 6:00 p.m. they reluctantly accepted them. A light rain turned into a downpour that drove many away. At 8:00 p.m., two brass cannons on nearby hills started firing. Soon the crowd heard the whistle and bell of an approaching locomotive. The train stopped at the platform and Allegheny City's mayor welcomed the distinguished visitor. Accompanied by his family, Lincoln walked quickly to the carriage, climbed in, and sat down. Responding to cheers and cries for a speech, he arose and said that given the late hour and bad weather, tomorrow morning would be a better time.[15]

Escorted by soldiers thoroughly soaked and covered with mud, the carriage left the station. Lincoln and his entourage traveled down streets still crowded in spite of the weather. Continuous cheering greeted them at the Monongahela House, and soldiers had to clear the way through the huge crowds so the presidential carriages could pass. Inside, supporters packed the hotel. The president-elect stopped in the lobby, stood on a chair, and made a few remarks. Reminded that they had given him a 10,000-vote majority, Lincoln replied:

> I have a great regard for Allegheny County. It is the banner county of the state, if not of the entire Union. I acknowledge with all sincerity the high honor you have conferred upon me.

He finished and stepped down to three cheers for "Honest Abe." The presidential party walked past the large registration desk and went up the winding, black walnut staircase to the Prince of Wales Room.[16]

These few comments did not satisfy his supporters who had waited outside for over three hours. The crowd on Smithfield Street became impatient and started chanting: "Lincoln, Lincoln," and "speech, speech." Lincoln stepped out on the hotel balcony that overlooked the Monongahela River and received several minutes of cheering and applause. When the noise finally ended, he postponed further remarks until morning, "when we hope for more favorable weather; and I have made my appearance now only to afford you an opportunity of seeing my beautiful countenance. Good night!" To laughter and further cheers, the president-elect left the balcony and joined his family for dinner.[17]

In spite of muddy streets and more rain, a large crowd, estimated at 10,000, had gathered by 8:30 a.m. in front of the hotel. Wearing a black dress suit with a large turndown collar and black tie, and showing "a judiciously cultivated beard and whiskers" that hid "the hollowness of his jaws," Lincoln returned to the balcony. He spoke of problems in the South, protecting local industries, and controlling Congress. The speech ended close to 9:00, one hour before his special train departed for Cleveland. While the crowd cheered and applauded, Lincoln left the balcony and followed his military escort to the waiting carriage. After acknowledging several rounds of cheers, the party departed. Accompanied by the militia units, they reached the station platform a few minutes before the train arrived. The president-elect departed Allegheny City on schedule, never to return to western Pennsylvania.[18]

2. The War Begins

"What more could be said?" — *The Pennsylvania Thirteenth*[1]

Immediately after news arrived of the fighting at Fort Sumter, Rowley and officers from three other local militias went to Harrisburg and volunteered their services, which Governor Curtin accepted. The Washington Infantry was initially reorganized into a three-company battalion (later Companies A, D, and F) with Thomas Rowley as its major. Seven additional companies soon joined them. The battalion became a regiment with Rowley promoted to full colonel and Joseph M. Kinkead appointed adjutant. Company D became the Rowley Infantry and Company F the Rowley Rifles. John W. Patterson recruited Company B in Birmingham, now part of Pittsburgh's south side. Teachers from the Sixth Ward's Franklin School sewed the regimental flags. On April 24, 10 companies marched to the school, received their flags, and left for Harrisburg's Camp Curtin. After a 200-mile journey on the Pennsylvania Railroad, Rowley's command reached the camp that evening. The next morning, the state's adjutant general designated the regiment the 13th Pennsylvania Volunteer Infantry. He mustered in the enlisted men and officers for three months of Federal service. The 13th departed Harrisburg on April 26 for Camp Scott near York, Pennsylvania, and six weeks of training.[2]

Capt. John Patterson wrote his wife June 6 that "we are encamped about 1 mile from Chambersburg [Pennsylvania] in the Fair grounds and are very comfortable." There were now six regiments stationed near Chambersburg under the command of Capt. Abner Doubleday. Patterson assumed that "Harpers Ferry will be our destination first; then Richmond." So far no one had been paid.[3]

June 11, the War Department assigned Rowley's regiment to Col. Dixon S. Miles's Fourth Brigade, stationed at Camp Brady outside Chambersburg. The 13th Pennsylvania joined the brigade's two regular army detachments and two volunteer infantry regiments. Miles reported to Maj. Gen. Robert Patterson, commander of the Department of Pennsylvania. Organized in late April and headquartered at Philadelphia, this department included Pennsylvania, Delaware, and Maryland, excluding Washington, D.C., and Annapolis. Most of General Patterson's 12,000 men were three-month volunteers. One exception was four companies of the Second Cavalry led by Colonel George H. Thomas. The enemy, Brig. Gen. Joseph E. Johnston's command of 11,000 effectives, originally occupied Harpers Ferry but later pulled back to Martinsburg, Virginia.[4]

Born in Ireland, Robert Patterson came to America in 1798. During the War of 1812, he first served in the Pennsylvania militia then the regular infantry. Promoted to major general of volunteers in 1846, Patterson commanded a militia division in the Mexican War, receiving a favorable citation from Winfield Scott for the capture of Jalapa. During the 1850s, Patterson promoted railroads and steamboats while still commanding a division of militia. When the Civil War began, he mustered into Federal service for three months. On June 11, 1861, General in Chief of the Army Winfield Scott felt that Patterson had the Shenandoah Valley well in hand.[5]

In late June, Miles positioned the 13th Pennsylvania near Williamsport, Maryland. Here they constructed a permanent fieldwork for Capt. Abner Doubleday's Battery. South of Washington, D.C., 20 miles separated Brig. Gen. Irwin McDowell's command of 30,000 from a Confederate force of 22,000, camped near Manassas, Virginia, and led by Brig. Gen. Pierre G. T. Beauregard. Winfield Scott requested and later approved McDowell's plan of operations against Manassas, an important railroad junction. Scott promised McDowell that Joe Johnston's troops would be kept out of the battle. The general in chief ordered Patterson to hold Johnston in check until McDowell defeated Beauregard's Confederate army.[6]

Scott gave Patterson authorization on July 2 to cross the Potomac. Early the next morning, Companies F and K, 13th Pennsylvania, accompanied Doubleday's two companies and battery to Martinsburg, Virginia. By this time, Joe Johnston had fallen back 20 miles to Winchester, Virginia. Col. Thomas J. Jackson and J.E.B. Stuart harassed the Federal columns with cavalry. Patterson's advance slowed to a crawl and then stopped all together at Charlestown, 20 miles northeast of the Confederate camp. His duty remained the same; hold Johnston in check at Winchester.[7]

The 13th Pennsylvania crossed into Virginia on July 4, and escorted Col. Ambrose Burnside's battery to Martinsburg. That day, the first edition of *The Pennsylvania Thirteenth,* the regimental newspaper, appeared. Page 1 contained a tribute to Thomas Rowley:

> Few persons have any idea of the responsibility which is thrown upon the Colonel of a green Regiment, and when many of the subordinate officers are entirely inexperienced in military affairs, the labor and responsibility is vastly increased. Col. Rowley started from Pittsburgh on the 24th of April with seven hundred and forty men, most of whom had never shouldered a

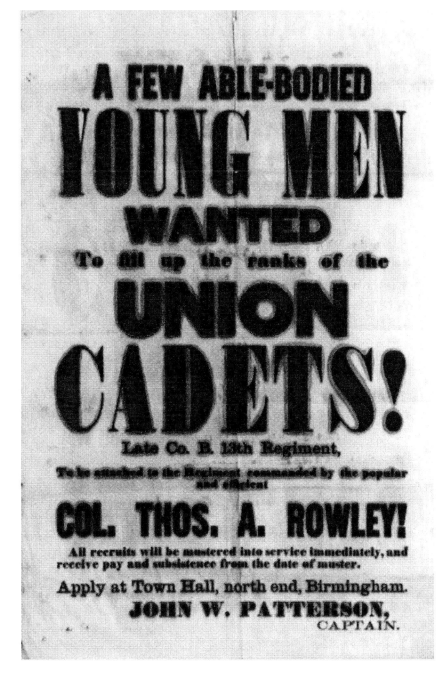

Recruiting poster for Capt. John Patterson's Company E, 102nd Pennsylvania, circa August 1861. Courtesy of William Phillis.

musket before, and but a few at all experienced in military discipline. Out of the inchoate mass of militia he has trained a Regiment of which he can well be proud. Of course, the Col. has labored hard and borne the many perplexities with the patience of a soldier, but the result is much owing to those qualities of head and heart which endeared him to his soldiers, as to his military proficiency. His kindness and attention to soldiers has given him a hold upon their affection which accomplishes more than the strong arm of military discipline could do. We doubt if there is a Regiment under better control in the whole army. What more could be said?[8]

The regiment spent several days there before making a forced march to Charlestown on July 17. As late as mid-July, an opportunity still existed to disrupt the Manassas Gap Railroad with Thomas's cavalry. Patterson failed to seize it. As a result, Johnston's men traveled east by rail and reinforced Beauregard in time to defeat McDowell at Manassas on July 21. Rowley took his command back to Harpers Ferry. Four days later, 16 companies of Pennsylvanians returned to Camp Curtin, northwest of Harrisburg. They were paid and mustered out August 6, most returning to Pittsburgh. The 13th passed into history without having fired a shot at the enemy. When his commission expired July 27, Robert Patterson left the army and returned to Philadelphia. He and Irwin McDowell filled the country's need for scapegoats following the defeat at Bull Run.[9]

The 102nd (or 13th) Pennsylvania Infantry

The Colonel of which is short, fat, and hearty
his name is Rowley.—*The Pennsylvania Thirteenth*[10]

Given direct authorization by Secretary of War Simon Cameron, Rowley set out immediately to raise a three-year regiment. It would ultimately be the only three-year regiment recruited almost entirely from Allegheny County. The remuster promoted Joseph Kinkead to lieutenant colonel and placed John Patterson in command of Company E. Two weeks later, the colonel, accompanied by his 14-year-old son, Henry, and five companies departed Pittsburgh. They reported to the Army of the Potomac on August 23. Initially assigned to Camp Sprague on Meridian Hill north of the capital, the regiment mustered 12 full companies September 30, over 1,000 effectives. A typical Civil War infantry regiment contained 10 companies. Because Rowley initially reported to Washington instead of Harrisburg, state recognition and officers' commissions did not arrive until October. As a result, several Pennsylvania regiments entered service ahead of the old 13th. Ultimately, Rowley's command would have no choice but to accept the higher number of 102.[11]

Posted to Brig. Gen. John J. Peck's brigade on September 13, the 102nd joined the 55th and 62nd New York and 6th New Jersey, about 3,500 effectives. John Peck graduated from West Point in 1843, the same year as U. S. Grant, and won distinction in the Mexican War. Five years later, he resigned from the army and began a successful business career. Even though Peck had served as a delegate to the Democratic National Conventions of 1856 and 1860, Lincoln appointed him a brigadier general of volunteers August 9. The brigade commander established a drill requirement of six hours per day. Frequently, his regiments marched across the hill to the sound of distant artillery.[12]

Born a French aristocrat but ineligible to inherit his father's title, Regis DeTrobriand became a lawyer and writer of prose and poetry. While touring the United States, he married Mary Mason Jones, an American heiress, in 1841 and they later settled in New York City. The day before First Bull Run, the Guards Lafayette, or 55th New York Militia, elected DeTrobriand, now an American citizen, their colonel. Accepted for Federal service, his regiment departed for Washington on August 31. That fall, DeTrobriand recorded his impressions of both the 102nd or 13th Pennsylvania and its colonel:

> The Thirteenth Pennsylvania had more than the maximum number of men, so that it was deprived of two supplementary companies. It was in good relative condition, under the command of an influential politician of Pittsburgh, a boon companion, round-faced and large in girth, who had no objection to exposing himself to fire, but who was not yet ashamed to protect himself from the showers from heaven, by an umbrella, under which I found him, one day going around camp, caring nothing for what any one might say.[13]

At midmonth, the 6th New Jersey departed, replaced by the 93rd Pennsylvania from the Lebanon area. Col. James M. McCarter, 38 years old and an ordained Methodist Episcopal minister, commanded this regiment. Thirteen months later, McCarter would be arrested and court-martialed on a charge of being drunk on duty. On September 26, most of the brigade departed Camp Sprague for Tennallytown but the 102nd remained behind and established Camp Holt. A reunion took place two weeks later. Saturday evening, October 9, Rowley marched his regiment into Washington. Under a full moon, they passed the White House and saw gaslights burning in its rooms. The column turned northwest on the Rockville Road and in about two hours rejoined Peck's Brigade at Camp Tennallytown. The ground was hilly but they quickly established camp, had supper and then went to bed. Three miles downstream stood the Potomac's Chain Bridge that provided access into and out of Virginia.[14]

In early October, Maj. Gen. George B. McClellan combined Brig. Gen. John Peck's, Darius Couch's and Lawrence P. Graham's brigades to form a new division led by Don Carlos Buell. An 1841 West Point graduate, Buell was commissioned brigadier general of volunteers on May 17, 1861. Joining the

Army of the Potomac that fall, he focused his efforts on organizing and training the inexperienced brigades. Only reviews and inspections took priority over drilling. The 98th Pennsylvania joined the brigade October 10, increasing Peck's command to five regiments.[15]

An enemy cavalry force on reconnaissance crossed the Potomac that month near Great Falls, 12 road miles northwest of Camp Tennallytown. The brigade went on alert but no orders came down from Army Headquarters. To reinforce pickets guarding the Chesapeake and Ohio Canal, Rowley sent Companies A and D on October 11 to Great Falls. Here, in a series of falls and rapids, the Potomac River drops 77 feet in the course of a mile. The men adopted buildings left over from construction of the Washington Aqueduct as quarters and named the camp Cantonment Rowley in honor of their colonel. About this time, Brig. Gen. George McCall's Pennsylvania Reserves, 12,000 strong crossed the river into Virginia. Peck's Brigade moved forward, occupied Tennallytown, and protected Georgetown. The 102nd sent one company to Fort Pennsylvania, located on a high hill. Rowley posted additional guard detachments at nearby Taylor Signal Station and Chain Bridge, nine miles down river from Great Falls.[16]

Good weather continued. With half of the 102nd detached for guard duty, the remaining companies practiced brigade drill with the other regiments. Since their August arrival, the 102nd had made considerable progress in mastering battalion and brigade drill and in firing rifled muskets. Morale was high when they mustered for pay October 31. Rowley served as mustering officer that day for the Anderson Zouaves (62nd New York). President Lincoln and McClellan reviewed Buell's Division November 8 at Meridian Hill. Having suspended publication after the July 4 edition, *The Pennsylvania Thirteenth* reappeared November 9. The Prince de Joinville and Comte de Paris, aides to McClellan, visited Rowley's regiment November 10. The next day, Buell departed for Kentucky where he relieved Brig. Gen. William T. Sherman as commanding general, Department of the Cumberland. Brig. Gen. Erasmus D. Keyes took over the division that McClellan reviewed again on December 6 at Meridian Hill. A member of West Point's Class of 1832, Keyes missed the Mexican War but later served as an aide and personal secretary to Winfield Scott. At First Bull Run, he commanded a brigade, receiving a promotion to brigadier general that August.[17]

December arrived with rain followed by snow and colder temperatures. Keyes briefly suspended daily drilling so that the men could build log cabins for the coming winter. On the 18th, division commander Keyes, Representative J. K. Moorhead, and a delegation from Harrisburg visited the camp. The delegates presented two stands of state flags to General Peck who in turn gave them to Colonel Rowley and John F. Ballier, 21st Pennsylvania. After the presentation and appropriate speeches, the visitors watched a brigade drill.

The day ended with a regimental pig chase. Rowley donated the pig that was shaved, greased, and released in front of the men. He announced, "The mess that catches him can eat him." The brigade's Pennsylvania regiments decorated their camps, "with evergreen arches, containing the letters of the respective companies and numbers of the regiments. In the company streets, pine trees were arranged in rows." Lt. John Large, Company C, observed that "our Camp is the prettiest that I have ever seen[.] The boys have decorated every street in it[,] each Co [Company] trying to excel in beauty & comfort[.] The Regt looks as well as any one in the District of Columbia[.]"[18]

Confusion still existed as to whether the regiment was the 13th or the 102nd. *The Pennsylvania Thirteenth* lamented the new state flag, "probably owing to the error of the painter who lettered the flags, the flag for the old Thirteenth had 102nd on it ... which will doubtless be corrected." In late December, the regimental officers decided to surprise Rowley with a new sword. They initiated a subscription drive, each individual asked to contribute $5. Everyone did except Capt. Thomas Duff, Company B. In spite of his refusal, they purchased a $165 sword with all the trimmings. Chaplain A. M. Stewart presented it to Rowley on January 27, 1862.[19]

On New Year's Eve, choruses from the brigade's four regiments sang appropriate songs in French, German, and English. The 102nd's Patriotic League serenaded Colonel Rowley and later entertained him at a dinner in the hospital tent. Organized in late December, the founders signed the following pledge: "The undersigned officers and non-commissioned officers and privates, actuated by motives of self-respect, patriotism, and love of country, do hereby pledge ourselves to abstain from the use of intoxicating liquors during the period of our service to the United States." Capt. John Patterson, a league member, wrote his wife that its "main feature ... is the total abstinence from the use of intoxicating drinks in any form whatever." The New Year's Day menu consisted of roast turkeys, oysters, lemonade, and other delicacies.[20]

During a January 2 snowstorm, Chaplain Stewart dedicated the 102nd's new church. Samuel Myers, Company H, wrote a friend the next day:

> The church is not built with brick nor wood but it is made out of canvas [.] [I]t cost one hundred and Seventy five dollars[.] [I]t was a pretty dear church to be in the regiment. The means was raised by the regiment to buy this tent for to have preaching and prayer meetings. I think it will do good in the regiment. Our colonel gave twenty five dollars to getting the tent. So you see that they want to do good in their regiment as well as drill their regiment... .

The men appointed a committee to heat the tent and to make arrangements so that it could also be used as a reading room. "Any body that wants to can go and spend an [h]our or too [sic] reading a good book or and newspaper."[21]

Maj. Gen. Darius Couch passed into and out of Rowley's military career for over two years. Courtesy of USAMHI.

News arrived in mid-January that fellow Pittsburgher Edwin M. Stanton was the new secretary of war, replacing Simon Cameron. John Peck went on sick leave and Brig. Gen. Darius M. Couch assumed brigade command. Couch, like McClellan and Stonewall Jackson, graduated from West Point in 1846. He was brevetted for gallant and meritorious conduct in the Mexican War. He resigned his commission in 1855. Returning to lead the 7th Massachusetts at First Bull Run, Couch received a promotion to brigadier in August. Rowley's son, Harry T., joined the 102nd that month serving as an unattached runner.[22]

"All's Quiet on the Potomac" continued for the first two months of 1862. In late January, Rowley sent a third company to Great Falls. Off-duty recreation at Cantonment Rowley centered on catching rabbits and riding down the canal in a small boat. Rain and snow fell throughout February. During this miserable weather, provisions briefly ran out at Great Falls. Companies H, I, and L now picketed the C & O Canal from Great Falls to the Chain Bridge. The Confederates remained south of the river. In early February, Captain Duff, who had not joined Rowley's sword subscription, presented his colonel a pair of heavy plated spurs of excellent workmanship. Congress confirmed John Peck's nomination as brigadier general.[23]

The old controversy, 13th or 102nd, was supposedly settled February 10. General Peck had delayed "publishing officially the number of the regiment commanded by Thos. A. Rowley, hoping that the old number might be retained." Brigade headquarters issued orders that the Old 13th would "hereafter be known as the 102nd Regiment of Pennsylvania Volunteers." Nevertheless, the arguments continued:

> We were in service and at Washington, three months previous to the organization of regiments which have a lower number. "A rose by any other name will smell as sweet." As good soldiers, we acquiesce and obey. Col. Rowley's commission having been issued on the 21st of April last, since which time he has not been out of the service of the United States, the change of number cannot affect the regiment otherwise than to render useless the numbers on the caps and the ornaments worn by the officers. Our friends at home are as much attached to the number 13 as we are; and as the Col. wore 13 on his cap in Mexico, the same in the "three months campaign," and for six months of the present campaign, 13 has figured on his frontlet, our paper will still be known as the *Penna. Thirteenth*.

Fifteen hundred copies of the February 15 issue failed to meet the demand in Tennallytown and Pittsburgh. Rowley and his adjutant, Capt. Joseph Browne, took an eight-day leave, spending Washington's Birthday in Pittsburgh. Back east, their regiment "was formed in line in the forenoon and fired thirteen rounds to celebrate the Father of our Country's birthday." Four days later, they watched "the drumming out [of] a soldier of the 62 New York Reg. for deserting; the letter D branded on his hip."[24]

Rowley and Browne returned to camp March 1. The 102nd received 1,000 pairs of pants that evening and held a dress parade the next day to show them off. Federal pickets discovered March 9 that Joseph Johnston's army had abandoned Manassas during the night. Orders arrived the next day at 3:00 a.m. to prepare to march. With each man carrying 100 rounds of cartridges, Keyes's division set out at 9:00 a.m. and followed the Pennsylvania Reserves across the Chain Bridge. With Peck commanding, the brigade marched nine miles down the Leesburg Road, stopped on Prospect Hill in Fairfax County, and for the first time bivouacked in Virginia. "The whole army of the Potomac is on the move," but "all quiet along the Potomac" continued. Four days later, the 102nd crossed Chain Bridge and returned in pouring rain to the old Tennallytown camp. Edward Hoon, 102nd Pennsylvania, wrote his father that it was nothing more than "a wild goose chase over into Virginia." Finding their winter quarters destroyed, Rowley's men spent the night either standing or sitting upon logs. There were not enough tents available so those without had to construct shelters the next day in a sea of mud. March 18, Rowley promoted Joseph B. Martin to Seventh Corporal of Company H.[25]

While in Virginia, the Army of the Potomac underwent a major reorganization. March 8, Lincoln issued General War Order No. 2 that created five army corps and assigned corps commanders. Five days later, McClellan's General Orders No. 101 announced division commanders. Except for Maj. Gen. N. P. Banks's Fifth Corps, each corps contained three divisions and each division three brigades. The 102nd became part of Peck's First Brigade, Darius Couch's First Division, Erasmus Keyes's Fourth Corps. Brig. Gen. W. F. "Baldy" Smith and Silas Casey commanded the corps's Second and Third Divisions respectively. Orders and counterorders reached Tennallytown almost daily followed by abortive marches. After drawing new gum blankets March 25, the 102nd set out the following afternoon for Georgetown.[26]

3. The Peninsula Campaign

*The cherry and pear and Apricots is all out
in full bloom. —Joseph B. Martin[1]*

The division's column that day included three regimental commanders who would meet two years later in a Culpeper, Virginia, court-martial. Colonel Frank Wheaton's 2nd Rhode Island belonged to Couch's old Third Brigade, now led by Col. H. S. Biggs, 10th Massachusetts. Col. Thomas H. Neill led David Birney's 23rd Pennsylvania in Lawrence Graham's Second Brigade. Thomas Rowley, of course, commanded the 102nd in Peck's First Brigade. Their career paths — Wheaton, Neill, and Rowley — would cross several times during the coming nine months.[2]

Rowley's regiment boarded the steamship *State of Maine* that evening at Georgetown. With Company H on deck for the night, the ship moved down river to Alexandria, and waited for the rest of Couch's division. For the 102nd, this marked the beginning of George McClellan's Peninsula Campaign. Geographically, the peninsula extends about 45 miles, southeast to northwest, between the York and James rivers. The coming military campaign would expand its boundaries north along the Pamunkey River to Hanover Court House and west to Richmond and the Virginia Central Railroad. McClellan's plan called for the Army of the Potomac to disembark and advance north and west about 80 miles to the Confederate capital. Here, he would place Richmond under siege then wait until it surrendered, ending the war. The starting point and initial supply depot was Fort Monroe, located on the peninsula's southern tip. Built during the 1820s and '30s, the stone and brick fortress guarded the entrance to Chesapeake Bay. Reinforced in May 1861 and commanded by the army's senior brigadier, John Wool, it now boasted a garrison of over 12,000 men. Given his seniority, Wool refused to accept McClellan's orders and remained independent in his Department of Virginia.[3]

With Peck and his staff standing on the pilot house with telescopes, the *State of Maine* left Alexandria at sunrise on March 27. Accompanied by Briggs's and Graham's brigades, the 102nd sailed down the Potomac and into Chesapeake Bay. After steaming all night, the transports reached Fort Monroe at

Once a peer and competitor, Brig. Gen. Frank Wheaton later served at Rowley's court-martial. Courtesy of USAMHI.

sunrise and passed what remained of the U.S.S. *Cumberland,* sunk March 8 by the *Merrimack* (C. S. S. *Virginia*). In the distance, John Large saw the *Monitor* at anchor and under steam but thought that it "looks more like a log raft with a Cheese box on it than anything I have ever seen." Private William Acheson recalled, "The bugle blowed and we fell in." Disembarking at Hampton, Virginia, on March 28, Peck's brigade marched about nine miles to Camp

A member of the court with Wheaton, Brig. Gen. Thomas H. Neill earlier commanded a regiment in Couch's Division. Courtesy of Mass. MOLLUS and USAMHI.

Hamilton and bivouacked not far from Newport News and Brig. Gen. Alexander Hays's 63rd Pennsylvania. They remained in camp on the brigade's right and "built shelters out of rails and gum blankets." Baldy Smith's and Silas Casey's commands joined Couch. John Patterson informed his wife April 2 that "we are about 2 miles east of Newport News and about 1 1/2 east of the James River." The day before, Patterson had visited Newport News where he saw enemy batteries across the James, the wrecks of the *Congress* and *Cumberland*, and the "notorious *Merrimack* ... flirting around, as saucy as could be." In Richmond, Jefferson Davis gave General Johnston command of all Confederate forces on the peninsula.[4]

General Keyes led Smith's and Couch's divisions out of camp at 7:00 a.m. on April 4. With a cavalry screen in front, they marched north on the Lee's Mill Road toward Warwick Court House, the James River a mile or two to the west. Brig. Gen. Samuel P. Heintzelman's Third Corps advanced on Keyes's right or east, its objective Yorktown. Narrow and muddy roads forced the regiments to march by flank, one after the other. After covering 12 miles, the 102nd camped that night at Young's Mill. The next morning, heavy rains made the roads almost impassable and the two divisions gained only five miles. Another day passed before Keyes's column reached the Warwick River's southern bank, about 20 miles north of Camp Hamilton. The 102nd took a position two miles east of the James. Pickets watched Confederate cavalry and infantry on the opposite side, about 50 yards away. The enemy line was thinly manned, at most 10,000 men. A majority of the Federal generals present recommended an immediate attack. North of the Warwick, Maj. Gen. John B. Magruder paraded his small command back and forth. Before long, he convinced the watching Yankees that they faced a sizable force. McClellan hesitated, missing the opportunity to push across and seize Yorktown. Magruder's theatrics won the day. Joe Johnston's reinforcements arrived in time to strengthen the Confederate Warwick line. McClellan's attention now focused on bringing up large siege guns to destroy Yorktown's fortifications.[5]

For several days the 102nd, eight miles southwest of Yorktown, waited for the guns assigned to its sector to arrive. Lieutenant Large described their camp. "[It] is in a thick pine forest with any amount of snakes[,] ticks & lots of wood ticks & musketoes [sic] so you can imagine we have a pleasant time." Along both banks of the river, skirmishers hid during the day and carefully searched for targets. After sunset, they traded and exchanged information. John Patterson wrote his wife, "The enemy appear in small parties across the river. Our batteries have shelled them out of one or two small fortifications." Rowley accompanied General Keyes and his staff on an April 11 inspection of the picket line. The next evening, Confederate pickets, under a flag of truce, crossed the Warwick and asked to see the commanding officer. Taken to Rowley's tent, they wanted to know if it was true that the Yankees held Manassas and Fort Donelson. The colonel replied that Johnston withdrew from Manassas on March 9 and U. S. Grant captured Fort Donelson on February 16. Assured that the information was true, the Rebels left and returned to their lines. Buoyed by news of victories at Island No. 10 and Pittsburgh Landing, Patterson observed: "We have 'Little Mac' with us and when he has everything ready we will get up and dust toward Richmond and when we get there we will have a Grand Circular Fox Hunt and capture them wholesale." Two weeks later, siege preparations were finally nearing completion and George McClellan decided to open his Yorktown bombardment at dawn May 5.[6]

On the evening of May 3, Confederate guns in front of Yorktown fired several rounds. When the bombardment ended, John Magruder quietly completed withdrawing his troops and retreated north to Williamsburg. He left behind empty tents and guns too large to move. The 102nd "left Warwick hastily on Sunday the 4th. Marched on through Rebel fortifications, and left Yorktown which had been evacuated, and took the road to Williamsburg." Brig. Gen. George Stoneman pursued the enemy with Federal cavalry, supported by Brig. Gen. Joseph Hooker's Third Corps division on the right and Couch's division followed by Casey's on the left. It rained all night and by the morning of May 5, the roads were nothing but great mudholes. With the 102nd leading on the left, the two Federal columns pushed north on separate and isolated roads. If the Confederates pressed hard, Hooker and Couch could not support each other. Seeing an opportunity, Joe Johnston ordered Maj. Gen. James Longstreet to conduct a fighting retreat.[7]

Battle of Williamsburg

> Colonels De Trobriand, Riker, Rowley, Ballier, and Johnston commanded
> regiments with coolness and discretion. — *Brigadier General Erasmus D. Keyes*[8]

Shortly after Longstreet received his orders, Hooker decided to push the retreating enemy. Lt. Col. Charles S. Wainwright, Hooker's chief of artillery, brought up a six-gun battery and opened fire on Fort Magruder, two miles southeast of Williamsburg. Hooker's infantry set out to flank the rebel stronghold by advancing northwest through dense woods. Without warning, Brig. Gen. Cadmus Wilcox's Alabama brigade struck the Federal left. As fighting spread down the line, Hooker's attack turned into a retreat and he called for help. Driving his division forward, Brig. Gen. Philip Kearny arrived at 3:00 p.m. and succeeded in stopping Longstreet's breakthrough on Hooker's left.[9]

Still leading Peck's Brigade, Rowley and the 102nd reached the battlefield just south of Hooker's center around 2:00 p.m. Assuming field command in McClellan's absence, the Second Corps commander, Brig. Gen. Edwin "Bull"

Sumner, ordered Peck to support Hooker's right. In 1819, Sumner was commissioned directly into the army. He gained the nickname "Bull" when a musket ball supposedly bounced off his head. Seniority earned him a corps command. With the 102nd in front, the brigade's five regiments double timed through ankle-deep mud and formed a battle line on the Williamsburg Road. To the left was a dense woods that marked Hooker's right. Artillery fire from Fort Magruder's guns, about 500 hundred yards away, struck the Federal line. Rowley's command now received its baptism of fire in a serious battle.[10]

DeTrobriand's 55th New York held the left. A road separated him from Rowley next in line and the 98th Pennsylvania farther right. The 102nd remained quiet and did not reveal its position. About 2:30 p.m., the 55th opened fire by file on advancing Confederate infantry. Rowley finished deploying his command, waited a short time, and then fired a volley with his entire second rank. For 90 minutes, Peck's three regiments held their ground and successfully fought off several enemy assaults. Out of ammunition the 55th and 102nd were relieved by the 62nd New York and 93rd Pennsylvania. Couch's Third Brigade, now led by Brig. Gen. Charles Devens, reached the field. Frank Wheaton's 2nd Rhode Island came forward in support of Peck's brigade. Graham's Second Brigade remained in reserve. John Large wrote his father, "after fighting for five hours we were relieved ... & marched some distance to the rear to partake of refreshments in the shape of Crackers & coffee & Biviouck [sic] on the mud with the rain coming down in torrents to bath our boys." Joseph Martin recorded his thoughts on their first battle: "We drove the rebels from their Forts, there was six forts. We fought till dark then fell back a half mile for the night."[11]

Early the next morning, Longstreet began pulling back and by daylight was gone. Col. Thomas Neill and two companies from the 23rd Pennsylvania advanced and occupied some works east of Fort Magruder. John Patterson felt that "our regiment did remarkable well for the first time it was under fire." He was not the only one. Corps commander Keyes commended Peck's regimental commanders. Rowley was so pleased with his regiment's conduct during their first engagement that he thought it unnecessary "to designate any particular instance of bravery."[12]

Battle of Fair Oaks or Seven Pines

> The Ninety-third Pennsylvania, Colonel McCarter, and One
> Hundred and second Pennsylvania, Colonel Rowley, behaved with
> great gallantry, both colonels wounded.—*Brig. Gen. Darius N. Couch*[13]

May 18 found the 102nd camped six miles from Bottom's Bridge over the Chickahominy River and 21 miles from Richmond. While positioned here, Colonel DeTrobriand became seriously ill and gave up command of the 55th New York. Silas Casey's Third Division crossed Bottom's Bridge on May 20 and Couch's followed two days later. Casey advanced west to Seven Pines and anchored the Fourth Corps's left flank, nine miles east of Richmond. On May 25, Couch positioned his command about three-quarters of a mile northwest of Casey and the Fair Oaks Station, its left flank on the Richmond and York Railroad. Before May ended, Heintzelman joined Keyes south of the Chickahominy and encamped near the Williamsburg Stage Road. Like their earlier advance toward Williamsburg, Heintzelman and Keyes were not within supporting distance. Recent organizational changes had reduced the Third and Fourth Corps to a combined four divisions, less than 30,000 effectives. Keyes did not like the new position but Heintzelman would not support sending an objection to McClellan. Seeing an opportunity to destroy both corps, Joseph Johnston decided to launch an attack before more Federals crossed the river.[14]

George McClellan was well aware that only two corps had crossed the river. Additional Chickahominy bridges were under construction and Sumner's Second Corps had orders to provide immediate support in case of an attack on the salient. McClellan's failure to take an active role in establishing defensive positions for the Third and Fourth Corps left the critical decisions to his subordinates. Like Sumner, Lincoln had chosen Keyes and Heintzelman for corps command according to seniority of rank. Williamsburg demonstrated their limited skills in handling large bodies of men on a battlefield. McClellan gave Heintzelman authority over both corps but this turned out to be little more than the blind leading the blind. Two of the army's best divisions, Joe Hooker's and Phil Kearny's, held reserve positions several miles to the east. Consequently, the impact of a frontal attack would fall solely on Couch's and Casey's commands, the latter one of the Potomac Army's worst. An 1826 graduate from West Point, Silas Casey distinguished himself in the Mexican War and later wrote a book on infantry tactics. Leading a Civil War division required skills he did not possess. Heintzelman's unwillingness to even raise an objection and McClellan's overconfidence set the stage for a Federal disaster.[15]

Joe Johnston's complex battle plan called for a coordinated attack by 22 infantry brigades in five separate columns. Scheduled to begin at 8:00 a.m., May 31, his initial target would be the Federal Fourth Corps's right and center. Heavy rains drove the Chickahominy to flood stage, isolating Keyes and Heintzelman even more. "On the nights of the 30th and 31st the regiment [102nd Pennsylvania] endured probably the worst storm of its experience." The next morning, nothing went right for the Confederates. Maj. Gen. D. H. Hill's four brigades finally began a frontal attack shortly before 1:00 p.m. Brig. Gen. Samuel Garland's brigade was the first to strike Casey's advanced and ill-prepared command. Garland's men quickly drove back the pickets and broke through the Federals' first line. Before long, Casey's division ceased to be an effective fighting unit.[16]

Couch's Division heard and saw the initial fighting. Just after 1:00 p.m., a few solid shot cleared the front lines and struck the ground near the brigadier's tent.

> The pickets [Casey's] broke and accompanied by camp followers, sick men, and stragglers retreated in a steady stream to the rear, giving the impression of a panic. Between 1 and 2 o'clock Casey's Division was forced back to our line [Couch's].

Keyes ordered Peck's Brigade forward to support Casey's left flank, now under attack by Brig. Gen. Robert Rodes's Alabamians. Charles Devens's Third Brigade moved up and covered the Williamsburg Stage Road, leading to Casey's center. Brig. Gen. John J. Abercrombie, Lawrence Graham's replacement, positioned his Second Brigade on Devens's right. Ordered by Keyes to support Casey's right, Couch took two regiments from the Second Brigade, Thomas Neill's 23rd and the 61st Pennsylvania, and led them forward in a counterattack about 2:30 p.m. They tried to stop Samuel Garland's advance but were soon cut off and fell back to Fair Oaks Station. Unable to communicate with Couch, his three brigade commanders fought the rest of the day on their own.[17]

Peck initially committed three regiments and they soon became scattered across the battlefield. The 93rd and 102nd Pennsylvania remained in reserve. About 4:30 p.m., General Keyes sent the last two regiments to the right. Moving at double-quick, the Pennsylvanians formed a battle line, then charged. Approaching on their right, an enemy column, most likely Colonel Micah Jenkins's brigade, "advanced under a heavy fire and formed a line oblique to the Nine Mile Road." Rowley halted the 102nd at a line of abandoned rifle pits and ordered them to open fire. After 30 minutes of intense firing, a musket ball struck the back of Rowley's head, knocking him down. Finding his colonel severely stunned, Lt. Col. Joseph M. Kinkead took command of the regiment. He brought the men slowly back, crossing the Williamsburg Stage Road into heavy woods. At 6:00 p.m., they formed their third and last line of battle. It held until dark. Reinforcements from Bull Sumner's Second Corps stopped Brig. Gen. W. H. Whiting's division at Fair Oaks Station. Here, Philip Kearny relieved Couch that evening. Peck later praised his regimental commanders and singled one out: "Rowley would not quit his regiment."[18]

General Peck felt justified in complimenting his four regimental commanders, one killed and two wounded at Seven Pines. After dark, orderlies took Rowley to an army hospital at Savage's Station. Here, M. P. Morrison,

Seriously wounded at Fair Oaks, Col. Thomas A. Rowley refused to quit his regiment. Courtesy of Mass. MOLLUS and USAMHI.

the 102nd's regimental surgeon, found the colonel's skull fractured and removed a detached bone fragment. During subsequent dressing changes, the doctor took out at least five additional pieces of bone. Morrison considered the injury serious but the patient refused to leave his command. In the same hospital lay a severely wounded Capt. John Patterson. A bullet had penetrated Patterson's chest, collapsed the left lung, and stopped just short of exiting his back. Attending physicians considered the wound probably fatal but the captain survived. Avoiding capture at Savage's Station, Patterson went by hospital steamer to Washington where he began a slow recovery.[19]

Kinkead submitted this battle report to the wounded Rowley:

> On reaching the line of rifle pits, the command was given from the rear to halt and commence firing. Captain Patterson (Company E) and Lieutenant Kenny were shot through the body and our men lay wounded and dying in the rear of each of the six companies that were in line. Although it may appear like making invidious distinctions, I cannot allow the opportunity to pass without calling your attention to the gallantry of Captain Patterson, who, as he lay bleeding, told his men to stay in their places and not trouble themselves about him until they had gained the victory.

The 102nd retired to White Oak Swamp and went on picket duty. Even though the 23rd Pennsylvania had suffered the highest casualties of Peck's regiments at Fairs Oaks, Couch failed to cite Thomas Neill's command in his report. Frank Wheaton and the 2nd Rhode Island did not come under fire at Seven Pines.[20]

Retreat to Malvern Hill

> Rowley would not quit his regiment. —*Brig. Gen. John J. Peck*[21]

For Rowley, the Civil War had become more than praise from commanding officers and regimental gifts. Like any person in the military spotlight, Thomas Rowley had detractors back home. In a May 28, 1862, letter to her recuperating husband, Almira Patterson discussed a story currently making the rounds in Pittsburgh:

> There is a report in the City about Col Rowley and not any to his credit either[.] Doubtless it may be false though the man that tell it says it is true. "That during the battle [Seven Pines] he got down from his horse (swearing he would be among his men). Took a gun and got *behind a stump*," where *he* was safe from harm while all the rest were exposed to the deadly fire. Moreover, it is said that the Col did this same thing in Mexico. I do wonder if there is any truth in this story{.} If you know do tell me!

Unfortunately, John Patterson's reply cannot be found.[22]

Events following the future Battle of Chancellorsville may explain Almira Patterson's rumor. In late May 1863, two line officers from the 102nd Pennsylvania charged Lieutenant Colonel Kinkead with cowardice before the enemy. Captain D. Kirk, Company L, then a sergeant major, claimed that Kinkead "did absent himself from his regiment without proper authority while said Regiment was engaged with the enemy [at Seven Pines] and did not rejoin his Regiment until after it had fallen back to the line of entrenchments near Savage Station." Second Lt. Thomas A. McLaughlin, Company I, charged Kinkead with lying "down behind a tree with his back to the enemy and did continue in this position while the men ... were standing up firing ... and that he afterwards left the field [Seven Pines] before the Regiment fell back" that evening. There is no discussion regarding the timing of these events relative to Rowley's wounding.[23]

Fortunately for George McClellan, his adversary did not destroy the Third and Fourth Corps on May 31. By mid-June, Sumner's Second and William Franklin's Sixth Corps had joined Keyes and Heintzelman south of the Chickahominy. Only Brig. Gen. Fitz-John Porter's Fifth Corps on the army's extreme right remained north of the river. Unhappy with Erasmus Keyes's performance at Seven Pines, McClellan posted the Fourth Corps "as far from the scene of any probable fighting as possible." Keyes's command occupied the army's left flank just south of Heintzelman's Third Corps. Brig. Gen. Innis N. Palmer, an 1846 West Point graduate and a prewar cavalry officer, took command of the Third Brigade from a wounded Charles Devens. In late June, McClellan sent Silas Casey to the army's supply depot at White House Landing and gave the division to John Peck. Brig. Gen. Albion Howe took over the First Brigade. Graduating from West Point in 1841, he earned a brevet promotion during the Mexican War, and spent the intervening years commanding an artillery battery. Promoted June 11 to brigadier, this would be Howe's first infantry command. To many, a Federal victory outside Richmond seemed imminent, just a matter of time. In any case, all remained quiet at the White Oak Swamp.[24]

Joe Johnston, seriously wounded near Fair Oaks Station the afternoon of May 31, was relieved of army command. Twenty-four hours later, President Jefferson Davis gave the Army of Northern Virginia to Robert E. Lee. Three and a half weeks passed, then George McClellan opened the Seven Days Campaign. At 8:30 a.m. on June 26, Joseph Hooker attacked Brig. Gen. Benjamin Huger's division, entrenched two miles west of Seven Pines. Later that morning, Darius Couch received orders from Keyes "to move forward two brigades to support Hooker." Howe's First and Palmer's Third advanced and remained in reserve until 2:30 p.m. Ordered forward by Heintzelman, Palmer advanced into some woods and came under enemy artillery fire. The fighting ended around sunset. Except for a 600-yard advance of the Third Corps's picket lines and a thousand Federal casualties, the Battle of Oak Grove gained nothing. The 102nd returned to its previous position.[25]

On June 26, Day 2 of the Seven Days, Lee responded to McClellan's opening move by attacking the Fifth Corps at Mechanicsville. The following day, he drove Porter from the field at Gaines's Mill. By sunset of Day 3, George McClellan had decided to make a change of base to Harrison's Landing on the James River. That evening, orders went out for the Army of the Potomac to begin a strategic withdrawal. Shortly after midnight, June 28, Erasmus Keyes received instructions to move three infantry brigades and all their artillery and baggage across White Oak Swamp before daylight. At that moment, there was not a single bridge across this broad stream capable of carrying a wheeled carriage. Engineering details went out immediately. After some confusion and conflicting orders, Couch's division vacated its entrenchments and began marching south and east on the James City Road toward a nonexistent White Oak Bridge.[26]

The 50th New York Engineers finished upgrading an existing bridge two hours before sunrise. Peck's division crossed first, followed by Couch's. At noon, Keyes ordered the two divisions to "take position at the junction of the James River, New Market, and Charles City Roads" located in a small hamlet called Glendale, four miles from White Oak Bridge. For the Army of the Potomac to escape Lee's pursuit and reach Harrison's Landing, this critical crossroads must be held. By noon, two Fourth Corps brigades and several batteries were in position. By sunset, the last two infantry brigades, Howe's and Abercrombie's, and most of the corps's artillery and wagons had joined them. That night Rowley and the 102nd watched as a continuous stream of infantry, artillery, and supply wagons flowed past. Overall, Day 4 was quiet, like the eye of the storm.[27]

Early the next morning, June 29, a regiment of North Carolina cavalry drove back Federal pickets on the New Market Road and mistakenly charged into Couch's lines. Musketry and a couple of artillery rounds stopped their advance. The Confederates quickly turned around and rode off, suffering over 80 casualties. Brig. Gen. George Sykes's Second Corps Division came up before noon and formed on Couch's right. During the afternoon, John Magruder's leading brigades struck Second and Sixth Corps units at the appropriately named Savage's Station, two miles east of Seven Pines. The battle ultimately ended in a stalemate. Federal casualties outnumbered Confederate two to one but Lee failed to disrupt McClellan's retreat.[28]

Keyes received orders about noon to "move my whole force to the James River, where I was to communicate with the gunboats, guard Turkey Bridge, the mill-pond and stream leading to the river." In case of attack, Fitz-John Porter would support the Fourth Corps. By evening, sufficient Second and Third Corps troops had reached Glendale to relieve Keyes. Leading the way, Couch's division made a night march south on the Quaker Road, crossed Malvern Hill, and stopped at Haxall's Landing on the James just before sunrise, June 30, Day 6. At the same time, farther north, the last Federal units safely crossed White Oak Swamp.[29]

Shortly after reaching the James, Col. Frank Wheaton led the 2nd Rhode Island from Haxall's, marched four miles west on the River Road, and occupied the bridge over Turkey Run. By midmorning only the Fourth Corps and two of Porter's Fifth Corps divisions had reached the James. Two-thirds of McClellan's army still guarded the crossings over White Oak Swamp and Glendale.[30]

On the far right of Lee's converging army, Maj. Gen. Theophilus Holmes commanded over 7,000 infantry and six batteries of artillery. His assignment June 30 was to advance eastward on the River Road about three and a half miles and disrupt the Federal supply trains driving south on the Quaker Road. Recognizing that an enemy column on the River Road posed a direct threat to Malvern Hill, General McClellan, between 3:00 and 4:00 p.m., sent orders to Keyes for Couch to be ready to move immediately. If the enemy threatened to break through Porter's two divisions on Malvern Hill, Couch should advance and attack. At Haxall's, the 102nd watched General McClellan ride by and board the gunboat *Galena,* which departed and steamed upriver. Holmes, 57 years old and almost deaf, could not manage a field command. He opened fire on Malvern Hill that afternoon with six guns but did not push his infantry forward. Fitz-John Porter replied with the Federal's artillery reserve that quickly silenced the enemy battery and panicked his infantry.[31]

Robert E. Lee's goal for June 30 was to cut McClellan's army in two at Glendale. On paper, Lee committed over 70,000 men. Less than half that number actually became engaged. The fighting began about 3:00 p.m. Three of James Longstreet's brigades opened the attack and broke through George McCall's Pennsylvania Reserves holding the Federal center on Frazier's Farm. Phil Kearny and Joe Hooker pushed their men forward, trying to contain the damage. During the next four hours, the divisions of Longstreet and A. P. Hill were fully committed. Darkness and Federal reinforcements combined to stop the Confederate assaults. The flow of McClellan's supply wagons continued unabated across Malvern Hill. Years later, Col. E. Porter Alexander, chief of artillery for Longstreet's corps, looked back at the day:

> I have often thought that in his [Robert E. Lee's] retrospect of the war no one day of the whole four years would seem to him more unfortunate than June 30, 1862. It was, undoubtedly, the opportunity of his life, for the Confederacy was then in its prime, with more men available than ever before or after. And at no other period would the moral or the physical effect of a victory have been so great as upon this occasion.[32]

Even though Holmes never threatened the Fifth Corps, Darius Couch received orders to move forward. Rowley called the 102nd into line at 2:30 p.m. and they marched toward the sound of the guns. Assigned to a reserve position, the division stopped short of the fighting and formed a battle line on the Quaker Road. That evening, Bull Sumner took charge of the Federal

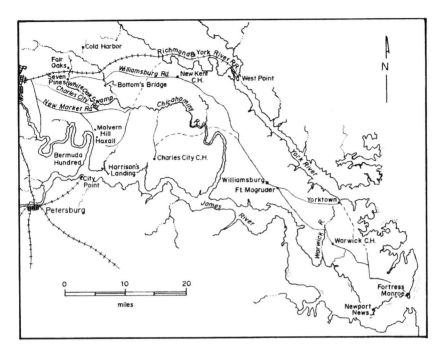

The Peninsula Campaign as seen by Thomas Rowley. Map by John Heiser.

withdrawal from Glendale. Shortly after dark, Couch received orders to advance to the crossroads and report to the Second Corps commander. Howe's and Abercrombie's brigades marched through town and occupied the afternoon's battlefield. Both sides were now tending their wounded. The 102nd watched as McCall's, Kearny's, and Hooker's divisions completed their pullback. Day 6 ended. At 2:00 a.m. on July 1, General Sumner told Couch to return to the same position occupied earlier that evening.[33]

George McClellan selected Malvern Hill as the army's rallying point. In truth, it was only an open plateau, roughly a mile and a quarter in length, north to south, and about 1,200 yards wide, east to west. Directly south and 130 feet below its crest was the James River. Turkey Run, flowing north to south, and Western Run, flowing northwest to southeast, generally defined the plateau's western and eastern boundaries respectively. Lee most likely would attack the Federal front and right flank. Consequently, McClellan massed seven infantry divisions and the artillery reserve facing north and east. The Federals formed an inverted "U." Two of Couch's brigades, Palmer's and Howe's, occupied the closed end's right half. The Quaker Road (James River Road) separated Palmer's command from Brig. Gen. Charles Griffin's brigade, Brig. Gen. George Morell's Fifth Corps Division. In front, oat and wheat fields extended north to a woods that bordered Western Run. Initially eight artillery batteries supported Couch and Morell, four divisional and four from the reserve. Still out of favor with the commanding general, Erasmus Keyes and John Peck's division remained at Haxall's Landing. Frank Wheaton's Rhode Islanders continued to hold the River Road Bridge over Turkey Run.[34]

For the first time since the Seven Days began, Robert E. Lee's Army of Northern Virginia was united on the same battlefield. The same could also be said of George McClellan's command. Beginning at Mechanicsville, the Army of the Potomac had continually eluded Lee's efforts to end its effectiveness. One more opportunity existed before the Federals would be under the navy's protection at Harrison's Landing. The massed infantry and artillery on Malvern Hill were intimidating. Fitz-John Porter had held a similar position at Gaines's Mill and only the enemy's last charge broke through his lines. Near daybreak, Lee decided to attack the Federal position. Stonewall Jackson's, Benjamin Huger's, and "Prince" John Magruder's commands would do the fighting on Day 7. From this point on, nothing seemed to go right for the Confederates.[35]

Inaccurate maps had already misled Magruder, who would waste over three hours getting into position. Confederate artillery would be ineffectively managed throughout the day. As a result, Col. Henry Hunt's Artillery Reserve and divisional batteries near the front dominated the battlefield. Poorly written field orders not only disrupted Lee's initial plan of attack but would also result in the general losing control of his army. To Colonel Rowley and the 102nd Pennsylvania that morning, the temperature was already hot and conditions could only get worse.[36]

Albion Howe's Brigade held the right or eastern half of Couch's position. About 8:00 a.m., the brigade formed a line of battle. Its right bordered a deep ravine that fell off about 60 feet to Western Run, edged by a thin belt of woods on both sides. This stream flowed obliquely across Howe's front. The line of trees expanded into heavy woods 500 yards north of the brigade's left center. From the right, Howe's line extended west toward Palmer. The only cover was a "tongue of woods," left of center. To the south or rear, the ground was open over a half mile to the River Road. One battery supported each brigade. Howe positioned his so that it could sweep the open ground in front and cover the woods bordering Western Run. By 9:00, the enemy completed placing two batteries, one 1,200 yards to the north, the second farther north and to the right. These guns opened fire and Howe ordered his men to lie down.[37]

The first enemy infantry appeared around 8:00 a.m. Brig. Gen. Lewis Armistead's Virginians pushed back Federal skirmishers, advanced toward Griffin, then took cover in a ravine. About 10:00 a.m., the Confederates launched a probing attack against Howe but Couch's and Morell's divisional batteries drove it back. Henry Hunt's artillery continued to duel with the enemy for several hours. Around noon, Berdan's Sharpshooters fell back as Brig. Gen. Rans Wright's Georgians moved against Griffin's left. Federal guns stopped Wright's advance. To this point, only the artillery had been engaged. Phil Kearny's division came up and took a position to the right and rear of Couch. Abercrombie's brigade, initially held in reserve, moved forward and reinforced both Howe and Palmer. At 2:30 p.m., the fighting shifted to Couch's front.[38]

D. H. Hill started his five brigades forward around 1:00 p.m., one on Morell's side of the Quaker Road, the other four on Couch's. The area of heavy woods near Western Run broke up Hill's command. Instead of attacking Malvern Hill as a unified division, the disorganized brigades made five separate attacks. About 2:30 p.m., Howe's, Abercrombie's, and Palmer's men watched as Brig. Gen. George B. Anderson's brigade, Hill's division, cleared the woods and nearby fence. The Confederate infantry formed a line of battle and started forward. Facing an isolated assault, Federal guns focused on Anderson's four regiments. When they came within musket range, Palmer's and Howe's men rose and fired. George Anderson's entire line stopped, wavered, and then fell back as Hill moved a second brigade forward.[39]

The 102nd Pennsylvania held a reserve position behind the brigade's front line. Just after 4:00 p.m., the musketry and artillery fire increased substantially. Brig. Gen. Robert Rodes's brigade, led that afternoon by Col. John B. Gordon, forced its way up Malvern Hill. Howe's men jumped up and fired. Gordon's five Alabama regiments stood their ground and volleyed back. Fortunately for the Federals, the enemy fire was high. Howe had the advantages of position and firepower. Staggered by the musketry, Gordon's line halted, then began falling back. At this point, Rowley, then in reserve, received orders to come up at once. While taking artillery and musket fire, the Pennsylvanians charged through a grain field and struck Gordon's line. Howe later remembered, "Nobly and gallantly did every man of the regiment respond to the order, and the impetuous dash of our men the enemy could not stand, but gave way." Rodes's command fell back to the woods and Howe's left wing advanced down the slope several hundred yards. The 102nd held this new position. It gave them the ability to open a crossfire on any subsequent attacks. Neill's 23rd Pennsylvania and a fresh battery came up and reinforced Albion Howe's line. With nothing left in reserve, Darius Couch concluded that his division needed immediate support. Since General Keyes was off the battlefield, Couch's request for help went to Second Corps Headquarters.[40]

Bull Sumner responded by sending Brig. Gen. John Caldwell's brigade. At Third Corps, Samuel Heintzelman released Brig. Gen. Daniel Sickles's command. Col. John Barlow led two of Caldwell's regiments to Howe's sector. Two fresh batteries took position behind the reinforced infantry. D. H. Hill ran out of brigades and could not find any reinforcements. There were no further assaults that afternoon on Couch's line. Shortly after 6:00 p.m., John Magruder launched the day's heaviest attack against Morell's division. Confederate infantry almost reached the supporting batteries but Griffin's, Abercrombie's, and Palmer's men advanced past the guns and drove the Confederates back. The rebels gave up the field, but it could have gone either way on Morell's front.[41]

The disjointed, unproductive charges made in response to Robert E. Lee's poorly written and misunderstood orders finally stopped. Earlier, Rowley's men had followed the retreating enemy taking a position in front or north of the day's original line. Before 6:00 p.m. the regiment was ordered to move by the left flank into a wooded ravine, possibly the one occupied earlier by Armistead. The 102nd now came under fire from Confederate batteries and sharpshooters hiding in tree-tops and behind shocks of grain. Howe brought them back to the main line at 2:30 a.m. on July 2. Couch's division suffered over 600 casualties on Malvern Hill and the 102nd Pennsylvania 60, their only engagement of the Seven Days.[42]

In spite of achieving a major victory July 1, McClellan ordered a complete withdrawal from Malvern Hill. The next day, Rowley's Regiment marched seven miles to Harrison's Landing where it encamped for over a month. For the first time, the Army of the Potomac became openly discouraged with McClellan's leadership. During July, the James River bottomland was continuously hot and humid.

> The want of room was prejudicial to the cleanliness as well as the well being of the private soldiers. The camps were unhealthy, water of bad quality. July heat was scarcely tempered by the dreadful storms we had almost every afternoon. An unhealthy odor infected the air around the tents and the heat, vermin, and flies left mighty little chance for rest or repose. Night alone brought a little relief.

The lists of those sick, dying, and dead from disease lengthened. In spite of replacements, new equipment, and plentiful supplies, the army grew weaker each day. While he was still a patient in Washington, the army promoted John Patterson to major July 3. Politics, intrigue, and reorganizations continued unabated.[43]

4. Second Bull Run, Antietam, and Fredericksburg

"Make Rowley General and hold me responsible."
—*James K. Moorhead*[1]

Lincoln visited Harrison's Landing on July 8 to learn what the commanding general intended to do. Two weeks earlier, the president had combined Maj. Gen. John Fremont's Mountain Department, Nathaniel Banks's Department of the Shenandoah, and Irwin McDowell's Department of the Rappahannock. They became respectively the First, Second, and Third Corps of the Army of Virginia, led by Maj. Gen. John Pope. The new commander was currently trying to concentrate his scattered commands. Wanting nothing to do with Pope, McClellan told Lincoln that his army should be reinforced and remain on the peninsula. Their discussion ended with little accomplished. The 102nd was "all in line this evening to receive the President, he past us at dusk." Returning to Washington, Lincoln promoted Maj. Gen. Henry Halleck to general in chief of the Union armies, then sent him to Harrison's Landing. The general in chief left the army commander with two choices: attack Richmond or leave the James. Finding McClellan's response unacceptable, Halleck issued orders August 3 for the Army of the Potomac to come north and join John Pope.[2]

Shortly after Malvern Hill, Howe's brigade was redesignated the Third. During July, Couch became ill and tendered his resignation. McClellan refused to forward it and appointed him major general instead. August 9, Stonewall Jackson forced the Army of Virginia's Second Corps to withdraw from Cedar Mountain, eight miles south of Culpeper, Virginia. This battle opened the Second Bull Run campaign. The next day, Rowley announced the coming departure for Harrison's Landing.

> Hospitals were vacated. Baggage and heavy artillery were loaded on transports. This proved to the army that we were to leave the hated Peninsula and the effect on the men was wonderful. They seemed to be transformed by joy. Everything we did not want to take with us was put on the bonfire.[3]

Robert E. Lee left Richmond by train August 15 to join his corps com-

33

manders, Jackson and Longstreet, at Gordonsville, Virginia. His adversary, John Pope, had positioned the Army of Virginia between the Rapidan and Rappahannock Rivers, just north of the Army of Northern Virginia. The 102nd departed Harrison's Landing the next morning and four days later reached the York River. They marched through Yorktown on August 24 and later encamped near Fort Monroe. Orders to embark finally arrived August 29. Rowley led his men on board the transports that sailed the next day. Near dawn, they reached Alexandria and found themselves in the middle of a Federal disaster.[4]

Four days before Rowley's return, Lee split his army, sending Jackson in a wide sweep around Pope's right. August 28, Brig. Gen. John Gibbon's Iron Brigade, supported by Abner Doubleday, engaged Maj. Gen. Richard S. Ewell's division, Jackson's Corps. The evening battle took place near Groveton, four miles west of Bull Run. In response to this fighting, John Pope hurriedly concentrated his forces on the old Manassas battlefield. Operating under the erroneous assumption that Jackson's corps was retreating, he attacked the Confederate position just north of the Warrenton Turnpike. The Army of Virginia, reinforced by Heintzelman's and Porter's corps, launched several isolated, uncoordinated assaults against Jackson, all of which failed. Longstreet's corps reached the battlefield about noon August 29, uniting Lee's army. Undaunted and ignoring warnings from his subordinates, Pope renewed his assault on Jackson the next day. Waiting until the Federals were fully committed against his left, Lee launched Longstreet, who quickly destroyed the Federal left. A stubborn defense of Henry House Hill, led by Brig. Gen. John Reynolds and George Meade, and Maj. Gen. Jesse Reno, enabled most of Pope's routed army to escape across the Stone Bridge.[5]

Henry Halleck issued orders August 30 for all arriving regiments to proceed immediately to Pope's headquarters near Manassas. After disembarking at Alexandria, Howe's brigade started for Fairfax Court House. Stragglers and skulkers led the Federal retreat from Bull Run toward the capital's fortifications. Stopping short of Centreville, the 102nd supported artillery during the September 1 fighting at Chantilly. That evening, the Federals lost two of their most promising commanders, Philip Kearny and Isaac Stevens. The Army of Virginia continued its retreat into Washington. To the west, nothing stood between Robert E. Lee and Pennsylvania.[6]

George McClellan placed Couch under the temporary command of Joseph Hooker on September 2 and positioned his Fourth Corps division at the Chain Bridge. After two days in Virginia, Howe's brigade crossed the river September 5, and marched through Tennallytown. The 102nd Pennsylvania passed their old camp, the campaign's starting point, with nothing to show for their losses on the peninsula. Couch's command, about 7,500 effectives, moved west and stopped at Offut's Crossroads on September 6. Elsewhere that day, John Pope departed for Minnesota and the Army of Virginia passed into history. General McClellan resumed command of the Army of the Potomac. It left Washington on September 7 and slowly headed northwest in pursuit of the Army of Northern Virginia.[7]

Now assigned to Major General William Franklin's Sixth Corps, Couch's Division guarded the Potomac fords from Offut's to Poolesville, Maryland. They marched northwest along the river road, leaving a detachment at each crossing. On September 7, Edward Hoon, 102nd Pennsylvania, optimistically wrote his mother:

> We have plenty to eat such as it is. We have small tents and three stay in a tent. We have good clothing.... We are about 75 miles from Washington City up toward Harpers ferry. the rebels is trying to git a cross the river in to Myrland [sic]. That is whare [sic] we want them.[8]

With Franklin protecting the left flank, McClellan cautiously moved his army toward Frederick, Maryland. Regiments from Nathaniel Banks's former Army of Virginia corps began relieving Couch's units September 11. Howe's brigade, now the Second, mustered five regiments, 93rd, 98th, 102nd, and 139th Pennsylvania and the 62nd New York. Charles Devens's First Brigade included the 10th Massachusetts, led by Col. Henry L. Eustis, and Frank Wheaton's 2nd Rhode Island. Brig. Gen. John Cochrane's Third Brigade contained Thomas Neill's 23rd Pennsylvania. In 18 months, the four regimental commanders, Rowley, Eustis, Wheaton, and Neill, would meet again in a Culpeper courtroom.[9]

While camped two miles south of Frederick, Robert E. Lee decided September 9 to divide his army again and issued Order 191. He committed 26 out of 40 available brigades to a three-pronged assault on Harpers Ferry. After crossing South Mountain, the remaining Confederate forces, Longstreet's command, would assemble between Boonsboro and Hagerstown. Lee assumed that by the time McClellan figured out what was happening, Harpers Ferry would be Jackson's and the Army of Northern Virginia reunited, its supply lines secured. By the evening of Wednesday, September 10, all of Lee's army except for Stuart's cavalry had left the Frederick area. Friday afternoon, Brig. Gen. Jacob Cox's Ninth Corps division drove Stuart out. At this point, no one, including McClellan, had the faintest idea of what Lee was going to do.[10]

Saturday morning, September 13, Army of the Potomac units continued to arrive and bivouac outside Frederick. Farther west, Stonewall Jackson closed the ring at Harpers Ferry and Lee waited for news at his Hagerstown headquarters. Shortly before noon, an aide handed George McClellan a copy of Lee's Order 191, the "Lost Order." Now aware that Lee had divided his army, McClellan decided to advance his right wing, three full corps, through

Turner's Gap towards Boonsboro. Maj. Gen. William Franklin's two Sixth Corps divisions were six miles to the south at Buckeystown and Darius Couch's five miles farther south at Licksville. Franklin would lead the left wing through Crampton's Gap and raise the siege at Harpers Ferry. Eighteen hours passed, however, before either Federal wing moved.[11]

Relieved by Nathaniel Banks's men September 12, the 102nd Pennsylvania resumed the slow march westward on the river road, checking the Potomac's fords and crossings for enemy activity. Even though his chest wound continued to discharge, Maj. John Patterson departed Washington on September 13 and began what would be a painful journey of over 35 miles to rejoin his regiment. While Lee's Order 191 passed up the Federal chain of command that morning, the 102nd marched through Barnesville and advanced a short distance farther to Licksville. After sunset, McClellan ordered Couch's command to Jefferson, six miles southwest of Frederick.[12]

The next morning, September 14, Rowley led his men down the Rohrersville Road toward South Mountain. Up ahead, William Franklin's two divisions departed Buckeystown at 6:00 a.m. Three miles later, they stopped in Jefferson and waited for Couch to catch up. "Learning that this division was still some distance in the rear," Franklin moved on to Burkittsville before noon. Four hours later, Maj. Gen. Henry Slocum's division captured Crampton's Gap, forcing Brig. Gen. Howell Cobb's brigade into Pleasant Valley. To the north, Maj. Gen. Jesse Reno's Ninth Corps and Joe Hooker's First were trying to drive D. H. Hill's division out of Turner's and Fox's Gaps. Couch did not reach Crampton's until 10:00 p.m., well after the fighting there had ended.[13]

Sunrise, September 15, found the four South Mountain passes in Federal hands, giving McClellan the initiative. Before Franklin could launch an assault against Maj. Gen. Lafayette McLaws's division south of Brownsville, the Harpers Ferry garrison surrendered. Seventeen miles to the north, McClellan watchfully advanced his four corps westward toward Sharpsburg. Late that afternoon, Jackson began moving his forces north to join Lee west of Antietam Creek. Only A. P. Hill's Light Division remained at Harpers Ferry that night. Back in Pleasant Valley, Franklin's three divisions established a position between Rohrersville and Brownsville and remained there for two days, protecting the Federal left and rear. The Sixth Corps's inactivity enabled John Patterson to reach the 102nd September 16.[14]

McClellan's battle orders reached William Franklin the evening of September 16. At daylight, two of the three divisions would start north toward Keedysville and rejoin the main army east of Antietam Creek. Couch's command, however, would move south and occupy Maryland Heights overlooking Harpers Ferry. The commanding general offered no explanation regarding this assignment. The next morning, Henry Slocum's and William "Baldy"

Smith's divisions set out at 5:30 a.m. for Antietam Creek, nine miles away. A. P. Hill's command departed Harpers Ferry two hours later. Hill's objective that day, Lee's right, lay 17 grueling miles to the north. Couch's three brigades marched south from Rohrersville toward Maryland Heights seven miles away. Shortly after Joe Hooker launched the day's opening attack on Lee's left, George McClellan had second thoughts and dispatched an aide with a recall order for Darius Couch. Franklin's leading units reached the battlefield around 10:00 a.m.[15]

Couch most likely received McClellan's recall close to noon. His three brigades stopped their ascent up Maryland Heights, climbed down, and began a 16-

Rowley considered Brig. Gen. Henry L. Eustis, shown here, and Frank Wheaton two of the most bitter members of the Culpeper court. Courtesy of USAMHI.

mile march toward the sound of the guns. Across the Potomac, A. P. Hill continued pushing his men forward. McClellan held Slocum's and Smith's divisions in reserve the entire day. Around 2:30 p.m., when Maj. Gen. Ambrose Burnside's Ninth Corps columns were ready to break through Lee's right, A. P. Hill's leading brigade came into line. Hill not only stopped the Federals but also drove back the Ninth Corps, ending McClellan's last chance for a victory on September 17. The 102nd's historian recorded that they arrived on the battlefield after sunset, probably around 8:30 p.m. Like A. P. Hill's, Couch's division had also completed a hard, 17-mile march in eight hours but accomplished nothing. McClellan and Franklin, however, reported their arrival on the morning of the 18th. Regardless, at sunrise September 18, Rowley advanced his regiment to the front near the Dunkard Church, expecting to attack, "but for some reason the order was changed to attack at daylight on the 19th." The Army of the Potomac spent the day "collecting the dispersed, giving rest to the fatigued, removing the wounded, burying the dead, and the necessary preparations for a renewal of the battle." Couch's command took "rest and refreshment." During the night, Confederate forces crossed the Potomac and by morning were safely in Virginia.[16]

Before leaving Maryland, General Lee sent Stuart's cavalry across the

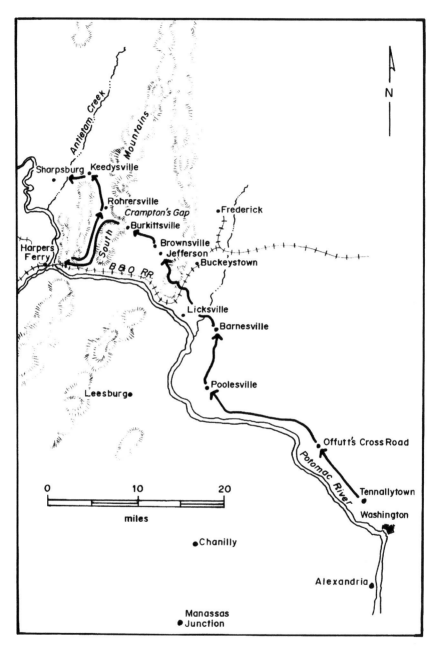

Route of March for Couch's Division — Washington to Antietam. Map by John Heiser.

river into West Virginia the afternoon of September 18. They recrossed the
river near Williamsport, Maryland, six miles southwest of Hagerstown, and
prepared to create a diversion. Stuart "was also aided in this demonstration
by a battalion of infantry and a section of artillery." To protect Lee's retreating columns, J.E.B. Stuart took up a position the next day overlooking
Williamsport and made "active demonstrations ... toward the enemy." George
McClellan received word "that General Stuart had made his appearance at
Williamsport with some 4,000 cavalry and six pieces of artillery, and that
10,000 infantry were marching on the same point." The major general ordered
Couch, accompanied by Pleasonton's cavalry, to advance at once. Franklin's
two divisions moved to within supporting distance. McClellan later recorded,
"General Couch made a prompt and rapid march to Williamsport and
attacked the enemy vigorously but they made their escape across the river."
J.E.B. Stuart saw it differently:

> On the 20th, the enemy were drawn toward my position in heavy force,
> Couch's division in advance. Showing a bold front, we maintained our
> position and kept the enemy at bay until dark, when, having skirmished all
> day, we withdrew to the south bank of the Potomac without loss.

McClellan ordered Franklin to Williamsport that evening. Arriving the next
morning, he learned that Stuart had already departed.[17]

The Antietam campaign had not been a good experience for either
Thomas Rowley or his regiment. John Large expressed frustration in a September 22 letter home:

> Couches division is now in no corps & is generally held in reserve[.] [W]e
> were not in the late battle near Sharpsburgh [sic] but get [got] there before
> it was over[.] we were marched night & day until we got there[.] [O]n sti-
> rarday the 20th [Saturday, September 19] we were marched to this place
> [Williamsport] & we found the rebs here in force & as no troops only
> Couches [Couch's] were here, our general [Couch] ordered us to retreat
> one mile back which we did....

Weeks passed before John Patterson's horse and baggage caught up with the
regiment. "But I get along very well as regards both. Col. Rowley on all
marches loans me one of his horses."[18]

Except for organizational changes, little happened during the next two
months. On September 26, McClellan assigned Couch's division to Franklin's
Sixth Corps. Lincoln reviewed the division October 3. A week later, the 102nd
Pennsylvania became part of the Second Brigade, Third Division, Sixth Corps.
The changes kept coming. Darius Couch went to Harpers Ferry on October
7 and relieved Edwin Sumner as commander of the Second Corps. Brig. Gen.
John Newton succeeded Couch at Third Division. Earlier that month, Robert
E. Lee had ordered J.E.B. Stuart to make another armed reconnaissance of

Maj. Gen. John Newton served as Rowley's commanding officer at Fredericks-burg and replaced Doubleday at Gettysburg. Courtesy of Cumberland County Historical Society Collection and USAMHI.

McClellan's army. Stuart and 1,800 cavalrymen departed the Army of Northern Virginia at dawn October 10 on "what proved to be a gaudy adventure."[19]

They crossed the Potomac upstream of Williamsport and headed north, reaching Chambersburg at dusk. Here, 20 miles to McClellan's rear, Stuart captured the town, collected over 1,200 horses, and destroyed Federal stores. The 102nd Pennsylvania was one of several units sent to capture the raiders. John Patterson wrote home:

> Since the 10th we have been moving around pretty briskly, after the "Rebs" who have had the *impudence* to invade Pennsylvania. We have not seen them yet, and I suppose they have as usual eluded us and gone back to Va. Our brigade [Howe's] is guarding one of the approaches, by which it is presumed they will return.

As Patterson predicted, Stuart safely returned to Virginia on October 12, creating another humiliation for Washington. Ambrose Burnside accepted Lincoln's offer to command the Army of the Potomac on November 7. Camped at New Baltimore, Rowley's command heard the news two days later. For the last time George McClellan watched the 102nd pass in review.[20]

The campaign to make Thomas Rowley a brigadier general began that fall. James K. Moorhead, a Democrat turned Republican, represented Pittsburgh's 22nd Congressional District. During the war, both Lincoln and Stanton sought his advice. On October 18, 1862, Moorhead sent his first letter to Stanton recommending Thomas A. Rowley's promotion to brigadier general. The secretary of war forwarded it to Maj. Gen. Ambrose Burnside. John Harper, the Bank of Pittsburgh's president and Stanton's close friend since childhood, echoed this recommendation November 15. Moorhead's second letter, dated November 18, suggested that Stanton "make Rowley General and hold me responsible for the wisdom of the act."[21]

Burnside announced a major reorganization November 14. William Franklin commanded the new Left Grand Division and Baldy Smith, now a major general, the Sixth Corps. Albion Howe left the brigade and took over the Sixth's Second Division. John Newton selected Rowley to succeed Howe as acting brigadier general, temporarily commanding the Third Division's Third Brigade, formerly its Second. On November 29, Lt. Col. Joseph M. Kinkead took charge of the 102nd. Given that Rowley had been cited three times during the Peninsular Campaign — Williamsburg, Seven Pines, and Malvern Hill — Newton's choice seemed logical and should not have come as a surprise. Colonels Eustis, Wheaton, and Neill most likely reacted differently to the announcement than John Patterson who wrote Almira:

> Genl Howe has been taken from us, and placed in command of Smith's Div. Col. Rowley is now acting Brigadier. All the Field & Co Officers of the Brigade are much pleased at his prospect of promotion, and are now preparing a proper petition for his appointment by the President. I hope it may be so, not only on his account but on my own also.

John Patterson advanced to lieutenant colonel in January 1863.[22]

November 13, the day before Rowley took command, dishonor struck his brigade. A general court-martial was appointed to hear the case of Col. James M. McCarter. The prosecution charged the colonel with being drunk on duty; the specification, "while in command of his Regiment [93rd Pennsylvania] at Regimental Drill at Camp near Downsville, Maryland, October 8, 1862, was drunk." Prosecution witnesses Maj. John Mark, Adjutant Jacob Embich, and three company officers, all from the 93rd, testified that the morning of October 8, an already drunken McCarter took command, issued undistinguishable orders, rode unsteadily, and marched the regiment into a stream. Lieutenant Colonel Kinkead, the defense counsel and Rowley's replacement, pointed out that the defendant had suffered a concussion at Fair Oaks that left McCarter partially paralyzed on his left side. This paralysis produced symptoms similar to inebriation. L. K. Haven, brigade staff surgeon, told the court that "all of the [McCarter's] actions ... October 8th, including the falling from his horse, could be attributed to ... Fair Oaks and that the taking of opium for relief of this condition would produce a stupor similar to the [e]ffects of alcohol." Regardless, the court found the colonel "of the Specification of Charge — Guilty, Of the Charge — Guilty" and sentenced him "to be cashiered." Division Commander John Newton referred the proceedings to Grand Division Headquarters with the recommendation that "cashiered" be changed to "dismissal." Major General Franklin approved the action December 18. This disreputable affair proved to be an accurate forewarning of what awaited Thomas Rowley.[23]

Rain, snow, and sleet accompanied Rowley as he slowly marched his brigade southward toward the Rappahannock River. Favorable news from Washington possibly reached him while encamped near Stafford Court House, Virginia. The War Department issued a preliminary list of individuals to rank as brigadier generals of volunteers from November 29, 1862. The order of appointment for these new generals placed Thomas A. Rowley 48th, next to last, and Col. Lysander Cutler, 6th Wisconsin, last. Two other officers from Newton's division also appeared on the list. Frank Wheaton, 2nd Rhode Island, was 29th and Thomas Neill, 23rd Pennsylvania, 44th. If the Senate approved this list as submitted, both Wheaton and Neill would rank ahead of Rowley, then serving as an acting brigadier.[24]

Enduring bitterly cold weather and muddy roads, Rowley's Third Brigade left Belle Plain on December 10 and advanced six miles to Falmouth. The next day they stopped two miles below or south of Fredericksburg.

> The whole army was moving. The weather was cold but clear, and the frost had hardened the ground, so that we [102nd Pennsylvania] avoided the mud pulling. As we descended from Stafford Heights to the valley along the river [Rappahannock], the fog was so heavy and dense that we could not see the opposite side of the river and it was 12 o'clock before the fog lifted. Soon after our batteries commenced to shell the town [Fredericksburg] thus starting fires in many places.

Before dark, the brigade marched back up the heights and bivouacked for the night. Burnside's headquarters issued orders for a dawn assault against Lee's seven-mile line.[25]

Franklin, commanding the Left Grand Division, spent December 12 moving John Reynolds's First Corps and part of Baldy Smith's Sixth across the river. At dawn, the air cold and foggy, Rowley's command crossed on the lower pontoon bridge and formed a line of battle on the Bowling Green Road, just above Hamilton's Crossing. High banks protected the men from enemy artillery fire. About 11:00 a.m., Reynolds launched an attack across the southern portion of the battlefield against Stonewall Jackson. Rowley moved up, becoming a reserve for the First Corps. George Meade's division advanced and broke Jackson's line. He failed to receive support and soon fell back. To the north, Edwin Sumner's and Joseph Hooker's Grand Divisions launched what turned out to be a series of suicidal charges against Longstreet's troops holding Marye's Heights. Rowley's command remained under artillery fire until 9:00 p.m. then returned to the road where a small eminence provided cover. Unaware of how badly he had damaged the Federals, Robert E. Lee prepared for a resumption of Burnside's fruitless assaults.[26]

Rowley's brigade advanced to the front and prepared to charge Jackson's lines at daybreak. The Army of the Potomac, however, did not renew the fighting December 14. Instead, they called a truce and men from both sides recovered the wounded and buried the dead. John Patterson recalled that very few shots were fired. "The skirmishers of the two opposing Army [armies] but 10 yds. apart, engaging in pleasant conversation and trading tobacco for coffee." Around 10:00 p.m. Rowley took his brigade back to the Bowling Green Road.[27]

During a heavy rainstorm the night of December 15, Burnside's troops withdrew to the Rappahannock's north bank. The Third Brigade later reported six men wounded and six missing at Fredericksburg. Before the army recrossed, Frank Wheaton and Thomas Neill received their commissions as brigadier generals. Wheaton immediately relieved Rowley of the Third Brigade and Neill took command of a brigade in Albion Howe's Division. Rowley, still a colonel, returned to the 102nd and joined them in winter quarters at White Oak Church near Falmouth, Virginia. Even though he held command for less than two months, the Third Brigade (62nd New York, 93rd, 98th, 102nd, and 139th Pennsylvania) became "my old brigade."[28]

Burnside ordered the army to leave camp the morning of January 20, 1863, and advance upriver to Bank's Ford. The 102nd Pennsylvania covered eight miles in good weather and bivouacked at about 5:00 p.m. Heavy rain started that evening and never stopped. The next morning, Rowley read an order to the regiment "informing us that we were about to meet the enemy once more." They packed up and resumed the march before daylight. With mud 10 to 18 inches deep, little progress was made. The regiment bivouacked near the Rappahannock, eight miles from Fredericksburg. Rowley prepared his command to move out January 22 but orders to do so never arrived. The troops received a ration of whiskey that afternoon. "After floundering in the mud for a day and a half, the army returned in squads to its camps," mercifully ending the "Mud March." The 102nd "fell in before daylight [January 23] and returned to our old camp ground." Major Patterson felt that "our move would no doubt have been successful but as usual we got stuck in the mud." Joseph Hooker took over the army January 26. Three days later, Thomas Rowley gave the 102nd to Col. Joseph M. Kinkead and departed on leave to Pittsburgh. He received his final pay as colonel, 13th Pennsylvania on January 31. Lieutenant Large wrote his brother February 6, 1863, "Colonel Rowley is now Brigadeer [sic]."[29]

5. First Corps Brigadier

*Our Division and Brigade commanders are also excellent,
and have the entire confidence of the men and
officers under them.—Colonel George McFarland*[1]

Secretary of War Stanton submitted to the Senate on January 14, 1863, a revised list of individuals to be commissioned brigadier generals in the volunteer force. The effective date would still be November 29, 1862. Since it was not in alphabetical order, the relative ranking between individuals became very important. Of the 63 recommended, Thomas Neill was third, Lysander Cutler 16th, Roy Stone 37th, and Thomas Rowley 45th. Surprisingly, the War Department failed to include Frank Wheaton. Stanton's list was referred to Senator Henry Wilson's Committee on Military Affairs. Wilson, a Massachusetts Republican and committee chairman since 1861, returned it to President Lincoln for further consideration. This meant political considerations; e. g., the number of brigadiers by state.[2]

Back in Pittsburgh, Capt. Henry B. Hays, U. S. Cavalry, mustered Thomas Rowley out of service as colonel, 102nd Pennsylvania, and mustered him in as a brigadier general of volunteers February 18, 1863. The State of Pennsylvania, however, did not recognize this promotion until April 18. In an acceptance letter to Adjutant General Lorenzo Thomas, Rowley reported his age as 45 and his year of birth as 1818. The new brigadier also wrote that day to Edwin Stanton requesting command of "my old brigade," Third Brigade, Third Division, Sixth Corps. Rowley closed the letter; "I believe there is now on file in your department the unanimous request of the Field Officers of the Brigade that I be assigned to that command." Stanton neither forwarded Rowley's letter to army headquarters nor acknowledged the request.[3]

In late February, Thomas Rowley returned from Pittsburgh and paid a farewell visit to the 102nd Pennsylvania and "my old brigade." Also rejoining the regiment after a brief leave, Lt. Col. John Patterson "met with a reception on the part of the officers that was truly gratifying." He then welcomed his former commander but others did not. "The reception given Genl Rowley was cold, so cold, that he does not remain in Camp at all, and says that the officers of his old Command do not treat him with common respect, which I can truly say is the fact." Three weeks later, he wrote Almira:

> I am glad Dave Jones told you of the manner I was received and the con-
> trast between my reception and that of Genl Rowley. If his was bad, [Colo-
> nel] Kinkead's was worse. Not an officer met him and did not go to his
> [Kinkead's] quarters until next day. I do not know how he and Rowley
> feels, but if I were either & was treated as they are, I would not stay long.

No one left an explanation for the cold February reception. Less than three
months earlier, the regimental officers had prepared a petition for Rowley's
appointment to brigadier by the president. This radical change in attitude
may have resulted from two factors. First, they knew now that Rowley would
not command either the Third Brigade or the 102nd. He was leaving the "old
13th" after two years and that may have generated resentment. Second, the
field and line officers disliked Kinkead and probably held Rowley responsible for his advancement to command. Events following Chancellorsville would
support the latter explanation.[4]

March 2, 1863, the U. S. Senate received Stanton's revised list of individuals to be promoted to brigadier general of volunteers. It reflected over a
month of political negotiations between the administration and interested
states. Since the January 14 submission, some names had been dropped,
including Roy Stone's, and others added. At first glance, the March revision
appeared to be in alphabetical order but exceptions became apparent. Lysander
Cutler, now eighth out of 74 candidates, began the C's, but Rowley, who fell
to 71st, followed the W's. Neill dropped to 44th. The newcomers included
two Sixth Corps peers of Rowley—William Morris at 52nd and the missing
Frank Wheaton at 58th. Chairman Wilson reported the revised list out of
committee the following day. On March 9, the Senate considered the general officer promotions including three posthumously. With a few exceptions,
it subsequently advised and consented "to the appointments of the said persons, agreeably to their nomination respectively." The final list would not be
released until September 18, 1863.[5]

Leaving his son Harry with the 102nd, Rowley departed and reported
to army headquarters. He waited here for an assignment from Maj. Gen.
Joseph Hooker. While Rowley had been home on leave, the 1st, 2nd, 6th,
and 13th Pennsylvania Reserves were ordered to Washington on February 21.
Four Pennsylvania regiments, the 121st, 135th, 142nd, and 151st, replaced the
Reserves in the First Brigade, Third Division, First Corps. Lt. Col. James R.
Porter, 135th Pennsylvania, served as the temporary brigade commander. On
March 26, Hooker instructed the new brigadier to report to Maj. Gen. John
F. Reynolds for assignment to a brigade. The next day, Reynolds sent Row-
ley to Maj. Gen. Abner Doubleday, Third Division, with the request "that
you assign him to the 1st Brigade now commanded by Col. Porter." Reynolds
also ordered Lysander Cutler to report to the First Division commander,
James Wadsworth, for assignment. Wadsworth gave Cutler command of his

Second Brigade. Lt. George A. Heberton, 110th Pennsylvania, received orders to report "without delay to Brigadier General Thomas A. Rowley ... for duty on his staff." Rowley relieved Colonel Porter on March 30 at Belle Plain, Virginia.[6]

Rowley's new division commander, Abner Doubleday, had experienced his own difficulties that winter. Secretary of War Stanton, with Lincoln's approval, nominated Doubleday for promotion to major general of volunteers January 26. Wilson's committee never took action. On March 6, the War Department resubmitted Doubleday's nomination and it received Senate approval March 9. The next day, Rhode Island's Republican senator, William Sprague, submitted a "motion for consideration that the vote agreeing to the resolution advising and consenting to the appointment of Abner Doubleday be reconsidered." The motion passed and the Senate secretary was ordered to "request the President of the United States to return to the Senate the resolution" that contained Doubleday's promotion. Senator Sprague withdrew his objection March 11 and Abner Doubleday finally became a major general. No explanation exists for Sprague's actions.[7]

Brigadier General Rowley and two close friends experienced a reunion. Col. Edmund L. Dana commanded the 143rd Pennsylvania in Roy Stone's Second Brigade, Doubleday's Third Division. He graduated from Yale College in 1838 becoming a member of the Luzerne County bar three years later. After the outbreak of fighting in Texas, Dana brought an artillery company to Pittsburgh in December 1846. It was redesignated Company I and assigned to the First Pennsylvania Infantry where he met Lieutenant Rowley. Dana accompanied Scott's army to Mexico City and fought at Cerro Gordo. Afterward, he returned to Pittsburgh and mustered out in July 1848. A Wilkes-Barre Democrat, his subsequent campaigns for U. S. House and state senate seats failed. In the summer of 1862, Governor Curtin placed Dana in charge of Camp Luzerne, a rendezvous camp near Wilkes-Barre. The 143rd Pennsylvania, recently recruited and organized, elected the camp commandant their colonel. On February 19, 1863, John Reynolds assigned the regiment to Stone's brigade. Edmund Dana welcomed his "Mexican friend" to the division April 8.[8]

Alfred B. McCalmont, a resident of Franklin, Pennsylvania, Venango County, was the 142nd's lieutenant colonel. Educated at Allegheny and Dickinson Colleges, McCalmont began practicing law in Pittsburgh in 1847 where he became friends with Rowley. Eight years later, McCalmont received an appointment as prothonotary of the Supreme Court, Western District of Pennsylvania. Three years later, he joined the staff of President James Buchanan's attorney general, Jeremiah S. Black, who appointed him assistant attorney general. After Lincoln's inauguration, McCalmont returned to Venango County and resumed law practice. In spite of being highly critical of the administration, he raised a company of volunteers, the Petroleum Guards, assigned to Colonel Robert P. Cummins's 142nd Pennsylvania Volunteers in August 1862.[9]

The brigade's three regimental commanders, however, were strangers to Rowley. After graduating from St. Mary's College in Baltimore, Chapman Biddle initially worked in his family's trading business and spent time in South America. Admitted to the bar in 1848, he did very well financially, specializing in wills and trusts. Biddle served in a Philadelphia militia group, commanded by John Cadwalader. Following Fort Sumter, an artillery battery elected him captain. In June 1862, he received authorization to begin recruiting what would become the 121st Pennsylvania. Next door to Biddle's Philadelphia office, Capt. Langhorne Wister embarked on a similar effort that resulted in the 150th Pennsylvania. These regiments would serve in the same division throughout the war. Promoted to colonel, Biddle succeeded in organizing seven companies. Three companies recruited in Venango County by Elisha Davis, now lieutenant colonel, completed the regiment with Alexander Biddle, the colonel's cousin, its major.[10]

Chapman Biddle took his men to the Chestnut Hill rendezvous camp, "determined to instruct them and himself properly and thoroughly in all duties which they might be called on to perform." Mustered in on September 1, the 121st remained in reserve during the Antietam campaign. The regiment was assigned October 7 to George Meade's Pennsylvania Reserve Division, Reynolds's First Corps. At Fredericksburg, they found themselves on the army's far left when Meade attacked A. P. Hill's breastworks December 13. The 121st sustained 24 killed, 115 wounded, and 10 missing. Reynolds and Meade later commended the regiment for its efforts that day.[11]

In late August 1862, recruits for the 142nd Pennsylvania Infantry were mustered into service when they arrived at Camp Curtin outside Harrisburg, "a very dirty place." On September 1, Robert P. Cummins, formerly a captain in the 10th Pennsylvania Reserves, was appointed colonel and McCalmont lieutenant colonel. Before the war, Cummins had been a director of Somerset County schools. Later elected sheriff, he resigned his commission in January 1862 but returned to the army that summer. The 10 companies that comprised this three-year regiment came from Venango, Somerset, Mercer, Fayette, Union, Monroe, Luzerne, and Westmoreland counties. Ordered to Washington, the 142nd arrived in time to watch the wounded come in from Second Bull Run. While they constructed earthworks, chopped trees, and dug rifle pits for Fort Massachusetts, the Army of the Potomac marched by on its way to South Mountain. Sent next to Frederick, the Pennsylvanians guarded the town, erected hospital tents, and cared for the wounded from Antietam.[12]

Assigned to George Meade's Third Division In early October, the 142nd joined four Pennsylvania Reserve regiments in the Second Brigade. At noon on December 12, they crossed the Rappahannock and held a position that night along the riverbank. The next morning, the regiment initially supported a battery on the left. During the division's afternoon charge against A. P. Hill, the 142nd came under enfilading artillery fire and suffered 270 casualties, killed, wounded, and missing, out of 550 men. Captain Horatio Warren never felt "so discouraged over the result of anything we ever undertook to do, as I did over the result of this [Fredericksburg] our first engagement." Except for the "Mud March," they saw no further action before Rowley's arrival.[13]

A friend before the Civil War, and his defense counsel at Culpeper, Col. Edmund L. Dana commanded the 143rd Pennsylvania. Courtesy of Mass. MOLLUS and USAMHI.

Col. Harrison Allen, previously a major in the 10th Pennsylvania Reserves, commanded the 151st Pennsylvania, a nine-month unit. Men from seven counties filled its ranks with over 60 of them being schoolteachers. Unfortunately, Allen did not work well with his division commander, Abner Doubleday, and his lieutenant colonel, George McFarland. There is no evidence of a problem, however, between Rowley and McFarland.[14]

In February, the 151st departed Alexandria for Belle Plain. They made camp and waited for a brigade assignment. George Fisher McFarland was a no-nonsense individual. "Religion and the temperance movement were also of great importance to McFarland. He strictly attended worship services, regularly studied the Bible, and abstained from using alcohol and tobacco." By March 1863, his personality as an officer had been formed.

> He attacked his military duties with the same alacrity, single-mindedness, and self-discipline that he displayed in his career and personal life prior to

Lt. Col. Alfred McCalmont's written affidavit gives a different view of the July 1, 1863, fighting near the Seminary. Courtesy of Mass. MOLLUS and USAMHI.

the war.... He was a perfectionist, quick to admonish those who did not approach their duties in a serious manner.[15]

Lieutenant Colonel McFarland wrote his wife March 1 that the regiment had been moved from the Second to the First Brigade. His diary entry for March 30 announced, "Genl. Rowley took command of brigade today." Doubleday and Rowley inspected the 151st by company April 12. Six days later, Colonel McFarland had his first discussion with Rowley and recorded that "he seemed to be a man of good sense, no fuss, and very approachable."[16]

Even though John Reynolds announced Rowley's assignment March 28, word that the First Brigade had a new commander spread slowly. On April 8, Pvt. Henry A. Cornwell, 121st Pennsylvania, wrote home, "Porter is our Brigadier Genl." At 6:00 a.m. April 9, Rowley informed his regimental commanders that the brigade would be reviewed that day. They fell in at 7:00, marched three miles, and then halted upon a flat. Here, President Lincoln and General Hooker reviewed the First and Sixth Corps. Mary Lincoln and Abner Doubleday's wife were also present. Capt. Albert Heffley, 142nd, remembered, "the string passed off with several blunders made by some of the Cols [colonels]." First Brigade returned to camp about 3:00 p.m. The next morning, Rowley, accompanied by his aide, Capt. Charles H. Flagg, inspected the 142nd. Afterward, McCalmont apologized for his regiment's appearance and told Rowley that "he could not expect our Regt to come out in the best of trim looking as though his men were kept in Band Boxes, for they had work to do every day." Four days later, the corps inspector visited the 142nd's camp. Following the inspection, Rowley told McCalmont that "we [the 142nd] had a very fine Camp."[17]

Returning to Henry Cornwell's April 8 letter, he told his sister that the Third Division "had been ordered to stay here [Belle Plain] this summer to guard the landing and railroad." He was very glad because "It will save us some very hard marching and a good deal of fighting." If fighting did occur, the Army of the Potomac "expected to whip every thing that comes in our way as long as he [Hooker] has command." Even though none of Cornwell's predictions came true, Joseph Hooker had succeeded in restoring the men's faith in their commanding general.[18]

Chancellorsville

> He [Rowley] paid no attention to either
> [shell].—*Lt. Col. George McFarland*[19]

By mid-April, General Hooker had completed his plans for the coming Chancellorsville campaign. One preliminary objective was to convince Robert

E. Lee that the main Federal attack would be made down river of Fredericksburg. To accomplish this deception, John Reynolds received orders to create a diversion on the Army of Northern Virginia's right. Reynolds initially selected his Third Division to execute this assignment. After being mustered for pay, Doubleday's division left camp at Belle Plain around noon on April 20 for Port Conway, Virginia, a small village on the Rappahannock River. Their objective was to cross the river using a canvas pontoon train and capture the enemy troops stationed at Port Royal. The 151st Pennsylvania led the column that afternoon toward Fletcher's Chapel. The men carried "three days rations and no knapsacks." Rowley selected George McFarland as his guide, the only officer who knew the way. The guide recalled, "We struck the River Side Road, passed a creek where the men had to wade knee deep, then halted an hour or more to make coffee," and later moved on. After enduring five hours of heavy rain and 13 miles of muddy roads, they reached King George Court House between 2:00 and 3:00 a.m. McFarland's exhausted men "lay down on the wet ground without fire or blankets" and were too cold to sleep. To Capt. Albert Heffley, "It was the hardest marching I ever experienced."[20]

After repairing the previous night's damage, the Third Division resumed the march at daybreak and soon passed through Federal cavalry pickets. They covered eight miles, then halted around 9:30 a.m. outside Port Conway and formed a line of battle with skirmishers deployed. Waiting for the pontoon train to catch up, Rowley's brigade spent the next four hours maneuvering and reconnoitering as ordered by the generals. About 3:00 p.m., the wagons finally arrived and proceeded down to the river. Now, according to George McFarland, Doubleday had at last decided to force a crossing. The major general picked Stone's Second Brigade to make the assault. Roy Stone ordered the 150th Pennsylvania to man the boats, row across the Rappahannock, and seize Port Royal. Company F from the 151st received a similar assignment. Dana's 143rd and Lt. Col. Walton Dwight's 149th began pontoon assembly by stretching the canvas over wooden frames. Eight companies of sharpshooters from the two regiments provided covering fire.[21]

The river was over 200 yards wide at Port Conway. Confederate rifle pits and breastworks lined the opposite shore. George McFarland remembered that "the rebels were quite numerous on the other side, and we could see them very distinctly." Company F's task was merely to provide a diversion in case the enemy started firing. He detailed 10 men to move forward and make pontoons out of feed boxes and tail boards. After several minutes, McFarland ordered them to lie down and wait. Colonel Allen and the other nine companies remained in reserve, 500 yards to the rear.[22]

The 143rd and 149th did not finish assembling the pontoons until after sunset. Having no artillery support, Doubleday concluded that a successful crossing at night was impossible and abruptly canceled the assault. He did order that some wooden guns be made and run down to the bank "as if regular 12 pounders." Maj. Thomas Chamberlin, 150th, remembered:

> Soon after nightfall, the pontoons were broken up and reloaded and the division began its return march. Proceeding a mile or two, a halt was made, fires were built in the woods (to give the impression of a large force) and the command bivouacked. About 4:30 AM, the march was resumed.

The sky cleared April 21 and General Doubleday returned to Belle Plain about 8:00 a.m. From his standpoint, they accomplished all they had intended to do. He later wrote that the operation was to be only a pretense of crossing. Rowley's regiments soon appeared after Doubleday. Even though they found a better road, the men straggled in until 5:00 p.m. The next day, Alexander Biddle received word of his promotion to lieutenant colonel, one of the few bright spots that month. McFarland wrote home April 23, "When we were ordered back without firing a gun, they [the men] thought it was marching too far and too hard to return without doing something." Evidently, John Reynolds agreed. Two days later, the 24th Michigan and 14th Brooklyn from Wadsworth's division successfully completed the Port Royal diversion. Lee regarded this down river activity as merely a deception and did nothing. The First Corps, however, knew who had succeeded and who had failed at Port Royal.[23]

Six days later, the Chancellorsville campaign officially began. Led by General Hooker, the Fifth, Eleventh, and Twelfth Corps left camp April 27. Advancing northwest, they began a turning movement around the Army of Northern Virginia's left flank. Twenty-four hours later, Hooker set in motion another feint on the left. The First and Sixth Corps would march down the Rappahannock's north bank and put across one division from each corps. This time Lee might be convinced that the main Federal attack would be at Fredericksburg.[24]

Reynolds's command broke camp at noon Tuesday, April 28, and started toward its selected position a few miles south of Fredericksburg. Rowley's brigade departed its "splendid old camp" between 1:00 and 2:00 p.m. The men carried knapsacks and eight days' rations. Passing First Corps headquarters and the White Oak Church, the column turned south and "struck the river five miles south of Fredericksburg." After marching 10 miles, the men "slept in a wet damp woods, one mile from the river." Captain Heffley recorded in his diary, "The weather is rainy & the roads from camp [Belle Plain] to the river are literally streun [sic] with woolen blankets & overcoats." That evening, George McFarland discovered two other men who shared his April 28 birthday: a private in Company I and Alfred B. McCalmont from the 142nd.[25]

McFarland described the activity that next morning for his wife:

> The men were up at 2:00 AM, April 29, had some coffee, then moved toward the river. After an hour or so, the brigade returned to camp. While the Second and Third Divisions remained in reserve at Pollock's Mill Creek, James Wadsworth's men rowed across the Rappahannock at daybreak and seized the south bank. Engineers hurriedly constructed two pontoon bridges and the other First Division brigades began crossing.

Around noon, Brig. Gen. John C. Robinson's Second Division advanced and stopped near the pontoon bridges. Rowley's brigade "laid around there until after dinner then were marched down to the river & again stacked arms & unslung knapsacks." Close to Robinson, Doubleday's command took position in a small cove. Intermittent rain continued all night and into the next morning.[26]

The 151st came to attention at 10:00 a.m. April 30. McFarland listened as Colonel Allen read a dispatch from General Hooker:

> The general announced with great satisfaction the entire sweep of the maneuvers of the last three days by the 5th, 11th, and 12th Army Corps, and that the enemies must now fight us on ground of our choosing, to his utter destruction, or make an inglorious retreat. This news was received with loud cheers and produced the best feelings in the ranks.

A Confederate long-range battery opened fire about 5:00 p.m. and dropped shells on the brigade for over three hours. McFarland recorded that "many narrow escapes were made. One of the shells struck within 2 or 3 feet of Genl. Rowley and sometime before another struck immediately behind him while riding on the bank of the cove. He paid no attention to either." After inspecting the 143rd's position and observing Wadsworth's troops across the river, Dana and Rowley spent the evening together. Both sides stopped firing their guns at dusk. On the morning of May 1, the heavy fog lifted around 9:00. Entrenchments and breastworks constructed by the First Division became visible on the far shore. Later that day, the men mustered for pay. Neither side resumed the artillery duel.[27]

At 1:30 a.m., Saturday, May 2, General Hooker decided to close the gap between Oliver Howard's Eleventh Corps and the Rapidan River with the First Corps. Having failed to mislead Robert E. Lee, Hooker ended the down-river feint and issued orders to withdraw from the river and march by way of United States Ford to Howard's right. Delayed for several hours, the orders did not reach John Reynolds until 7:00 a.m. A withdrawal across the Rappahannock by Wadsworth's division should have been made during the night. Now it would be executed in daylight. Because existing roads did not follow the Rappahannock's north bank, it would be dark before Reynolds's leading division reached Howard's right.[28]

Just after sunrise on May 2, George McFarland heard artillery firing to the right. Lee had begun his own feint, this one against Hooker's left. Doubleday's and Robinson's commands set out at 8:00 a.m. for the army's right flank, about 30 road miles from Fitzhugh's. When their withdrawal began, Confederate guns opened fire with shell, shot and slugs. One of them struck the jaw of Col. Robert Cummins's horse. Cover provided by the cove protected the brigade as it set out for Falmouth with the men carrying "haversacks, knapsacks, and 8 [4?] days provisions besides gun and accouterments and 60 rounds of cartridges." After marching over 24 miles, the column reached United States Ford just before 7:00 p.m. Some regiments unslung knapsacks and piled them just off the road. When Doubleday's pioneers reached the far shore, a roar of musketry erupted to the west. Stonewall Jackson's men had just overwhelmed the Eleventh Corps's final line of resistance.[29]

Stone's and Rowley's brigades hurried across the pontoons and started down Old Mine Road. They soon met survivors from Howard's corps fleeing Jackson's infantry. Reaching their assigned position shortly before midnight, Rowley's brigade went into line between 1:00 and 2:00 a.m. on the right of Robinson's division. Most laid down and slept soundly until the fighting resumed at 6:00 a.m. McFarland described this action in a letter home:

> Such terrible and constant sounds of musketry and artillery and desperate attack, we thought none could stand. The rebels charged time and again with all the desperation of madman, and seemed to think they *must* and *could* break our lines. At 8 O'clock and again at 10, the contest was most desperate, and the rebels advanced with the shouts and yells of demons.

The Federal center bent and pulled back, but did not break May 3. On the right, the First Corps was "drawn up in order of battle, in 2 to 4 lines." They threw up breastworks and waited but the enemy continued to concentrate on the center. Only stray shots reached the brigade.[30]

That afternoon, Rowley ordered out five companies as brigade pickets with George McFarland in command. They advanced in line of battle and followed the retreating Confederates about a half mile. The rebel pickets then stopped, turned around, and opened fire. Before the skirmish ended, both sides rightfully claimed many prisoners taken. Rowley's brigade expected to make an attack May 4 but nothing happened. In preparation for the army's withdrawal, the men spent the next day building bridges and roads. Between 1:00 and 2:00 a.m., May 6, the First Brigade fell in and "marched through mud up to our knees & and got to the pontoon bridge [over the Rappahannock] just at the break of day." When the two bridges at U. S. Ford cleared, the First Corps recrossed the river. The Third Division marched until 11:00 a.m. when it stopped briefly for breakfast. Shortly after passing Hooker's headquarters, Doubleday called a halt and they spent the night near the Wallace House. May 7, John Reynolds assembled his corps at Pollock's Mill, about five miles below Fredericksburg. For Rowley's brigade, the Chancellorsville campaign had ended where it began, "in a beautiful woods 6 miles below Fred-

ericks & about ½ a mile north of the Rappahannock River," near White Oak
Church. Brigade returns listed only 48 casualties: 1 killed, 11 wounded, and
36 taken prisoner.[31]

The Chancellorsville campaign did not end so favorably for the 102nd
Pennsylvania. West of Fredericksburg and south of the Rappahannock River,
Maj. Gen. John Sedgwick's Sixth Corps operated as an independent command
that first week of May. Except for capturing Marye's Heights on May 3, the
largest Federal corps accomplished little. Around midnight May 4, the major
general decided to give up his current position and retire to the north bank.
"By 4:00 AM, the infantry and artillery were across the two Bank's Ford pontoon bridges, and the engineers cut the cables on the south bank and let the
current drift the bridge spans over to the north bank." Unfortunately, most
of the 102nd Pennsylvania remained behind. Assigned to the rear guard, they
manned the brigade's picket line while the other regiments fell back toward
the river. The regiment did its job but recall orders never arrived. Lt. Col.
John Patterson refused to abandon his post. Surrounded by the enemy, 94
officers and men of the 102nd, including Patterson, "tried to get away but
could not." Taken to Richmond's Libby Prison, they received a parole May
25. To make matters worse, charges accusing Col. Joseph Kinkead of cowardice before the enemy at Seven Pines, Malvern Hill, Fredericksburg, and
Salem Church near Chancellorsville were formally filed May 23. Brigade commander Frank Wheaton and John Sedgwick quickly approved Kinkead's May
27 resignation. Lt. Col. John Patterson replaced him, becoming a full colonel September 2. Kinkead, not Rowley, was the probably the subject of Almira
Patterson's May 28, 1862, "report in the city."[32]

Rowley took a second oath of office on May 8, this time at Doubleday's
headquarters. In Harrisburg, the promotion to brigadier became effective May
8. In a confirming letter to Adjutant General Lorenzo Thomas, the new
brigadier gave his age as 47 and his year of birth as 1816. Edmund Dana called
on Roy Stone and Rowley on Sunday, May 17. Both of Doubleday's brigades
camped that day on the Fitzhugh estate in woods containing oak and hick-
ory, four miles south of Falmouth and a mile north of the Rappahannock.
Wadsworth's division was a mile to the north and Robinson's a short distance
to the northeast. A week later, the 135th Pennsylvania departed for mustering out. This left Rowley's brigade with only three regiments, about 1,000
effectives.[33]

John Reynolds reviewed the Third Division on May 30. Afterward, Doubleday detailed Company D, 149th Pennsylvania, to be the division's provost
guard and Capt. James Glenn provost marshal. The next day, orders arrived
giving Rowley his first experience at divisional command. "Gen Doubleday
desires me to inform you that, Gen Reynolds having gone to Washington for
a few days, he has assumed command of the Corps, that you are therefore in

His commander on July 1, 1863, Maj. Gen. Abner Doubleday remained support-ive of Rowley during and after the Civil War. Courtesy of USAMHI.

command of the Division." Lt. W. L. Wilson, Rowley's acting assistant adju-tant general, directed Col. Chapman Biddle, 121st Pennsylvania, to "take com-mand of the 1st Brigade." Speculation grew that Lincoln would offer Reynolds army command. McCalmont and Rowley visited Edmund Dana on June 2 and they most likely discussed Reynolds's absence. Company D reported for duty at Third Division Headquarters on June 3. John Reynolds returned that evening but said nothing about his trip to the capital.[34]

Colonel McFarland had seen much in the past six months. Writing to his wife on June 5, he answered criticisms of the army made earlier by "Mrs. Sutton's brother."

> We have many very unworthy men and officers of all grades in the army — some the "Devil" would not know what to do with. But we have many very good ones — noble fellows worthy of the cause and of God's protecting care and blessing — if human beings are ever worthy of it.

Unfortunately, he gave no examples of either type.[35]

Friendly fire shattered Stonewall Jackson's left arm the evening of May 2. Complications followed its amputation and Jackson died May 10. His death forced Robert E. Lee to reorganize the Army of Northern Virginia. It now contained three corps commanded by Lt. Gen. James Longstreet, Richard S. Ewell, and Ambrose P. Hill. Three divisions made up each corps. Lee also developed plans for a June invasion of the North and presented them to Jefferson Davis on May 15. In spite of serious problems at Vicksburg and in Tennessee, the president approved. The commanding general returned to Fredericksburg and started writing orders.[36]

6. The Gettysburg Campaign

Lee's campaign plan called for Ewell's corps to lead the Confederate advance toward Maryland, driving off any Federals found in the Shenandoah Valley. Longstreet would move along the Blue Ridge with J.E.B. Stuart's cavalry on his right flank, protecting the passes against enemy probes. After A. P. Hill's corps, the last to withdraw from the Rappahannock, had passed behind them, Longstreet and Stuart would follow the general advance. On June 3, Longstreet's and Ewell's corps began pulling back from their river line and moving northwest toward Culpeper Court House. Back at Fredericksburg, Hill actively demonstrated to hold the Army of the Potomac in place. Hooker, unsure of Lee's intentions, ordered Maj. Gen. Alfred Pleasonton's three cavalry divisions to cross the Rappahannock and find Stuart, a reconnaissance in force. Union infantry defended Beverly and Kelly's Fords as Pleasonton's columns crossed over the morning of June 9. The resulting Battle of Brandy Station, the largest cavalry fight of the war, ended as a standoff. In spite of having a day that "made the Federal Cavalry," little was learned about Lee's plans. Ewell resumed his march toward the Shenandoah Valley.[1]

By June 11, Federal intelligence clearly indicated that at least part of the Army of Northern Virginia was on the move but no one knew where or why. One result of this uncertainty was Washington telling Hooker to do what he considered impossible: cover the capital and Harpers Ferry while holding the Fredericksburg line. Accepting the need to keep all options open, the general decided to move part of his army north. Hooker selected Bealeton, Virginia, as a central point for supplies and issued orders that evening to move before daybreak. Corps commanders received instructions directing that all civilians must leave at once and extra baggage be sent to the rear.[2]

Around noon that day, Adjutant Wilson sent out this circular:

> Regimental commanders are hereby notified to have their commands in readiness to move at any moment they may be called upon. Tents may be left standing until orders to march. Every thing else will be expected in readiness. By command of Brig Gen Rowley.

Sgt. Jacob J. Zorn, Company F, 142nd Pennsylvania, predicted a move at 4:00 p.m. Reynolds's orders reached divisional headquarters four hours later. The First Corps left White Oak Church at 8:00 a.m. June 12, beginning what would be a long and arduous march north to Gettysburg. Rowley's brigade moved northwest first on the Falmouth and Warrenton Pike, then along the Post Route. They covered 12 miles before halting after sunset. Unbeknownst to Joe Hooker, the Confederate army had already "cut loose from Richmond," and was up ahead on his left, their goal: Pennsylvania.[3]

The First Corps advanced 13 miles June 13 and camped near Bealeton Station on the Orange and Alexandria Railroad, four miles from the Rappahannock River. Late that evening, John Reynolds received word that Hooker had decided to transfer his entire army to the line of the Orange and Alexandria Railroad. News that Ewell's corps was in the Shenandoah Valley had created an immediate need to swing the Army of the Potomac northward and cover Washington. Given right wing command, John Reynolds would coordinate withdrawal of the First, Third, Fifth, and Eleventh Corps from the Rappahannock line and their movement by forced marches to Centreville, Virginia.[4]

With Rowley's brigade leading, Third Division set out at 6:00 a.m. Sunday for Manassas Junction. The First Corps, Abner Doubleday commanding, found itself in a race to reach Centreville before the enemy. They began "one of the most tortuous and torturing marches on record." Heading northeast along the Orange and Alexandria Railroad, the column passed through Warrenton Junction and forded Cedar Run. Maj. Thomas Chamberlin, 150th Pennsylvania, described the June 14 ordeal:

> The heat of the sun was withering. Not a breath of air stirred the leaves; the dust rose like a white cloud, powdering the hair and clothes of the troops ... not a drop of water was to be had at times for a distance of five mile.... No man was allowed to fall out of the ranks, under any pretext, without a pass from his company commander, approved by the regimental surgeon. Those who did were driven in again by the field officer at the rear of each regiment, or "gobbled up" by the rear-guard.

Decades would pass before army medical officers fully understood and accepted the danger from heat exhaustion. Leaving Catlett's Station, the brigade crossed Broad Run at 8:00 p.m., where it expected to stop. Instead, orders came to move on. They reached Manassas Station at 2:00 a.m. June 15, having covered over 25 miles.[5]

After five hours' rest, the advance resumed. Leaving the Orange and Alexandria Railroad, they turned north and advanced over the old battlefield, crossing Bull Run at Blackburn's Ford. Reynolds stopped the column at 3:00 p.m. near Centreville. Zorn remembered, "We marched 12 miles through a fine country." Having advanced 64 miles in 78 hours, the division spent June

16 at Centreville, washing bodies as well as clothes. General Hooker arrived at Fairfax Station and Reynolds returned to corps command. The Army of the Potomac, now concentrated at Centreville and Fairfax, had won the race. Unfortunately, the Army of Northern Virginia was never a participant. Lee's objective was neither Washington nor Baltimore but Pennsylvania. Word reached Hooker that Ewell's men had driven the Federal garrison and Maj. Gen. Robert H. Milroy out of Winchester, Virginia. For the second time in less than a year, Lee had an open road to Pennsylvania. Just before 8:00 p.m., Joe Hooker decided to shift the army from Centreville to Leesburg and suggested that marching be limited to early morning and late at night.[6]

Reveille sounded at 2:00 a.m. June 17. Rowley's men marched north toward Leesburg. This seemed to be the hottest day so far and hundreds fell out because of either heat stroke or exhaustion. The brigade covered over 20 miles. The next day, they passed through Chantilly and stopped at Herndon Station on the Loudoun and Hampshire Railroad that ran to Leesburg. The men slept for a second night close to the tracks. The Third Division led a four-mile advance to Guilford Station on June 19, bivouacking by Broad Run. The worst was over. Rest and rain with cooler temperatures gave the men an opportunity to recuperate. Doubleday ordered both brigades to take precautions against raids by John Mosby's partisan raiders. George McFarland estimated the distance marched from White Oak to Broad Run at 100 miles.[7]

After capturing Winchester, Ewell's infantry pushed north and on June 15 crossed the Potomac at Williamsport. The next day they occupied Hagerstown and Sharpsburg and Ewell sent his cavalry toward Chambersburg. Even though Joe Hooker was still undecided whether this marked the beginning of a full-scale invasion, the citizens of Pittsburgh were not. Representative Moorhead, a spokesman for the city's Executive Committee of Public Safety, sent a telegram to the president requesting that Maj. Gen. William Brooks, commander of the Department of the Monogahela, be given the authority to declare martial law in Pittsburgh. From Fairfax, Virginia, General Hooker engaged in a telegraphic debate with Lincoln and Halleck. Hooker wanted more freedom and more men to deal with the enemy. Unfortunately, the president no longer had confidence in his commanding general and kept a tight rein on the Army of the Potomac.[8]

Before reaching Broad Run, hundreds had fallen out of the ranks because of the heat. Among them were stragglers with a different reason for falling behind. This group soon left the route of march to loot nearby farms. Rain and cooler temperatures did not eliminate the problem. Doubleday received a communique June 23 from corps headquarters:

> Maj Genl Reynolds directs me to say that he has found your men straggling over the country and that he wishes you to take measures to prevent it. He sends back several to your Div under guard.

Congressman J.K. Moorhead told Secretary of War Stanton, "Make Rowley General and hold me responsible for the wisdom of the act." Courtesy of James Wadsworth Family Papers and the Library of Congress.

S. M. Weld, Capt and A. D. C.
(Stephen Minot Weld Jr., 18th Mass.)

The major general immediately issued an order to Rowley and Stone that a "proper pass" would be required "to leave defined brigade limits."[9]

While waiting for orders near Broad Run Creek in Loudoun County, over halfway to Gettysburg, General Doubleday put his division through brigade drill the afternoon of June 22. Afterward, Captain Flagg, Rowley's aide, inspected the regimental camps. The men heard heavy cannonading from a cavalry encounter at Snicker's Gap. McCalmont recorded that relations between the division's field officers and him "are very agreeable." He regarded Edmund Dana as "quite an accomplished gentleman, and a [fellow] Democrat." Rowley was ill June 24 and did not attend the "Masonic Brethren meeting" held in Dana's quarters.[10]

Army headquarters informed Reynolds that Ewell occupied Chambersburg, Pennsylvania, June 22 and that Robert E. Lee's two other corps crossed the Potomac on June 24. Hooker reacted to this news by giving John Reynolds command of the army's left wing, First, Third, and Eleventh Corps. He instructed Reynolds to cross the Potomac and seize the National Road passes, Crampton's and Turner's Gaps, as quickly as possible. This would shield both Washington and Baltimore from a potential breakout by the Army of Northern Virginia. Hooker assigned additional cavalry and artillery units to Reynolds. After six days of rest, Rowley issued orders at 8:00 a.m. June 25 to Colonels Biddle, Cummins, and McFarland for "Commanders of Regiments to pack up and form in line, ready to march."[11]

With Reynolds commanding the left wing, Doubleday took over the corps. Rowley assumed command of the Third Division, Chapman Biddle the First Brigade, and Alexander Biddle the 121st Pennsylvania. Finding the Potomac too deep to ford at Young's, the First Corps moved on three miles to Edwards Ferry. Here, they forded Goose Creek, crossed the river June 25 on pontoon bridges, then marched 18 miles in steady rain to Barnesville, Maryland. Doubleday informed his divisional commanders that Lee's two remaining corps had passed through Hagerstown, Maryland, on their way to Pennsylvania. In spite of heavy rain, the First Corps crossed Sugar Loaf Mountain, the Monocacy River, and Catoctin Mountain on June 26 then camped near Jefferson, Maryland. John Reynolds rode back that evening to Edwards Ferry to confer with Hooker.[12]

At 6:00 a.m. on Saturday, June 27, Rowley's division moved northwest toward Middletown. When the 151st set off that morning, someone forgot to call in the pickets. Forced to remain behind, McFarland organized the pickets into squads then hurried forward to rejoin his command. Unfortunately, the 151st led the corps that day and everyone soon became aware of the problem. George McFarland remembered the event well. "There was much straggling and bad work and complaint by Genl. Rowley in comd. of the Div." They later bivouacked close to South Mountain where Howard's Eleventh Corps held the passes.[13]

While Middletown's church bells rang out the next morning, the Army of the Potomac became aware that Lincoln had replaced Joseph Hooker with George Meade. Concluding that Lee must be followed north, the new army commander instructed Reynolds to immediately turn east, recross the mountains, and advance the left wing's three corps to Frederick, Maryland. With regiments closed up and minimal straggling, Third Division moved out at 3:00 p.m. Four hours later, they stopped one mile outside Frederick. Meade's instructions for the next day called for an advance by Reynolds and Howard to Emmitsburg, Maryland. They set out on June 29 at 6:00 a.m. Two miles south of Emmitsburg, Mount St. Mary's College for men came into view. In town, the Sisters of Charity watched as the column marched by the extensive grounds and buildings of St. Joseph Convent House. They marched 25 miles before halting that evening. Passing through Emmitsburg near sunset, the First Corps took up a defensive position facing north and west. Rowley complimented McFarland for his regiment's fine performance during the 24-mile march.[14]

The next morning, the trek toward Gettysburg resumed as heavy rain turned the roads into quagmires. Wadsworth's and Robinson's divisions accompanied by Wainwright's artillery advanced north on the Emmitsburg Road (Gettysburg Pike). To the west, the Third Division moved on parallel farm roads protecting the corps's left flank. Rowley's command crossed the Mason-Dixon Line and around noon stopped midway between Emmitsburg and Gettysburg, 160 miles from the Rappahannock. To the west, north, and east was the Army of Northern Virginia. Maj. Gen. Jubal Early's Second Corps division had advanced to York, Pennsylvania, and Maj. Gen. Robert Rodes's division held Carlisle. A. P. Hill's Third Corps and Longstreet's First were spread out from Greencastle to Cashtown. Brig. Gen. John Buford's First Cavalry Division encountered one of Hill's brigades in Fairfield, Pennsylvania, five miles from the First Corps.[15]

From his Taneytown headquarters, nine miles to the south, Meade reassigned John Reynolds to command the army's left wing, First, Third and Eleventh Corps. With a new army commander, no one was sure what this meant. General Howard and the Eleventh Corps, south at Emmitsburg, had previously accepted Reynolds's leadership but Daniel Sickles, having returned to command the Third Corps, might resist the change. Sickles, once a Democratic congressman, was a political general. Like Rowley, he made up "for his lack of military training by acting on the battlefield with reckless courage, and was much admired for it by his men." Officers in Wadsworth's and Robinson's divisions most likely discussed the First Corps command changes. Solomon Meredith, Lysander Cutler, Gabriel Paul, and Lt. Col. Rufus Dawes, 6th Wisconsin, remembered well what had happened six months earlier.[16]

On December 18, Ambrose Burnside assigned James Wadsworth to the Left Grand Division, commanded by William Franklin. Five days later, John Reynolds selected Wadsworth to replace fellow New Yorker Abner Doubleday as commander of the First Division. Brigadier Doubleday departed divisional headquarters and returned to an earlier posting of brigade command in the same division. From there, he would report to Wadsworth, making a difficult situation worse.[17]

This was the second time in less than two months that Abner Doubleday had been removed from First Division command. The first, ordered by George McClellan, took effect November 7, 1862. Ambrose Burnside, McClellan's successor, granted Doubleday an unexpected reprieve by transferring his replacement, Brig. Gen. C. C. Augur, to General Banks's Army. John Reynolds initiated Doubleday's second removal. In late December, Maj. Gen. George Meade departed the First Corps's Third Division for command of the Fifth Corps, replacing Fitz-John Porter. Three weeks passed before Reynolds announced on January 18, 1863, that Doubleday would replace Meade. Neither McClellan nor Reynolds left an explanation concerning their treatment of Doubleday. Regardless, the First Corps remembered the action taken.[18]

Before leaving the Rappahannock, James Longstreet dispatched his favorite scout or spy telling him not to return until he could bring information of importance. Harrison caught up with Longstreet the night of June 29 and told him the approximate location of five Federal corps and that George Meade had replaced Hooker. At first reluctant to accept this news, Lee quickly countermanded orders issued the night before. His army would now concentrate east of the mountains at Cashtown.[19]

Earlier that day, George Meade informed his corps commanders that Longstreet's and Hill's corps were near Chambersburg, and Ewell's was scattered between Carlisle and York. With pressure on Philadelphia and Harrisburg relieved, Meade expressed a desire to optimize the army's position for either offensive or defensive operations. In a later circular, the army commander disclosed that the enemy was now advancing in strong force on Gettysburg. There would be no major changes regarding Federal corps dispositions, however, until Meade better understood Lee's plans.[20]

On the afternoon of June 30, John Reynolds placed the First Corps in a defensive position. He posted the First and Third Divisions to guard against attack from either north or west. Wadsworth held the Emmitsburg Pike that led north to Gettysburg, and Rowley the two parallel farm roads that ran southeasterly from Fairfield to the Emmitsburg Pike. Stone's Second Brigade covered both roads, connecting with Colonel Biddle's First Brigade near Middle Creek. Lt. Col. Alexander Biddle's 121st Pennsylvania extended the corps' picket line about a mile eastward to the 19th Indiana from Meredith's Iron Brigade. General Reynolds and his staff established headquarters on the pike at Moritz's Tavern, southeast of Doubleday and south of Wadsworth. Doubleday established corps headquarters at the J. Brown farm on Bull Frog Road. Rowley set up his tent nearby. Capt. John Glenn, divisional provost marshal, and Company D, 149th Pennsylvania, joined them. Glenn mustered his men in front of the barn for pay. The First Corps held the extreme left of Meade's line, which extended that night over 30 miles east to Sedgwick's 6th Corps at Manchester.[21]

Two days earlier, General Reynolds had ordered Col. Theodore B. Gates

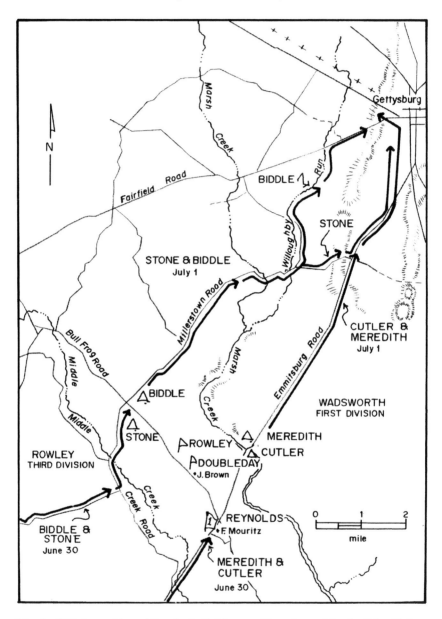

March of Wadsworth's and Rowley's divisions to Gettysburg. Map by John Heiser.

and the 20th New York State Militia to join the First Corps when relieved from provost guard duty at Edward's Ferry. The New Yorkers left the Potomac River on June 27 and followed the corps's route of march north. Near sunset on June 30, Gates finally found Doubleday, who assigned the regiment to

Biddle's First Brigade. They spent the night watching one of the roads from Fairfield.[22]

At noon on June 30, Buford's cavalry column passed through Gettysburg and stopped just outside the town near a Lutheran seminary. To the northwest, they observed Brig. Gen. J. J. Pettigrew's North Carolina Brigade, Maj. Gen. Henry Heth's division, Hill's Corps, withdrawing along the Chambersburg Pike. Federal cavalry cautiously followed Pettigrew. That evening, Buford positioned his troopers to monitor all roads coming into Gettysburg from the west, north, and east. Col. William Gamble's brigade observed the roads from Fairfield and Cashtown; Col. Thomas C. Devin's the ones from Carlisle, York, and Harrisburg. Buford knew that Hill's corps was camped to the northwest and that Ewell's corps was approaching from the northeast. He expected trouble the next day.[23]

In addition to resuming division command, Rowley faced a painful, personal problem, boils on his upper thighs. His staff surgeon, Thomas J. Keely, was absent on sick leave. Dr. William T. Humphrey, originally in the 13th Pennsylvania Reserves and now the 149th's surgeon, examined the general June 29. He concluded that night, "It would be difficult for him to ride a horse." The next morning at the Brown farm, Humphrey considered Rowley "not competent to go into any engagement on horseback." The Potomac Army reported 287 cases of boils for June 1863.[24]

Morning, July 1, 1863

> General Rowley held the left wing under the most
> adverse circumstances and with a portion of Wadsworth's men,
> covered the retreat of the main body by successive
> echelons of resistance.—*Maj. Gen. Abner Doubleday*[25]

On the evening of June 30, Abner Doubleday prepared to advance the First Corps to Gettysburg. Observing the standard army practice or custom, he sent his divisional commanders a marching order for July 1 establishing this sequence: Rowley, Robinson, and Wadsworth. Marching first was the favored position, fresh road and minimal dust or mud. Reynolds's divisional postings, however, created a problem. The Third Division was nearby but the Second was a few miles south at Emmitsburg. As Doubleday's order stood, Wadsworth would be forced to wait until Robinson's command had cleared Marsh Creek.[26]

Shortly before 7:00 a.m., John Reynolds rejected Doubleday's order and told the First Division to move immediately. Their objective was to support

John Buford as he pushed out from Gettysburg. Reynolds did not expect any trouble and, possibly for that reason, issued only verbal march orders. Wadsworth immediately sent orderlies to inform his two brigade commanders, Solomon Meredith and Lysander Cutler, of the change in march sequence. Reynolds returned to Moritz Tavern and summoned Abner Doubleday for a briefing. Arriving around 7:30, the First Corps commander listened as Reynolds read the latest dispatches from Meade and Buford and summarized the tactical situation. The wing commander would accompany Wadsworth's division and Capt. James A. Hall's 2nd Maine Battery to Gettysburg on the Emmitsburg Road.

> He [Reynolds] then instructed me [Doubleday] to draw in my pickets, assemble the artillery, and the remainder of the corps, and join him as soon as possible. Having given these orders he rode off at the head of the column and I never saw him again.

Doubleday amended his orders and began readying the Second and Third Divisions to follow Wadsworth.[27]

Ten miles south of Moritz's, George Meade did not anticipate any problems this morning either. Given what John Buford had learned June 30, it is difficult to understand the optimism of either Meade or Reynolds. If fighting did break out, John Reynolds would decide whether to stand or pull back. By 8:00 a.m., five Federal corps were advancing on Gettysburg. Their commanding general chose to remain at his Taneytown headquarters. The probability of dilatory, incomplete, or misunderstood communications increased as the army moved closer to Gettysburg and farther away from its commanding general. Meade's earlier decision for Reynolds to resume wing command should have mitigated this problem. Unfortunately, when the crisis peaked that afternoon, John Reynolds was not available to assume field command.[28]

One of Doubleday's aides gave Rowley the new marching orders, who then informed Biddle and Stone. The Third Division would continue to protect the corps's left by staying west of the Emmitsburg Road. Before they left the Brown farm, Surgeon Humphrey walked over to Rowley's tent and repeated last night's warning not to ride a horse. The brigadier ignored his doctor again. To minimize the pain, Rowley decided to avoid sitting astride the horse. Instead, every riding position possible except the natural one would be tried that day. The brigadier went over to Chapman Biddle's tent, reviewed Doubleday's new march sequence, and said that he would accompany Biddle to Gettysburg. Shortly before 9:00 a.m., First Brigade's 1,300 officers and men set out for Gettysburg, about six miles away. McFarland's 151st left its bivouac on George Spangler's farm and Alexander Biddle's 121st departed the crossroads near W. R. White's farm. The Third Division would arrive too late to support either Meredith or Cutler mainly because a sense of urgency did not yet exist in the First Corps. Rowley's perceived sluggishness that morning became another factor straining relations between the two divisions.[29]

The First Brigade led the Third Division's northeasterly advance up Bull Frog Road as follows: Company of Sharpshooters, 121st with two companies deployed as flankers, 142nd, 151st, and 20th NYSM followed by Capt. J. H. Cooper's battery, First Pennsylvania Artillery. Rowley's column passed by "orchards, meadows, fields of grain, substantial fences, and comfortable farmhouses," with large barns. About 10:00 a.m., while crossing a covered bridge that spanned Marsh Creek, they heard artillery fire to the north. The 142nd immediately threw out flankers. Spaced about 16 feet apart, these skirmishers formed a single line, perpendicular to the road, that extended out over a half mile on both sides. Keeping up with the main column, they climbed fences, forded streams, and passed through woodlots. As the brigade advanced up the west bank of Willoughby Run, Capt. Jacob F. Slagle, divisional judge advocate, reached the column with Doubleday's instructions "to hurry it up." Rowley ordered quick time then double quick. The irregular cadence of route step march abruptly ended.[30]

Around 11:00 a.m., the brigade reached the Fairfield or Hagerstown Road, a mile southwest of Gettysburg. Troopers from the 8th Illinois Cavalry told them that fighting was just ahead. The men climbed a fence, filed to the right, and formed a line of battle in the road facing north. With the sharpshooters leading, Rowley ordered an advance by the right flank. They passed through a grove of trees, entered a wheat field, and then crossed Willoughby Run for the third time. On their left, John Buford's dismounted cavalry was fighting near a brick house (Harmon's) and large stone barn. Coming under fire from enemy skirmishers, First Brigade took position on the eastern slope of McPherson Ridge, a woodlot on their right and the Lutheran seminary behind them. Battle smoke hung above the trees. Over three-quarters of a mile directly west on Herr's Ridge stood another grove paralleling the Federal line. Physically, there was nothing in these open fields to either anchor the brigade's left flank or impede an enemy advance. Rowley ordered knapsacks unslung. The men lay down and listened to the shriek of rebel shells passing overhead.[31]

While the brigade was forming a battle line on the Fairfield Road, John Reynolds fell mortally wounded in the woodlot on McPherson Ridge. Yesterday's informal command changes became official. Rowley's brigade staff— Capt. Charles H. Flagg, acting assistant inspector general; 1st Lt. William L. T. Wilson, 142nd Pennsylvania, acting assistant adjutant general; and 1st Lt. George A. Heberton, Battery F, Pennsylvania Light, aide-de-camp — moved to Third Division Headquarters. The general elevated 1st Lt. Oliver K. Moore, Company A, 143rd Pennsylvania, to acting aide-de-camp. Colonel McFarland remembered that

(Top) Looking west at the Lutheran Theological Seminary circa July 1863. (Bottom) Looking east at the building today. From *In Memoriam: James Samuel Wadsworth, 1807–1864* (New York Monuments Commission, 1916).

Brigadier General Thomas A. Rowley, our able Brigade Commander, took charge of General Doubleday's Division and Colonel Chapman Biddle of the 121st P. V. the First Brigade. During the period under consideration, some hard fighting and daring charges took place, resulting in our favor.[32]

While Rowley awaited orders from Doubleday, James Wadsworth's division finished driving back two brigades from Henry Heth's division. Meredith's Iron Brigade chased the survivors from Brig. Gen. James Archer's brigade across Willoughby Run and west to Herr's Ridge. A half-mile farther north, men from Brig. Gen. Joseph Davis's brigade surrendered to Rufus Dawes's 6th Wisconsin, the 95th New York, and 14th Brooklyn at the Middle Railroad Cut. Aware that Biddle had reached the seminary and Stone was approaching, Doubleday now set out to strengthen the Federal line.

Keeping a short leash on his inexperienced replacement, the major general instructed Rowley to close up on Meredith, then occupying the woodlot, northwest of Biddle's right. Finding the brigade's advanced guard "on the field and near the woods and the road where the brick house and the barn [Harmon's] were burned," Captain Slagle gave the orders to Rowley. Facing north, the First Brigade advanced over the crest and down into a ravine south of Meredith that contained Willoughby Run. Rebel musketry and artillery fire from Herr's Ridge concentrated on the exposed infantry. After a short time, Biddle's men about-faced and returned to their original position on McPherson Ridge. The resulting gap between brigades never closed. Col. Charles S. Wainwright, commanding the corps artillery, posted Cooper's battery between Meredith and Biddle. The Third Division's pioneers tore down fences so that the 3-inch guns could advance. Initially facing northwest, Cooper exchanged fire with Maj. W. J. Pegram's artillery on Herr's Ridge. About 11:30 a.m., Rowley left divisional headquarters to join Doubleday at the Lutheran seminary.[33]

Reaching the crest, he could now see the morning's battlefield. Three ridges, roughly parallel, ran north to south. The first, Seminary, was highest in elevation and longest in length with open woods covering its top in both directions. Moving west, the ground fell away, leveled off, and then rose forming Middle Ridge. It was lower in elevation and the smallest of the three. Less than a quarter mile west of Middle Ridge stood the third, McPherson. Similar in elevation to the second, it seemed to be the widest. Running northwest from Gettysburg, the Chambersburg Pike followed the land's contours. South of where the road intersected McPherson Ridge stood a house, large barn, and smaller buildings with an orchard and woods on one side and a lane running from house to pike on the other. This was the farm of Edward McPherson. One hundred fifty yards north and running almost parallel to the road was an unfinished railroad bed having neither ties nor rails. In the valleys, the bed's surface was close to ground level but deep cuts — the East,

Middle, and West — marked its passage through the three ridges. North of the first or East Cut, Seminary Ridge became Oak Ridge that continued on to Oak Hill. About 250 yards north of the railroad bed, the second and third ridges merged, forming a plateau.[34]

The two generals and their staffs waited west of the seminary as Stone's three regiments climbed the ridge and then halted. Doubleday and Rowley gave brief speeches, offering words of encouragement, and urging them to fight for the soil of Pennsylvania. At that moment, Roy Stone most likely resented Rowley's presence as a brigadier and his divisional commander. Competitors since the war began, Stone had failed to get his star last November. Their paths would cross again. While Pegram's artillery shells passed overhead, Doubleday reviewed what had happened that morning and instructed Colonel Stone to position his brigade at the McPherson farm, between Meredith on the left and Cutler on the right. Col. Langhorne Wister's 150th Pennsylvania led the advance followed by Dana's 143rd. Captain Glenn initially positioned his company, the Divisional Provost Guard, south of the seminary. Sheltered by rocks and trees, they formed a skirmish line that extended across the Fairfield Road. A section of Capt. G. T. Stevens's Fifth Maine Battery stood in the road facing west and a squad of Gamble's cavalry occupied woods to the south.[35]

While Doubleday and Rowley greeted Roy Stone at the seminary, James Wadsworth, temporarily elevated to corps command, rode south along the Federal line. He found an old acquaintance, Colonel Gates, who complained about enemy sharpshooters in the Harmon farmhouse and stone barn across the run. The general told his former subordinate to seize the buildings. Gates ordered Capt. Ambrose N. Baldwin and Company K, 20th NYSM, forward. They drove out the enemy skirmishers and took possession of the brick house and nearby farm buildings.[36]

To the southeast, Oliver Howard led his Eleventh Corps into Gettysburg. He climbed the stairs to Fahnestock's Observatory and studied the northern battlefield through field glasses. Guards led Confederate prisoners, captured in the Middle Railroad Cut, south on Baltimore Street "past my post of observation." Around 11:00 a.m., Capt. Daniel Hall yelled up from the street, "General Reynolds is dead, and you are the senior officer on the field." The major general came down, rode south to Cemetery Hill, and established his headquarters east of the Baltimore Pike. Because he ranked Doubleday, Howard issued orders assuming command of the field and the army's left wing. A reassignment of duties in the Eleventh Corps followed. Doubleday and others felt that the wing commander's position was unique to John Reynolds and ended with his death. This became the first command controversy at Gettysburg. Close to noon, Abner Doubleday returned to leading the First Corps and Wadsworth the First Division.[37]

John Reynolds's death would plague the Federals until George Meade finally reached the field that night. Seniority was not yet an issue between the generals this morning but it would be by evening. The baggage that Oliver Howard carried to Gettysburg would impair his relationship with the other corps commanders: Doubleday, Slocum, and Hancock. Many in the army unjustly blamed his Eleventh Corps for the Chancellorsville defeat. Many in the Eleventh Corps blamed their commander for the complete surprise and success of Stonewall Jackson's attack. Regardless of who was right or wrong, the ongoing dissension weakened Howard's position. Chancellorsville finger-pointing and seniority squabbling were symptomatic of a more debilitating problem that July 1: the inability of Federal general officers to concentrate on stopping Robert E. Lee.[38]

At 12:30 p.m., John Buford brought word that Ewell's Second Corps would soon reach the battlefield. Howard quickly prepared dispatches for Henry Slocum and Daniel Sickles informing them of the clash between Heth and Wadsworth and the approach of Ewell's infantry. Slocum, the army's senior major general, had just finished marching his Twelfth Corps to Two Taverns, five miles southeast of Cemetery Hill. Sickles and the Third Corps occupied Emmitsburg, 10 miles away. Inexplicably, Howard failed to mention Reynolds's death and to request immediate support. He then discussed placement of the Eleventh Corps with Maj. Gen. Carl Schurz and accompanied Brig. Gen. Francis Barlow's division north through town.[39]

From Taneytown, George Meade tried to get control of the rapidly changing situation. Informed of Reynolds's death and well aware of Howard's and Doubleday's limitations, he ordered Maj. Gen. Winfield Scott Hancock to take command of the First, Third, and Eleventh Corps and determine if this was a good place to fight. Hancock raised questions about seniority. Both Slocum and Howard outranked him. Three days earlier, Henry Halleck gave Meade "the authority to appoint anyone to a command regardless of seniority." Able to promote and dismiss officers as conditions warranted, he brushed Hancock's concerns aside. Except for Meade's immediate staff, the army was unaware of the unusual authority Lincoln and Stanton had delegated to the new commander. Consequently, many general officers would react unfavorably whenever George Meade employed this power. With justifiable reservations, the new left wing commander set out for Gettysburg at 1:30 p.m.[40]

Northwest of Gettysburg, Meredith's brigade occupied the woodlot, Herbst Woods, south of the McPherson farm. Cutler's battered regiments were reforming on Oak Ridge. Before long, they would advance west and reoccupy Middle Ridge, north of the Chambersburg Pike. Provost guards escorted the last prisoners into town. Chapman Biddle's infantry held the crest of Middle Ridge. On their right, Cooper engaged Pegram's batteries. After several minutes, the enemy rate of fire started dropping off. By 1:00 p.m., the Confederate guns on Herr's Ridge became silent. John Robinson's Second Division reached the field and started constructing breastworks that overlooked Biddle's position.[41]

As Rowley prepared to return to the First Brigade, he observed a small group of line officers approaching the seminary on foot. The general rode over and learned that they belonged to the 7th Wisconsin. Aware that this regiment had earlier repelled Archer, he strongly rebuked them for being absent during the fighting. After reaching the 7th's position in Herbst Woods, they told their colonel, W. W. Robinson, about the confrontation with Rowley.[42]

Afternoon, July 1, 1863

The relative lull at the seminary lasted for almost an hour. Then, between 1:00 and 1:30 p.m., Capt. W. P. Carter's and C. W. Fry's batteries, Ewell's corps, opened fire from Oak Hill, a mile to the north. These guns enfiladed the Federal infantry and artillery on Middle Ridge. Cooper quickly changed front to the right or north and resumed firing. Ordered by Doubleday to vacate the crest and change front to the right, First Brigade took position on the low ground between McPherson and Middle Ridges facing north. This widened the gap between Meredith and Biddle even more. South of the Herbst woodlot, the only Federal infantry still facing west was Gates's two companies at the Harmon farm.[43]

Cutler's brigade withdrew to Oak Ridge. Federal artillery on McPherson Ridge north of the pike quickly vacated their exposed position. In an attempt to reduce casualties from the enemy shells, Rowley and Biddle repositioned the four regiments several times but gained little. After firing a few rounds, Wainwright ordered Cooper to withdraw and reposition his guns in front of a house north of the seminary. Commanded now by Lt. George Breck, who replaced a wounded Capt. G. H. Reynolds, Battery L, 1st New York, moved forward replacing Cooper.[44]

Informed that enemy artillery and infantry units were arriving from the northeast and that lead elements of Howard's Eleventh Corps were just coming into line, Doubleday belatedly decided to strengthen his right. He ordered two regiments, the 97th New York and 11th Pennsylvania from Brig. Gen. Henry Baxter's brigade, John Robinson's division, up Oak Ridge beyond Cutler. Baxter's remaining regiments and Gabriel Paul's brigade accompanied by John Robinson soon followed. Their goal was to prevent Ewell's fresh troops from rolling up the First Corps's right flank. Doubleday ordered Rowley to detach and relocate the 151st to Seminary Ridge. Here the regiment became the corps's final reserve. McFarland initially positioned his command behind a fence south of the seminary. After a short time, he moved them north to a

Commanding the First Corps's Second Division at Gettysburg. Brig. Gen. John Robinson later presided over Rowley's court-martial. Courtesy of USAMHI.

grove of trees and manned the breastworks built earlier by Paul's brigade. McFarland's departure left Biddle with less than 850 effectives.[45]

James Glenn found Rowley in the grove with McFarland. His entire company was no longer required on the Fairfield Road. Glenn asked the general, "Where I should take position with my men and what my duties would be." Rowley instructed him to go into town, gather up all stragglers, and send them forward to their respective regiments. Part of Glenn's company moved into Gettysburg and carried out the assignment.[46]

General Howard left the Eleventh Corps, rode west, and began an inspection of the First Corps's position. Moving south along Oak Ridge's eastern slope, the field commander met Wadsworth near Capt. James Stewart's Battery B, 4th U. S., and told him to hold Seminary/Oak Ridge as long as possible then withdraw to Cemetery Hill. Howard rode on to find General Doubleday, who wrote afterward:

> About 2 P. M., after the Eleventh Corps line was formed, General Howard rode over, inspected, and approved it. He also examined my position and gave orders, in case I was forced to retreat, to fall back to Cemetery Hill. I think this was the first and only order I received from him during the day.

Howard also expressed concern about the First Corps's unsupported left flank. Doubleday, however, considered it well secured. So far, all Confederate attacks had been directed against either the center or right. From his standpoint, the key to this battlefield was Herbst Woods. Except for Gamble's brigade, Biddle's left flank remained in the air. Evidently, the two generals never considered a pullback of the First Corps to Seminary Ridge or a complete withdrawal to Cemetery Hill. Doubleday and Howard "naturally supposed" that John Reynolds wanted Gettysburg defended to the last. Failure to discuss the eventual retreat of both corps was probably their most costly oversight. Howard returned to Cemetery Hill and waited for the Twelfth Corps.[47]

Before meeting Doubleday, Howard sent a second message to Slocum, this one an urgent request for both aid and counsel. Henry Slocum was already aware that Doubleday and Howard were in serious trouble, outnumbered by Hill and Ewell. At 1:30 p.m., three courses of action were available to him: ride to Gettysburg and find out what was happening, send a courier to Meade for orders, or wait. Unfortunately for the men then fighting and dying, Slocum chose the path of least resistance: wait. Thirty minutes later, a dispatch from Meade arrived informing the right wing commander, Fifth and Twelfth Corps, of Reynolds's death and Hancock's assignment to field command. It also contained orders to concentrate the Twelfth Corps at Gettysburg. The army commander had given field command to a junior, an oversight not easily forgotten by Slocum. The march from Two Taverns toward the sound of the guns did not begin until after 3:00 p.m. The Twelfth Corps's tardy response ruled out any chance of supporting the First and Eleventh Corps north of Gettysburg. It would also jeopardize their stand on Cemetery Hill.[48]

Just after 2:30 p.m., Henry Heth received Lee's approval to attack Doubleday's line south of the Chambersburg Pike. Heth employed three brigades, right to left, Archer's now led by Col. B. D. Fry, James Pettigrew's, and Col. J. M. Brockenbrough's. Only two would be important this afternoon. John

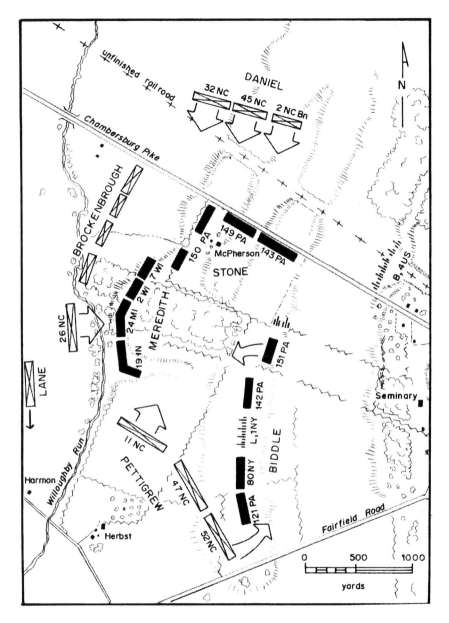

Pettigrew and Brockenbrough assault McPherson Ridge 3:00 pm (80th NY ~ 20th NYSM). Map by John Heiser.

Brockenbrough commanded over 900 effectives and Pettigrew 2,500, the largest brigade Lee brought to Gettysburg. Given Meredith's casualties that morning, the opposing sides between the Fairfield Road and Chambersburg Pike appeared to be about equal. Stone's brigade, however, was heavily engaged with Brig. Gen. Junius Daniel's brigade, Rodes's division. Langhorne Wister could commit only one full regiment, the 150th Pennsylvania, against Brockenbrough. Hill's artillery on Herr's Ridge exceeded the ground available for deployment. Doubleday, however, had only 18 guns south of the pike. The three Federal brigades, Biddle's, Meredith's, and Stone's, shared a third problem: unsupported flanks. Brockenbrough and Pettigrew would take full advantage of this weakness.[49]

Five hundred yards west of the seminary, Pettigrew's four North Carolina regiments, Federal left to right, 52nd, 47th, 11th and 26th, came out of the woods and filed south. They halted, formed a double line of battle, then with flags flying advanced eastward toward Biddle and Meredith. Left of Pettigrew, Brockenbrough's four Virginia regiments moved forward against Stone and Meredith's right. After crossing a wheat field and Willoughby Run, the 52nd and 47th North Carolina, 1,100 muskets, continued marching through open pasture directly at Biddle's Brigade. Approaching a wooded hill, the 11th and 26th North Carolina began to wheel left toward the Iron Brigade's exposed left flank.[50]

The sudden appearance of Pettigrew's brigade in the west found Biddle's three regiments facing north to minimize the impact of Carter's artillery fire from Oak Hill. Two regiments, the 121st and 142nd, were also out of position. For over an hour, Stone's brigade had been fighting to stop Daniel's North Carolinians from seizing the Chambersburg Pike. Langhorne Wister, 150th Pennsylvania, assumed brigade command after Roy Stone received a serious wound. Doubleday ordered Rowley to support Wister with his right two regiments, the 121st, and 142nd plus Breck's artillery. Carrying out these instructions, Thomas Rowley rode past the 142nd yelling, "Honor the Old Keystone State." The men applauded and their brigadier retired to the rear. Line officers yelled, "By the right flank, march," and the men advanced north toward the pike. McCalmont later wrote, "they had just been put in motion when the appearance of a large body of the enemy on our left made a change of front necessary."[51]

Without waiting for Doubleday's approval, Rowley quickly recalled both regiments. The general came riding across to them from the seminary. He passed the 142nd, located Alexander Biddle, and gave him instructions on where to place the 121st. Finding Chapman Biddle with the 20th NYSM, Rowley ordered the brigade to change front to the left and reform on Middle Ridge facing west. While the infantry changed position, Lieutenant Breck immediately moved his six guns to the left, placed them on the ridge's crest facing west, and opened fire on Pettigrew's advancing infantry. Earlier, Gates's men had "greatly annoyed" the 52nd North Carolina by sharpshooting from Harmon's second floor. Seeing the enemy's approach, they quickly vacated the farm and fled south. Col. J. K. Marshall, 52nd North Carolina, ordered the house and outbuildings burned.[52]

Confederate shells struck the ridge and confusion reigned in the Federal ranks for several minutes. Forced to take a new position on the brigade's left, the 121st marched south. They passed in front of Breck's Battery, forcing its guns to stop firing. The brigade's new battle line would be, left to right, 121st, 20th NYSM, Battery L's six guns, and 142nd. The artillery placement split the brigade. With commands thrown so far apart, Chapman Biddle directed Gates "to take charge of the two regiments on the left," 121st and 20 NYSM. Biddle remained with the 142nd. Wainwright now ordered Lt. B. W. Wilbur and Battery L's right section to the McPherson farm. Lt. William H. Bower commanded the remaining four guns on Middle Ridge.[53]

From the new battle line, Confederate officers could be seen "stepping in front swinging their swords." Thomas A. Rowley rode down the 142nd's line and yelled, "Here's for the Old Keystone State! Stand up for the Old Keystone! There the rebels are coming! Give it to them!" The men cheered and started firing a few minutes later. McCalmont felt that "his [Rowley's] exposure was perhaps rash but the emergency required something to be done promptly." Maj. Horatio N. Warren watched Rowley ride toward the seminary. When about halfway there, the general's horse stumbled, throwing his rider forward. Thinking that Rowley was wounded, Warren rode up and asked if he was hurt. Rowley said no and they parted company.[54]

Alexander Biddle's 121st finally reached their position on the left. They faced west, advanced a short distance, and took cover behind a wooden fence. Across their front, the 52nd North Carolina marched diagonally to the southeast. Soon, it would be well beyond the Federal left. When Pettigrew's men had advanced to within 200 yards, Wainwright ordered Breck's two sections taken back and posted south of the seminary. By now the rebel front line was less than 100 yards away. Edwin Gearhart, 142nd Pennsylvania, remembered:

> Suddenly a cloud of smoke arose from their [Confederate] line and almost instantly the balls began to whistle about us and the men next to my right fell. The order rang out along the line, fire! fire! And we all discharged our guns and commenced to load and fire at will ... I think we fired about five rounds.[55]

Chapman Biddle's three regiments volleyed, their musketry directed at the 47th and 11th North Carolina. Pettigrew's men halted and fired again. His right regiment, the 52nd, kept advancing and when opposite the 121st, wheeled left or north, and fired. Alexander Biddle attempted to change front and refuse his exposed flank. The North Carolinian's enfilading musketry broke the Pennsylvanians. The retreat spread north and soon the entire brigade was falling back. Oliver Howard's earlier evaluation of their Middle Ridge position proved to be correct.[56]

Abner Doubleday decided there was no choice but to commit his last reserve. As shells burst overhead and solid shot bounced off tree trunks, Rowley carried the order to McFarland. The nine-month unit crossed the breastworks assembled earlier by Gabriel Paul's brigade and advanced west into the gap between Biddle and Meredith. Taking a position between the 142nd Pennsylvania and 19th Indiana, the 151st soon found its battle line split; the right wing within the woods and the left on open ground. The North Carolinians welcomed these new arrivals with a volley from the trees. McFarland's right wing took careful aim and fired back but could not match the severe and destructive musketry from the 11th and 26th North Carolina. His left wing succeeded in taking a heavy toll of the Confederates assaulting the 142nd.[57]

Grasping the regimental colors, Chapman Biddle rode to the front and ordered the 142nd to charge the advancing 47th North Carolina. To many, Biddle's conduct was "an act of personal gallantry." To Maj. Horatio Warren, the charge was "hopeless ... unwise, rash, leading to misfortune that might not otherwise have occurred." McCalmont considered it an order to "charge bayonet against a double line of infantry twice as strong as our own." The 142nd followed Biddle, climbed a "broken down rail fence," and pushed into a wheat field. After struggling forward a short distance, Colonel Cummins rallied the small group that remained at the flag. They fired one round then "were running in retreat without order." A few halted at the fence. Turning round, the Pennsylvanians fired at the North Carolinians now on the ridge's crest, only 30 feet away. Gearhart remembered, "The rebs did not return our fire but came rushing down the hill yelling." Carrying a mortally wounded Robert Cummins, the survivors ran toward Seminary Ridge. Three of Cummins's litter bearers were shot and the colonel's body left in the swale. Bower's guns, south of the seminary, opened with canister.[58]

Pettigrew's attack from flank and front overwhelmed efforts to rally and reform the First Brigade units. Chapman Biddle's broken regiments fell back a quarter mile to the seminary. While under fire from three directions, McFarland withdrew his men and once again took position behind Paul's breastworks. Federal artillery stopped the Confederates on the crest of Middle Ridge. Here, the 26th North Carolina found that "his [McFarland's] dead marked his line of battle with the accuracy of a line at a dress parade." Their advance halted, Pettigrew's and Brockenbrough's men tended the wounded. The musketry trailed off and for 15 minutes only the artillery was active. Doubleday, Wadsworth, Rowley, and Wainwright used this brief respite to form a defensive line from the remnants of three brigades and three batteries. Rowley's new line, right to left, was the 151st, 142nd, two sections of

Reynolds's Battery L under Breck, 20 NYSM, and 121st. Col. William Gamble's cavalry brigade continued to hold the ground south of the Fairfield Road.[59]

Because there was no response to a 3:00 p.m. request for help, Howard sent his brother, Maj. Charles Howard, an hour later to hurry the Twelfth Corps forward. Two miles out on the Baltimore Pike, the major found Henry Slocum, who refused to "assume the responsibility of that day's fighting." From Seminary Ridge, the Federals watched as two fresh Confederate brigades — Brig. Gen. Abner Perrin's and A. M. Scales's, Maj. Gen. Dorsey Pender's Division — passed through Pettigrew's and Brockenbrough's infantry. Two days earlier, Perrin's four South Carolina regiments had camped on the western slope of the Blue Ridge Mountains, just north of the Mason-Dixon Line. The next morning, June 30, they marched in light rain down the macadamized Chambersburg Pike and passed the burned remnants of Thaddeus Stevens's iron works. Around 2:00 p.m., the column halted and they bivouacked on South Mountain. Orders came that evening to "cook one day's rations and have it in haversacks and be ready to march at 5:00 AM."[60]

Setting out the next morning behind Henry Heth's division, the brigade had marched about two miles when they first heard artillery fire up ahead. The division halted and Perrin's brigade turned right into a country road (Knoxlyn Road) and formed a line of battle facing southeast. Their advance resumed while in front "the cannonading increased in fury." From the crest of Belmont Schoolhouse Ridge, Maj. William Pegram's Napoleons and 3-inch rifles became visible on Herr's Ridge, over a mile away. The open countryside made it easy for the South Carolinians to see all that was going on. They found the ground "clear and open, a succession of wheat and clover fields with any number of fences." Perrin's lines opened to clear farmhouses, passed through woodlots and forded a small stream. In front, Federal artillery returned Pegram's fire.[61]

Pender's division slowly moved forward, staying about a half mile behind Heth's last two brigades. Spencer G. Welsh, a surgeon in the 13th South Carolina, recalled that he "could see from one end of the division to the other as it moved forward.... It was nearly a mile in length. The scene was certainly grand." Dorsey Pender's brigade alignment, right to left, was Brig. Gen. James H. Lane's, Perrin's, and Scales's, his left on the Chambersburg Pike. North of the pike, A. P. Hill held Brig. Gen. Edward Thomas's Georgians in reserve. The first line reached Herr's Ridge and stopped just behind the guns. "Suddenly we heard artillery fire open on our left and after a short interval, the artillery was followed by a musket fire." To the northeast, Robert Rodes's division, Ewell's corps, had opened its attack on the brigades of Lysander Cutler and Henry Baxter. After waiting here about an hour, Perrin's regiments moved forward through the massed artillery and advanced down the slope

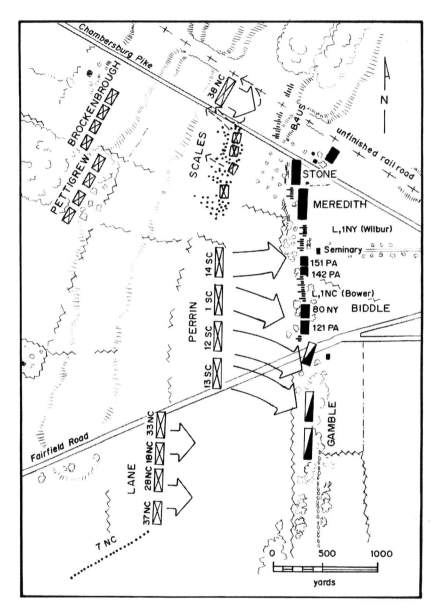

Pender's division attacks Doubleday's Seminary line 4:00 pm (80th NY ~ 20th NYSM). Map by John Heiser.

toward Willoughby Run. In front, Heth's Division struck the Federals positioned in a woodlot and adjoining field. Perrin's line advanced about 300 yards when the "fire and smoke and dust and noise and confusion and disorder of battle had begun." After 20 to 30 minutes of heavy fighting, Pettigrew drove the enemy back. Now it was Pender's turn.[62]

Perrin's and Scale's commands advanced in two lines, crossed Willoughby Run, and climbed McPherson Ridge. Up ahead, Pettigrew's advance stalled, then stopped. Wounded men struggled to the rear. Blue and gray bodies covered the ground. Coming into position, Pender's battle line drew an arc from south of the Fairfield Road to the Chambersburg Pike. Lt. James Stewart positioned three guns from his Battery B, 4th U. S., on each side of the East Railroad Cut. Standing near these guns, Rufus Dawes, described the scene:

> For a mile up and down the open fields in front, the splendid lines of the Army of Northern Virginia swept down upon us. Their bearing was magnificent. They maintained their alignment with great precision. In many cases the colors of regiments were advanced several paces in front of the line.[63]

Once again, rebel infantry extended well beyond the Federal left. John Buford had seen the danger earlier and positioned William Gamble's brigade on Biddle's left. The troopers moved forward at a trot, stopping south of Fairfield Road. Half of them dismounted and took position behind a low stone fence. A few crossed the road and almost reached the 121st's left. Rapid fire from their single-shot, breech-loaded, carbines disrupted the Confederate right. Like Colonel Fry during Heth's earlier attack, James Lane halted his brigade south of the road and redeployed to face Gamble's men.[64]

Perrin's infantry received a cheer as they passed through Pettigrew's ranks and climbed Middle Ridge in this order: Federal left to right, 13th, 12th, 1st, and 14th South Carolina, roughly 1,500 men. Remaining behind, the 1st Rifles guarded the wagon train. To their front, they saw the last of Biddle's men struggling to reach cover. Capt. Washington Shooter, 1st South Carolina, later wrote:

> We could see the Yankees running in wild disorder and everything went merry as a marriage bell until we ascended a hill where we saw their batteries and their last line of entrenchment — a stonewall. When we rose [climbed] the hill [Middle Ridge] their batteries opened with shells in earnest and made wide gaps in our ranks. We passed over the hill into the bottom and before the ascent of the second hill [Seminary Ridge] when their batteries opened with [canister?] at easy range.[65]

The 14th South Carolina charged straight ahead toward the 142nd and 151st Pennsylvania and Breck's guns. Earlier that spring, before leaving Virginia, Perrin issued general orders:

> Whenever the charge bayonets was ordered, no one was to fire his gun under any circumstances until the enemy's line was broken or the command to commence firing was given by the officer in command of the line.

Leaving Middle Ridge, the command echoed down the line, "At the charge bayonets." A member of the 14th's Company K recounted:

> The enemy were behind a rock fence, and we could hear their officers distinctly encouraging their men to hold their fire, until the command to fire was given. They obeyed their command implicitly, and rose to their feet and took as deliberate aim as if they were on dress parade, and to show you how accurate their aim was, 34 out of 39 men fell at the first fire of the enemy.

The South Carolinians also obeyed their commanding officer and did not return the Pennsylvanians' volley.[66]

Wainwright's 24 guns — Breck, Cooper, Stevens, and Stewart — opened with shell and canister. On the Federal right, artillery fire and musketry from Stone and Meredith devastated Scales's brigade. Their advance abruptly halted and the men lay down to fire back. Using the breastworks and trees for cover, Biddle's infantry and Breck's guns stopped Perrin's left regiment, the 14th South Carolina, short of the grove. Abner Perrin considered it "the most destructive fire of musketry, grape, and canister I have ever been exposed to during the war." Afterward, Spencer Welsh wrote his wife:

> Such a rattle of musketry I have never heard surpassed ... many brave fellows went down in death.... Officers who have been in all the fights tell me that they never saw our brigade act so gallantly before. When the order was given to charge ... our men rushed forward with a perfect fury, yelling and driving them, though with great slaughter to themselves as well as to the Yankees.... As the enemy were concealed, they killed a great many of our men before we could get at them.

Captain Shooter described the scene for an absent fellow officer. "Scales's Brigade faltered then stopped and left the field. The left and center of the 14th faltered and then gave way. Lane's brigade halted on the hill. Saw Yankee cavalry on their right."[67]

Biddle and Rowley rode the line trying to steady their men. At the breastworks, Captain Warren heard Rowley cry distinctly, "We must hold this hill! You must hold this ridge!" Most of them stayed in line. While riding toward the seminary, the general saw Lt. Frank M. Powell lying on the ground. "You're wounded?" he asked and Powell nodded. Rowley got down and gave him directions to the division hospital, St. Francis Xavier Church. He then asked a surgeon nearby, "If he could not do something for me [Powell]."[68]

Federal success at the seminary grove was only temporary. Abner Perrin rode to the front and led the second charge himself. Captain Shooter described the Confederates' quick recovery:

> Our brigade halted for a moment.... Albert Owens and Larkin [color bearers] pushed forward, waved their colors and called to the Regiment to "Come on." Larkin was shot down. Albert picked up his flag and with both

colors moved on. He was directly shot down.... The old 1st sprang forward with a yell — the 12th and 13th moved rapidly forward. Our regiment [1st SC] cleared its front then wheeled to the left [north] and poured a flank fire into the enemy.[69]

Alexander Biddle saw the 1st South Carolina driving toward a gap in the fence. He sent an aide to warn Rowley who replied that the fence must be held. The 1st struck the seam between Biddle and Gamble. At the same time, Col. Joseph N. Brown's 14th South Carolina changed direction,

Competent commander of the First Corps's artillery, Col. Charles Wainwright openly criticized Doubleday's, Wadsworth's, and Rowley's performance at Gettysburg. Courtesy of USAMHI.

broke through south of the seminary and then on the north side. The 1st South Carolina also changed direction and fired on Alexander Biddle's exposed left. Raked by this musketry, the 121st disintegrated. Shooter remembered that "they [Biddle's men] left the woods and we followed them running." Chapman Biddle spoke with Gates and then, without instructions from either Doubleday or Rowley, ordered a retreat. The Federal left center fell back but both flanks held. Perrin's two remaining regiments, the 12th and 13th South Carolina, swung farther right and assaulted Gamble's men south of the Fairfield Road. Under fire from two directions and aware that the infantry and artillery were leaving the seminary, the troopers slowly fell back to their mounts.[70]

Confusion later existed whether the First Corps ever received specific orders to retreat from the seminary. With no reserves available, Howard later wrote that he ordered Doubleday at 4:00 p.m. "to fall back fighting to Cemetery Hill if he could no longer remain in his [current] position." From Doubleday's standpoint, "I did not get the order and I guided myself to Cemetery

Hill the best way I could by making inquiries and noticing which way the retreating masses were going." The First Corps fell back with or without the field commander's concurrence. One of Doubleday's aides gave Wadsworth the order to withdraw. Most likely Rowley also received one. Neither Howard nor Doubleday attempted to direct the Federal retreat to Cemetery Hill. Both corps would pay a high price for the lack of leadership within Gettysburg.[71]

During this melee at the seminary, when the chaos was at its worst, the South Carolinians captured the First Brigade's flag. The exact time and location are not known because no one on the Federal side ever admitted its loss. In a July 29, 1863, letter to South Carolina's governor, Milledge Luke Bonham, Abner Perrin claimed the capture of

> Four standards, two of which I intended to send to you to be placed in the State House at Columbia but they ordered me to turn them in here [Culpeper Court House, Virginia] to be sent to Richmond I suppose. These were the Corps Standard of the 1st Army corps, commanded by Reynolds whom we killed, and a beautiful flag of the 104th New York Regiment [Paul's Brigade, Robinson's Division].

The First Corps standard left the field with Abner Doubleday and the Third Division's headquarters flag remained with Rowley east of the seminary. Perrin's error in identifying his trophy is understandable. Army of the Potomac brigade flags were triangular, four and a half by six feet overall. They incorporated the corps badge (disc for the First) and divisional color (blue for the Third). First Brigade's standard was a triangular version of the Third Division's flag, blue disc on a white field. Maj. C. W. McCreary's 1st South Carolina most likely collared it. Captain Shooter told George McIntyre that they "captured ten pieces of artillery [incorrect], three stands of colors, and any number of prisoners." The flag went from Culpeper to the Confederate War Department in Richmond.[72]

As it had happened earlier on Middle Ridge, the collapse of Biddle's line began on the left and spread to the right. For the second time that day, Biddle's (or Rowley's) brigade had failed to hold its assigned position, endangering the Iron Brigade. If something were not done quickly, Perrin's South Carolina troops would seize the Chambersburg Pike, closing off an escape route for Wainwright's artillery. Seeing the division's Provost Guard starting to fall back, Rowley shouted at Captain Glenn, "Rally the men and hold that place, if possible." The general added, "For the sake of Allegheny County do not fall back and let them in there." Glenn reformed those who remained and positioned them behind a stone wall north of the seminary. Rowley saw Capt. Craig Wadsworth, an aide to the deceased John Reynolds. Pointing toward Gamble's men who were holding the horses, the general asked, "Why didn't [don't] they charge?" Wadsworth replied, "The Cavalry was under command of General Buford ... the horses there belonged to men who were dismounted and behind the stone wall." Not satisfied, the general said, "By God, I shall order them to charge," and left to find Colonel Gamble.[73]

West of the seminary, McCalmont saw Captain Cooper and told him "that the infantry on the left had gone and unless he immediately withdrew he would be captured." The battery limbered up at once and withdrew. The 142nd Pennsylvania followed the 121st Pennsylvania and 20th New York in the retreat eastward. They did not recover Colonel Cummins's body. After ordering the 151st to fall back, George McFarland found himself severely wounded in both legs. Chapman Biddle received a scalp wound. At the same time, his horse, struck by a bullet, threw off the colonel and fell to the ground. Biddle briefly gave brigade command to Gates. He later returned with a bandaged head and led the retreat through Gettysburg. The 142nd followed McCalmont who, with Lt. Daniel Wilkins's help, carried the regimental colors. Breck limbered up his guns and departed for Cemetery Hill. Glenn's company became the division's rear guard. Because of their efforts, Wainwright lost only one gun, the second piece in Lieutenant Wilbur's section. Perrin captured the disabled cannon and three caissons on the seminary's entrance road.[74]

Unable to find William Gamble, Rowley dropped the cavalry charge and returned to Glenn's position at the stone wall. Dismounting, he walked the line trying to rally the men. Cpl. Henry B. Callahan told the general to leave or he risked capture. After a few moments, Rowley "mounted a horse and galloped off the field." The brigade's dead and wounded remained behind. Earlier that morning, Wadsworth's surgeons had converted the seminary into a hospital. Stretcher bearers carried Col. Robert Cummins and George McFarland into the building now in enemy hands. Placed in the basement's southwest corner, Cummins died the next day but McFarland managed to survive the coming ordeal.[75]

Meredith's Brig. followed Biddle's toward Cemetery Hill. Farther north, Robert Rodes's division finally seized Oak Ridge. The First and Eleventh Corps had now been driven from their positions north and west of Gettysburg. After breaking Biddle's line and capturing the brigade's colors, the 1st and 14th South Carolina surged forward down Chambersburg Street and into town. They pursued Biddle's survivors, taking many prisoners. Col. Abner Perrin issued orders for the two regiments to halt and return to Seminary Ridge. This relieved the pressure somewhat on Rowley's men running toward Baltimore Street. John Glenn and five others followed the Fairfield Road into Gettysburg, crossed Steven's Run, and joined the retreat. Shortly after reaching Cemetery Hill, Doubleday sent Captain Slagle back to find Rowley and to "tell him to make a stand on the edge of town if possible." Slagle remembered what then happened:

> I went back to the field outside of town but could see no troops. I then
> came in and saw a great many gray backs coming up the first street [Cham-
> bersburg Street] as we entered town. I thought they were prisoners our men
> were bringing with them. I turned to the right and went up the forks of
> the road [Fairfield Road] but could not find General Rowley. I then turned
> to go back the same way but concluded that he had gotten further up in
> town and took the other fork [Middle Street] which just saved me, for if I
> had gone in the road I came, I would have been taken prisoner.[76]

Conditions faced by John Robinson's and Cutler's men as they withdrew
from Oak Ridge became worse. Entering Gettysburg from the north, Brig.
Gen. George Doles's Georgians followed the Carlisle Road south and took
position behind fences and buildings. They began a harassing flank fire that
increased the disorder and chaos. Confused by the pattern of Gettysburg's
streets, many Federals panicked and tried to escape by climbing fences and
running down alleys. Most were later captured. William Locke, chaplain of
the 11th Pennsylvania, Paul's brigade, saw "the men crowding through the
streets, and up the alleys, and over fences in utter ignorance of whither they
were going, every moment increased the confusion and dismay."[77]

Sgt. Jacob Zorn followed the Chambersburg Pike into Gettysburg. He
found the streets "jammed full of retreating soldiers and artillery." Up ahead
was the Diamond, a town square formed by the intersection of Chambersburg, Carlisle, York, and Baltimore Streets. The rebels brought a gun down
one of the side streets and opened fire. Zorn remembered:

> They threw Greap [Grape] and canister through the streets just raking
> them from one end to the other [.] [T]he men broke out in every direction
> through houses and any thing that come in the way.... I scurried up Main
> St. [Carlisle] to the upper end of town where we were cut off and had to
> surrender....

Later paroled, Zorn returned to the 142nd Pennsylvania on October 25, 1863.[78]

Thomas Rowley, accompanied by Lt. Oliver Moore, galloped toward
town. Two lengths in front was Lt. William Wilson, wounded and heading
for the hospital at St. Francis Xavier Church. To relieve pressure on his boils,
the general changed riding position several times. Up ahead, Wilson's horse
almost threw him when forced to jump an overgrown and partially concealed
ditch. Without warning, Rowley's mount bolted and abruptly stopped at the
ditch's edge, throwing him to the ground. Captain Wadsworth saw Rowley
fall but rode on.[79]

Ignoring the pain, Rowley remounted and rode east on High Street. He
stopped frequently, giving orders to the retreating soldiers. Wounded men
limped along the sidewalks and rebel skirmishers fired from the side streets.
Having walked in from the seminary, Powell stood outside St. Francis Xavier
and watched as Rowley approached the Baltimore Pike intersection. For some

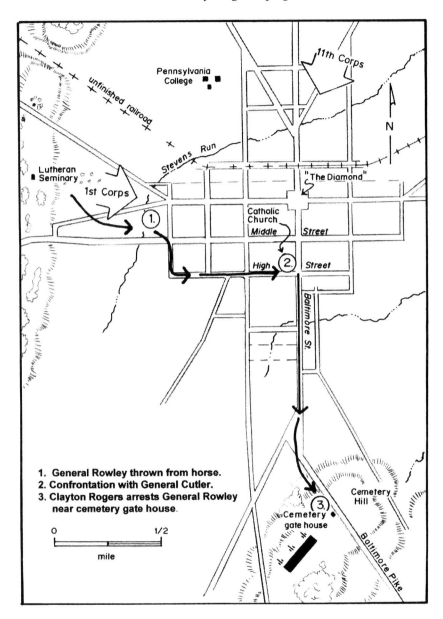

Rowley's retreat to Cemetery Hill, 4:30–5:30 PM. Map by John Heiser.

reason, the Third Division's retirement down High Street came to a standstill. The general forced his horse ahead to find out what was wrong.[80]

The simultaneous retreat of two Federal corps had clogged and overflowed Gettysburg's narrow streets. On the Baltimore Pike, Eleventh

Corps units headed south on the left or east side, First Corps on the right, and artillery moved down the center. At the intersection with High Street, just east of St. Francis Xavier, Biddle's, Stone's, and Meredith's survivors heading east from the seminary met the remnants of Baxter's, Paul's and Cutler's brigades pushing south. Officers shouted: "First Corps this way; Eleventh Corps this way." Confederate shells struck building fronts, showering the road with brick fragments and mortar.[81]

Troops, ambulances, and artillery moving south on the Baltimore Pike temporarily stopped Third Division units trying to exit High Street. Rowley became incensed at this delay and began looking for someone to vent his frustration on. After ordering a First Division officer named Stevens to stop looking for a horse and rejoin his command, Rowley saw an unfamiliar brigadier forcing his way down the crowded street. He asked, "What is your name sir?" Hearing "General Cutler," Rowley unwisely decided to complain about the earlier behavior of officers from the 7th Wisconsin near the seminary. When Cutler defended them, the Pennsylvanian lost his temper and said that they would settle the issue another time. One of Cutler's aides, Lt. Thomas Miller, came up in time to hear Rowley's "oath" and threat. Miller followed Cutler toward Cemetery Hill where the two generals would meet again.[82]

Born in Massachusetts, Lysander Cutler settled in Penobscot County, Maine. Here, he taught school, managed several businesses, and married Catherine Bassett. Bankrupted by the 1856 depression, the Cutlers moved to Milwaukee, Wisconsin. On July 16, 1861, he became colonel of the 6th Wisconsin Volunteers. At Brawner's farm the evening of August 28, 1862, Cutler was wounded in the right thigh. Granted a leave of absence, the colonel returned in time for Fredericksburg. During this battle, a horse kicked him, aggravating the gunshot wound. Deemed unfit for duty, Cutler spent two months in a Washington hospital. Belatedly promoted to brigadier general, he took command of Wadsworth's Second Brigade on March 1863. Two horses had already been shot from under him July 1. There is no question that by 4:30 p.m., Cutler and Rowley were enduring both physical pain and mental anguish from what was sure to be another defeat for the Potomac Army. Neither individual forgot their afternoon encounter in Gettysburg.[83]

The congestion finally broke. Rowley led their advance onto Baltimore Street and the brigade resumed its retreat southward. Near the northern foot of Cemetery Hill, Col. Charles Wainwright met Rowley, who claimed that he now commanded the First Corps. Failing to persuade the brigadier that both Wadsworth and Robinson ranked him, Wainwright rode up the hill, convinced that Rowley was drunk. General Wadsworth and his staff were visible on the hill's crest. To Jacob Slagle, Cemetery Hill at 5:00 p.m. "was a pitiable sight; the tired, worn out remnants of our fine regiments who had gone so proudly into the field in the morning, were collecting together, and when all was told — what a miserable sight."[84]

Remembering well the unpleasant confrontations of July 1, 1863, Brig. Gen. Lysander Cutler filed charges against Rowley in April 1864. Courtesy of Mass. MOLLUS and USAMHI.

As line officers reformed the survivors from the First Brigade, Rowley directed Colonel Biddle to take a position in the rear of Cemetery Hill. Lt. W. M. Dalgliesh, an aide to Colonel Stone, informed Rowley that Second Brigade had come up and was forming behind Biddle's. One regiment, however, became separated from the others. The general ordered that it "should be brought into [the] Cemetery lot with the balance of the Brigade." While his staff watched the division reform, Rowley spoke with McCalmont and invited the colonel to his headquarters later that evening.[85]

Edmund Dana found Rowley and gave him the brigade's status. A severely wounded Roy Stone had been taken prisoner at McPherson's farm. Langhorne Wister replaced Stone and suffered the same fate. Dana assumed brigade command around 3:30 p.m. Falling back to the seminary, the three regiments formed a battle line that straddled the Chambersburg Pike. To their right rear was the East Railroad Cut, defended by Stewart's Battery B and Dawes's 6th Wisconsin. When Wadsworth's order to withdraw arrived, Dana and the 143rd Pennsylvania followed the railroad embankment into town. They fell in with Cutler's brigade and were among the last to reach Cemetery Hill. The colonel received further instructions from Rowley on where to post the Second Brigade.[86]

While Colonel Robinson and Lt. Col. Mark Finnicum watched the 7th Wisconsin re-form on Cemetery Hill, Rowley rode over and asked which regiment they commanded. The colonel replied, "Seventh Wisconsin." Remembering again what had happened at the seminary, Rowley said, "Your men are damned good and brave fighting men but the officers are a worthless lot, ... a damned pack of cowards. I saw them on the road and know them ... Keep them with the regiment." Choosing not to reply, Finnicum walked away and located General Doubleday, who ordered the 7th to form on the left of an artillery battery. Leaving the 7th Wisconsin, Rowley rode off to find Abner Doubleday.[87]

Frank Powell walked by the cemetery gate and saw Rowley holding his horse and talking to Doubleday. Nearby was Captain Baird, assistant adjutant general, Third Division. Rowley returned to the 7th Wisconsin just as Finnicum gave the command to move out. Addressing Robinson and Finnicum, the brigadier ordered the latter to place his men on the right (east) side of the road (Baltimore Pike). The lieutenant colonel replied that Doubleday told him to form on the left side. Rowley shouted, "I gave you the first order and will hold you responsible for the execution of it. By God I command this Corps." The general then departed. With Robinson's approval, Finnicum marched his command "to the point designated by General Doubleday." Near the gate a few minutes later, Doubleday overheard Rowley again claim corps command but said nothing.[88]

Rowley, Finnicum, and Robinson were not the only confused and angry officers on Cemetery Hill that afternoon. Shortly after 4:00 p.m. Hancock arrived and, according to Howard, simply said, "General Meade has sent me to represent him on the field." They proceeded to divide the duties and establish a defensive line. Meade's dispatch announcing Hancock's new assignment did not reach Howard until 7:00 p.m. Like Slocum, he now realized that a junior (Howard was promoted to brigadier first) had replaced him as field commander. Experiencing deep mortification, Howard sought out Hancock and in essence requested that George Meade be informed of the fine job he had done. Hancock's version of what happened that afternoon was much different and their disagreement persisted long after the war. Doubleday complicated the situation even more by offering a third version of the encounter. In any case, it is a reasonable assumption that command effectiveness on Cemetery Hill deteriorated further following the first meeting between Howard and Hancock. The whole that afternoon did not equal the sum of the parts. Unfortunately, this incident was only the beginning.[89]

Around 5:00 p.m., Hancock engaged Abner Doubleday in a loud and animated conversation. Ordered by Meade to take field command, Hancock wanted to stop the Federal retreat immediately and establish a defensive line. To the east, a ravine separating Cemetery and Culp's Hills offered the enemy a favorable line of attack. Having personally assigned Steven's 5th Maine Battery to cover this approach, Hancock wanted a First Corps brigade to occupy the western slope of Culp's Hill. Doubleday recounted "that he [Hancock] at once directed me to send a force to support a battery that had been established on a lower range of hills some one hundred yards to the East of our position." An intense argument between Doubleday, Hancock, and Lt. Col. Charles H. Morgan, Hancock's chief of staff, ensued. The First Corps commander reluctantly ordered Wadsworth to provide the requested support.[90]

Lt. Clayton E. Rogers, a Wadsworth aide, carried the general's instructions to Colonel Robinson: "assume brigade command and prepare to occupy the western slope of Culp's Hill." Rogers then left to find and bring up the 6th Wisconsin. Replacing the wounded Solomon Meredith, William Robinson sent his aides to inform the brigade's scattered regiments of their new assignment. Assuming regimental command, Finnicum prepared the 7th Wisconsin to move out. Lieutenant Rogers finally found Rufus Dawes and the 6th Wisconsin on Cemetery Hill's northern slope. The 6th prepared to join Robinson's column. About this time, Oliver Howard met Hancock and Doubleday near the cemetery gate. Still reluctant to accept Hancock as field commander, Howard issued orders that would send the Iron Brigade in a different direction. The resulting disagreement delayed the occupation of Culp's Hill, essential to stopping Ewell's advance. Most likely, Rowley was close enough to hear both arguments and saw the ensuing command confusion that followed Howard's arrival. The stage was now set for this tragedy's final act.[91]

While the Iron Brigade reformed, Cutler's command finally reached the northern slope of Cemetery Hill. The decimated regiments halted behind Col. Orlando Smith's Eleventh Corps brigade and Capt. Michael Wiedrick's lunettes. Exhausted men fell to the ground while officers sorted out their commands. Having escorted an ammunition train north from Emmitsburg, Maj. Ira G. Grover and the 7th Indiana joined Cutler at this time. Orders to occupy the crest of Culp's Hill reached Grover and he marched off with his regiment. A few minutes later, Wadsworth, Robinson, and four Iron Brigade regiments set out for the western slope of Culp's Hill.[92]

Their departure left a gap in the Federal defensive line on Cemetery Hill. Continuing to operate under the erroneous assumption that he commanded the First Corps, Rowley decided to close it. Unfortunately, he selected troops from Wadsworth's division to do so. Earlier, Lysander Cutler had posted Lieutenant Miller at the cemetery gate to "show the regiments of his command where the brigade would form." Thomas Miller had just finished positioning the 147th New York when General Rowley came over and spoke directly to Maj. George Harney, acting commander. The general ordered Harney to a different location. Lieutenant Miller interrupted and said that these troops were part of Cutler's command and pointed out where they were forming. Rowley replied "that he was in command there and the major must form his regiment where he directed." Having overheard the conversation between Rowley and Miller, another aide departed to tell Cutler.[93]

Informed that the same officer encountered earlier in town had stopped the 147th, Lysander Cutler went over and asked Rowley, "Did you stop this regiment?" Receiving a positive answer, Cutler replied, "General Doubleday ordered the brigade to this position." "I don't care a damn about General Doubleday! I command the corps and will place the troops where I please," Rowley replied. Having heard enough, Cutler left to find Doubleday.[94]

Between 5:00 and 5:30 p.m., Clayton Rogers and Rufus Dawes approached the crest of Cemetery Hill. They saw "everything in disorder. Panic was impending over the exhausted soldiers. It was a confused rabble of disorganized regiments of infantry and crippled batteries." Near the crest, Dawes looked over and saw Rowley, Major Harney, and Lieutenant Miller. To Colonel Dawes, "Rowley had become positively insane. He was raving and storming, and giving wild and crazy orders." To Rogers, it seemed that "Rowley, in great excitement, had lost his own 3d division, and was giving General Wadsworth's troops contradictory orders, calling them cowards." Concluding that Rowley's conduct "was so unbecoming a division commander and unfortunately stimulated with poor commissary ... [Rogers] did not hesitate to arrest this crazy officer, on his own responsibility, and called on Col. Dawes to execute the order with the bayonets of the 6th Wisconsin." Rufus Dawes watched as "Clayton Rogers rode up and boldly placed General Rowley under arrest and called on me for bayonets to enforce the order." Bayonets of the 6th Wisconsin were not required. Brig. Gen. Thomas A. Rowley probably surrendered his sword to Rogers then left the area with Lieutenant Colonel Dawes.[95]

The 27th Article of War gave Lieutenant Rogers the authority to arrest a brigadier general and required that brigadier to cooperate fully with his junior. Acts of impropriety, such as drunkenness, provided sufficient justification for taking such action. It was Rogers's responsibility to immediately inform Major General Doubleday. Additionally, the arresting officer must provide "the prisoner a copy of the charges within eight days" or by July 9. No record exists that Rogers ever filed or served the charges.[96]

Dawes, not Rogers, reported the arrest to Abner Doubleday and later claimed that "the Major-General commanding the corps endorsed the act after the fact." The corps commander left no record of this conversation. William Robinson's orders to move to Culp's Hill reached Dawes. Accompanied by caissons from Stevens's battery, Dawes, Rogers, and the 6th Wisconsin left the cemetery. Around this time, Doubleday sent Capt. Stephen Weld, one of Reynolds's aides, to get entrenching tools. On his return, Weld met Gen. Winfield Hancock who told him to take the tools back.[97]

After two hours of inactivity, Henry Slocum decided to take action at

1st Lt. Clayton Rogers (left) arrested Rowley the evening of July 1 on Cemetery Hill. Courtesy of Sawyer County, Wisconsin, Historical Society. Lt. Col. Rufus Dawes (right) executed Rogers's order. Courtesy of USAMHI.

3:30 p.m. Without bothering to either look at the field himself or to consult the officers already there, Slocum instructed Brig. Gen. Alpheus Williams to seize Benner's Hill with the Twelfth Corps's First Division. Supposedly, this movement would menace Richard Ewell's left flank. Consequently, when the Confederate threat to seize Cemetery Hill peaked, Federal reinforcements were advancing on an unoccupied hill a mile away. Lee did not attack that evening. In spite of a series of command blunders, remnants from the First and Eleventh Corps held their position. Slocum relieved Hancock of field command between 5:30 and 6:00 p.m. Howard relinquished his authority at 7:00 p.m. The curtain finally came down on July 1, 1863.[98]

Returning to Rowley's predicament, "Any person in the military service of the United States arrested for a capital crime must be kept in close confinement." For noncapital offenses, officer confinement could include "being limited to his quarters, or tent, or to camp, garrison, or other defined boundaries." Charges filed just before the April 1864 court-martial placed Rowley under arrest for a capital crime. It is not clear what followed his July 1 arrest. Rowley should have been deprived of his sword. Physical removal was usually avoided but an officer under arrest could not wear his sword. Later correspondence with defense counsel Edmund Dana indicated that someone took Rowley's sword either July 1, 1863, at Gettysburg or April 21, 1864, in Culpeper. Besides confinement, the arrested officer could not exercise "even the minor functions of his office."[99]

Corps, divisional, and brigade records fail to mention either Rowley's arrest or the ensuing events. In 1878 and 1898, exasperated War Department clerks reported, "No record of arrest or trial." Only the "Organization of the Army of the Potomac at the battle of Gettysburg, July 1–3, 1863," mentions Rowley's removal or replacement as both a divisional and brigade commander. Chapman Biddle stated that Rowley resumed brigade command the morning of July 2. There is no evidence that Doubleday took any action against the brigadier either that evening or the following day.[100]

Satisfied that the brigade was properly positioned, Rowley withdrew a short distance to the rear and established his headquarters for the night. Lieutenant Moore joined him and they reviewed the day's casualty reports. The 151st Pennsylvania left Spangler's farm with 466 enlisted men and 21 officers. Only 92 answered evening roll call. Sixty-three percent of McCalmont's command had been killed, wounded, or captured at the seminary. About 80 survived the retreat through town. Under orders to support batteries posted in the cemetery, they lay on their arms that night. With three quarters of yesterday's muster missing, the 121st also slept under arms on the hill's south slope. The two companies sent by Gates to occupy the Harmon house now comprised almost half of his remaining command. Before sunset, Maj. Gen. Daniel Sickles and his staff rode by and the First Corps survivors greeted them with cheers. Sickles's presence indicated that the Third Corps would soon be on the field.[101]

A week before, Brig. Gen. George J. Stannard received word that his brigade of five, nine-month Vermont regiments was detached from John Abercrombie's division and assigned to Doubleday's. A sister brigade led by Brig. Gen. Alexander Hays became part of the Second Corps's Third Division. Both brigades left Washington's defenses and set out to join the Army of the Potomac. Stannard's aide, Lt. George Benedict, found and spoke with John Reynolds at Moritz's Tavern the evening of June 30. He later returned to the brigade, bivouacked near Emmitsburg. Marching north July 1, Stannard's column was eight miles from Gettysburg when orders from Doubleday "to hasten forward as fast as possible" arrived around noon.[102]

"Four or five miles from the field the heavy roar of cannon in front reached all ears." Looking north, Benedict saw that "the smoke of the battle was now mounting high over the field and the sultry thunder of artillery, rolling continuously and heavily, filled the air." Just before sundown, the Vermonters approached the Round Tops. Informed earlier that Rowley commanded the Third Division, Stannard sent his aide forward to report their arrival. Benedict "found Rowley stretched on the ground by a little white house. He was asleep, overcome by fatigue, or something, and his aides would not wake him. They told me to guide the brigade to that point." Stannard brought his column forward and they camped that night in a nearby wheat field. George Meade reached the cemetery around midnight. He gave John Newton First Corps command, returning Doubleday to the Third Division. Jacob Slagle considered Doubleday's removal "at that time ... a gross outrage." Rowley's reaction to the promotion of his former Sixth Corps divisional commander is not known.[103]

End of the Campaign

> General Rowley himself displayed great bravery. He was several times struck by spent shot and pieces of shell, and on the third day his horse was killed by a cannon-shot while he was holding him by the bridle and conversing with me. —*Abner Doubleday*[104]

On the morning of July 2, Chapman Biddle placed the 121st in a field just south of the cemetery, taking cover behind a stone fence. Nearby, an aide wrote his general's farewell to the First Corps.

> Major General John Newton being the senior officer having been assigned to the command of the 1st Corps. General Doubleday hereby resumes the command of the 3rd div. In doing so he desires to express his pride and

gratification at their splendid achievements of yesterday against overwhelming numbers and his deep sorrow at the many [casualties?] which the corps
has sustained. It gives him great satisfaction to resign the command to so
capable and distinguished an officer as Major Gen. Newton

Captain E. P. Halsted A.A.G. 3rd Div.

Unfortunately, Doubleday's initial magnanimity soon ended, replaced by out-
right hostility toward Meade, Howard, and Newton. Before noon, the major
general reorganized his Third Division into three brigades: "the First under
... Thomas A. Rowley, the Second under Colonel E. L. Dana ... and the Third
under Brigadier General George J. Stannard." Meade posted the division in
a reserve position behind Cemetery Hill.[105]

Near sunset, Doubleday ordered Rowley to move the First Brigade to
the left or south of Cemetery Hill and support the Second Corps then under
attack by Longstreet. The four regiments moved out and crossed the Taneytown Road. While marching southeast, troops trying to escape the fighting
split the brigade in two. Unable to follow Rowley, the 151st Pennsylvania and
20th New York continued to the top of a hill where the Second Corps's Brig.
Gen. John Gibbon stopped and positioned them in the front line. The two
regiments remained there and later played a critical role in the fighting that
followed.[106]

Early on July 3, the 142nd and 121st Pennsylvania shifted a half mile to
the south, placing them near the center of Hancock's Second Corps line. During the rebel cannonade that afternoon, Rowley moved both regiments farther left. Shell fragments struck the general as he rode down the ridge. Taking
a position on Dana's right, the men piled up rails for protection. Located about
midway between the cemetery and Little Round Top, both brigades had a
full view of the afternoon attack. Their role, however, was limited to firing
a few shots at rebel sharpshooters and dodging projectiles. Near dusk, a bursting shell killed Capt. C. H. Flagg of Rowley's staff; his body was found the
next day. Before retiring, Edmund Dana invited the general to have an Independence Day dinner with him.[107]

Learning July 5 that John Newton was junior in commission, Abner
Doubleday refused to obey his orders. Edwin Coddington described the
standoff. "For some reason Doubleday did not inspire confidence as a commanding officer.... [He] requested permission to leave the Army of the
Potomac if Meade would not allow him to command the First Corps." No
one changed his mind. Relieved from duty and ordered to report to the adjutant general, Doubleday departed for Washington on July 7. The major general and Rowley would meet again. Brig. Gen. John R. Kenly and his
Maryland Brigade arrived at First Corps headquarters Saturday, July 11. John
Newton gave him command of the Third Division. Since the previous fall,
Kenly had been guarding the Baltimore and Ohio Railroad. Reynolds's death,

Doubleday's departure, Stone's absence, and Kenly's arrival caused considerable confusion in the division. Some unit histories reported that Rowley commanded the First Brigade, others said the Third Division. The confusion became worse.[108]

Thomas Rowley began a medical leave of absence July 10 and made plans to return to Pittsburgh. He stayed with Edmund Dana at Second Brigade Headquarters July 12 then departed the next day. Chapman Biddle assumed brigade command. John Kenly's first recorded reference to Biddle in this capacity appeared July 30 in Special Order #84. Rowley briefly returned to the Army of the Potomac in mid-August and relieved Biddle. The First Brigade return for July 1863 listed Rowley "absent due to sickness" and "in arrest" for August. The brigadier general received another two-week, medical leave beginning September 14 "on account of total disability occasioned by boils upon his person." That week, Abner Doubleday reported to Major General Banks in New Orleans for assignment. Near the end of September, General Newton placed John Kenly under arrest for intoxication. Released October 3, Kenly returned to Third Division Headquarters. In Pittsburgh, Assistant Surgeon J. C. McKee recommended a third extension of Rowley's medical leave because of "remittent fever and general debility." The brigadier general was listed "absent sick" on brigade returns for September and October. Lysander Cutler began a 30-day leave of absence August 17.[109]

In the weeks that followed Gettysburg, the divisional and brigade ranks grew smaller. One of Stannard's Vermont regiments left July 8 and the remaining three July 18. Theodore Gates and the 20th NYSM returned to provost guard duty July 17. While George McFarland recuperated, the 151st Pennsylvania departed for Harrisburg on July 19 and mustered out August 6. Lt. Col. Alexander Biddle and McCalmont led the 121st and 142nd Pennsylvania, respectively. A familiar and popular Abner Doubleday was gone, his replacement an outsider without combat experience. Rumors circulated about Rowley going on medical leave and what exactly had occurred July 1 on Cemetery Hill.[110]

If this was not enough, army headquarters issued a circular August 4 demanding that battle reports be submitted immediately. Responsibility for preparing the division's July 1 report fell on Lieutenant Wilson, who had served as acting divisional AAG that day. In a letter to Col. Edmund Dana, Wilson described his current problem.

> Genl Rowley [on medical leave in Pittsburgh] having been in command of the Division the 1st day is looked to for a division report and has thus far received the report of the 1st Brigade [Biddle's] upon which to base his. Genl Doubleday [in Louisiana with Banks] intimated in a letter a few days since that he would be compelled to make his Corps report without any mention of the 3rd Division that day unless he got its report soon. As the

> order received this morning is peremptory it will be necessary to make the division report from the report of the operations of the 1st Brigade alone if that of the 2nd Brigade is not furnished.
>
> I am called upon for Gen Rowley's report and having received the authority from him to sign his name, I will be compelled to make use of it at the foot of such a report as my feeble abilities may dictate.

This bureaucratic crisis, like most in the army, ultimately went away.[111]

Dana finally finished his brigade report August 5 and gave it to Biddle who then wrote the divisional report for July 2 and 3. All three, Rowley, Dana, and Biddle, predated their submissions to July 28, thereby complying with Meade's orders of August 4. In his July 1 report, Thomas Rowley took pleasure in commending brigade and regimental commanders and their replacements for bravery. The brigadier's list included future supporters and critics. Chapman Biddle made "mention of the excellent conduct of" Lieutenant Colonel McCalmont and "valuable services rendered" by Capt. Horatio Warren.[112]

Abner Doubleday did not submit a Gettysburg report until December 14. Many considered it "the longest battle report of the Union Army." Well aware of his subordinate's July 1 arrest, he strongly endorsed Rowley's behavior throughout the three days.

> General Rowley himself displayed great bravery. He was several times struck by spent shot and pieces of shell, and on the third day his horse was killed by a cannon-shot while he was holding him by the bridle and conversing with me.... General Rowley held the left wing under the most adverse circumstances and with a portion of Wadsworth's men, covered the retreat of the main body by successive echelons of resistance.

The "List of Officers of First Brigade, Third Division, First Corps, Killed and Wounded in Action at Gettysburg" reported T. A. Rowley wounded July 1 and 3, 1863. First Brigade's list of casualties included "Thomas A. Rowley, Brigadier General, Wounded." There is no information on the type of wound received either day.[113]

September 18, the War Department issued General Orders No. 316. This 100-page document listed all "promotions and appointments in the Army of the United States made by the President, by and with the advice and consent of the Senate, and by the President alone since the publication of General Orders No. 181 of November 1, 1862, and up to July 1, 1863." The final selection and ranking had changed considerably from March, no doubt reflecting Chancellorsville and Gettysburg. Effective November 29, 1862, 83 officers advanced to brigadier general of volunteers. Within this group, Thomas H. Neill ranked 10th, Frank Wheaton 13th, Lysander Cutler 36th, William H. Morris 62nd, and Thomas A. Rowley 75th. The document did not list Rowley's original regiment, the 102nd Pennsylvania, because he was detached from

Brig. Gen. William Morris, who earlier carried John Peck's orders to Rowley on the Peninsula, became a member of the court. Courtesy of USAMHI.

it and would never return. General Orders No. 316 listed 44 brigadiers promoted to major general of volunteers. The final ranking supported personal grievances expressed on and after July 1 at Gettysburg. Among the new major generals, Oliver Howard ranked 13th, Winfield Hancock 17th, Abner Doubleday 24th, and John Newton 38th. The last entry announced the January 21, 1863, cashiering of Maj. Gen. Fitz-John Porter.[114]

Whatever his feelings regarding the July 1 arrest, Rowley could not demand a trial. If he considered himself "aggrieved by the arrest" or the charges preferred against him were later withdrawn, redress under the 34th Article was available. There is no indication that Rowley ever considered seeking redress before the trial. Naively, he may have assumed that in time the army would forget the incident. The problem should have been discussed with Abner Doubleday, but he was gone. Even though Rowley had previously reported to John Newton at Fredericksburg, no record exists of a conversation between the two officers at Gettysburg.[115]

A deadline for the army taking formal action against Rowley did exist. "No person shall be liable to be tried and punished by a General Court Martial for any offense which shall appear to have been committed more than two years before the issuing of the order for such trial." A different limit was applicable in Rowley's case. The arrested "must be brought to trial within ten days after the serving of the charges, unless the necessities of the service prevent; and unless tried within forty days after serving of charges, the arrest ceases." It appears that, based on this aspect alone, Rowley's arrest would become invalid August 19, 1863, assuming that Lieutenant Rogers filed charges before July 9. The relief, however, was only temporary. "Officers thus relieved from arrest without trial may be tried at any time within twelve months after such release." For Thomas Rowley, this meant until August 18, 1864.[116]

7. Camp Berry, Maine

With my knowledge of the military, I should say
that General Rowley proved himself a very superior general
and a brave man. — *Captain Oliver K. Moore*[5]

On October 14, 1863, the War Department ordered Thomas Rowley to "repair without delay to Portland, Maine and relieve Major Charles J. Whiting, Second U. S. Cavalry, in command of the depot for drafted men." A later explanation for this posting was that having been wounded at Gettysburg and physically unfit for field service, he was assigned to command the Department of Maine. Actually, it was a "depot for drafted men" called Camp Berry.[2]

On July 4, 1863, the War Department created 15 depots for drafted men. By August, brigadier generals of volunteers commanded 10 of them. As was the case for Maj. Charles J. Whiting, captains, majors, and colonels of the regular army filled the remaining vacancies. That fall, Maj. Gen. Abner Doubleday found himself assigned to the Buffalo, New York, depot. The War Department revoked the order a few days later and he remained in Washington, his new assignment after Louisiana. Rowley's posting to Portland appeared to be the norm rather than the exception for brigadiers either recuperating or out of favor.[3]

By mid-June 1862, Lincoln had concluded that McClellan's Peninsular Campaign would not end the war. His judgment confirmed by the Seven Days fighting, the president on July 11 sought 300,000 additional men to serve three years. Recognizing an immediate need for more infantry, the War Department ordered Maine to establish three mustering camps for the coming wave of volunteer recruits. One facility, initially called Camp King, was located just south of Portland in the Ligonia section of Cape Elizabeth. Renamed Camp Abraham Lincoln, it filled enrollment quotas for Cumberland, York, Oxford, and Androscoggin counties.[4]

The heady days of mustering and training entire regiments of Maine volunteers ended that winter. By January 1, 1863, 28 of Maine's 32 infantry regiments were in the field. On March 3, Congress passed the Enrollment [Conscription] Act that required three years of military service from all able-bodied males between 20 and 45 years of age. Conscripts would be called up by Federal decree, not by the governors. Names of the first draftees were drawn in New York City on July 11. Two days later, draft riots broke out in several northern cities. Less violent changes took place in Maine.[5]

Camp Lincoln became a rendezvous point for draftees with volunteers sent elsewhere. The permanent garrison focused on collecting, training, and controlling conscripts. After taking the oath for three years of service, recruits received uniforms and rudimentary drill instruction. They later went to Virginia and became replacements for the Army of the Potomac. To discourage those experiencing a "change of heart" regarding military service, the authorities moved the camp north in August 1863 to Mackworth Island near Falmouth and renamed it Camp Berry. Maj. Gen. Hiram G. Berry from Rockland, Maine, was mortally wounded at Chancellorsville on May 3, 1863, a loss the army could ill afford. Isolation on Mackworth Island failed to stop desertions and three months later, just before Rowley's arrival, Camp Berry returned to Cape Elizabeth. A high stockade fence, 800 feet by 200 feet, now surrounded the original wooden barracks and drill field.[6]

The date that Thomas Rowley relieved Major Whiting was not recorded. The post record shows a marked change in penmanship October 13. Whatever the day, Brigadier General Rowley soon realized how far he had fallen in the military world. For the first time a general officer was present for duty at Camp Berry. The camp's permanent garrison, Company A, mustered three officers and 95 enlisted men. Eighty-seven conscripts and three officers comprised Company B. Attached to the post were 17 additional officers, one from each of Maine's 15 infantry regiments and two artillery batteries assigned to either the Army of the Potomac or Burnside's Ninth Corps. Assisted by 51 enlisted men, they conducted conscripts from Camp Berry to their respective regiments.[7]

Not everyone saw Rowley's glass as half empty. In an October 29 letter to his brother, Alfred McCalmont complained of serving under a division commander (John Kenly) "who is drunk two-thirds of the time and incompetent when sober" and of being unable to secure a promotion to full colonel. He also expressed little sympathy for a close acquaintance. "General Rowley has procured a nice berth. All goes by political and personal favoritism. Rowley has been ordered to Portland, Maine. He was under arrest, but that made no difference. He is to superintend the draft." Fortunately, McCalmont's opinion regarding the brigadier changed by spring.[8]

Initially, Rowley was the sole Pennsylvanian at the camp and would become its only out-of-state commandant. On November 1, George Meade approved Special Order No. 292, Army of the Potomac. "Lieutenants J. F. Denniston and G. A. Heberton, Aides de Camp to Brig Gen T. A. Rowley, are relieved from further duty at the Headquarters of the 1st Brigade, 3rd Division, 1st Corps, and will at once proceed to join General Rowley at Portland,

Maine." Evidently, William Wilson and O. K. Moore were either not available or not considered. Just promoted to captain, John Denniston, Company C, 155th Pennsylvania, received orders November 10 transferring him to Rowley's staff. George Heberton, an aide at Gettysburg, rejoined the general in December, followed by a surgeon.[9]

Little is known about the relationship between Rowley and Portland's citizens. The *Portland Daily Press*'s December 2, 1863, issue carried this notice:

> Headquarters Draft Rendezvous
> Portland Dec. 1, 1863
>
> Orders No. 47 — The streets of Portland will hereafter be patrolled by a guard from Camp Berry, and all soldiers found upon the streets not having proper passes will be arrested and sent to Camp Berry, and any soldier found drunk or behaving in a disorderly manner will be immediately sent to jail. The fact of a soldier not belonging to this camp will not shield him from the penalty of the order.
>
> By order of brig. Gen. Rowley
> J. H. Harrison, Capt. 5th Cav. Act. Asst. Adj. Gen.

No discussion of street conditions either before or after the order exists. Another Portland newspaper, *The Eastern Argus*, reported December 17: "Gen. Rowley has at Camp Berry about six hundred men, a large portion of whom are volunteers under the last call. They all go into regiments and batteries now in the field." December's post record showed a total garrison of only 204 with 85 conscripts and no volunteers. The paper proved to be correct, however, in predicting future changes.[10]

The new year did not begin auspiciously for Rowley's former commander Abner Doubleday. On December 31, 1863, Edwin Stanton requested that the major general of volunteers be promoted in the regular army from major, 17th Infantry Regiment to lieutenant colonel, 5th Infantry, effective October 16, 1863. The Senate did not approve the change.[11]

During January, the army assigned a third company, consisting of two officers and 82 enlisted volunteers, to Camp Berry. On January 22 and 30, Maj. Gen. John Sedgwick, George Meade's temporary replacement, ordered several Maine regiments to send small details of commissioned officers and enlisted men to General Rowley. Camp Berry reached a high-water mark for Rowley's tenure when two companies from the "U. S. Invalid Corps" reported in February. This brought the total garrison, excluding attachments, to 465. Both Invalid Corps units soon disbanded and the men were sent to the 11th Maine Infantry. Thomas Rowley was by no means the army's only general officer holding an assignment far below that to which he was entitled.[12]

In mid-January, Secretary of War Stanton sent the Senate a list of "Major-Generals and Brigadier-Generals without commands equal to a brigade." Monthly pay for both the general and his staff plus the secretary's opinion as to the general's value were to be included. The *Army and Navy Journal's* recap, which did not report the latter, turned out to be a Who's Who of the Federal Army. George B. McClellan, John C. Fremont, David Hunter, Irwin McDowell, W. S. Rosecrans, Don Carlos Buell, Lewis Wallace, Samuel Heintzelman, Erasmus Keyes, Daniel Sickles, Abner Doubleday, James Wadsworth, John Gibbon, Charles Griffin, Francis Barlow, Solomon Meredith, and Gabriel Paul made the list. Near the end appeared: "Thomas A. Rowley, $229.50; relieved July 14, 1863. Wounded at the battle of Gettysburg; commanding depot for drafted men at Portland, Me. No staff." The War Department evidently overlooked Lieutenant Denniston and Heberton.[13]

Twenty major generals and 47 brigadiers with commands below a brigade cost the nation over $27,000 a month. Congress questioned the need "to assign officers of such high rank with their numerous staff to such duties." Stanton attempted to defend the situation.

> The Generals assigned to temporary duty, such as commanders of draft rendezvous, Courts-Martial, etc., are generally disabled by wounds or sickness incurred in the field. Their staff officers in such cases are generally employed at the depots as Commissaries, Quartermasters, Adjutants, etc.

This explanation failed to silence the secretary's critics.[14]

During February, Lincoln asked Congress to restore the rank of lieutenant general. The bill passed February 26. Three days later, the Senate approved U. S. Grant's nomination to the position. Lincoln presented the commission and Grant accepted it March 9. The next day, Grant visited George Meade at Brandy Station, Virginia. After reaffirming Meade as the Army of the Potomac's commander, he returned to Washington then traveled to Nashville to meet with Sherman. Returning to the capital, Grant established his headquarters in Culpeper, Virginia, on March 26, six miles south of Meade's and 12 miles north of the Rapidan River. The lieutenant general started preparing plans for his overland campaign in a plain brick house near the railway station.[15]

The *Army and Navy Journal's* March 19, 1864, issue reported the latest in the ongoing battle between Abner Doubleday and George Meade:

> It is authoritatively announced that General Doubleday did not prefer charges against General Meade to the Committee on the Conduct of the War; that he did not request the Committee to investigate General Meade's conduct, nor did he ask to be summoned before the committee as a witness; and lastly, General Doubleday never claimed to have received any order to retreat at Gettysburg, Pa.

Future events would show that Doubleday had not agreed to a truce. On the same page appeared a notice that President Lincoln ordered Brig. Gen. George Henry Gordon to be tried by court-martial "for disrespect to his superior officer." The article concluded, "The trial will probably consume some time."[16]

Col. E. L. Dana became the last commander of the Third Division's First Brigade on February 24, 1864. A month later, George Meade announced a major reorganization of the Army of the Potomac. The First Corps, its divisions, and brigades, passed into military history. The Third Division made its final order book entry March 20. The active regiments became part of Maj. Gen. G. K. Warren's Fifth Corps, headquartered across the river at Rappahannock Station. John Newton departed and reported to Major General Sherman, commanding the Division of the Mississippi, Cincinnati. His grade of major general of volunteers was revoked April 18. Newton later led a division in Oliver Howard's Fourth Corps, Army of the Cumberland. John Kenly reported to Lew Wallace, commanding the Middle Department, who assigned him to command the District of Delaware. Two days later, Edmund Dana received his field orders. The 121st, 142nd, 143rd, 149th, and 150th Pennsylvania regiments now comprised Col. Roy Stone's Third Brigade, James Wadsworth's Fourth Division, Warren's Fifth Corps. Returning from leave Friday, April 1, Jacob Zorn found the Third Division's headquarters abandoned. Dana attended an April 8 dinner at Wadsworth's headquarters. He enjoyed the evening conversation with Brigadier General Cutler, John Robinson, and James C. Rice. Within two weeks, they would be participants in Rowley's court-martial. Roy Stone organized a brigade board April 16 to prepare for the spring advance. He placed Dana in charge of the detail.[17]

In early April, orders came ending Rowley's exile to the Pine Tree State. Having completed his "penance" for July 1, 1863, he could now return to the Army of the Potomac and receive a field command; or so he thought. The name of his replacement at Camp Berry is not known.[18]

8. The Culpeper Court-Martial

April 2, 1864, Special Orders No. 135, War Department

This evening General Rowley come back it is said to take command
of the brigade and ... the 142nd Regt ... gave him three
hearty cheers of welcome.—*Sgt. Jacob J. Zorn, 142nd Pennsylvania*[6]

The War Department's Special Orders No. 135 relieved Rowley from command of Portland's draft rendezvous April 2, 1864. He received instructions to "turn over his command to the next senior officer and proceed, without delay, to Headquarters, Army of the Potomac, and report in person to Major-General Meade, commanding." E. D. Townsend, assistant adjutant general, did not specify what would happen at Culpeper. Another list of "Appointments by the President, by and with the Advice and Consent of the Senate" appeared in the *Army and Navy Journal*'s April 9, 1864, issue. Three members of the new group "to be Brigadier-Generals of Volunteers" would soon enter Rowley's life: #8 Captain Alexander S. Webb, effective June 23, 1863; #20 Colonel James C. Rice, August 11, 1863; and #21 Colonel Henry C. Eustis, September 12, 1863.[2]

Thomas Rowley had not been home since leaving for Portland, Maine. Most likely, a personal appeal to the War Department was successful in changing his orders from "proceed, without delay" to those granting a 10-day leave in Pittsburgh. While the general prepared to depart Camp Berry, his old regiment, the 102nd Pennsylvania, left Brandy Station, Virginia, on a 30-day leave. Two weeks earlier, Col. John Patterson had announced the opportunity to reenlist. His March 17, 1864, circular stated that "the number required ... to have the Regiment go home as a veteran Regiment is 334." Patterson added: "your dead comrades on many well fought fields, look to you to preserve the honor and glory of their death, by the preservation of the name of the old regiment." They met the quota and the entire regiment began their leave April 4. A hometown reunion took place that month between Rowley and his former command. The surviving Washington Infantry officers gathered and chose to remember the occasion with a group photo. Rowley in civilian attire occupies the place of honor on the far left. This photo is all that remains from what must have been an emotional experience, the last time that Rowley spoke with John Patterson. The general's obvious willingness to

During an April 1864 reunion in Pittsburgh, the Washington infantry honored their former commander, Thomas Rowley. From *History of the Washington Infantry* and courtesy of William Phillis.

participate supports the view that he expected to receive a command at Culpeper.[3]

Generals Grant and Meade spent Monday, April 18, reviewing John Sedgwick's Sixth Corps. That evening, Rowley arrived at Culpeper, 62 miles or six and a half hours by rail from Washington. The news spread quickly throughout what remained of his "Old First Brigade." Sergeant Zorn recalled that "this evening General Rowley come back it is said to take command of the brigade which he commanded last summer and was a favorite of and to the 142nd Regt[.] [W]hen he come[,] the Regt turned out and gave him three hearty cheers of welcome." Those were probably the last cheers Thomas Rowley ever received as a general officer.[4]

Accompanied by Edmund Dana and aide George Heberton, the general rode to army headquarters Tuesday morning, April 19, but found General Meade absent. Initially optimistic in Maine, Rowley knew this morning that all brigade commands had been filled. No one at Meade's headquarters mentioned a pending court-martial. G. K. Warren, Fifth Corps commander, heard that Meade was calling a general court-martial and asked Brig. Gen. Seth Williams, Meade's assistant adjutant general, for details. William replied at 6:10 p.m.: "The Court to try Brig Genl Rowley upon charges preferred against him some time since. He reported here this morning." Two and half hours later, Williams asked Warren "please telegraph the name of a suitable officer to serve as judge advocate in the Court about to be ordered for the trial of General Rowley." The general's son and aide, Capt. George Meade, in his April 19 diary entry correctly predicted, "Gen. Rowley to be court martial for drunkenness at Gettysburg."[5]

Even though many already knew on April 19 of the coming court-martial, Meade's Special Orders No. 110 issued the next day failed to mention the coming trial.

> April 20, 1864
>
> 1. Brig Gen Thomas A. Rowley, US Vol, having reported to the Major General commanding in compliance with Part 46 of Special Orders No. 135 of the 2nd Instant from the War Department will report for further instructions to the commander of the 5th corps.

That evening, April 20, Rowley heard unofficially of his pending court-martial and asked Edmund Dana to help prepare a defense.[6]

Under the 97th Article, any officer "being mustered and in pay of the United States" was subject to be tried by court-martial. The gravity of the offense and offender's rank determined the type of court-martial that had jurisdiction. A commissioned officer could not be tried by either a garrison or regimental court-martial. "A General Court-Martial takes exclusive cognizance of all offenses committed by commissioned officers." Rank alone, however, did not prescribe Rowley's fate. Certain crimes by noncommissioned officers and enlisted men also required a general court-martial. Qualifying offenses included drawing a sword upon another officer and disobedience of a superior officer's lawful command.[7]

Thursday, April 21, 1864, Special Orders No. 713, Army of the Potomac

> I saw Brigadier General Thomas A. Rowley frequently during that day (July 1, 1863). I saw him frequently during the next two days (July 2 and 3), but there was no appearance of intoxication about him from first to last. I have never seen General Rowley intoxicated and I have known him many years.—*Lieutenant Colonel Alfred B. McCalmont, 142nd PA*[8]

During the Civil War, only a general officer commanding an army, division, or separate brigade could appoint a general court-martial. When the division or brigade commander was the accuser, the next higher commander must appoint the court. Lysander Cutler, who filed the charges, did not command the Third Division at Gettysburg. Abner Doubleday who did no longer served in the Army of the Potomac. Neither Cutler's immediate superior, James S. Wadsworth, nor his corps commander, G. K. Warren, initiated legal action against Rowley. The army commander started the process.[9]

At 9:45 a.m. April 21, George Meade issued orders for Warren to "place Brig Gen Rowley in arrest." Under bright sunshine and blue skies, Thomas Rowley received Special Orders No. 713 which announced that his court-martial trial would begin in less than 24 hours. Meade approved Warren's recommendation that recently promoted Lt. Col. DeWitt C. McCoy, 83rd Pennsylvania, serve as judge advocate. Before the war, McCoy practiced law in Crawford County, Pennsylvania, and served as its district attorney in 1859. He volunteered in August 1861 and joined the Army of the Potomac as captain, Company F, 83rd Pennsylvania. Wounded at Gaines's Mill, McCoy saw more action at Antietam, Fredericksburg, and Chancellorsville. The 83rd was part of Col. Strong Vincent's successful fight to hold Little Round Top.[10]

The judge advocate served as "the medium of communication between the court and the accused." Since Rowley had counsel, McCoy would function as the army's prosecutor, "conducting the case with care and caution." Normally, he spoke with the accused and the witnesses (prosecution and defense) before the trial began "to obtain a clear view of the facts." Given Meade's demanding schedule, it is doubtful that McCoy did this in Culpeper. The judge advocate furnished the defendant a copy of the charges and specifications, a list of the court members and of the prosecution's witnesses. The detailed charges and specifications first appeared in the court proceedings for April 23. It could not be determined when the defendant first received them. Concurrent to these responsibilities for the judge advocate, Thomas Rowley prepared and submitted to McCoy on April 22 a list of witnesses he intended to call.[11]

Warren ordered his chief quartermaster to find suitable accommodations for the trial, one having "all things necessary for the court's use and comfort." Most likely, he chose one of the many Culpeper homes already taken over by the Federals. To minimize court delays, witnesses would remain "in immediate attendance," but "kept at such distance" to avoid overhearing any of the proceedings. The room arrangement actually employed was probably close to one of those shown in Figure 22.[12]

Dana and the accused went to Army Headquarters that afternoon to see Colonel McCoy, but the judge advocate was not available. Jacob Zorn learned at battalion drill that: "Col. Roy Stone Commands the brigade and not Genl Rowley as we expected." The evening turned out to be more pleasant than anyone had a right to expect. The 142nd's regimental band serenaded Rowley. Nearby was the 121st Pennsylvania. Both regiments had changed considerably since Gettysburg. Two weeks earlier, Alfred McCalmont departed Culpeper for Harrisburg and command of Camp Curtin. Maj. Horatio N. Warren now led the 142nd Pennsylvania. Col. Chapman Biddle, First Brigade commander on July 1, resigned his commission the previous December because of poor health. The 121st, mustering less than 100 effectives, gave their colonel a formal farewell on December 12, 1863. Biddle passed down the line "shaking the brawny hand of every man present." Maj. Alexander Biddle continued as regimental commander until he resigned in mid-January.[13]

It is not clear whether Special Orders No. 713 arrived before or after the general was placed under arrest. Something had gone wrong because Seth Williams sent Warren this message at 8:00 p.m. April 21:

> A copy of Special Order No. 110 of April 20 was sent to General Rowley in an envelope through your headquarters yesterday morning with a slip of paper requesting you to have it delivered to him at Headquarters of the brigade in which Colonel Dana's regiment is serving in your corps.

Already aware of his coming trial, Rowley did not receive Special Order No. 110, which instructed him to report to Warren April 20, until late the following day. Williams was concerned because army protocol evidently dictated that Rowley be instructed to report to Warren before being arrested.[14]

The most effective defense witnesses would be those individuals who were with Rowley throughout the day and evening of July 1, members of his personal staff. Dana's biggest problem was getting them to Culpeper in time

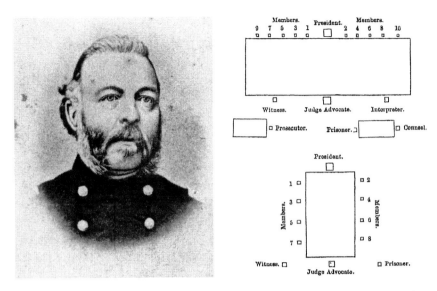

Lt. Col. DeWitt McCoy (left) from Crawford County, Pennsylvania, served as the judge advocate during Rowley's trial. Courtesy of USAMHI. Two possible seating arrangements (right) for officers participating in a Civil War court-martial. From *Field Manual of Court Martial* and courtesy of USAMHI.

for the trial. A shell burst killed Capt. C. H. Flagg, 142nd Pennsylvania, July 3. First Lt. William L. T. Wilson, honorably discharged on surgeon's certificate December 12, 1863, lived and worked in New York City. Capt. Oliver K. Moore resigned his commission January 24, 1864, and returned to Wilkes-Barre. Dana finally found McCoy midday April 21 and the judge advocate belatedly sent out summonses by telegraph that afternoon to Colonel McCalmont in Harrisburg and civilians Wilson and Moore. The trial would begin in less than 24 hours.[15]

The 75th Article of War states "no officer shall be tried by officers of an inferior rank, if it can be avoided," and "the number of members should not be less than thirteen, if possible, and, under no circumstances less than five." If the optimal 13 were not present, it should be stated in the order that "no other officers but those named can be assembled without injury to the service." Special Order #713 contained this statement. Meade's nine selections to the general court-martial were brigadier generals. John C. Robinson, Alexander Hays, John H. H. Ward, Joseph J. Bartlett, Frank Wheaton, Thomas H. Neill, William H. Morris, Alexander S. Webb, and Henry L. Eustis received Special Orders No. 713. The most senior, John Robinson, would serve as the presiding officer, charged with keeping order and ensuring that the court followed established procedures. Members would sit "according to the order in which they are named in the detail [S O #713]." In all deliberations, however, they were considered equal. The trial would begin at 10:00 a.m. the next day or "as soon thereafter, as practicable." S O #713 did not specify the charges.[16]

The nine court members would administer justice to the best of their understanding and ability. Neither the prosecution nor the defense could object to a member's question. All had to be present during the examination of witnesses. George Meade also established the court's hours and location. If necessary, this authority could be delegated to John Robinson. Special Order #713 stated, "the court can sit without respect to hours," which gave Meade and Robinson considerable latitude in setting a schedule. The daily proceedings would be transcribed and then read by the judge advocate at the next session. If the court and defendant agreed, the reading could be dropped.[17]

Before a trial began, President Lincoln had authorization "to dismiss, without referring the case to a court martial, any officer of the Army, volunteer force, or militia, if in his judgment such officer is unsuitable for [the service] or whose dismissal would promote the public service." It is not known when he first became aware of Rowley's trial. Lincoln would take no action until the court issued its verdict.[18]

Friday, April 22, 1864, Day 1

> The Judge Advocate [McCoy] was not prepared to proceed....
> The Court, therefore, at his [McCoy's] request adjourned.[19]

The court held its first session April 22. Generals Hays and Ward were absent, probably caught up in Grant's and Meade's review of their Second Corps brigades. Dana was officially "assigned to defend the general and take charge of his case." Assistance provided by a defense counsel was restricted to giving advice and submitting written questions to the judge advocate. Dana subsequently prepared a list of six questions that he directed to all defense witnesses. McCoy first read the question and entered it into the record. The judge advocate or any court member could object to it. If someone did, the court was cleared, a vote taken, and the majority ruled. If no one objected, the witness had to answer the question. Dana could neither address the court nor interfere in its proceedings. "His presence is only tolerated as a friend of the prisoner."[20]

McCoy informed the court that he was not prepared to proceed because "the witnesses for the prosecution not having been summoned for want of time." John Robinson, the president, adjourned the board until 11:00 a.m. the next day. Colonel Roy Stone issued no orders at the brigade's 5:00 p.m.

dress parade. Zorn and others in the 142nd erroneously concluded "that Genl Rowley will be in command." Rowley and Dana spent the evening at Col. Richard E. Coulter's headquarters, 11th Pennsylvania, Henry Baxter's brigade, John Robinson's division, Warren's corps.[21]

Saturday, April 23, 1864, Day 2

> The trial on the part of the prosecution to proceed with
> the court declining to entertain the motion [Rowley's
> to postpone] at this time. —*Lt. Col. D.L. McCoy*[22]

John Robinson announced that Brig. Gen. John C. Rice had replaced Joseph Bartlett. Alexander Hays and John Ward said their absence Friday resulted from not having received the order "until the evening of the twenty-second." The court president asked Rowley "if he had any objection to any member named in the order." The accused said no and McCoy duly swore in the board.[23]

Rowley requested and received permission to introduce his counsel, Edmund Dana. The application granted, he now asked that the trial be postponed "to enable him to procure the attendance of absent witnesses," and submitted a sworn statement supporting this position. In it, he stated that Moore, Wilson, and McCalmont were "indispensably necessary for my defense in this proceeding." Rowley specifically requested "the Court to grant me, at least before closing the case, such reasonable time as may be required to secure either the attendance or the evidence of the material and essential witnesses above mentioned." The previous day, without any discussion, Robinson granted McCoy a delay. Today, however, he cleared the room for deliberation regarding Rowley's request. After several minutes, the doors reopened and the judge advocate reported that the court would not entertain the motion either for postponement that day or in the future. Coppee's *Field Manual of Courts Martial* recommended, "the court grants him [defendant] a proper time" to prepare his case and "either adjourns, or proceeds to the trial of other cases." This court followed neither option. There was no assurance that McCoy's April 21 summonses had even reached Moore, Wilson, and McCalmont.[24]

All court-martial deliberations were done in secret. The president, judge advocate, or any member could request that the room be cleared. Rowley, Dana, and all witnesses went elsewhere. "No person can be present except the members and the judge advocate." Once cleared, the orderly "guards the door against intrusion." A simple majority decided procedural questions. Rowley requested a postponement to provide more time to secure defense witnesses. He did not have the right to demand a delay. After clearing the room, the court decided to refuse his application. This procedure would also be followed whenever a member objected.[25]

The judge advocate now formally arraigned Thomas A. Rowley on four charges. The first, "Drunkenness on duty on the battlefield," was based on one specification claiming that Rowley, "While commanding the Third Division, First Corps, was drunk ... at the battle of Gettysburg, July 1, 1863." Three specifications supported the second charge, "Conduct to the prejudice of good order and military discipline." The first specification said that Rowley, while in the presence of Major General Doubleday, his staff, and officers from the First Division (Wadsworth's), declared, "By God, I am in command of this Corps. By God, I am the ranking officer here, or words to that effect." The second described how the defendant rode up to Col. W. W. Robinson, 7th Wisconsin, and said, "The 7th Wisconsin is a good fighting regiment but the officers are not worth a damn, that the officers were not with their regiment and ordered Colonel Robinson to join his regiment." This conversation took place in Gettysburg the afternoon of July 1. The third claimed that on Cemetery Hill in the early evening of July 1, Rowley attempted to direct units not under his command (147th New York) and, "used threatening language and gestures to compel them to march in another direction."[26]

"Conduct unbecoming an officer and a gentleman" was the third charge, its single specification stating that Rowley: "was drunk and fell from his horse ... July 1, 1863." The only specification given for the final charge, "Disobedience of orders," was Rowley's failure to obey an order from Doubleday "to relieve the 1st Brigade (Meredith's), 1st Division (Wadsworth's), then in his front." Lysander Cutler's signature followed the charges and specifications, filed nine months after the incidents occurred. The charges did not cite Clayton Rogers's arrest on Cemetery Hill. Subsequent testimony by the prosecution's witnesses failed to mention the actions of either Rogers or Rufus Dawes. The defendant pleaded not guilty to all charges and specifications.[27]

The military accuser, General Cutler, could attend the court-martial but his role was limited to that of adviser or assistant to the judge advocate. When preferring charges, the time, location, and date of every act had to be specified. Details, if they existed, could be stated in general terms. For all six specifications against Rowley, the prosecution stated the time and location: Battle of Gettysburg, July 1, 1863. A description of each incident followed but it failed to specify the time and location. Rowley was entitled to a copy of the charges and a list of prosecution witnesses, a reasonable time before the trial began. In this case, "reasonable" was 24 hours.[28]

Thomas Rowley faced the crisis of his life. Disobedience of orders, the worst military crime, was a penal offense punishable by death. The Federal Army executed 267 men during the Civil War, the highest ranking a first sergeant. It is unlikely that the Culpeper court ever considered death or incarceration. Any commissioned officer found drunk on duty must be cashiered. If the court found Rowley guilty of "conduct unbecoming an officer and a gentleman," he would be subject to immediate dismissal. The need to court-martial a general officer became an embarrassment to both the army and the administration. In some instances, the War Department severely restricted communication of the proceedings and findings. By April 1864, however, all the Culpeper participants were well aware of the outcome of two earlier court-martials: Fitz-John Porter's and Joseph Revere's. Either or both could influence this trial.[29]

Maj. Gen. Fitz-John Porter, George McClellan's favorite subordinate, commanded the Fifth Corps from its inception during the Peninsular Campaign until December 1862. That month he was charged and tried for failure to obey orders and misbehavior before the enemy. On January 21, Lincoln approved and confirmed the court's proceedings, findings, and sentence. Porter was to be "cashiered and dismissed from the service of the United States." Stripped of rank "as Major General of Volunteers and as Colonel and Brevet Brigadier General in the Regular Service," he would also be "forever disqualified from holding any office of trust or profit under the Government of the United States." Fitz-John Porter became not only a convenient scapegoat for Second Manassas, but also provided the administration a means to contain and damage McClellan's continuing influence within the army's officer corps. This message from Washington surmounted the misery of Burnside's Mud March. George Meade replaced Porter.[30]

Hiram G. Berry, Camp Berry's namesake, led the Second Division, Dan Sickles's Third Corps at Chancellorsville. In the early morning of May 3, 1863, he fell mortally wounded "at the age of thirty-eight, one of the most promising generals that the Civil War had produced." At 7:30 a.m., divisional command went to Joseph B. Carr, the senior brigadier and commander of the First Brigade. Brig. Gen. Joseph W. Revere, grandson of Paul Revere, "thought that he [had] succeeded to the command of the division" and could act on his own discretion. About 8:00 a.m., Revere marched his Second or Excelsior Brigade and part of Carr's First Brigade off the field. Without either consulting or informing fellow officers, he took the equivalent of nine regiments out of the front line and marched them three miles to the rear. This unauthorized withdrawal significantly weakened the Federal right, exposing the batteries at Fairview. Revere later attempted to justify the move, "I moved them back down the road for the purpose of reorganizing and bringing them back to the field comparatively fresh."[31]

Daniel Sickles relieved the brigadier immediately and later filed charges. Joseph Hooker called a general court-martial that first met May 13. Its nine members included Winfield Scott Hancock as president, John Newton, James

Wadsworth, John Gibbon, and Francis Barlow. The court found Revere guilty only "of conduct to the prejudice of good order and military discipline," and sentenced him "to be dismissed from the military service." Hooker approved May 15 and forwarded the case record to Washington. Initially, Lincoln accepted the verdict and ordered its execution August 10, 1863. He later changed his mind, revoked the sentence, and offered Revere the opportunity to resign instead. Against this background, the army opened its case against Thomas Rowley.[32]

The prosecution's witnesses would be sworn and examined first by the judge advocate, then by the accused, and finally by court members. McCoy called Lysander Cutler, who had seen Rowley twice before the court-martial. Based on the defendant's appearance and conversation in Gettysburg the afternoon of July 1, Cutler considered Rowley drunk. A second encounter taking place that evening on Cemetery Hill confirmed this opinion. Here, Rowley had supposedly halted the 147th New York and later interfered with placement of the 7th Wisconsin. When challenged by Cutler, the accused claimed to be commanding the First Corps and would place the troops where he pleased.[33]

Even though the witness had discussed three of the six specifications, Dana declined to cross-examine. Members of the court submitted three questions. Addressing the first, Cutler considered Rowley, who had halted the 147th New York on Cemetery Hill, unfit for duty. In response to another question, he admitted that the defendant did not use either threatening language or gestures in his presence on Cemetery Hill. "He [Rowley] used none to me."[34]

Col. William Robinson, 7th Wisconsin, took the stand. He had never seen Rowley before July 1 and did not know what unit the accused commanded at Gettysburg. Like Cutler, Robinson considered Rowley intoxicated and described their encounter that evening on Cemetery Hill. This incident was the basis for the second charge's second specification. Dana asked Robinson to describe the noon confrontation between Rowley and officers from the 7th Wisconsin near the seminary. The colonel replied: "Ten were absent ... I think most of them were back to the regiment by Eight o'clock in the morning. Two did not probably return until Eleven o'clock." Rowley greeted Stone's Brigade no earlier than 11:00 a.m. on July 1.[35]

Lt. Thomas W. Miller, 55th Ohio Infantry and Cutler's aide-de-camp, took the stand and described Rowley's July 1 encounter with George Harney, 147th New York. "He rode in front of the regiment flourishing his sword as though he would force them to go in the direction he wanted." Miller considered Rowley drunk during the afternoon retreat and described the confrontation with Cutler in town. The witness felt that Rowley was still drunk on Cemetery Hill because "he appeared very excited, his pretensions to command all the troops within his reach, his general appearance, language and actions."[36]

Two questions submitted by Dana were approved and read to the witness. Lieutenant Miller responded that Rowley was accompanied by two lieutenants when ordering the 147th New York to a new position and reaffirmed that the general "had his sword drawn and flourished it at this time." John Robinson excused Miller and adjourned the court until Monday.[37]

Alexander Hays had been relieved from one court-martial board only to be reassigned to Rowley's. His copy of the April 21 order did not identify the defendant, leaving Hays to initially speculate that it must be "an important prisoner or one of rank." A same-day trip to Meade's headquarters disclosed the "victim's identity but not the charges." On April 23 he wrote his wife, Annie: "went to Culpeper this morning, to court-martial, and tried our friend all day." While trying to locate the court that first morning, Hays found "Sam Grant," his West Point classmate and former comrade in arms, smoking a cigar and asked him where the trial was being held. Grant did not know "as he was not a member of our court."[38]

Sunday, April 24, 1864, Day 3

> Am acting as counsel for a friend — a Brigadier General, who is
> on trial for matters which occurred at the Battle of Gettysburg....
> My tent is crammed full of officers calling on General Rowley
> who is staying with me.... — *Col. Edmund Dana*[39]

Edmund Dana found time April 24 to write a Wilkes-Barre friend describing his current duties and hopes for the future:

> I have been engaged during the past week upon a Court Martial for the trial of officers brought before us, and in addition to this and my duties with the regiment, am acting as counsel for a friend — a Brigadier General, who is on trial for matters which occurred at the Battle of Gettysburg... . My tent is crammed full of officers calling on General Rowley who is staying with me... . How much there is grandly beautiful and imposing in the parades and daily exercises and reviews of a large army — and how much that is sad and at times heart rendering. I suppose Wilkes-Barre begins to wear its spring dress — I should be happy to enjoy again its quiet — unbroken by fife or drum or the heavy tramp of marching columns.[40]

During that first week of the trial, Rowley and Dana discussed the nine members of the court. They were Rowley's jury and like a jury their backgrounds could determine the final verdict. This narrative will now consider the qualifications of each member.

In future correspondence with Dana, Rowley was most critical of the three who had served with him in Darius Couch's Fourth Corps Division: Henry Eustis, Thomas Neill, and Frank Wheaton. There is no record of personal clashes or disagreements between them. In early September 1862, however, the four were full colonels commanding regiments and competing for the same prize, a general's star. Considering what happened at Fredericksburg during Rowley's brief tenure as brigade commander, it is reasonable to conclude that whatever the previous feelings were between them, greater tension existed after December 13, 1862.[41]

Born in Providence, Rhode Island, and commissioned directly into the cavalry as a first lieutenant in 1855, Frank Wheaton served on the western frontier until 1861. Promoted to lieutenant colonel, 2nd Rhode Island, he reported the battlefield death of Maj. Sullivan Ballou at First Bull Run. His father-in-law, Samuel Cooper, became the Confederacy's ranking general. Wheaton received regimental command July 31, 1861. Thomas Hewson Neill spent two years at the University of Pennsylvania then transferred to West Point, graduating in 1847. Assigned to the 5th Infantry, he missed the Mexican War but spent many years on the frontier. After the Civil War began, Captain Neill joined George Cadwalader's staff. Commissioned colonel in February 1862, he took over the 23rd Pennsylvania.[42]

McClellan assigned Wheaton's, Rowley's, and Neill's regiments to Couch's Division, Keyes's Fourth Corps. Rowley received three citations during the Peninsular Campaign, Neill one, and Wheaton none. To some extent, it was a matter of being in the right place at the right time. Given the opportunities, Rowley went on to earn battlefield recognition. All three appeared on the November 29, 1862, list of newly commissioned brigadiers. Army records indicate that Wheaton and Neill received their promotions either just before or during the Battle of Fredericksburg. Rowley did not.[43]

Henry Lawrence Eustis graduated from Harvard in 1838 and from West Point in 1842, the same class as John Newton and Abner Doubleday. He resigned from the army in 1849 and accepted a teaching position at Harvard. In spite of poor health, Eustis secured a leave of absence and became colonel of the 10th Massachusetts on August 21, 1862. Cited by division commander John Newton for gallant service at Chancellorsville, he took command of the Second Brigade before Gettysburg. Eustis received a promotion to brigadier September 10, 1863.[44]

After Rowley's transfer to the First Corps, Wheaton and Neill led their brigades at Chancellorsville and Gettysburg. Detached from the Army of the Potomac in late December, Wheaton's command served several months at Harpers Ferry in the First Division, Department of West Virginia. Returning March 29, 1864, the unit became the First Brigade in Brig. Gen. George Getty's division, Sedgwick's Sixth Corps. Thomas Neill commanded Getty's Third Brigade and Henry Eustis his Fourth. At the time of the court-martial, it is reasonable to assume that they knew each other quite well. Three court members currently commanded brigades in the same division and two had earlier commanded regiments in the same division as Rowley.[45]

West Point dismissed Cadet John Cleveland Robinson in 1836. Three years later, he received a second lieutenant's commission in the 5th Infantry. On September 1, 1861, Colonel Robinson commanded the 1st Michigan Infantry. Promoted to brigadier, he temporarily took over David Birney's brigade in Philip Kearny's division, Heintzelman's corps, June 9, 1862. Birney later replaced Kearny following his death at Chantilly on September 1. John Robinson led the First Brigade, First Division, Third Corps until December 29 when Burnside gave him command of John Gibbon's Second Division, Reynolds's First Corps. During the March 1864 reorganization, the First Corps was consolidated into two divisions that became the Second and Fourth in Warren's Fifth Corps. John Robinson took command of the Second and James Wadsworth the Fourth.[46]

During the Peninsular Campaign, Capt. William H. Morris served as an assistant adjutant general to Brig. Gen. John J. Peck. At Williamsburg and Seven Pines on the peninsula, he carried orders to Colonel Rowley and later brought back Rowley's reports for both battles. Promoted to colonel that summer, he commanded heavy artillery, first outside Baltimore then in John Kenly's Maryland Brigade at Harpers Ferry. An 1851 graduate from West Point, Morris received a brigadier's commission the same day as Rowley and took command of the Second Brigade, Maj. Gen. Robert C. Schenck's division, Eighth Army Corps. Following Gettysburg, his fellow brigade commander, John Kenly, replaced Abner Doubleday. During the Bristoe and Mine Run campaigns, Morris led the First Brigade, Brig. Gen. Joseph Carr's Third Division, Maj. Gen. William French's Third Corps. At this time, the division's brigade commanders included J. Hobart Ward and Regis DeTrobriand. In April 1864, Morris took command of a brigade in Brig. Gen. James Ricketts's Sixth Corps Division.[47]

An unknown to Rowley, James Clay Rice graduated from Yale University in 1854 and quickly gained admission to the New York bar. Initially commissioned a lieutenant in the 39th New York Infantry, he received a promotion to lieutenant colonel, 44th New York, after First Bull Run. During McClellan's Peninsular Campaign, this regiment was part of Brig. Gen. Daniel Butterfield's Fifth Corps Brigade and saw action at Gaines's Mill and Malvern Hill. Rice became a full colonel in July 1862 and assumed brigade command following the death of Col. Strong Vincent on Little Round Top. Promoted to brigadier August 17, 1863, he later commanded the Second Brigade in Lysander Cutler's First Corps Division. That fall, Rice temporarily replaced Cutler, who went on medical leave. He now led the Second Brigade and Cutler the First in Wadsworth's Fifth Corps Division.[48]

Brig. Gen. James Rice, the only "civilian" member of Rowley's court. Courtesy of USAMHI.

John Ward, another stranger to both Rowley and Dana, enlisted in 1842 as a private, served in the Mexican War, and remained in the commissary general. Commissioned colonel in the 38th New York Infantry, he led the unit at First Bull Run. Assigned to Brig. Gen. David Birney's Second Brigade, Philip Kearny's First Division, Samuel Heintzelman's Third Corps, the 38th fought on the peninsula at Second Bull Run and Chantilly. Phil Kearny praised Ward's bravery at Williamsburg and Fair Oaks. Promoted to brigadier general October 4, 1862, he temporarily led the brigade in Birney's absence. In November, Burnside formally assigned the First Division to Birney and its Second Brigade to Ward. At this time, John Robinson commanded Birney's First Brigade but later moved to the First Corps. Ward retained brigade command throughout 1863. In March 1864, Major General Birney's division was redesignated the Third Division, Second Corps. John Ward led that division's First Brigade and Alexander Hays its Second.[49]

After graduating from Allegheny College, Meadville, Pennsylvania, in 1840, Alexander Hays immediately entered the Military Academy. Commissioned a second lieutenant four years later, he served throughout the Mexican War, receiving a commendation from Gen. Winfield Scott and a promotion to first lieutenant. Failing to recover from a battle wound, Hays resigned his commission in 1848 and later worked as a civil engineer on the railroads in western Pennsylvania. During this period, he became friends with Thomas Rowley, most likely through the Masonic Order.[50]

Like Rowley, he initially led a three-month regiment then returned to Pittsburgh. Here, Hays recruited a three-year regiment, the 63rd Pennsylvania, and was commissioned its colonel. During the Seven Days, the 63rd served in John Robinson's brigade, Philip Kearny's Third Corps Division. He received a brevet of major (regular army) "for gallant and meritorious service in the battles of Fair Oaks and Glendale," and brevetted lieutenant colonel for Malvern Hill. During Second Bull Run, Kearny ordered Hays to charge James Archer's Tennessee brigade, holding the railroad cut in A. P. Hill's line. While leading his men from up front, a Confederate bullet shattered Hays's ankle. Returning to active duty after a one-month leave of absence, the War Department assigned Hays to the forces defending Washington.[51]

He was commissioned brigadier general of volunteers and confirmed a lieutenant colonel in the regular army. While still recovering near the capital, Hays took command of the Third Brigade, Silas Casey's division, Samuel Heintzelman's Twenty-second Corps on January 8, 1863. One of his five regiments was the 151st Pennsylvania. On February 15, the 151st departed Washington for John Reynolds's First Corps. George McFarland recorded in his diary, "all regretted parting with our esteemed commander Brig Genl Alexander Hays." In late June, John Abercrombie's division left Washington to reinforce the Army of the Potomac. The largest brigade, George Stannard's nine-month Vermonters, went to Abner Doubleday's division. On June 25, Hays's command became the Third Brigade, Third Division, Hancock's Second Corps. Three days later, Alexander Hays commanded the division. The new division performed well on Cemetery Ridge and remained under Hays until the army's March 1864 reorganization.[52]

Letters written during April reflected Alexander Hays's disappointment and bitterness. Not only did he fail to receive a promotion to major general but his command no longer existed. On March 26, 1864, military necessity disbanded the Third Division that Hays had led since Gettysburg. George Meade showed no interest in finding the brigadier a new assignment. Winfield Scott Hancock's suggestion to Grant finally brought action on March 25. Grant gave Hays the Second Brigade in David Birney's Second Corps Division. Nine regiments, including the 63rd Pennsylvania and Berdan's Sharpshooters, comprised the new brigade that mustered about 5,000 effectives.[53]

Alexander Hays remained a good friend and supporter of Rowley. Whatever benefits he brought to the trial, however, may have been offset by the presence of Alexander Webb.

Born in New York City, Alexander Stewart Webb attended private schools, graduated from West Point in 1855, and later taught mathematics at the Military Academy. Given a New York City upbringing and the status of his parents, Webb held a social position at the opposite end of the spectrum from Alexander Hays and Rowley. Beginning the war as a lieutenant, 2nd Artillery, he won distinction on the peninsula and rose to major, 1st Rhode Island Light. In August 1862, Webb joined Fitz-John Porter's Fifth Corps staff. Shortly before the Battle of Gettysburg, he received a brigadier's commission

A court member and close friend of Rowley, Brig. Gen. Alexander Hays, carried his own baggage to Culpeper. Courtesy of Mass. MOLLUS and USAMHI.

and his first infantry assignment as commander of the Second Brigade, John Gibbon's division, Hancock's Second Corps.[54]

On July 3, Webb's Second Brigade occupied the portion of Cemetery Ridge later called "the Angle." On its right was Alexander Hays's Third Division. Both generals played a major role in stopping the Pickett-Pettigrew-Trimble Charge. Both Federal commands paid a high price for this victory with Webb being wounded. Instead of nobly sharing the glory and celebrating as comrades in arms, their success led instead to a serious personal rift.

Two of Hays's brigades, totaling eight regiments, held the Second Corps's right. Samuel S. Carroll's Third Brigade, minus the 8th Ohio, remained with Howard's Eleventh Corps on Cemetery Hill. Except for John Robinson's division coming up on the right, Third Division received no reinforcements that afternoon. During the fighting, Webb came over and reported to Hays, "The enemy had broken through his lines." Alexander Hays curtly replied, "They did not get to his." The conversation abruptly ended and Webb departed. The second incident occurred after stopping the Confederate attack.[55]

George Fleming later described the scene. "The men of the Third Division [Hays's] individually ran out when the assault was seen to have failed and were picking up the enemy's colors on the ground... . The enemy were careful to drop their colors and took no chance of being shot with them in their hands, and our men brought in these colors." Col. Clinton D. McDougall, 111th New York, Hays's Third Brigade, recalled, "that twenty-three captured flags lay in front of a tent." Hays and his staff viewed them as "spoils of victory justly won." The colors had been found in front of the Third Division, proving conclusively that the Confederate regiments to which they belonged had fought there. Alexander Webb did not agree.[56]

Webb felt that some of the colors rightfully belonged to his brigade and sent an aid to get them. After hearing the request, Hays retorted, "If Webb captured them, how in the hell did I get them?" Receiving no answer, the general directed Capt. George Fleming "to deliver to Webb's aide six flags from those taken." The aide rode off with the flags. To Fleming, "Webb had no shadow of a claim to these flags and his credit for them came from General Hays's generosity."[57]

Time did not immediately heal this wound. In an August 8, 1863, letter to his wife, Alexander Webb described his new adversary. "Alex Hays is not capable of commanding a Brigade even. He is a real specimen of a weak ignorant political appointment. He is nothing but a personally brave man ... no education & vulgar beyond measure." Throughout Meade's fall campaign, Webb commanded the Second Division, while a wounded John Gibbon recuperated. On the evening of March 23, 1864, Webb and Hays had dinner with G. K. Warren. Hays remembered, "We had a pleasant time and talked over the past as well as prognosticated for the future." Three days later, the reorganization occurred and Webb now led the First Brigade in Brig. Gen. Francis C. Barlow's Second Corps Division.[58]

Dana and Rowley must have been discouraged after examining the court. Five of the nine, Hays, Webb, Morris, Eustis, and Neill, were West Point graduates. Three, Robinson, Wheaton, and Ward, career army officers. Only one, James Rice, had volunteered like Rowley. A Yale graduate and practicing attorney, Rice came from the other side of the social and business tracks. The court's nine members did not accurately reflect the Army of the Potomac. That month, its three corps of infantry mustered 32 brigadiers, nine of whom were volunteer officers. At least two volunteer brigadiers should have been members of the court. Joseph Revere's court mustered three volunteer officers. For Rowley, the number never exceeded one. James Rice merely replaced Joseph Bartlett. Many regular field officers in the Army of the Potomac held an indefensible prejudice against the volunteers. They tried to justify their position by citing the perceived behavior of Daniel Sickles and Daniel Butterfield. It will never be known how many court members considered Rowley guilty before the proceedings even began.[59]

Monday, April 25, 1864, Day 4

> *Question by Judge Advocate*: Do you know whether General Rowley was at the battle of Gettysburg July 1, 1863 or not?
>
> *Answer Lieutenant Colonel George Harney, 147th NY*: I am not positive.[60]

The trial resumed at 11:00 a.m. with all members, the judge advocate, the accused, and his counsel present. McCoy called Lt. Col. George Harney, 147th New York Volunteers. Upon questioning, Harney was not sure if he had ever seen Rowley before the trial. His inability to remember a drunken brigadier general waving a sword and giving improper orders undercut the earlier testimony of both Cutler and Miller relative to the second charge's third specification. Dana obviously declined cross-examination and McCoy quickly moved on to his next witness, Capt. Craig W. Wadsworth, currently "an additional aide de Camp on the Staff of Genl. Fremont."[61]

This officer, son of James Wadsworth and former aide-de-camp to John Reynolds, saw the accused "five or six times during the day [July 1]." Captain Wadsworth first thought Rowley drunk just before the retreat from the seminary. He based this observation on the defendant's excited behavior that afternoon. Rowley's later fall from his horse only confirmed the captain's opinion that he was drunk and "unfit to command the Division." Dana later established that the witness was unaware of either Rowley's boils "which rendered it painful and difficult for him ride," or "that shortly after the battle he [Rowley] was relieved and sent home on account of total disability occasioned by boils upon his person." Further questioning also brought out that Craig Wadsworth did not know that Rowley had positioned the Provost Guard (Glenn's company) on the Cashtown Road with orders "to hold that position until Captain [James A.] Hall's [2nd Maine] Battery should be gotten off the field." Before stepping down, he confirmed that the defendant "continued in command of the 3rd Division ... throughout and during the day of July 1st."[62]

Lt. Col. Mark Finnicum, 7th Wisconsin, was duly sworn. He first met the accused the evening of July 1 and concluded from "actions and conversation that he was drunk." The witness observed that Rowley "appeared to be very much excited and sat unsteadily on his horse" while speaking to Colonel Robinson on Cemetery Hill. Finnicum gave his version of the conversation between Rowley and William Robinson. Generally, it was in agreement with Robinson's prior testimony. In reply to Dana's question, Finnicum said, "The remarks of the General [Rowley] were addressed to Colonel Robinson as I understood."[63]

Only three witnesses testified April 25. Assuming a maximum of one hour per individual, the court adjourned no later than mid-afternoon. The judge advocate went to Meade's headquarters and reviewed the proceedings with either the commanding general, members of his staff, or both. Evidently dissatisfied with McCoy's report, Meade sent the following telegram to Washington:

> April 25 PM
> To: Hon E. M. Stanton Sec of War
>
> The testimony of General Doubleday is needed before the Court Martial now sitting in Culpeper for the trial of General Rowley. In view of the delay which would be caused by sending a commission to Washington to take General Doubleday's deposition, I suggest General Doubleday be ordered to attend the court Martial tomorrow, he can come down by regular passenger train, give his testimony before the court and return to Washington on Wednesday
>
> Major General Commanding

Stanton agreed and issued orders for Doubleday to testify the next day in Culpeper.[64]

The April 25 trial record, approved by McCoy and John Robinson, cannot be reconciled with the previous discussion of what happened after the court's adjournment. The closing statement for this session says, "The Court then adjourned to meet again at four o'clock on the afternoon of the 26th instant to await the arrival of gen. Doubleday." Given the state of military communications in 1864, it is impossible to understand how the court was even aware of Doubleday's summons when it closed that afternoon. At the time of adjournment, the involved parties did not know who the prosecution's last witness would be.[65]

Abner Doubleday, three colonels, one lieutenant colonel, and a captain then comprised a "Military Commission for the trial of such cases as may be brought before it." The sessions took place at "Pennsylvania Avenue, north side, near 18th Street." That week, three general court-martial trials and a commission "for examination of cases of officers published for dismissal" were underway in the capital. The most newsworthy was the trial of Brig. Gen. W. A. Hammond, Surgeon General U. S. Army.[66]

Tuesday, April 26, 1864, Day 5

> *Question by the Court*: Did you form your opinion on anything you saw in the actions of Genl Rowley or on anything he said in your presence that he was unfit for the performance of duty through the influence of liquor, or is your opinion based on hearsay since?
>
> *Answer Major General Abner Doubleday*: It is based on representations of others since.[67]

The court reconvened Tuesday at 4:00 p.m., the second delay in proceedings to accommodate prosecution witnesses. Neither delay was subject to court deliberation. Having traveled that morning by train from Washington, Maj. Gen. Abner Doubleday took the stand. McCoy's initial list of witnesses did not include the major general. Witnesses not identified initially by either the prosecution or the defense, however, "may be called at any stage of the proceedings." A summoned witness on active military duty must testify. Abner Doubleday had no choice but to appear at Rowley's trial. The reason for his hurried summons soon became evident.[68]

Cutler's fourth charge accused Rowley of disobeying Doubleday's order "to relieve the 1st Brigade [Meredith's], 1st Division [Wadsworth's], then in his front. This at the battle of Gettysburg July 1, 1863." Lysander Cutler offered no explanation as to how he became aware of this problem. The charges did not specify the time and location of the alleged disobedience. Abner Doubleday testified only that the incident occurred the evening of July 1 on Cemetery Hill. The Maj. Gen. could not remember which brigade was supposed to be relieved and added at that time, he was receiving

> [c]ontradictory orders from Generals Howard and Hancock one directing the troops to go to the right and the other directing them to go to the left. One set of these orders I did not carry out of course and did not enforce. This [the order to Rowley] is one of the orders I felt in doubt about and

hesitated whether I could obey. I did not execute it immediately and did not require him [Rowley] to do so. I do not consider that I had any cause of complaint that any order was not carried out under the circumstances except that he [General Rowley] was somewhat inattentive. I think that his troops moved very quickly to the points designated.[69]

McCoy moved to the second charge, first specification. The major general did remember hearing the accused claim "to command the 1st Corps apparently under the impression that I succeeded General Reynolds by rank who had commanded the right [left] wing of the army." Except for Cutler, the other officers present were of "inferior rank and I do not remember [their names]." In reply to the judge advocate's questions, Doubleday felt that "he [Rowley] was somewhat under the influence of liquor," on Cemetery Hill but could not "state the precise language," the defendant used in claiming corps command. Court members later raised additional questions as to Rowley's exact words. The witness's final answer on the subject was, "I have stated I do not now remember the exact words further than that he said he was in command of the 1st Corps." No one asked and Doubleday never volunteered an explanation as to why he had not corrected Rowley as to whom commanded the corps.[70]

The judge advocate now asked his last question, "When you saw General Rowley at the Hill [Cemetery], did you think him capable of performing his duties properly on the battle field?" The prosecution's key witness answered, "He spoke distinctly and sat uprightly on his horse but he spoke slowly with a little effort. I did at that time think he was capable of doing his duty properly on the battle field." There is no question that this statement severely undermined the prosecution's efforts to show that Rowley was drunk and unable to perform his duty.[71]

Edmund Dana submitted a question concerning the Third Division's deployment on Cemetery Hill. The witness replied, "It was promptly formed. I don't know whether it was due to General Rowley or to the brigade commanders [Dana and Chapman Biddle]." The court raised a question similar to McCoy's last, "Was General Rowley in your opinion so much under the influence of liquor as to be unable to do his duty properly on the battle field at any time during the battle?" Doubleday now said, "In my opinion, he was." The major general based his conclusion on the facts that "his [Rowley's] face was very red and he enunciated his words slowly." This comment contradicted his earlier statement that "he [Rowley] was capable of doing his duty properly on the battle field."[72]

A member of the court questioned Doubleday's second reply concerning Rowley's ability to command:

> Do you form your opinion on anything you saw in the actions of General Rowley or on any thing he said in your presence that he was unfit for the

performance of duty through the influence of liquor, or is your opinion
based on hearsay since?

A different member immediately objected, "Because the answer to it has been
previously given in General Doubleday's testimony." John Robinson cleared
the court for deliberation. After reconvening, McCoy announced the court's
decision that "the question be answered, the objection having been withdrawn." Abner Doubleday took the chair and said, "It [opinion regarding the
influence of liquor on Rowley's fitness for duty] is based on representations
of others since." One can easily visualize the silence that must have pervaded
the room.[73]

The defense counsel submitted a last question. "Did General Rowley and
his Division behave well and to your satisfaction during the battle of the 1st
July, 1863?" Doubleday's closing comment followed, "The Division behaved
admirably and I was perfectly satisfied with General Rowley's conduct except
this conversation with General Cutler." Testimony from the defendant's former commanding officer not only failed to support the charge of disobedience of orders but also added very little if anything to the prosecution's case
regarding the other three charges.[74]

Two principal actors in this drama were absent from Culpeper. First Lt.
Clayton E. Rogers, who arrested Rowley, resigned his commission July 14,
1863, and returned to Viroqua, Wisconsin. Lt. Col. Rufus R. Dawes, who
executed Rogers's July 1 arrest, was serving as president of a general court-
martial for Wadsworth's Fourth Division. Like Doubleday, Dawes would have
no choice but to testify. There is no evidence, however, that McCoy tried to
secure him as a witness. The prosecution closed its case and the court
adjourned to meet the next day at 11:00 a.m.[75]

During the prosecution phase, all testimony substantiating the charges
and specifications had to be presented. Once closed, no further evidence could
be introduced. At this point, the defendant might deem it advisable to devote
one or two days to preparation. Normally, a court granted this request. For
Thomas Rowley the courtesy was denied.[76]

Oliver K. Moore wrote to Dana on April 21 that he could not appear as
a defense witness because his brother was very sick but offered to prepare a
deposition. Moore had served as an acting aide-de-camp being with the general during most of the Gettysburg campaign. The letter stated, "At no time
did I see General Thomas A. Rowley under the influence of intoxicating
liquor, to my knowledge." He closed with a request, "To General Rowley in
particular say, if it is necessary to save him I will come down at all hazards."
Colonel McCoy sent a second telegram to Moore on April 26 requesting his
presence at the court-martial.[77]

Wednesday, April 27, 1864, Day 6

> *Question by the defense*: Describe his manner of riding in consequence of these boils and whether he could without great suffering sit firmly in his saddle.
>
> *Major W. T. Humphrey, Surgeon*: He would ride at times sideways and not straddle. He would sit in most every position except the natural one to ride easy.[78]

All defense witnesses would first be examined by the accused, then the judge advocate, and lastly by the court members. Edmund Dana called the first defense witness, Maj. Horatio N. Warren, commanding 142nd Pennsylvania Volunteers. Commissioned a captain in August 1862, the rank held at Gettysburg, he received a promotion to major February 2, 1864. Warren first met Rowley in April 1863.[79]

Horatio Warren proceeded to describe "all that he [Rowley] said and did on those four occasions" he saw the general at Gettysburg July 1. The major praised the defendant's effectiveness in rallying men at the seminary and considered him "perfectly sober ... and fit to command." Warren did not see Rowley after the retreat to Cemetery Hill.[80]

Capt. Frank M. Powell, commander of Company A, 142nd Pennsylvania, took the stand. Seriously wounded at Gettysburg, the witness received a promotion to his current rank February 2, 1864. Horatio Warren enjoyed telling the story that Powell's "faithful Bible, carried in a side-pocket nearly over his heart, saved his life [July 1]."[81]

From 2:00 to 6:00 p.m. July 1, Powell saw Rowley five times at four different locations. The captain felt that "he [Rowley] always appeared cool and determined. If I can judge what a sober man is, I would suppose him sober. I saw nothing to the contrary." McCoy and members of the court challenged without success the witness's memory.[82]

The next defense witness was Maj. James Glenn, 149th Pennsylvania. At Gettysburg, he commanded Company D then serving as Third Division's Provost Guard. His promotion to major occurred April 5, 1864. A resident of Allegheny County, Pennsylvania, Glenn had known Rowley for about 16 years. Recalling the two occasions on July 1 that Glenn received orders from the accused, "He [Rowley] appeared to be perfectly sober as near as I could judge and appeared to be perfectly cool and seemed to know what he was doing."[83]

McCoy asked the witness, "Did the question whether General Rowley was drunk or sober at the time enter your mind?" Glenn replied, "No Sir." A member of the court posed the question, "What induced you to say that General Rowley was perfectly sober in answer to the first question as to his

Lt. Col. George Harney (left), 147th New York, did not remember Rowley interfering with the placement of his regiment. Courtesy of Mass. MOLLUS and USAMHI. Commanding the division's provost fuard, Capt. James Glenn (right) saw nothing wrong with Rowley's behavior the afternoon of July 1. Courtesy of Richard Matthews, Ron Palm, and USAMHI.

condition?" The witness responded, "I thought because I never thought anything else of General Rowley but that he would be sober in a place of that kind."[84]

Dana called Surgeon William T. Humphrey. Mustered in June 21, 1861, the witness initially served as an assistant surgeon in the 13th Pennsylvania Reserves, 42nd Pennsylvania Volunteers. He received a promotion to surgeon with the 149th Pennsylvania on September 8, 1862, and currently held the rank of major. At Gettysburg, Humphrey served on Rowley's staff because Surgeon Seely was on sick leave. He described the defendant's health status the morning of July 1: "boils on the upper third of the thigh on the inside of the thigh. He had two or three smaller ones lower down — two I am positive of. One — the largest about the size of a hen's egg — very large."[85]

A court member asked, "Was there anything in the appearance or conversation of General Rowley during the first of July that led you to think that he was drunk and unfit to discharge his duties?" The major answered, "I discovered nothing." The judge advocate had no questions.[86]

Capt. George W. Jones, currently commanding the 150th Pennsylvania, took the stand. At Gettysburg, Jones led Company B. The witness saw Rowley three times July 1 beginning at noon and ending that evening on Cemetery Hill. As to the general's condition Jones stated, "I think he was sober ... to the best of my knowledge, I think he was sober." McCoy asked, "Did the question as to whether General Rowley was drunk or sober occur to your mind at that time?" Captain Jones replied, "No Sir."[87]

The day's last defense witness was Lt. W. N. Dalgliesh, acting aide-de-camp to Col. Roy Stone. During the Gettysburg campaign, he served Stone in the same capacity. On April 5, 1864, Dalgliesh received a promotion to first lieutenant, Company D, 149th Pennsylvania.[88]

Having known Thomas A. Rowley "by sight and reputation" since boyhood, Dalgliesh first saw the accused July 1 between "one and two o'clock" and later on Cemetery Hill "between five and six o'clock." Dana asked his standard question, "What in your opinion was the condition of General Rowley as to sobriety on those occasions?" "I presume that he was sober." Dana followed up with, "Did you see anything in General Rowley's manner indicating that he was drunk or disqualified to attend to his duties as commander of the Division?" Dalgliesh answered, "No Sir, I did not — not that I noticed at all about him." The judge advocate posed the same question to this witness that he had to Jones, "Did the question as to whether General Rowley was drunk or sober occur to your mind at that time?" Dalgliesh gave the same reply, "It did not. I never thought of such a thing at the time."[89]

John Robinson adjourned the court and delayed scheduling the next session until 10:00 a.m., Friday, April 29. Supposedly, he took this action to provide time for the arrival of three defense witnesses: A. B. McCalmont, Oliver K. Moore, and W. L. T. Wilson. That evening, however, James Rice told Dana, "It made no difference what was shown for the defense." The defense counsel never recorded his reaction to Rice's observation.[90]

Thursday, April 28, 1864, Day 7

> To General Rowley in particular say, if it is necessary to save
> him I will come down at all hazards. — *Oliver K. Moore*[91]

In spite of Robinson's earlier announcement, the court met in closed session. No record exists of the proceedings and "witnesses [Dana and Rowley] not present."[92]

Friday, April 29, 1864, Day 8

> It made no difference what was shown for the
> defense. — *Brigadier General James C. Rice*[93]

The defense counsel called 1st Lt. Charles B. Stout, Company C, 143rd Pennsylvania. The lieutenant saw Rowley on Cemetery Hill near sunset, had no conversation with him, and "thought him sober." Charles H. Reilay, Company C, 143rd Pennsylvania, took the stand. Promoted to first lieutenant on January 25, 1864, Reilay saw the defendant twice July 1, the first time at the foot of Cemetery Hill and the second after sunset in an apple orchard, "about midway between Cemetery Hill and Round Top." Dana asked his standard question and Reilay replied, "I should think he was sober both the times I saw him."[94]

Arriving from New York City the night before, Mr. William L. Wilson was duly sworn. At Gettysburg, First Lieutenant Wilson, adjutant, 142nd Pennsylvania, served on Rowley's staff as acting assistant adjutant general. Now he was a Wall Street bank cashier for Mylert and Company. Except when carrying orders, the witness was with Rowley the entire day of July 1. Wilson discussed his understanding of what caused the accused to fall from his horse and described the congestion at the corner of High and Baltimore Streets. In response to Dana's questions, he replied that Rowley did not draw a sword July 1 and frequently complained about his boils. The witness not only considered the defendant sober but added that he would have noticed "had he been drunk and unfit to command."[95]

Even though Oliver Moore and Alfred McCalmont had neither testified nor submitted statements, Dana had no choice but to close the defense. Rowley read a final statement to the court. The defendant pleaded innocent to all charges and dismissed falling off his horse with the comment, "Its partial absence [skill in horsemanship] either through physical conformation, corpulency or sickness is not militarily a capital offense nor the crime at which the 83rd Article of War is leveled." Acting under the misunderstanding that Doubleday had succeeded Reynolds as wing commander and "temporarily at least the command of the 1st Corps devolved upon me," the accused tried to reposition two of Cutler's regiments. He also admitted to "reprimanding with much severity the officers of the 7th Wisconsin" that was not warranted. Colonel Robinson's version of what happened that evening on Cemetery Hill "should be taken in preference to that of the other witness Lt. Col. Finnicum."[96]

Rowley went on to acknowledge the court's difficulty in reconciling the conflicting testimony "without imparting the crime of perjury to a single witness; much more so when a large and respectable body of witnesses is concerned." Defense witnesses, who had known and worked with him prior to Gettysburg and saw him several times July 1, were in a better position to judge his behavior and condition. They either "could not be mistaken in the fact and are correct in the opinion they express, or *they have willfully misstated both the facts and their opinion*" (author's emphasis). Prosecution witnesses who had never seen the defendant before "based their opinions upon a hasty interview, a few words dropped, an order issued, a single act or position occurring in the excitement and confusion of a retreat after a desperately contested battle." The defendant reminded the court, "All the witnesses who saw me on foot thought me perfectly sober." His statement closed with the hope: "It will be the pleasure of this court to relieve me from lifelong disgrace, and return me to the post of duty and of danger, to my command which is awaiting anxiously and hopefully my return to it." Appendix III contains Rowley's entire statement.[97]

McCoy submitted the case without remark and the room cleared. When all members had finished their deliberations, John Robinson informed McCoy, who then read the first specification. The judge advocate polled the court and recorded their votes. Everyone had to vote on each specification, punishment, or acquittal. In Rowley's case, they might have written their name and opinion, guilty or not guilty, on a slip of paper. McCoy would have collected these slips, announced the aggregate verdict, followed by each member's position. This procedure would be repeated until all specifications and charges had been voted on. When finished, the tabulation and ballots were destroyed and only the court's verdict reported. If it was not unanimous, the minority was bound by the decision. "The will of the majority binds the minority."[98]

If found guilty, the defendant faced either peremptory or discretionary punishment. For charges not discretionary, the sentence must be "in obedience to the law, regardless of individual sympathies or opinions." A minority, if present, was bound by the majority's finding in determining sentence. The only penalty requiring a two-thirds vote was death.[99]

The members returned and gave their verdict. With two minor exceptions, they found Thomas A. Rowley guilty of all charges and specifications except the fourth — disobedience of orders — and sentenced him to be cashiered or dismissed at once. John Robinson adjourned the court and sent the verdict to George Meade who immediately approved it.[100]

Earlier that morning Alexander Hays had written wife Annie:

> Last night [April 28] I came home late after a most protracted and tedious session of our court. In anticipation of a movement, we were required to "sit without regard to hours." We finished the case, and you will hear the result in good time.... The court meets again today at Culpeper to confirm our proceedings.

This letter and Dana's diary entry confirm that the court held a closed session April 28. Hays goes on to infer that they reached a verdict before hearing the testimony of Rowley's final witnesses, confirming Rice's comment to Dana. Leaving a sick brother in Wilkes-Barre, Oliver Moore reached Culpeper on April 30 "too late to be sworn." At Rowley's request, Moore prepared a two-page statement May 2, sworn to and subscribed before the 143rd Pennsylvania's adjutant. His comments regarding Rowley's fall from the horse, behavior on Cemetery Hill, and sobriety July 1 reinforced Wilson's April 29

verbal testimony. Even though a regimental adjutant witnessed this document, the court had adjourned, closing the case. Rowley knew this. He
requested the deposition for a different audience, one in the White House.[101]

Most likely unaware of what the general had said at Culpeper, Stanton
resubmitted Doubleday's promotion to lieutenant colonel April 30. It would
become effective September 20, 1863, about four weeks earlier than Stanton's
first submission. This time the Senate approved it on May 18.[102]

No matter how he felt about the outcome, George Meade's options were
limited. On one hand, he could neither pardon nor mitigate Rowley's punishment. The 89th Article stipulated that "every officer authorized to order a
general court-martial shall have the power to pardon or mitigate any punishment ordered by such court except the sentence of death or of cashiering." On
the other hand, Meade could not carry out the court's decision. Three types
of cases required the president's approval before a sentence could be executed:

- The defendant was a general officer.
- The defendant was sentenced to imprisonment in a penitentiary.
- The defendant was sentenced to death but was neither a spy, deserter,
  mutineer, nor murderer.

Consequently, Maj. E. R. Platt, Meade's judge advocate, sent a complete
record of the proceedings with the general's endorsement to Washington.
Only Lincoln possessed the authority to pardon Thomas Rowley.[103]

On May 1, 1864, Platt directed the following to Col. Joseph Holt, once
Buchanan's secretary of war and now Lincoln's judge advocate general.

> By this mail there will be sent to your office the record of the Court in the
> case of General Rowley which requires the action of the President under
> the 65th Article of War. General Meade desires me to remind you of the
> great importance of having this officer's status determined and to request
> [that] you will obtain the proper action on it as soon as possible.[104]

The May 1 "record of the Court" sent to Holt differed from the original
set of charges and specifications introduced April 23. The words "Major General Doubleday, commanding the 1st Corps, and staff and many others," and
"as well as the 1st Division" were deleted from the second charge, first
specification. These changes meant that Doubleday, his staff, and First Division personnel did not hear Rowley exclaim, "By God I am in command of
this Corps; By God, I am the ranking officer here," or "words to that effect."
Since the court found Thomas Rowley "Not Guilty of Disobedience of
Orders," Doubleday ceased to be a trial participant. This court-martial now
became a struggle between colonels and brigadiers, First Division versus the
Third, Pennsylvania versus Wisconsin, regular army versus volunteer, or so it
appeared. Edmund Dana recorded that the court met briefly May 2 "to consider the case submitted" and adjourned. Two days later, Warren's Fifth Corps
crossed the Rapidan River and entered the Wilderness.[105]

9. The Defendant Reacts

> To be found guilty of drunkenness by fellow officers
> would be the ultimate disgrace for most men unless
> the verdict was unfounded or the man was incredibly
> insensitive and arrogant. — *Richard Matthews* [1]

Thomas Rowley still faced the crisis of his life. Doubleday's testimony did not support the disobedience of orders charge and it was dropped. In spite of conflicting testimony from prosecution witnesses and circumstantial evidence, the court found Rowley guilty on all remaining charges, sentencing him to immediate dismissal. The closed session of April 28 and the court's treatment of Rowley's key witnesses — Wilson, Moore, and McCalmont — confirmed Rice's comment to Dana, "It made no difference what was shown for the defense." If that comment accurately described the attitude behind closed doors, this trial had two objectives: find Rowley guilty and finish the proceedings by May 1. Failing to find justice in Culpeper, the defendant prepared what would be his final appeal.

After hearing the verdict, Rowley went immediately to army headquarters and requested permission to travel to Harrisburg, Pennsylvania. In response, Meade sent the following:

May 2, 1864 — 9 AM
Grant, Lt. General,

Brig gen. Rowley has been tried by Court Martial and is now awaiting the promulgation of proceedings, the record having been transmitted to Washington. He is without command and desires to go to Harrisburg, Pa. to await further action. I would be glad if an order to that effect can be issued or authority to that effect given me.

Grant agreed and issued Special Orders No. 133. The generals may have thought that Rowley merely wanted to await the president's verdict, but this was not the case. He went to Harrisburg to secure McCalmont's written statement and forward it with Moore's to Washington, hopefully, in time to influence the president. [2]

At Camp Curtin outside Harrisburg, Alfred McCalmont explained his absence at Culpeper. "I received a subpoena to attend ... but it did not reach me until two days after the time named in it for appearing." At Rowley's request, the colonel prepared on May 4 a two-page statement, sworn to and subscribed before a Harrisburg alderman. He first stated, "I knew him [Rowley] intimately. I saw nothing in his conduct or appearance on that day [July 1] to indicate that he was under the influence of liquor or any stimulant. His conduct during the fight was in my opinion very gallant." Moving on to the evening of July 1 on Cemetery Hill, McCalmont remembered "some conversation with him [Rowley]. He appeared to be perfectly self possessed and sober but was mortified at the result of the fight." The colonel closed with: "I have never seen General Rowley intoxicated and I have known him many years." George Snowden, captain in the 142nd Pennsylvania, received an army discharge April 18, 1864. A diary entry reported that "on a long, circuitous journey home to Franklin (Pennsylvania)," he met Rowley and McCalmont on May 4 on a Harrisburg street and walked with them to the State Senate Chamber.[3]

The next day, Rowley sent a plea for help to Representative Moorhead.

> I do not know how my case has gone. And with you to take my papers to the War department, as I am anxious to be in the field. I am not guilty of the charges against me. And I have always done my duty and have never had a black mark against me ... and can explain my record on the day I am charged with intoxication[.] If I had been even so willing I could not have got drunk for [neither] I nor my staff [had] any Liquor until that evening [July 1, 1863] and then it was only one drink. Examine the testimony yourself.

The letter went on to say again, "I am anxious to be in the present move. I send this to you as I have ever found you my friend but am sorry to trouble you, but I hope sometime to be able to pay you in part." Rowley suggested that Moorhead contact Thomas Williams, who represented the Twenty-third Congressional District, and seek his support. Included with this letter were the signed affidavits from McCalmont and Moore. The congressman gathered up the papers and went to the War Department.[4]

A week later, the Harrisburg newspapers reported that the "old 13th" had seen heavy fighting in Virginia. Having reenlisted as a veteran volunteer regiment in April, the 102nd Pennsylvania led by Col. John Patterson crossed the Rapidan River on May 4 and entered the Wilderness that afternoon. The morning of May 5, Sedgwick's Sixth Corps was to pass behind or east of Warren's Fifth Corps and follow Hancock's Second Corps to Spotsylvania Court House. Robert E. Lee never let it happen. Around 10:30 AM, George Getty received new orders to push his division down the Brock Road and seize its critical intersection with the Orange Plank Road before A. P. Hill did. Frank Wheaton's brigade got there just in time to stop Henry Heth's advance. Maj. Gen. David Birney's Second Corps Division came up on Getty's left. At 4:15 p.m., Wheaton's brigade advanced into the dark woods immediately north of

This photograph of Col. John Patterson was taken in Pittsburgh, one month before his death in the Wilderness. Courtesy of William Phillis.

the Orange Plank Road. While leading his men across the Brock Road, a bullet struck John Patterson in the face, passed through, and lodged in his shoulder. The colonel died before his body touched the ground. To relieve enemy pressure on Wheaton, Birney ordered Alexander Hays's entire brigade forward. Coming under heavy fire, Hays stopped to rally his old regiment, the 63rd Pennsylvania. "With a sickening thwack, a stray bullet tore through the general's skull and toppled him from his saddle." Thomas Rowley lost a close friend and a loyal company commander. The situation was no better in his former command, now part of Roy Stone's Third Brigade, Wadsworth's Fourth Division, Warren's Fifth Corps.[5]

Wadsworth's division marched south the evening of May 5 and stopped just short of the Orange Plank Road. A short time later, Col. Roy Stone abruptly left the Wilderness, his Third Brigade, and the Army of the Potomac. General Wadsworth was mortally wounded the next day and Lysander Cutler took over the Fourth Division on May 7. Col. Edward S. Bragg, 6th Wisconsin, filled Stone's vacancy and led Doubleday's Gettysburg regiments to Spotsylvania. Four weeks of heavy fighting followed with no Federal victories. From Major General Warren's perspective, the Third Brigade had not performed well since beginning the Overland campaign. Following the defeat at Cold Harbor, Warren made several changes. First, he transferred Stone's former command to Gen. Charles Griffin's First Division, where it became the First Brigade. Second, Col. Joshua Chamberlin replaced Edward Bragg. This left Cutler's division with only the two brigades that had once been Wadsworth's at Gettysburg. Warren explained to Meade, "I did it because this brigade [Stone's] had not sustained its former good reputation, and its apologists laid all the blame on General Cutler." These events were still to come. Let us return to Harrisburg in early May.[6]

George McFarland had endured a very slow and painful recovery from his Gettysburg wounds. Wednesday, May 11, he went to Harrisburg and discussed various issues with state officials, including Samuel P. Bates. McFarland's diary entry for Thursday said that he "saw my old commander, Brig. Genl. Thos. A. Rowley. Very pleasant and sociable, said he would get my pay, which I deserved and should have." McFarland never mentioned Rowley's arrest and trial in either his diary or letters.[7]

The judge advocate general completed his first review of the court's proceedings on May 6 and sent an 11-page summary to the president. Colonel Holt concluded that "the Court possessed superior advantages for arriving at a just decision in the case, and there is no reason suggested by the record why their judgment should not be relied on as correct."[8]

Congressman Moorhead delivered McCalmont's and Moore's affidavits to the War Department. After reading them, Colonel Holt changed his mind. The judge advocate general wrote May 11:

The opinion is still entertained that the weight of proof addressed at the trial warranted the Court in their decision: but when these papers which were not before them, are considered in connection with other evidence in the case, it must be admitted that so decided a conflict in the testimony relating to the gravest of the charges is presented, as would probably justify the President in withholding his approval from so severe a sentence as dismissal. This course would be the more proper if it shall be known to the Government that the previous record of this officer is altogether free from marks of such irregularities and excesses as are alleged against him, in the present instance. This office has no knowledge of his antecedents and therefore can express no opinion.

Lincoln read Holt's revised report then passed it on to Stanton.[9]

Being experienced trial lawyers, Edwin Stanton and Abraham Lincoln had three choices: accept the court's verdict, revoke the finding, or, like Joseph Revere, give Rowley the opportunity to resign. The secretary of war reached a decision May 23. He disapproved the court's finding and sentence and so informed the president two days later. Lincoln concurred. E. D. Townsend issued General Court Martial Orders No. 120 May 27. After restating the charges, specifications, and findings, it closed, "The finding and sentence are disapproved and Brigadier-General Rowley will be at once released from arrest and returned to duty."[10]

Return to the Army of the Potomac — Petersburg

> And will take any responsibility rather than give him [Rowley] a
> command in this Corps if it can be avoided under the circumstances.
> All the charges were proved against him and grosser ones
> could not have been framed. — *Maj. Gen. G.K. Warren*[11]

"Released from arrest and returned to duty," Rowley searched for a field assignment. The War Department offered little if any advice. Since his last active command was now part of the Fifth Corps, the brigadier decided to report to G. K. Warren. There is no evidence that anyone tried to discourage Rowley from doing so.[12]

The War Department sent copies of General Court-Martial Orders No. 120 to Grant and Meade. Neither general thought to inform Warren that Lincoln had disapproved the trial's findings and sentence. It is difficult to accept that Thomas Rowley traveled through a war zone to Petersburg without someone knowing at either Grant's or Meade's Headquarters. No one notified the Fifth Corps of the brigadier's coming arrival. Unfortunately for Rowley, not only did his June 19 request for a new assignment come as a complete surprise, it followed Warren's confrontation with Meade.[13]

The only favorable omen that day was the army's need for combat-effective brigadiers. Three general officers would determine whether Thomas Rowley filled one of these vacancies: Grant, Meade, and Warren. One of them had to be his advocate. Shortage or not, George Meade could be quickly ruled out since he had authorized the court-martial and approved its findings. Ulysses Grant had been generous in victory but Petersburg turned out to be one more in a series of Federal setbacks. Under normal circumstances the Fifth Corps commander might have given the brigadier an audience but not on June 19. Thomas Rowley had unintentionally stumbled into an emotional morass.

It resulted from the extreme bitterness that the Fifth Corps commander felt toward George Meade, once his staunchest advocate. Even though his Mine Run performance had been an embarrassment, Meade still favored giving Warren a corps command last March. John Newton, William French, George Sykes, and Alfred Pleasanton lost theirs in the reorganization. Ambitious, young, brilliant, and meticulous, Warren initially impressed the lieutenant general. After the Wilderness, Grant no longer left the details to Meade but now assumed an active role in the Army of the Potomac's daily affairs. Hancock, Warren, and Sedgwick found themselves in the supreme commander's spotlight. Warren was the first to suffer. At Spotsylvania, Grant became so concerned about the Fifth Corps's failure to execute orders promptly "that he directed Meade to relieve Warren if he did not attack promptly." Influential general officers now considered him to be nervous, snappish, finicky, and too willing to tell others what they should do while he was executing his move. Overly cautious on the battlefield, "peculiarities of temperament, or defects of personality," or whatever the reason, G. K. Warren failed to meet Grant's expectations. Petersburg provided the spark for a major confrontation with Meade. To understand why, turn the clock back one week.[14]

While Rowley made arrangements to rejoin the Army of the Potomac, U. S. Grant reached a decision. From May 5 through June 12, 1864, starting in the Wilderness and ending at Cold Harbor, the Federals had suffered almost 53,000 casualties — 7,400 killed, 37,000 wounded, and 8,100 missing. With apparently little to show for having lost half of his army, the lieutenant general decided to give up the Rapidan to James line and shift his campaign 25 miles southward. Retaining the initiative, Grant set out to do what Maj. Gen. Benjamin Butler had failed to accomplish south of the James River, namely capture Petersburg. This would stop the arrival of essential armaments and supplies from the southeast. Three Federal corps quietly abandoned their Cold Harbor lines the night of June 12. They embarked on a 50-mile turning movement that would take them around Lee's right and behind Butler to attack the Confederate extreme right. Initially, Warren's Fifth Corps remained behind to screen the pull out and to create a diversion by crossing the Chickahominy River on June 12. After marching a short distance toward Richmond, the Fifth entrenched and waited for the Second Corps to pass behind it.[15]

Unaware of Grant's decision, Robert E. Lee set into motion his own chain of events that would soon impact the North and Thomas Rowley as much as Petersburg. Having stopped the Army of the Potomac at Cold Harbor, Lee returned Maj. Gen. John C. Breckinridge's division to the Shenandoah Valley. He then detached Early's Division from Ewell's Second Corps. Supported by a large cavalry force, Jubal Early caught up with Breckinridge and took command of the column. His orders to drive the enemy out of the valley and threaten Washington would relieve the pressure on Richmond. Ironically, by transferring his army south of the James, Grant uncovered the capital in time for Early's advance.[16]

Like Hooker's flanking march at Chancellorsville, everything went well initially. Meade successfully withdrew four corps from Lee's front. Shortly after sunrise June 14, transports began ferrying Hancock's infantry across the James River. The remaining three corps reached the river's north bank, 10 miles below City Point, before evening. Early the next morning, Hancock's artillery and wagons crossed over on a new pontoon bridge. Grant issued orders for the Second Corps to move south immediately and support William "Baldy" Smith's assault on Petersburg, 16 miles away. Hancock's leading infantry reached the Cockade City at dusk. Charles Dana, assistant secretary of war, optimistically wired Stanton, "Lee appears to have no idea of our crossing the James River. General Grant moves his headquarters to City Point this morning. Weather splendid."[17]

"Baldy" Smith commanded the Eighteenth Corps in Maj. Gen. Benjamin Butler's Army of the James. After Beauregard stopped Butler's spring advance at Bermuda Hundred, Grant detached the corps and it joined the Army of the Potomac just before Cold Harbor. While Hancock crossed the James on June 14, Smith's command returned by steamer to Bermuda Hundred and moved into position to attack and seize Petersburg.[18]

At daybreak June 15, "Baldy" Smith's two divisions crossed the Appomattox River on a pontoon bridge at Point of Rocks. Eight miles to the south, Beauregard's 2,500 effectives manned Petersburg's well-designed and constructed entrenchments. Mustering 14,000 infantry and 2,500 cavalry the Eighteenth Corps easily drove back the Confederate cavalry, advanced to the enemy's outer line, and deployed around 1:30 p.m. Smith hesitated and did not launch his first attack until 7:00 p.m. In spite of this delay, they quickly seized a mile and a half of entrenchments and 18 guns. Unaccountably, "Baldy" Smith stopped the advance. "Tomorrow would be time enough to renew the attack." Hancock did not overrule his junior and arriving Second Corps troops merely relieved units from the Eighteenth. Within both Federal corps, the magnitude of the opportunity lost June 15 would grow as each ensuing day passed. For over three hours that night, "the Federals could [have walked] into Petersburg just about as they chose." Beauregard considered the city to be "clearly at the mercy of the Federal commander who had all but captured it."[19]

Shortly after daybreak June 16, transports began ferrying Burnside's infantry across followed by Warren's and Maj. Gen. Horatio Wright's Sixth Corps. The steamer *Exchange* carried Colonel Chamberlin's First Brigade infantry from Windmill Point to Guiney's Landing. Supply trains and artillery caissons used the pontoon bridge. Once on the south bank, the Ninth Corps moved out immediately but Warren's column did not depart until 2:30 p.m.[20]

Earlier that morning, Grant wired Meade, "Hurry Warren up by the nearest road to reach the Jerusalem Plank Road, about three miles out [east] from Petersburg." Maj. Gen. Andrew Humphreys, Meade's chief of staff, informed Warren at noon, "The major-general commanding [Meade] directs that you push forward your corps as rapidly as possible toward Petersburg, and that as soon as a division is ready you move it forward without waiting for your corps to get together." Meade wanted at least one Fifth Corps division to move south about eight miles past Burnside's left, turn right, head west and seize the road. When the Ninth Corps later came into line that afternoon, the Federals outnumbered Beauregard five to one.[21]

George Meade rode across the James and met with Grant around noon. In spite of Smith's and Hancock's failure to seize Petersburg the night before, the commanding general remained optimistic and ordered an assault by the Second and Ninth Corps at 6:00 p.m. Around 2:00 p.m., a piqued G. K. Warren replied to Meade's noon message:

> I have just received a copy of General Grant's dispatch to you, telling you to hurry up my corps. I am on the road and will make as good time as possible, and reach there before camping. It, of course, could not be expected of me to be there before dark, but I certainly will be there before morning.

Fifth Corps infantry did not reach the front until after dark and failed to capture the Jerusalem Plank Road. Burnside and Hancock probed both enemy flanks but gained little. By midnight, Grant's entire army was south of the James. Lee took no action to reinforce Beauregard.[22]

East of Petersburg, General Beauregard massed 10,000 defenders in trenches opposite the Second and Ninth Corps. Farther south, Confederate lines west of the Jerusalem Plank Road remained empty. Well aware of this problem, Beauregard later remembered "that if Meade had put so much as one army corps over on the Jerusalem Road and told it to march due north, I would have been compelled to evacuate Petersburg." Warren's relatively fresh command could have been the "one army corps" that Beauregard feared. Instead, they advanced slowly, cautiously pressed back Confederate skirmishers and saw little fighting June 17. North of Warren, the Ninth and Second Corps fought hard, enjoyed initial success, and seemed ready to break through, but complete victory eluded them. Poor leadership and a lack of coordination between and within the three corps continued. After the fighting ended at midnight, Beauregard pulled back his forces to a shorter and stronger line, newly constructed and unknown to the Federals.[23]

At 3:30 a.m. June 18, Lee finally accepted the fact that Grant had crossed the James 48 hours earlier and began shifting the Army of Northern Virginia southward. Maj. Gen. Joseph Kershaw's division, Longstreet's corps, marched that night from Drury's Bluff to Bermuda Hundred then on to Petersburg. His leading brigade would not reach Beauregard's trenches until 7:30 a.m. "Meade issued orders for an attack all along the line at the moment of dawn." He thought that Hancock and Burnside had broken Beauregard's main line the day before and it remained vulnerable. At 4:00 a.m., columns from the Second, Fifth, Ninth, and Eighteenth Corps advanced. An overwhelming assault by four corps soon deteriorated into a series of divisional probes that accomplished little. Fifth Corps's four divisions, led by Cutler's, should have crossed the Jerusalem Plank Road, wheeled north, and pushed the Confederates across the Appomattox. Instead, they advanced westward toward the city and came across an entrenched enemy battle line, Beauregard's right. Unfamiliar with the ground, Warren stopped the advance about 7:30 a.m., short of the key road, and sent out patrols.[24]

Except for Kershaw, Longstreet's corps was still hours away from Petersburg. The Federals had another chance for victory. At 10:00 a.m., Meade queried Burnside and Warren, "You will please advise me at what time your columns of assault will be prepared to attack the enemy in your front ... I desire the enemy attacked at all hazards by each corps and desire to arrange for its being simultaneous." Meade's tactics were simple. Assault in mass Beauregard's new and shorter line of entrenchments, about a mile east of Petersburg. An hour later, Meade told Warren: "The attack ordered will be made by your command punctually at 12 m [noon]. Neither general suggested a turning movement around the Confederate right.[25]

At 11:36 a.m., the Fifth Corps commander informed Army Headquarters, "I am gradually forcing the enemy's skirmishers back and getting batteries forward. I cannot be ready to attack in line or column before 1:00 PM." Meade retorted, "I cannot change the hour in the order of attack just issued. Everyone else is ready. You will attack as soon as possible after the hour designated." Second, Sixth, and Eighteenth Corps divisions attacked at noon. Beauregard ultimately repulsed every Federal assault, imparting severe losses. Meade fumed and stewed in the rear. His corps now ready, Warren suggested a 3:00 p.m. rush. "I think it would be safe ... and will give time to notify all to make another effort." He badly misjudged the enemy opposition by adding,

"I am willing to try alone. The enemy does not seem strong in infantry force." Surprisingly, Burnside concurred with Warren's afternoon assessment.[26]

Offering no tactical guidance, Meade curtly replied to both corps commanders at 2:20 p.m.:

> I am greatly astonished at your dispatch of 2 p. m. What additional orders to attack you require I cannot imagine. My orders have been explicit and are now repeated, that you each immediately assault the enemy with all your forces, and if there is any further delay the responsibility and the consequences will rest with you.[27]

The Fifth and Ninth Corps attacked just after 3:00 p.m. Federal artillery opened fire, then Joshua Chamberlin led his command toward the earthworks. "From every point dominating the scene of the assault came shot and shell and rattling grape and canister, coupled with a murderous fire of musketry, against which no troops could make an effective stand." Out front, the colonel was seriously wounded during the second charge. For the first time, Grant awarded a battlefield promotion. Not expected to recover, Chamberlin was elevated to brigadier general. In an interview that appeared in the *New York World*, January 15, 1893, the major general remembered his old brigade:

> It consisted of Doubleday's Division of veterans, Roy Stone's and Rowley's old brigades, to which was added a fine new regiment, the 187th Pennsylvania, and these made up a brigade. I was called to command it while I held the rank of colonel in another brigade. It was with this magnificent command that I made the now famous charge at Petersburg.[28]

It was too late for either brave words or charges. "The morning's opportunity gone with the morning mists." Once again, the Federals demonstrated convincingly that properly manned fortifications could not be taken by storm. Kershaw's entire division was now in reserve and General Lee on the field. Grant had heard and seen enough. At 6:50 p.m. he wired Meade: "I think after the present assault, unless a decided advantage presents itself, our men should have rest, protecting themselves as well as possible. If this assault does not carry, we will try to gain advantages without assaulting fortifications." Forty minutes later, Meade ordered Warren to "secure your lines and look to your left flank.... All that men could do under the circumstances was done." A formal siege would replace frontal assaults. "That night the Union Army made a line of works from the Appomattox to the Jerusalem Plank Road in front of the Confederate line." The Federals listened as belfry clocks in Petersburg struck the hours.[29]

Neither side renewed the fighting on June 19. By noon, Confederate forces south of the James were "within the entrenched lines of the city, and all felt perfectly safe and secure." Petersburg turned out to be Grant's best opportunity throughout the 1864 campaign of winning a great victory. Like the preceding Overland campaign, there was little to show after four days of intense fighting and 11,000 casualties. Grant claimed to be satisfied "that all had been done which was possible." Even if the commanding general had truly felt this way, that view did not prevail throughout his army. Many concluded that the best chance of the war had been missed and "the blame of the failure to take Petersburg must rest with our generals, not with our army."[30]

Shortly after sunrise, G. K. Warren informed Army Headquarters, "All of their dead and wounded were recovered last night [June 18]," and "all is quiet in my front except light musketry ... and occasionally a cannon-shot." Officers waiting outside Warren's tent watched as George Meade rode up about 9:30 a.m., dismounted, and entered Fifth Corps Headquarters. Later correspondence described the ensuing confrontation.[31]

July 22, 1864

Major-General MEADE:

DEAR GENERAL: I send herewith the *Pittsburgh Commercial* of July 14, which has an allusion to you and myself, which I have marked. Seeing this in the papers I have thought it best to indicate at least one way in which it may have been started. About two weeks ago General Smith told me that it was common talk at General Grant's headquarters that you had told General Grant that you had threatened me with a court-martial if I did not resign. As you had never done so, I could not believe for an instant that you had ever said so to General Grant, and yet I believe the story circulates as coming from the highest authority. I wish to make some public denial of the statement contained in this newspaper.

G. K. WARREN

Enclosure from the Pittsburgh Commercial

A late letter from the Army of the Potomac states that General Meade and General Warren have had a disagreement; that the former preferred charges against the latter for disobedience and tardy execution of orders, but that nothing has yet come of it. The same writer says a great deal of jealousy, fault-finding, and mutual derogation has been awakened in the army, at which the country would be astonished, if not disgusted, were the facts to be given. Important changes are rumored.[32]

In his same day reply to Warren, George Meade recalled in some detail what had been said at Warren's headquarters the morning of June 19:

Maj. Gen. G. K. WARREN

GENERAL: Although I cannot be responsible for the newspaper correspondents, or the talk of staff officers, I have enclosed a note denying the statement in the *Pittsburgh Commercial*, which you can make any use of you think proper.

I could not deny the existence of a disagreement, because there was a serious one between us on the 19th ultimo, and I don't think you ought to be surprised at the publicity, as your conversation in the presence of General [Samuel] Crawford, and within the hearing of several officers outside your tent, precluded the possibility of its being kept private. I frankly confess to you I was very much irritated, and felt deeply wounded by the tone and tenor of your conversation on that occasion, and fully determined, on leaving you, to apply to have you relieved.

I did speak to General Grant upon the subject, with whom I have frequently spoken about you, and I even went so far as to write an official letter giving my reasons for desiring you to be relieved, but upon further reflection, in view of the injury to you, and in the hope the causes of disagreement would not occur in the future, I withheld this letter, and have taken no official action.

I do not desire any concealment of my views from you; on the contrary, am glad of this opportunity of an explanation. I have never entertained any but the most friendly feelings toward you, and have always endeavored to advance your interests, but I cannot shut my eyes to what I think is wrong in you, and on several occasions I have differed from you in what you seemed to consider was your prerogative.

In your conversation of the 19th ultimo I thought you exhibited a great deal of temper and positive ill feeling against me, not justified, as I think, by anything I have either said or done. It is my earnest desire to have harmony and co-operation with my subordinate officers, but I cannot always yield my judgment to theirs, and if it is impossible to have these relations, necessary for harmonious co-operation, a separation is inevitable. I do not make these remarks for any other purpose than to explain the reason I felt called on to speak to General Grant about you.

GEO. G. MEADE.

Meade's enclosed note regarding the *Pittsburgh Commercial*'s July 14 article follows.

HEADQUARTERS ARMY OF THE POTOMAC
July 22, 1864

Major-General WARREN:

GENERAL: I have received your note of this date, calling my attention to an article in the Pittsburgh Commercial of the 14th instant. The statement therein made that I had preferred charges against you for disobedience and tardy execution of orders is entirely without foundation in fact.

GEO. G. MEADE[33]

Warren recorded his reaction to this disagreement in a July letter to Meade but never sent it.

As to my being relieved, I have always maintained that in your place you should have the choice of your Corps Commanders, nor will I allow my efforts, or any friends of mind to force me upon you.... I would not resign under any circumstances nor apply to be relieved, while in the presence of the enemy. To relieve you from initiating such action, I told you on the 19th [June 1864] that if I did not suit you, it was best you should have someone put in my place.

Returning to June 19, the acrimonious conversation in Warren's tent finally ended and George Meade angrily rode off to discuss the problem with U. S. Grant.[34]

While he waited outside Fifth Corps Headquarters that morning, Rowley probably overheard the heated exchange. An aide brought in the brigadier who requested an assignment in the Fifth Corps. Given the past 24 hours and Warren's emotional state of mind, Rowley could not have picked a worse time to make the request. If the major general had known in advance Rowley's purpose, he probably would have refused to see him. The brigadier general soon heard that he did not warrant a second chance in the Army of the Potomac. Dismissing Rowley, Warren immediately wired Brig. Gen. Seth Williams, the army's acting adjutant general:

General Rowley has just joined me under General Court Martial Orders No. 120 of War Department. Have you seen the orders? I don't know what to do with him. And will take any responsibility rather than give him a command in this Corps if it can be avoided under the circumstances. All the charges were proved against him and grosser ones could not have been framed. The order says without comment or reason, "The finding and sentence are disapproved and Brigadier Rowley will be at once released from arrest and returned to duty."[35]

Seth Williams replied that the army commander would be given the message when he returned from City Point. After reading Warren's dispatch George Meade sent a recommendation to Grant.

June 20, 1864 — 9.10 PM

The following dispatch from Gen Warren is submitted for the consideration of the Lieut. Gen commanding. About the circumstance of the case I think it would be prejudicial to the interests of the service to again give Gen Rowley a command here, and I trust that he may be assigned to duty elsewhere.

Brig. Gen. John Rawlings, Grant's chief of staff, replied to Meade the next morning, "You will not permit General Rowley to be assigned to a command. Orders on the subject will be sent to you tomorrow." No one that day had either the time or interest to find out why Washington had overturned the verdict. From the army's standpoint — Grant, Meade, Warren, and Rawlings — Rowley remained guilty as charged. On a different subject, Charles Dana wired Stanton from City Point, Virginia, "General Meade notified Warren this morning [June 20] that he must either ask to be relieved, or else he [Meade] would prefer charges against him."[36]

Rowley's case struck a respondent cord at City Point. If General Grant was guilty of drinking excessively, intoxication had never interfered with his execution of military responsibilities. A personal affliction sometimes provides insight to understanding the problem in others. Grant probably assumed that he understood Rowley's situation quite well. In this instance, a general officer supposedly had permitted drinking to jeopardize his battlefield effectiveness. The charge of falling off a horse brought back unpleasant memories.[37]

Following Vicksburg's surrender July 1863, Grant traveled to New Orleans and discussed future operations with Nathaniel Banks. During their meeting, Banks presented his famous visitor with a large, recently broken horse and boasted that his horses were the fastest in the army. On September 4, the generals and their staffs went out to review Maj. Gen. Edward Ord's 13th Corps and William Franklin's 19th. Grant, who enjoyed a challenging horse, decided to ride Banks's gift. Before long, the horse became very difficult to control. Always confident of his riding skills, the conqueror of Vicksburg decided to return to quarters at a gallop. While racing down the road, a nearby train's shrill whistle startled Grant's horse which then struck a passing carriage. The animal lost its footing and fell down, pinning the general. Even though doctors found no broken bones, the rider spent several painful days in bed. Rumors started circulating that Grant was guilty of being drunk on duty and falling off his horse. His critics either ignored or forgot the mitigating circumstances.[38]

To refresh his memory, the lieutenant general on June 21 requested a copy of Rowley's court-martial verdict. Seth Williams found it necessary to send a messenger to Colonel Locke at Fifth Corps Headquarters. "Please send me by special message a copy of General Court Martial Order No. 120, War Department, Case of General Rowley. General Grant asks for a copy and unfortunately I have sent away all the copies we had." After reading the order, reviewing Meade's recommendation and considering his own views, Grant reached a decision that evening. Special Orders No. 40, issued the next day, concluded that it was "inadvisable to place him [Rowley] on duty because of the feeling in the Army of the Potomac of distrust of his fitness to command." Special Orders No. 40 also removed Thomas Neill, a member of Rowley's court, from Sixth Corps divisional command. Following Grant's orders, Rowley went to Washington and reported to the adjutant general. Three days later, Stanton told the brigadier general to report in person to Maj. Gen. Darius Couch, commanding the Department of the Susquehanna, headquartered at Chambersburg, Pennsylvania, for assignment.[39]

The battlefield deaths of James Wadsworth, Alexander Hays, and James Rice plus the poor performance of others created a serious shortage of competent general officers in the Army of the Potomac. A week after Rowley's dismissal, George Meade requested that Regis DeTrobriand be relieved from his current assignment and rejoin the army as soon as possible. Rowley's friend from the peninsula took command of John Hobart Ward's Second Corps Brigade in July. A second court member had lost his command [40]

Charles Dana reported July 1, "Grant thinks the difficulty between Meade and Warren has been settled without the extreme remedy which Meade proposed last week." Meade might have agreed with Dana but Warren did not. A July 24 letter to his wife confirmed that Warren was not ready to either forgive or forget:

> I believe Genl Meade is an unjust and unfeeling man and I dislike his personal character so much now that it is impossible we shall ever have again any friendly social relations. I have also lost all confidence in his ability as a general. He has quick perception but does not know how to act with patience and judgment.

The final act did not take place until April 2, 1865, at Five Forks. Here, under orders from Phil Sheridan, Maj. Gen. Charles Griffin relieved G. K. Warren of Fifth Corps command.[41]

Besides George Meade, Warren faced another problem that July, the need to reorganize his command. The Fifth Corps currently mustered only 16,000 men. Six weeks of heavy fighting and the Third Brigade's (Stone's) transfer to Griffin had reduced Cutler's division to less than 2,000 effectives. The major general's first approach was to simply disband the unit by distributing its two brigades to other divisions. Still resentful of the March consolidation, First Corps veterans strongly objected. Some at corps headquarters felt that the acrimonious dispute, would be resolved only when Cutler was transferred out of the Fifth Corps. Warren changed his approach and on September 8 submitted a plan to concentrate the old First Corps regiments in one division, Samuel Crawford's. Meade approved and the reorganization took place four days later. Relieved from field duty at his own request, Lysander Cutler left the Army of the Potomac. Units once part of Rowley's and Stone's Gettysburg brigades were now in Crawford's First and Third Brigades.[42]

Before leaving Petersburg, return once more to the morning of June 19. Assume that the court-martial had never occurred and Thomas Rowley was returning to field duty after a long convalescence. Even under this scenario, Warren could not have given him command of either his former First Corps brigade or division. The five remaining regiments from Doubleday's division had suffered such high losses since May 1 that they failed to meet the brigade minimum. Joshua Chamberlain was their last commander.

10. Jubal Early's Invasions of Pennsylvania

The unpopularity of Gen. Couch from his lack of activity,
has destroyed his usefulness....—*Philadelphia Inquirer, August 3, 1864*[8]

The Department of the Susquehanna was created June 9, 1863, to organize defensive forces in central and eastern Pennsylvania against Robert E. Lee's invasion. Darius Couch, who left the Army of the Potomac after Chancellorsville, commanded this new department. Originally, the area west of Johnstown, Pennsylvania, and the Laurel Ridge remained the Department of the Monogahela, headquartered in Pittsburgh. On April 6, 1864, it was annexed to the Department of the Susquehanna and ceased to be a separate department. Edwin Stanton demoted the Department of the Monogahela's last commander, Maj. Gen. William T. H. Brooks, to brigadier general and reassigned him to Benjamin Butler's Eighteenth Corps. On June 24, the War Department ordered Thomas Rowley to report in person to Darius Couch for assignment. Three days later, the major general issued General Orders No. 37, creating a post for his new subordinate: "That portion of the department of the Susquehanna west of Johnstown and the Laurel Hill range of mountains will comprise the Monogahela District, head-quarters at Pittsburgh, Pa."[2]

The *Army and Navy Journal's* July 9, 1864, issue announced that General Rowley had "been ordered to command the old department of the Monogahela." In addition to William Brooks, several precedents existed for giving Rowley the command of a military district. Stanton's January 1864 report to the Senate listed two major generals and seven brigadiers as commanding military districts. Couch and Rowley had little time to reminisce about the peninsula. Word came July 3 that they faced a new problem, Jubal Early.[3]

Beginning with Stonewall Jackson in 1862, the Shenandoah Valley had been the scene of one Federal defeat after another. The *New York Times* described the region as the "kitchen garden of the Rebels." The paper went on to lament, "A short distance from Washington, the Rebels have, from year to year, garnered its precious products and made the valley one of the chief reliances of its commissariat." Events soon indicated that 1864 would be no better. As part of U. S. Grant's plan to simultaneously strike the Confederacy on four different fronts, Maj. Gen. Franz Sigel advanced southward or up the valley that spring. His force consisted of one infantry and one cavalry division, totaling 6,500 effectives. Brig. Gen. John Imboden's cavalry brigade stopped Sigel's advance at New Market, Virginia. Two infantry brigades, led by John Breckinridge, hurried forward and joined Imboden. The combined Confederate force of 5,000, including 258 cadets from the Virginia Military Institute, attacked shortly after sunrise May 15. After sustaining several assaults, Sigel ordered a general retreat north toward Strasburg. A few days later, Maj. Gen. David Hunter relieved Sigel and immediately set out to disrupt enemy supply lines and communications in the Shenandoah Valley.[4]

The new Federal commander won a victory at Piedmont, burned the VMI buildings including its library in Lexington, and spread destruction throughout the region. Confident that his Petersburg and Richmond lines would contain Grant, Robert E. Lee detached Jubal Early's division from Ewell's corps June 12 and sent it north to support Breckinridge. Unaware of Lee's decision, Hunter moved eastward and on June 18 attacked enemy forces near Lynchburg. Breckinridge reinforced with Early's leading regiments stopped the Federal assault. Knowing now who opposed him, Hunter abruptly departed the valley and began a retreat that night into the mountains of West Virginia. Once again, the Confederates possessed an unobstructed invasion path into Maryland.[5]

Brushing aside Hunter's rear guard at dawn, Early advanced down (north) the Shenandoah Valley to Winchester. Forewarned of the enemy's approach, Sigel retreated and concentrated Hunter's reserve division at Harpers Ferry. Turning east, Early's 10,000 infantry and 4,000 cavalry bypassed Sigel and crossed the Potomac on July 3 at Shepherdstown, Falling Waters, and Dam No. 4. At this time, the Department of the Susquehanna reported less than 1,100 officers and men present for duty. To defend Chambersburg, Pennsylvania, Couch brought together an assortment of cavalry, Signal Corps, infantry militia, and two artillery sections, totaling no more than 400 effectives. Assured that Washington would pay all costs during the emergency, Governor Curtin made plans for a new militia callup. Lincoln and Curtin issued a joint proclamation July 5 calling upon the commonwealth for 12,000 militia or volunteer infantry "to serve at Washington and its vicinity for one hundred days, unless sooner discharged." The president's primary objective was not defending the Keystone State but to avoid withdrawing Army of the Potomac units from outside Richmond. Militia units subsequently raised in Pennsylvania went to the capital, doing nothing to alleviate local manpower shortages.[6]

Couch issued orders July 5 for Rowley to come to Chambersburg immediately. Rumors of a Rebel push into Maryland appeared in the *Pittsburgh Gazette* on July 6. This issue also contained a news update from Maryland:

> General T. A. Rowley, commanding the District of the Monongahela, has
> received the following dispatch relative to the reported invasion.
>
> Chambersburg (PA), July 4
>
> Latest information from the cavalry in front, as well as dispatches from
> Hagerstown [Maryland], show that there are no rebels on this side of the
> Potomac.

This erroneous communiqué marked the beginning of a miserable two months
for both Couch and Rowley.[7]

Jubal Early drove off a small Union cavalry force and captured Hagerstown the same day that Rowley reached Chambersburg. After giving the
brigadier general command of the troops in the Cumberland Valley, Couch
and his staff left for Harrisburg on July 7. The situation appeared to offer
Rowley an opportunity to redeem his military reputation. Unfortunately, he
lacked both the resources and authority to strike Early in Maryland. Governor Curtin had already begun mobilizing the state militia. Rendezvous camps
for his new callup of 12,000 would be established at Harrisburg, Philadelphia, and Pittsburgh. General Couch asked the mayors of these cities to use
their influence immediately to raise more troops under the recent calls. Newspapers announced, "The old Pennsylvania Reserves are flocking to the res-
cue."[8]

On July 1, the War Department instructed Rowley to "report in person,
on Wednesday, July 6th, 1864, to Lieutenant-Colonel H. B. Burham, Judge
Advocate of a General Court Martial, in this city, as a witness in the case of
Captain Thomas Dain." Army bureaucracy took precedence over Early's ongo-
ing invasion. After a brief meeting with Couch, Rowley left Chambersburg
July 6 for Washington.[9]

The defendant, Thomas Dain, was a member of Company E, 102nd
Pennsylvania. When Rowley commanded a brigade at Fredericksburg, Dain
served as an aide-de-camp. Earlier he had held a similar position on Albion
Howe's staff when that general commanded the same unit. The charges against
Captain Dain included desertion and misbehavior before the enemy. Lieutenant Colonel Burham claimed that on December 13, 1862, near Falmouth,
the captain "did, without lawful authority, absent himself from his duty, and
from his said Company and Regiment." While serving as an ADC during the
battle, he "did misbehave himself before the enemy by absenting himself" and
failed to report to either the 102nd or Rowley. Burham called on Howe and
Rowley to testify. Found guilty of desertion but not misbehavior, Thomas
Dain was cashiered and sentenced to three years of hard labor at the Albany,
New York, Penitentiary. No record exists of Rowley's role during the trial. At
its conclusion, he returned to Chambersburg and General Howe to the War
Department.[10]

Stanton belatedly attempted to strengthen an inefficient and unwieldy command structure. On July 7, Rowley's former commanding officer and fellow witness, Albion Howe, took "command of the Military District of Harper's Ferry, from the Monocacy to Hancock, subject to the orders of Major General Hunter." Howe relieved Sigel and told him to report to Hunter at Cumberland, Maryland, for orders. These changes, long overdue, however, did nothing to deter Early's invasion.[11]

The Confederates routed Maj. Gen. Lew Wallace's force of 6,000 at the Monocacy River on July 9, then moved on to Frederick, Maryland. Having extorted a ransom of $20,000 from Hagerstown, "Old Jube" demanded and received $200,000 from Frederick. By now, the invading force of four Georgia, five North Carolina, four Mississippi, eight Louisiana, and three Virginia regiments had the nation's full attention. Farther west, "General Rowley's troops reoccupied Hagerstown." His mixed command of cavalry, infantry, and artillery entered the city that afternoon and captured 15–20 rebels. The general's aide, Lieutenant Heberton, announced, "Trains are now running as usual." The next day, Rowley informed Couch that Early held Middletown, Maryland, with 12,000 infantry. While the rebels enjoyed Maryland's hospitality, George Getty's division, Wright's Sixth Corps, boarded transports at City Point, Virginia, and departed for Hampton Roads. The 102nd Pennsylvania and Frank Wheaton's brigade bid Virginia farewell and headed north for the Potomac River. Lee achieved his primary objective of weakening the Army of the Potomac.[12]

The *Pittsburgh Gazette's* July 11 morning edition carried Darius Couch's latest pronouncement: "All responding to the [Governor's] call west of Johnstown and the Laurel Hill range of Mountains will report to the commanding officer Camp Reynolds near Pittsburgh." At noon that day, Wheaton's men disembarked from the transports *Dictator* and *Guide* at Washington's Sixth Street wharf.

> Erect and armed, three brigades bounded down the gangplanks. Greek crosses gleamed in the summer sun, and the crowd hailed the Sixth Corps with jubilant, tumultuous cheers, incongruous in a beleaguered city.... The column quickly formed and went swinging up Seventh Street.... The rhythm of tramping feet brought people running to the sidewalks to welcome back the Army of the Potomac...."It is the old Sixth Corps!" the soldiers heard voices exclaim. "The danger is over now!"[13]

General Wright initially directed Frank Wheaton to move northwest toward the Chain Bridge. While marching up Pennsylvania Avenue, word came that Confederate infantry was driving in the Federal picket line and threatening to capture Fort Stevens. The column turned right and headed north on 11th Street. They now heard artillery fire from the northern forts. Wright rode by and gave instructions to gather near Crystal (Silver) Springs.

While Sixth Corps troops marched through the capital, Jubal Early's column reached Silver Spring, Maryland. Fortunately for the Federals, he decided to reconnoiter before attacking Fort Stevens. After studying Federal defenses, Early scheduled a major attack for the next morning. Wheaton's command reached the objective about 4:00 p.m. and relieved Veteran Reserve Corps soldiers, War Department clerks, and civilian volunteers now retreating toward the fort. William Acheson, 102nd Pennsylvania, remembered being the first to enter the fortifications. Shortly after arriving, orders came to recover the abandoned picket line. Troops from the 98th, 102nd, and 139th Pennsylvania easily seized the position before sunset but advanced no farther. "Skirmishing continued through the night."[14]

After receiving confirmation of the Sixth Corps's arrival, Early canceled his July 12 assault. He decided instead to probe Federal defenses northwest of Washington. Getty's division, commanded now by Wheaton, spent the day skirmishing. Orders finally came at 5:00 p.m. to push back the enemy picket line and "to occupy, if successful, two strong, wooded hills in our front." Federal batteries from nearby forts opened fire on the Confederate position. While Lincoln watched from Fort Stevens, the First Brigade's (Wheaton's) skirmish line and three regiments from Third Brigade surged forward. They soon learned that Early's line was much stronger than expected, forcing Wheaton to bring up reinforcements from both brigades, including the 102nd Pennsylvania. The division captured both hills but went no farther. Back in the capital, Abner Doubleday received orders from the Department of Washington to "assume command of the force on the south side of the Eastern Branch [Anacostia River]." This would be the closest that Doubleday ever came to receiving a field command after Gettysburg.[15]

Concluding that the day's results were not favorable, Early withdrew after sunset. Crossing the Potomac between the Monocacy and Goose Creek on July 14, the Confederates returned to Virginia. With the threat of invasion evidently eliminated, Couch relieved Rowley at Chambersburg. The brigadier general arrived in Pittsburgh on July 13. Local newspapers considered him a returning hero. "The general has been in charge of the troops in the Cumberland Valley and succeeded in wrestling Hagerstown on Saturday last [July 9], from the hands of the marauders." Rowley formally took command of the Monongahela District. Eight officers and four enlisted men reported for duty, a much smaller contingent than even Camp Berry.[16]

To achieve Curtin's goal of 12,000 men, the state adjutant general assigned western Pennsylvania a quota of 4,000 volunteers and Allegheny County 1,488. After one week, the region's response was no better than lukewarm. Representative Moorhead, Rowley's supporter and the National Party's current nominee for the 22nd District, "delivered a [July 13] speech to spur recruiting in the city." Couch announced from Harrisburg, "Colored troops will be accepted by companies under the late calls for one hundred days. Men will be later organized into regiments." The major general gave Samuel Solan, 9th Pennsylvania Reserves, authority "to recruit a company of colored one hundred days men from Allegheny County." Commanded by white officers, the recruits would "receive the same pay and commutation as other troops," and be transported at no charge to Camp Penn. In spite of Moorhead's, Couch's, and Solan's exhortations, Pittsburgh returned to its preinvasion routine and local volunteering continued to languish.[17]

General Wright and two Sixth Corps divisions followed Early to Poolesville, Maryland. While waiting for reinforcements to catch up, Wright received orders to return to Washington. At Harpers Ferry, David Hunter sent his Second Cavalry Division, commanded by Brig. Gen. William Averell, south. On July 20, they caught up with Early's wagon train at Stephenson's Depot. Here, Averell defeated Confederate forces commanded by Maj. Gen. Stephen Ramseur. After the fighting ended, Brig. Gen. George Crook arrived with Hunter's infantry and took command. The two Federal columns occupied Winchester on July 22. Crook left the next day in hot pursuit of the enemy. Like Stonewall Jackson two years earlier, Early eluded his pursuers and momentarily disappeared from Federal view.[18]

Assuming that the Confederate forces leaving Maryland had rejoined Lee, Grant was ready to pull back the Sixth Corps but Henry Halleck objected. The two generals and Lincoln also disagreed over who should lead a new, separate command to seize and hold the Shenandoah Valley. This distraction coupled with the fact that units from four separate commands — the Middle Department (Lou Wallace) and the Departments of the Susquehanna (Darius Couch), Western Virginia (David Hunter), and Washington (Maj. Gen. Christopher Augur) — were now involved, ended any hope of an effective pursuit through Virginia. Horatio Wright received new orders from Grant to leave Washington and take his two divisions back to Richmond. Jubal Early upset everyone's plans when he soundly defeated Crook's command at Kernstown, Virginia, on July 24. Confederate cavalry chased Crook and Averell north through Winchester, Martinsburg, and finally across the Potomac. The beleaguered Federals regrouped in Hagerstown while their pursuers stopped briefly at Williamsport, Maryland.[19]

Early quickly burst the Federals' bubble by resuming the offensive. Brig. Gen. John McCausland's brigade destroyed Martinsburg, West Virginia's railroad facilities. Reinforced by newly promoted Brig. Gen. Bradley T. Johnson and his brigade, the Confederate column continued north. McCausland, a graduate of VMI and assistant mathematics professor under Thomas Jackson, ordered Johnson to cross the Potomac River at daylight at McCoy's Ford on July 28. Brushing aside enemy pickets, the two Confederate brigades, 2,600 men strong, entered Maryland and headed northwest to Clear Spring.

Here they took on Averell's troopers. Maj. Harry Gilmor, leading the First Regiment and Second Battalion, Maryland Cavalry, promptly drove the Federal forces five miles east toward Hagerstown. Averell withdrew his division from Maryland to Greencastle, Pennsylvania. While Congress still debated how to compensate Pennsylvania for Lee's 1863 invasion, John McCausland moved north, crossed the Mason-Dixon Line, and began reconnoitering the Keystone State.[20]

The only opposition facing McCausland's column was a small detachment of the 6th U. S. Cavalry. Lt. Hancock T. McLean and 44 men departed the Carlisle Barracks in early June and headed southwest, their immediate objective Chambersburg. The next day, they continued on through Greencastle and at Mercersburg turned south. McLean's small command joined William Averell's division and spent the next three weeks picketing the Potomac crossings from Hancock, West Virginia, east to Antietam Creek. The repetitious and boring duty abruptly ended.[21]

"About 3 p. m. July 29 my [McLean's] pickets were driven in from McCoy's Ferry and Cherry Run to Clear Spring from which place they were driven back within two miles of Shimpstown [Pennsylvania]." McLean reformed his men and held the Confederates at bay briefly, then retreated. The lieutenant checked them several times that afternoon but ultimately fell back through Mercersburg around 5:00 p.m. Later, at St. Thomas, five miles west of Chambersburg, a detachment from the 3rd U. S. Cavalry joined McLean. The combined cavalry force was steadily driven back to within two miles of Chambersburg. Reinforced by 40 infantry and a single piece of artillery from Battery A, First New York, the Federals formed a battle line and managed to delay McCausland for about two hours. Finally, outflanked, McLean withdrew through Chambersburg at 5:00 a.m. July 30, stopping in Shippensburg. Averell, who reported to Hunter, not Couch, fell back from Greencastle without engaging the enemy column. Bradley Johnson later acknowledged McLean's efforts. "At 9 p. m. we moved on Chambersburg, which place we reached just before day. My advance had skirmished all night with a party in front and on the outskirts of the town, being fired into with canister from a field piece. Our further progress was delayed until broad day disclosed the weakness of the enemy." Hancock McLean was one of the few Federals who knew what needed to be done and did it that last week in July.[22]

Responding to orders from Major General Halleck, Couch had earlier sent six companies of 100-day volunteers to General Averell at Hagerstown and one company to Maj. Gen. Lew Wallace, most of them recruited in Pittsburgh. This left the major general nothing to fight with outside Chambersburg. Shortly before 4:00 a.m. July 30, Couch and a few remaining staff officers completed evacuating supplies and records and then departed the town on a northbound train. Two hours later, John McCausland formed a line of battle in the fairgrounds overlooking Chambersburg, a mile and a half away. After firing a few artillery rounds, he sent the 21st Virginia Cavalry followed by the 8th and 36th Virginia Infantry, about 500 men, into Chambersburg.[23]

When these regiments were in position, McCausland rode to the Franklin Hotel for breakfast. Major Gilmor arrested some of the leading citizens and took them to the general. Hearing that Jubal Early wanted $500,000 cash or $100,000 gold, the citizens left to raise what they could. After waiting six hours, McCausland decided that the demand would not be met and gave the order, "The town must be burnt." The fires they set destroyed two-thirds of the community. Early considered this act fair restitution for Hunter's raids in the Shenandoah. Once Chambersburg was burning, around 11:00 a.m., the Confederates withdrew and moved west on McConnellsburg, reaching Johnson's Brigade at 5 p.m. General Averell entered Chambersburg three hours later from the direction of Fayetteville. Jubal Early's second invasion was almost over. To many in Pennsylvania, however, Chambersburg marked the beginning, not the end, of this campaign.[24]

Embarrassed twice in less than a month, Washington and Harrisburg now panicked. "The Sixth Corps was marched from Georgetown to Frederick, from Frederick to Harper's Ferry, from Harper's Ferry back again to Frederick." Romney, West Virginia, and Cumberland, Maryland, sent requests for help to Pittsburgh. Rowley could not respond because his remaining five companies of 100-day men had already been sent to General Hunter. Governor Curtin made plans to convene the legislature and announced a second callup of 30,000 100-day men.[25]

Early's second invasion had already induced the citizens of Harrisburg to convene a vigilance committee. In addition to the burning of Chambersburg, July 30 marked the reemergence of former Secretary of War Simon Cameron, now chairman of Harrisburg's Committee of Public Safety. He wired President Lincoln: "Rebels entered Chambersburg at 3 o'clock this morning in three columns. This is fifty miles from here [Harrisburg]. Send us a general fit to command and we will try to take care of ourselves. General Couch is said to be at Bedford." John Hay responded, "The President directs me to refer the enclosed to the Secretary of War." Chairman Cameron publicly recommended that martial law be declared immediately in Harrisburg. General Couch disagreed and from his Harrisburg headquarters that evening sent this reply:

> After having carefully considered the matter, do not believe it is for the interest of the State and country at this present time or moment to comply with your request. I am also of the opinion that it will be productive of more injury than good unless the state looks to Harrisburg to furnish all of the men for her defense.

Both sides had fired their opening round July 30. Couch left the next day for Pittsburgh.[26]

News of a second invasion reached Pittsburgh on July 29. Rumors quickly spread that Early was preparing to attack Pittsburgh; Wheeling, West Virginia; and Cincinnati, Ohio. From Harrisburg, Darius Couch sent Rowley an unsettling dispatch the evening of July 30. He announced that "Averell had driven the Rebels from Chambersburg and that they had retreated westward." General Couch expressed the opinion that "they might intend to come this way [Pittsburgh] and that it would be best to be prepared to meet them." A "furore of excitement" now swept Allegheny County. At 11:00 a.m. Sunday morning, July 31, "a public meeting of citizens [Pittsburgh and Allegheny City] was held at Wilkins Hall for the purpose of taking such measures as might be deemed prudent and necessary, under the exciting circumstance [rebel invasion]." The citizens selected Pittsburgh's mayor James Lowry Jr. to be their chairman.[27]

A motion was made and approved that the chairman "be authorized to appoint a Committee on Home Defense, consisting of fifty members ... to consult with General Rowley, and assist in the organizing of companies and regiments." They later agreed to use the existing Committee of Public Safety, chaired by Gen. Thomas M. Howe, a prominent and successful businessman in Pittsburgh. A second motion followed requiring "General Rowley to declare martial law whenever, in his opinion, it might become necessary to do so." Before a vote could be taken, N. P. Sawyer moved that the chairman "telegraph immediately requesting the presence here of Gen. Buell, Gen. Fremont and Gen. McClellan" to give the committee "the benefits of their counsel and take command of the defenses of the city." This motion "excited considerable ridicule and was laid upon the table." Maj. Russell Errott sarcastically suggested adding James Buchanan to Sawyer's list. Mr. Wesyer felt that there were already competent officers to defend the city and that passing Sawyer's resolution would be an insult to General Rowley. After others had risen to denounce the resolution as being both foolish and impractical, it was dropped from consideration and the public meeting adjourned.[28]

A short time later, the Committee of Public Safety and Rowley met in Mayor Lowry's office and made several decisions that afternoon. First, they asked General Rowley "to appoint suitable persons ... for the purpose of organizing troops for the defense of the two cities and vicinity." Second, business would be suspended and all employers would be asked to assemble their employees the next morning (Monday, August 1) to determine how many would volunteer for local defense. Veteran officers, detailed by General Rowley, would then organize the men into companies and regiments, all reporting to the district commander. Third, if requests from General Rowley and the two mayors to suspend business failed, martial law would be declared immediately. That evening, General Rowley issued a statement: "In accordance with the resolution of the committee appointed by the citizens, I now request the suspension of all business in the cities of Pittsburgh and Allegheny, and all adjoining boroughs, as far as the same is practicable. The time for prompt action is at hand." At 8:00 a.m. Monday, selected officers met the volunteers at local schoolhouses to organize home defense companies.[29]

During the afternoon meeting, Rowley received a message from John Cessna in Bedford, Pennsylvania: "Rebels left McConnellsburg [Pennsylvania] this morning [Sunday, July 31] going southward. Gen. Averell in close pursuit.... No Rebels in this county." A second message soon followed claiming that McCausland's column was heading westward, rather than southward. Estimates of Confederate strength ranged from 500 to 10,000. The *Pittsburgh Commercial* expected the rebels to move north through the Monogahela Valley. Couch informed Rowley that it was absolutely necessary that an army of at least 15,000 men be organized to defend western Pennsylvania. Before adjourning, Pittsburgh's Committee of Public Safety concluded that they had no choice but to prepare for the worst.[30]

Even though the fires in Chambersburg were out, the issue continued to burn elsewhere. Philadelphia, like Harrisburg, voted to accept martial law. Secretary of War Stanton gave the final responsibility to Couch. The general refused Philadelphia's request as he had Harrisburg's and recommended a militia callup in only Pittsburgh. Harrisburg's Committee of Public Safety retaliated July 31 by asking Chairman Cameron to send the president a letter requesting Couch's removal and the appointment of General Cadwaladar to the position of department commander. Born in Philadelphia, Cadwalader served with distinction in the Mexican War and received a promotion to major general April 25, 1862. Since August 1863, he had commanded the post of Philadelphia. Cameron went on to publicly claim, "The unpopularity of Gen. Couch, from his lack of activity, has destroyed his usefulness and has shaken public confidence in him."[31]

Following John Hay's earlier advice, Simon Cameron also wired Stanton that morning. The secretary of war replied at noon:

> General Couch having been assigned to the command of the department by the President, he can only be removed by order of the President, who is not in the city today; but your telegram will be referred to him for his instructions. In the mean time, General Halleck [the Army's Chief of Staff], who is in the general military command under General Grant's instructions, will immediately direct General Couch to assign General Cadwalader to the defense of Harrisburg, according to your wishes.

Stanton's reply failed to stop the unwarranted criticism of Darius Couch.[32]

The *Pittsburgh Gazette* announced August 1, "Gen. Couch is here, and Gen. Rowley is laboring indefatigably to bring things into military trim."

Couch met with the Committee of Public Safety at 9:00 a.m. then issued a general order. First, he informed the local populace "that the enemy are already within ... our state and a much larger force [may be] marching westward." Couch ordered an active force of not less than 15,000 be immediately organized and directed the mayors of Pittsburgh and Allegheny to start signing men up. After receiving enrollment reports from designated authorities, Rowley would take command of all organized companies. The major general revoked the committee's earlier decision to suspend business, but reemphasized, "It is imperative that these enrollments be made without delay."[33]

In spite of rumors and potential threats, the response throughout Pennsylvania to Curtin's militia callup continued to lag. Like Couch in Pittsburgh, Maj. Gen. George Cadwalader now appealed to Philadelphia to respond to Curtin's call but did not specify a quota. The poor response may have resulted from continued criticism of military officials. The *Philadelphia Inquirer* reported August 3: "The excitement along the line of the railroad [Pennsylvania Railroad], against Gen. Couch is most intense. His public acts are being freely criticized, and there is a great deal of indignation manifested." The *Pittsburgh Gazette* followed suit that day. According to "an old citizen of Chambersburg":

> General Couch, whose headquarters were at Chambersburg at the time of the raid, informed the citizens on Friday afternoon last [July 29] at 2:00 PM that the rebels were coming and immediately afterward commenced to pack up his effects and actually left Chambersburg that evening accompanied by all the soldiers then in the town, numbering to our informant about fifty.... Our informant asserts ... that if Gen. Couch had remained in Chambersburg during Friday night and organized the citizens, they in connection with the fifty soldiers would have been abundantly able to prevent the burning of the town. Our informant also says that if Gen. Couch Friday afternoon had telegraphed to Harrisburg for assistance, it would have been possible to reinforce the soldiers and citizens of Chambersburg that night so as to have made impossible the burning of the town on the following day.[34]

Admittedly, the *Gazette* could not "vouch, of course, that the information be correct" but lamely went on:

> If that information be correct, we cannot come to any other conclusion that Gen. Couch manifested great incapacity on the occasion referred to. We cannot otherwise account for his failure to ascertain, as nearly as possible, by means of scouts the real force of the enemy, instead of taking it for granted as he seems to have done that they were in overwhelming numbers.

The editor now remembered:

> On the 4th day of July when the invasion of Maryland was about commencing, Gen. Couch then at Chambersburg acted in much the same way. Without knowing definitely that the Rebels were coming toward Cham-

bersburg, he sent word to all the farmers in the neighborhood to drive their horses and cattle at once. The result was, that the people were panic stricken, while the rebels did not approach near to Chambersburg.

Newspapers in Pennsylvania's three principal cities vilified the commander of the Susquehanna on August 3. No one cared whether McCausland had overwhelming numbers or not. Unable to defend himself, Darius Couch became a convenient scapegoat for everything that had gone wrong the past 30 days. Time failed to improve the situation.[35]

Couch's decision to leave Harrisburg the evening of July 31 and join Rowley in Pittsburgh made the uproar even worse. Harrisburg and Chambersburg became "inflamed against General Couch for not concentrating his attention upon them." To make the situation even worse, "Pittsburgh and Wheeling fancied it was they who were threatened with attack" and demanded more protection than either Couch or Rowley could provide. A reporter observed August 3, "the General [Couch] seemed to take things very coolly and was evidently in no way alarmed at the situation of affairs." Two days later, the major general telegraphed Stanton, "after having made all proper dispositions with general Rowley, I intend leaving for Harrisburg tonight [August 5]."[36]

McCausland and Jones attacked New Creek, Maryland, on August 4. A spate of new rumors quickly spread. Breckinridge was moving toward Wheeling or Pittsburgh. Jubal Early had recrossed the Potomac and occupied Hagerstown. Mosby's and Imboden's cavalry and mounted infantry roamed at will throughout Maryland. The next day, Governor A. G. Curtin issued a new call for 30,000 volunteers to serve during the emergency. Couch's same-day General Order instructed those organized west of Johnstown to rendezvous at Camp Reynolds at Pittsburgh. Earlier that morning, about 300 troops left Camp Reynolds by train for Uniontown. Here a New York battery would join them. The Federals intended to "concentrate a considerable force at this point [Uniontown] for the purpose of securing the country in that vicinity." In another circular "to the People of the Southern Tier of Counties of Pennsylvania," General Couch announced "that a raid by the enemy is not impossible at any time during the summer and coming fall." He called upon the citizens "to put your rifle and shot guns in good order," and to be ready to find "favorable places for cover ... and kill the marauders, recollecting, if they come it is to plunder, destroy, and burn your property." This disheartening circular also contained instructions on how to construct barricades across farm roads.[37]

Pennsylvania's current plight gained nationwide attention. *The New York Times* pointed out, "No state asks and receives as many special favors in the matter of raising troops as Pennsylvania; and yet she never has a corporal's guard to keep the horse thieves from crossing her borders." The tide quickly turned. "General Averell attacked the combined forces of McCausland, Johnson, Gilmor, and McNeil," the morning of August 7 and "completely routed their entire command." In spite of this victory, Governor Curtin addressed a special session of the state legislature August 9. He reminded the assembly of the support given to the national government. From his viewpoint his state had fulfilled all its obligations. Consequently, Pennsylvania had a right to be defended by Federal forces. Recalling Couch's earlier circulars, "How could an agriculture people, in an open country, be expected to rise suddenly and beat back hostile forces which had defeated the organized veteran armies?" The governor severely condemned "the gibes, and sneers, and scoffs, which have been thrown upon the people of Pennsylvania by the newspapers and citizens of other states."[38]

The *Pittsburgh Commercial* announced August 6 that Rowley's adjutant, Albert M. Harper, would command the troops being sent to the Uniontown area, including a full battery. Since Harper was still recovering from his Wilderness wound, Lieutenant Heberton would act as both commissary and quartermaster to the troops being sent from the District of the Monongahela. Many local citizens considered the military activity too little, too late.[39]

Andrew Curtin was not the only one agitated by Early's second invasion. Repeated failures to take control of the Shenandoah Valley upset U. S. Grant even more. On August 1, he ordered Maj. Gen. Philip Sheridan and two cavalry divisions to western Maryland. Grant then telegraphed Henry Halleck to "put Sheridan in command of all troops in the field and to give him instructions to pursue the enemy to the death." Sheridan arrived in Washington on August 3 but Halleck hesitated to take action. In an evening dispatch to his lieutenant general, Lincoln approved Grant's proposal but added, "It will neither be done nor attempted unless you watch it every day and hour and force it." Grant left City Point the following evening for Washington.[40]

While the lieutenant general was en route August 5, Early's troops occupied Hagerstown for the second time. U. S. Grant conferred with Stanton, Halleck, and Lincoln on August 7. They approved a reorganization of existing military departments, giving Phil Sheridan command of the Middle Military Division and the new Army of the Shenandoah. The latter would ultimately consist of the Sixth and Nineteenth Corps, three divisions of cavalry, and a large supply of artillery, about 43,000 effectives. Grant left immediately for General Hunter's headquarters at Monocacy Station, Maryland, where he ordered all the troops in the area to move that night to the Shenandoah valley. Senior to Sheridan who held field command, David Hunter asked to be relieved from duty. Grant accepted this unselfish offer, and Sheridan received orders to come at once from Washington. Jubal Early pulled back his cavalry into West Virginia, ending the current crisis. While newspapers announced these command changes August 8, Grant returned to City Point on the steamer *Diamond*. Sheridan and Hunter went by train to Harpers Ferry.[41]

David Hunter's replacement was only the first of many changes. A cumbersome and overlapping Federal command structure disappeared. Grant and Stanton organized the Middle Military Division to permanently end Confederate threats to Maryland and Pennsylvania. In addition to the newly created Army of the Shenandoah, this division encompassed Hunter's former Department of West Virginia and Couch's Department of the Susquehanna that included Rowley's District of the Monogahela. With headquarters at Harpers Ferry, Sheridan assumed command August 9 and started announcing staff and field assignments immediately.[42]

Early never attacked the Pennsylvania Railroad, Lincoln left Couch alone, and Sheridan took command. The second invasion, however, remained a bitter pill for Darius Couch. Many still felt that he fled Chambersburg without notice on a special train. Political wounds in Philadelphia, Harrisburg, and Pittsburgh continued to fester. The critics demanded their pound of flesh. Thomas Rowley had served two major generals. Abner Doubleday presided over a backwater court-martial. The second was now a political liability to Washington. Like Petersburg on June 19, the brigadier general lacked an effective advocate. For Doubleday, Couch, and Rowley, Early's invasions and the new Army of the Shenandoah proved to be nothing more than lost opportunities.

Resignation

> Our Book Contains no Braver Soldier or True Gentleman than
> Thomas A. Rowley. —*James Onslow, 62nd Pennsylvania*[43]

For the next few months, Thomas Rowley dealt with real and imagined Confederate threats, some of them directed against Erie, Pennsylvania. John Harper was president of the Bank of Pittsburgh and a close friend of Edwin Stanton. He supported Rowley's 1862 promotion to brigadier general. His second son, Albert M., joined the 139th Pennsylvania on August 25, 1862. Rowley assisted Albert in securing an appointment as regimental adjutant. Severely wounded in the Wilderness, Lieutenant Harper slowly recovered in Washington. On August 17, he received a promotion to captain and an assignment to the District of the Monongahela. Rumors arose in September of another Confederate invasion. Rowley again gave Captain Harper command of a small force of infantry, cavalry, and artillery stationed near Uniontown but the enemy never materialized. In October, the general made contact with his friend and former defense counsel, Edmund Dana.[44]

After the court-martial, Colonel Dana and his 143rd Pennsylvania marched into the Wilderness. Wounded and captured May 5, he set out on a long journey south. Reaching Charleston, South Carolina, in June, Dana was one of 50 Federal officers "placed under the fire of their own guns." (Appendix IV) Word reached Charleston in July of Rowley's acquittal. Exchanged on August 3, Dana rejoined his command in early September outside Petersburg and led them through the battles at Hatcher's Run and the Weldon Railroad. Rowley wrote Dana on October 8 and expressed pleasure with his friend's return but regret at the continued absence of a promotion.

> I am sorry you have not the command of the Brigade but I think there is a good time coming. I have been talking with some friends (General Moorhead our member of Congress) in regard to your promotion and will work as well as talk for I know your value as an officer and am sure if the facts were known to the President, you would get what you deserve [a general's star].

With some bitterness Rowley continued.

> I would [have] liked much to have had the command of the Olde Brigade [First Brigade, Third Division, First Corps] but as General Warren said that they did not want me and said to General Grant they had no confidence in me, I was ordered to Washington. I hope General Warren will get his reward for telling an untruth but I should not mummer for I have a very agreeable place at home with my family.

He went on to discuss the summer campaign against Early, his current staff in Pittsburgh, and the wedding of William L. Wilson, his former aide, then abruptly turned to members of the court-martial.

> Did you ascertain from General Ward what side he was on at my trial? How unfortunate all the officers of that court have been. Robinson lost a leg, Generals [James] Rice and [Alexander] Hays killed, [Frank] Wheaton dismissed or asked to resign, [William] Morris wounded, and [John] Ward is in difficulty. Wheaton will get his reward some of these days ... Neil [Thomas Neill] has lost his command.

Rowley went on to speculate about the April verdict, "I believe the court stood 5 for convection and 4 for acquittal and that Eustice [Eustis] and Wheaton were two of the most bitter." He closed on a warmer note, commenting on Dana's efforts to recover the sword Rowley surrendered either July 1, 1863, at Gettysburg or April 21, 1864, at Culpeper, Virginia.[45]

Edmund Dana received a December letter informing him that Rowley now belonged to a military commission in Harrisburg trying rebel spies from Canada and draft resistors from Columbia County, Pennsylvania. At first, Rowley tried to console his friend.

> I have been looking for your promotion anxiously and have been speaking to my friends in the House and Senate about you. I expect to be in Wash-

ington in a few days and will ask my friends to have your name brought
before the President.... Has General Warren never sent your name up?

With regret and sadness, he turned to a familiar topic:

> Have you ever said anything about my case to General Warren? He was
> under the impression that my old command did not want me and I believe
> said so to General Grant. I would like to be with you. Give my kind
> regards to all the officers of the old command and say to them I have been
> watching their army this campaign and I have never found them wanting
> in a single instance and would glory to command them once more.

Rowley told Dana that Alfred McCalmont had left Harrisburg in November
to take command of a black regiment assigned to Major General Butler. Evidently misinformed, Colonel McCalmont and the 208th Pennsylvania Volunteer Infantry, a one-year unit, departed Camp Curtin on September 13.
Looking ahead, Rowley said that he would try to secure a leave and visit Dana
in February 1865. In what may have been his last letter as a commissioned
officer, he never discussed resignation.[46]

About the time he wrote to Dana in October, one company from the
109th Pennsylvania and two from the Veteran Reserve Corps reported to the
brigadier general in Pittsburgh. James Moorhead, representing Rowley's 22nd
district, enjoyed reelection to Congress in November. Moorhead either could
not or would not alter the events leading to Rowley's forced resignation.[47]

On December 1, 1864, another reorganization took place. The Department of the Susquehanna ceased to exist and Darius Couch left for Tennessee.
With the Confederacy no longer an offensive threat, the complex array of military departments and districts in the East was superfluous. Stanton resur-
rected Robert Patterson's Department of Pennsylvania and placed Major
General Cadwalader in command with headquarters in Philadelphia. On
December 23, Rowley sent Adjutant General Thomas a brief letter: "I most
respectfully tender my resignation as Brigadier General Volunteers to date
from February first A. D. 1865." No reason was given and none can be found.
Thomas forwarded the letter to Henry Halleck, who returned it December
28 with the notation, "approved to take effect immediately."[48]

Rowley issued an order December 20 informing Pittsburgh that "a salute
of one hundred guns will be fired by Battery A, 1st New York Artillery from
the hill over Bayardstown tomorrow ... at 12 o'clock M, in honor of the recent
great victories achieved by Major General [George] Thomas ... in Tennessee."
A similar salute was fired December 27 in recognition of William T. Sherman's accomplishments. Albert M. Harper, A. A. G., signed both orders, the
general's last. During the Christmas holidays, he journeyed to Harrisburg
and Philadelphia, most likely to say good-bye to friends and associates.[49]

The War Department announced December 31 that Lincoln had accepted
Rowley's resignation effective December 29. First Lt. George A. Heberton,

Brig. Gen. Thomas Rowley resigned his commission December 23, 1864. Courtesy of USAMHI.

ADC, was mustered out and honorably discharged December 27, "to date November 30th, 1864, he being a supernumerary officer." First Lt. John T. Denniston, ADC, resigned December 31. Department returns listed General Rowley as commandant of the Monongahela Department from July through December 1864. The January 1865 entry was "Resigned." Following instructions from the Department of Pennsylvania Headquarters, Capt. G. P. Davis assumed command of the District of the Monongahela January 10, 1865, and announced, "The Military Post of Pittsburgh is for the present abolished." Physically unable to return to the 1 39th, Capt. Albert Harper joined Cadwalader's Philadelphia staff. On January 30, Edwin Stanton sent another long list of appointments to the Senate including a promotion of Col. John M. Oliver, 15th Michigan Volunteers, to brigadier general effective January 12. Oliver filled the vacancy created by Rowley's resignation.[50]

11. Aftermath

Few men were better or more favorably known in Pittsburgh
than General Rowley. — *New York Times*, May 15, 1892 [9]

Thomas A. Rowley

Before the war ended, George McFarland set out to write a history of
the First Corps's Third Division. He asked its former officers and enlisted men
to submit "a satisfactory biography of himself ... incidents of the camp, the
march, the hospital and the battlefield ... plus copies of official reports, orders,
circulars, addresses, &c." A submission from Pittsburgh reached McFarland
in late July.

> July 23, 1865
>
> Dear Col.
>
> I should have attended to this matter before this but I have been absent
> from the City for some weeks.... I hardly know what to write you, here
> goes.
> I was born in this city and have held a different office in both the city
> and county. I served in the Mexican War first as a Lieut in the First Pa
> Vols. and 2nd as a captain of Company H. D. C. and Maryland Regiment.
> Was at the taking of Vera Cruz and National Bridge and different other
> battles. Have been in the U. S. Service since the Pronouncement of the
> Rebellion. 1st as Col. of the 13th Pa Vols. three months men, 2nd as Col.
> of the Old 13th Pa Vols. (now called the 102nd) three years men. Was
> appointed Brig Genl 29 Nov. 1862. Took part in the following battles
> Yorktown, Williamsburg, Fair Oaks (2 days), White Oak swamp, Charles
> City X roads, Malvern Hill, Chantilly, Antietam, Fredericksburg, Chancel-
> lorsville, and Gettysburg (3 days). Was severely wounded in the head at
> Fair Oaks. Had horse killed under me at Gettysburg.
> I hope Col. you can make something out of this. It is impossible for me
> to write anything more. I think this covers all my life in short hand.
>
> Very truly your friend
> Thomas A. Rowley

Ten months later, McFarland received James Onslow's seven-page biography of Thomas Rowley that concluded, "Our book contains no braver soldier or true gentleman than Thomas A. Rowley."[2]

The willingness of veterans to submit material and buy a copy exceeded McFarland's initial expectations. A subsequent update sent "to the Officers and Enlisted Men of the Old Third Division of the First Corps" announced his decision "to enlarge the size and scope of the work." At first McFarland had "intended to issue a 12 'mo' volume of 350 pages" but now found this to be insufficient, and believed "that the increased cost of a larger and finer edition would be cheerfully paid." The proposed larger volume, 8 "vo," would contain "steel portraits of 18 (perhaps more) officers, [and] diagrams of battlefields" at prices of $2.50 and $3.00. "Subscribers and those wishing copies of the book" should "remit their orders and money at once." The colonel misjudged the readiness of the Third Division's veterans to "cheerfully" pay more and his literary effort ended unsuccessfully. Today, the submitted biographies, personal records, and battle reports can be found at the Pennsylvania State Archives. McFarland left no explanation as to why he never published a divisional history.[3]

On February 13, 1867, President Johnson nominated Thomas Rowley to be "marshal of the United States for the Western District of Pennsylvania, in the place of Samuel McKelvy, whose nomination was not confirmed." Rowley's nomination was referred to the Judiciary Committee, chaired by Senator Lyman Trumbull, a moderate Republican from Illinois. The committee reported favorably and the Senate confirmed Thomas Rowley as the new Federal marshal in Pittsburgh on February 25.[4]

After less than a year, Johnson removed Rowley from office in January 1868. The president proposed Robert H. Kerr as Rowley's successor January 28. This time, however, the Judiciary Committee reported adversely. The Senate rejected several of Johnson's nominations on July 17, 1868, including Kerr's. A week later, the Judiciary Committee received the nomination of H. L. Brown to be marshal in place of Rowley. Senator Roscoe Conkling, a New York Republican and antagonist of the president, recommended, "that it lie on the table." The Senate, by unanimous consent, voted on a large block of presidential nominations including Brown's and "ordered that said nominations lie on the table." Trumbull later voted against Johnson's impeachment. The Pittsburgh position remained vacant until President U. S. Grant nominated Alexander Murdoch to be marshal of western Pennsylvania. Senator Trumbull reported favorably April 7, 1869, and the Senate approved Murdoch the next day.[5]

Returning veterans reorganized the Washington Infantry and elected Rowley captain on February 18, 1870. A year later, he became a brigadier general in charge of the Third Brigade, 18th Division, Pennsylvania Militia. Rowley returned to the contracting business but evidently never ran for office

Seated on the front row's extreme left, Thomas Rowley attended the 102nd Pennsylvania's 1878 reunion on Pittsburgh's south side. From *History of the Washington Infantry* and courtesy of William Phillis.

again. Survivors of the 102nd held their first official reunion August 16, 1875. Those present decided to organize a permanent regimental association and elected Thomas Rowley its first president.[6]

The brigadier assisted former comrades in filing their pension claims. A need then arose to file his own claim. On January 30, 1878, Dr. M. P. Morrison completed an officer's certificate of disability that described the Fair Oaks injury. The next day, Rowley filed a pension application stating that because of the 1862 head wound, he saw little with his left eye and endured severe migraines. In April, a board of surgeons concluded that Rowley was one-fourth incapacitated and granted him a pension of $7.50 per month. After an investigation by the Adjutant General's Office, the War Department gave final approval July 14, 1878.[7]

In late 1883, Rowley experienced a mild stroke that partially paralyzed his left side. Facing financial as well as physical problems, he requested a pension increase February 18, 1884. A month later, the general's disability increased to one-half and Rowley's pension doubled to $15 per month. On June 24, 1886, Congress approved by Special Act No. 422 a second increase of $10 per month effective immediately. Except for one summer spent in Ireland, he remained close to western Pennsylvania. Thomas Rowley faced one more ordeal.[8]

In August 1889, members of the 102nd, 134th, and 137th Pennsylvania Volunteers held a joint reunion in Butler, 35 miles north of Pittsburgh. The formal program ended August 15 but several guests, including Rowley, decided to stay another night in Butler. Three coaches filled with veterans and their wives departed Butler the next day at 2:35 p.m. on a West Penn express train to Pittsburgh. Twenty-five minutes passed and the train started crossing Bridge #6 over Buffalo Creek. With no warning, the first passenger car derailed, breaking both couplers. The car rolled over and tumbled down a 15-foot embankment, coming to rest upside down in the creek.[9]

One end of a bridge rail broke loose and came through the second car's floor. This car also derailed, tipped over, but did not careen down the embankment. Three were killed in the first car, one a veteran from the 102nd. Most of the survivors, including Rowley, found themselves pinned in the wreckage. A relief train left Pittsburgh at 6:15 p.m. It returned to the city shortly after 11:00 p.m. carrying the dead and injured. Bruised around the head and shoulders, Rowley "was carried out on a stretcher. His gray hair tumbled about his smoke-begrimed face. The old general was placed in an ambulance and taken to his home on Devillier Street." *The Pittsburgh Post* reported that the bridge rails had spread because of rotten ties. Railroad management claimed that the accident was unavoidable.[10]

Shortly after the Butler reunion, Rowley's health began to steadily decline. George W. Perkins had served under the general in the Washington Infantry and the 13th and 102nd Pennsylvania. On January 30, 1891, the survivors organized the Washington Infantry Veteran's Corps with Perkins as its secretary. They participated in a local parade February 13 and the secretary recorded:

> The Veteran Corps was assigned the position of honor and in addition to carrying the two beautiful silk Guidons also carried the old torn Battle Flags of the old 13th and the 102nd Penna. Regt. that were carried through the war from the battle of Falling Waters in 1861 to Five Forks April 1865. The old veterans marched well all things considered and came in for a good share of applause at many points on the line of march. It was a matter of universal regret that our old Commander Genl. Thomas A. Rowley was unable to walk with us, but the Old Veteran put in an appearance in a carriage and started out with us but in some manner got flanked on the line of march and was lost for the greater portion of the Route.[11]

At 5:00 a.m. Saturday, May 14, 1892, Robert Rowley found that his father had died during the night, reportedly from heart failure. The Washington Infantry called a special meeting that evening to take action. Mexican War veterans, members of the 102nd Pennsylvania, and the Union Veteran Legion also met and passed appropriate resolutions. Sunday, Company A, Washington Infantry, "turned out strong to pay the last sad tribute to its honored dead." The *Pittsburgh Commercial Gazette* credited Rowley with commanding the First Corps after John Reynolds's July 1 death at Gettysburg. No doubt, the brigadier would have found that claim ironic. In a five-paragraph obituary, *The New York Times* correctly reported that Rowley "took command of the Third Division [at Gettysburg]" and in 1864 had resigned his commission and returned to Pittsburgh. The *Pittsburgh Post* devoted a single paragraph to the general. Family and veterans attended a May 16 funeral service at the Webster Avenue home, followed by internment in Allegheny Cemetery. Buried nearby was Mary Ann, his wife of 37 years. Before her October 15, 1887, death, she had given birth to five children. Two daughters died before age 6. One daughter and two sons, Robert and Harry T., reached adulthood. Neither son had children. Unlike his friend Alexander Hays, the general's gravesite is not included in Allegheny Cemetery's "Points of Interest" brochure and is easily forgotten on Memorial Day.[12]

The Arresting Parties

George Meade accepted Clayton E. Rogers's resignation and honorably discharged him from military service July 14, 1863. The lieutenant who arrested Rowley on Cemetery Hill returned to Wisconsin. He raised a full company and rejoined the army February 1865 as captain, Company B, 50th Wisconsin Infantry. Assigned to the western theater of operations, the regiment served in Missouri. Using his earlier experience with McDowell, Doubleday, and Wadsworth, Captain Rogers joined Maj. Gen. John Pope's staff and became provost marshal for the district of central Missouri. After Appomattox, he spent time on court-martial boards and special commissions. Honorably mustered out January 6, 1866, Rogers resumed working as a sawmill operator.[13]

Rufus Dawes, who carried out Rogers's arrest order, later led the 6th Wisconsin, Cutler's brigade, Wadsworth's division, into the Wilderness. They also fought at Laurel Hill (Spotsylvania) with Cutler commanding the division and W. W. Robinson the brigade. The 6th crossed the North Anna River on May 23 and successfully turned back an assault by A. P. Hill. At Bethesda Church, Dawes commanded three regiments, 6th and 7th Wisconsin, and 19th Indiana. During the march to Cold Harbor, Col. E. S. Bragg relieved William Robinson as brigade commander. At Petersburg on June 19, Cutler's division charged Beauregard's fortifications that afternoon, losing a third of the men as killed and wounded. In early July, Cutler proposed combining the 2nd, 6th, and 7th Wisconsin into a single regiment with Dawes as its colonel. State authorities in Madison approved this change but the War Department did not.[14]

Dawes was not offered a full colonel's commission that June because the 6th Wisconsin's number of effectives fell below the manpower minimum. On August 10, 1864, his term of enlistment expired and he left the army. Returning home, Rufus Dawes became a wholesale lumber merchant in Marietta, Ohio. He did receive on March 13, 1865, a promotion to brevet brigadier general of volunteers for his meritorious services during the war.[15]

The first public discussion of what had happened on Cemetery Hill that July 1 evening occurred in the *Chippewa Herald*'s January 4, 1884, issue. A two-column tribute to Clayton E. Rogers, who had recently departed Chippewa Falls for Hayward, Wisconsin, contained a sketch written by Rufus Dawes. Approximately half of the article focused on Rowley's arrest. Dawes lavished praise on Rogers "for his cool, clear-headed, and quick-witted actions [and who] did more than any other one man to get the troops in line of battle." It then went on to quote Robert E. Lee: "the appearance of a strong line of battle on Culp's Hill caused him [Ewell] to withhold the attack." The incident gained state and possibly national attention when "A Gallant Officer" later appeared in the February 3, 1884, edition of the *Milwaukee Sunday Telegraph.*[16]

The article's timing is not clear. First elected to Congress in 1880, the Republicans renominated Dawes two years later but he lost the election. Whether Dawes or Rogers were considering a run for political office in 1884 cannot be determined. Five years later, Rufus Dawes tried but failed to secure the Republican nomination for governor of Ohio.[17]

Court-Martial Participants — Members of the Court

> It was a war in which officers from regiment to division
> level were required to display personal courage in
> the field of fire — targets on horseback. —*Richard Matthews*[18]

A sweeping tragedy unfolded as the members of Rowley's court marched into the Wilderness and later fought at Spotsylvania. By July 1, 1864, eight of the nine brigadiers had lost their life, health, or reputation, Frank Wheaton being the only exception. For many, the price they paid that spring exceeded the defendant's loss. Rowley's October 8 letter to Dana briefly mentioned what each general officer had sustained. A detailed discussion follows.

On the morning of May 5, 1864, Henry Heth's division, A. P. Hill's corps, marched east along the Orange Plank Road. Pushing aside Federal cavalry, Hill threatened to drive a wedge between Warren's Fifth Corps and Hancock's Second. For Meade and Grant, the key was holding the Brock Road intersection. Under orders to attack, Hancock advanced two Second Corps divisions, David Birney's and Brig. Gen. Gershom Mott's. Already in position, George Getty grew impatient and pushed ahead before Birney and Mott arrived. His two brigades north of the Orange Plank Road, Eustis's and Wheaton's, were stopped and fell back. Coming up on Getty's right, Alexander Hays led his brigade forward. Thick woods and heavy undergrowth isolated the regiments, ending command integrity. Hays tried to rally the 63rd Pennsylvania. A bullet struck his head and he fell to the ground. Col. Horace Porter later described Grant's reaction to the news.

> General Grant was by no means a demonstrative man, but upon learning the intelligence I brought, he was visibly affected. He was seated upon the ground with his back against a tree, still whittling pine sticks. He sat for a time without uttering a word, and then speaking in a low voice and pausing between sentences said, "Hays and I were cadets together for three years. We served for a time in the same regiment in the Mexican War. He was a noble man and a gallant officer. I am not surprised that he met his death at the head of his troops; it was just like him. He was a man who would never follow, but would always lead in battle."

Hays was later buried in Pittsburgh's Allegheny Cemetery. In 1867, Lieutenant General Grant visited the gravesite and paid an affectionate tribute to the memory of his fallen classmate.[19]

The afternoon of May 5, Alexander Webb's brigade, positioned south of the Orange Plank Road intersection, stopped the Confederates from capturing the Brock Road. The next day Frank Wheaton, Henry Eustis, Alexander Webb, and James Rice fought north of the Plank Road under James Wadsworth. Longstreet's flank attack that morning first broke Birney's line and then Wadsworth's. Once again, Hancock was fighting to hold the Brock Road. Lee's final attack stalled and the Wilderness campaign ended. The opposing armies moved on to Spotsylvania. At 4:30 a.m. May 12, Hancock's corps assaulted and captured the Confederate salient or Mule Shoe. As the Federals regrouped to break the enemy's second line, Lee counterattacked, driving the Second Corps back. Hours of intense hand-to-hand fighting followed. At sunset, Hancock still held the outer line, Lee the inner. Severely wounded, Alexander Webb was fighting for his life in a nearby field hospital. "The bullet which struck him had passed through the corner of the eye and came out behind his ear." The brigadier not only survived but 10 days later was "detailed for temporary special recruiting service."[20]

That fall, first Hancock then Meade recommended Webb for promotion, whether by brevet or otherwise. November 2, Stanton and Meade agreed that as of August 1, 1864, Alexander S. Webb held a brevet appointment to major general of volunteers. They formally announced the promotion November 12. Relieved from duty in New York City, Webb returned to the Army of the Potomac on January 11, 1865, and served as George Meade's chief of staff until Appomattox. On May 31, Meade added his name to the list of corps and divisional commanders who should be promoted to major general in the regular army as vacancies occurred. While serving as lieutenant colonel, 44th Infantry, Webb requested and received a discharge in December 1870 to accept the presidency of the City College of New York.[21]

On August 27, 1883, veterans of the 72nd Pennsylvania Volunteers gathered in Gettysburg to dedicate their Cemetery Ridge monument. One of the speakers was their former brigade commander, Alexander Webb. Reflecting on his right flank that earlier July 3 afternoon, he said, "There was 'old' Alex. Hays, a glorious fighter, probably a man without a newspaper in his interest. He tells of his front without one attempt to take from any one their laurels fairly won." Webb later remarked that there was "no braver, and but few more observing officers" on the Gettysburg field than Alexander Hays. Time heals most wounds.[22]

Following the court-martial, Henry L. Eustis resumed command of the Fourth Brigade, George Getty's Sixth Corps Division. The brigade fought in the Wilderness (relieved May 5 by Alexander Hays), Spotsylvania, North Anna, and Cold Harbor. While George Meade began quietly moving four army corps out of the Cold Harbor lines and south toward the James River, Charles Dana sent a June 12 dispatch to Stanton:

> General Owen [Joshua T., Brigade commander, John Gibbon's Second Corps Division] is under arrest for misconduct in face of the enemy and ordered to Fort Monroe, where court will sit to try him. Same court will try General Ward [John Hobart, Brigade Commander, David Birney's Second Corps Division]. General Eustis is relieved of his command and ordered to Washington. He is to be informed that if he does not resign, charges of neglect of duty and general inefficiency will be preferred against him. He is said to eat opium.

Grant announced that Eustis "is relieved from duty with the Army of the Potomac, and will at once proceed to Washington, D. C. and report to the Adjutant-General of the Army and await orders." Four days later, Stanton ordered him to Cambridge, Massachusetts, where he was to remain until he received new orders. Eustis resigned June 27, 1864, stating impaired health. What specifically triggered Dana to take this action against Eustis is not known. Twenty-two months of continuous field service no doubt made the general's health problems worse. A narcotic may have provided relief during the Overland campaign.[23]

John Henry Hobart Ward, former commander of the First Brigade, Birney's division, was also mentioned in Dana's June 12 dispatch. As Alexander Hays had already done on the Federal right, Ward moved his brigade into position the afternoon of May 5 to support Getty's left, south of the Orange Plank Road. Three regiments were committed but accomplished little. Before

On April 27, 1883, Alexander Webb made peace with his Gettysburg antagonist, Alexander Hays. Courtesy of USAMHI.

long, Mott's nearby division started giving way and then collapsed. Ward pushed his remaining regiments forward and held the line, safeguarding the Brock Road behind them. Overnight, Birney made plans to attack at dawn, break through the enemy lines, and seize Lee's supply train. Ward's brigade south of the Plank Road pushed forward at 5:00 a.m. Initially successful, they joined in the rout of A. P. Hill's two divisions. Longstreet arrived around

7:00, however, and before noon had pushed the Federals back to the morning's starting point. That afternoon, Robert E. Lee set out to wrest the Brock Road from Hancock. During this fighting, brush near the Plank Road caught fire and the resulting smoke drifted into Hancock's lines. Unable to see their enemy, some of Mott's men broke and fled eastward, abandoning the Brock Road. The resulting panic spread north to Ward's regiments.[24]

As Mott's and Ward's men streamed to the rear, artillery caissons at the Plank and Brock Road intersection started pulling back to join the infantry. While trying to stem the rout a mile behind or east of the vacated rifle pits, Col. Charles Morgan, Hancock's staff, saw on one of the caissons "Gen. Ward riding through his troops but making no exertion to rally them." Finding that the general wasn't wounded, Morgan said that "he had better get off that caisson and help rally his command." Ward complied and soon led several hundred men back to Brock Road. Two officers from Birney's staff later submitted statements supporting Morgan's story.

Until this incident, David Birney felt that "Ward had maintained a high reputation in the country and Army for bravery and soldierly qualities, and before charges are made against him, or he is placed under arrest, I hope he will be heard by Major General Hancock." The brigadier got his audience with Hancock and the corps commander decided to give him a second chance.[25]

The army moved to Spotsylvania and on May 12, Hancock launched his dawn assault against the Bloody Angle. David Birney was on the field positioning Brig. Gen. Samuel S. Carroll's brigade (Gibbon's division) when he saw Ward walking to the rear for a horse. Birney told one of his aides to secure a mount and ordered Ward to rejoin his brigade. Before this could be done, however, the brigadier general encountered Winfield Scott Hancock, who later described the scene. "Along the enemy's works ... I noticed Gen Ward laboring under great excitement, was disposed to do some things which I thought foolish. He was being reckless ... I warned him to be careful and obey my directions.... His appearance and actions indicated that he had been drinking more than proper."[26]

Hancock informed Birney, who went to see for himself and immediately placed Ward under arrest. On June 12, Grant instructed Meade to relieve the brigadier general at once and send him to Fortress Monroe for trial. The court-martial never took place. Regis DeTrobriand replaced Ward, who honorably mustered out of service July 18, 1864. In spite of extensive lobbying by Ward's supporters, Stanton refused to revoke the dismissal order.[27]

On the morning of May 5, 1864, Thomas Neill's brigade was detached from Getty's Second Division and remained with the Sixth Corps. During Longstreet's counterattack the next morning, George Getty was seriously wounded south of the Orange Plank Road and carried off the field. That eve-

A former court member, Brig. Gen. John H.H. Ward's army career ended at Spotsylvania. Courtesy of USAMHI.

ning, Neill's command played a key role in stopping Ewell's flank attack on Sedgwick's right. The next day, he took command of the Second Division and later fought at Spotsylvania and Cold Harbor before moving on to Petersburg. With no explanation, U. S. Grant's Special Orders No. 40 announced

June 21 that Neill was relieved from duty in the Sixth Corps. Assigned to Benjamin Butler's Department of Virginia, he became the Eighteenth Corps's inspector general.[28]

September 12, Grant relieved the brigadier general from duty in the Eighteenth Corps and sent him to Washington. In late October, the War Department issued orders for Neill to report to Major General Sheridan," commanding the newly created Middle Military Division. After a few days, Sheridan directed Neill to report for duty to the commanding officer of the Sixth Corps. The major general changed his mind September 20 and sent Neill to Martinsburg instead. The *Army and Navy Journal* reported October 1, "General Neal [sic] has been relieved from duty with the Eighteenth corps and ordered to report for duty with Major-General Sheridan." A week later, it announced, "Neill is in command of the post at Martinsburg, Va." Edwin Stanton sent a puzzling October 2 query to Brig. Gen. John D. Stevenson at Harpers Ferry. "Do you know anything about General Neill, commanding at Martinsburg? What are his antecedents?" A squabble had already developed as to whether Neill reported to Stevenson or had an independent command. Stevenson replied to Stanton:

> Upon receiving telegram of Major General Halleck, directing me to assume command of all forces in this district, including Martinsburg and lower Shenandoah Valley, I immediately communicated the order to General Neill. Yesterday I visited him ... when he stated that he considered himself aggrieved by the order [Neill was senior], and informed me that he had applied to be relieved.

The War Department relieved Thomas Neill on October 3 and instructed him to report to the adjutant general for orders. The *Journal* announced October 15: "Brigadier-General Neil (sic) has, at his own request, been relieved of the command at Martinsburg, Va."[29]

Two weeks passed, then Stanton sent Neill back to Sheridan. On October 27, the major general gave the brigadier "the duty of inspecting that portion of the Department of West Virginia west of Martinsburg." Sheridan's assistant adjutant general sent a dispatch that listed specific duties and closed, "You are directed to report frequently to these headquarters your address. Special instructions will be sent you, from time to time, as may be necessary." Thomas Neill disappeared for the rest of the war.[30]

Except for Brig. Gen. Henry Baxter's brigade that fought with Wadsworth May 5 and 6, John Robinson's Fifth Corps Division saw little action in the Wilderness. With Robinson in the lead, Warren's corps made a forced march the night of May 7–8, their goal being the seizure of the Spotsylvania crossroads. Maj. Gen. Richard Anderson, who had replaced a wounded James Longstreet, won the race. Before Robinson could organize his command, he received orders to charge the Confederate position. The brigadier led the first assault at Laurel Hill. It failed and he was shot in the left knee. Col. Theodore Lyman, a member of Meade's staff, remembered that this "division behaved badly. Robinson rode in among them, calling them to attack with the bayonet when he was badly shot ... and carried from the field." His leg was amputated that evening. Brevetted major general of volunteers June 27, 1864, Robinson reported to Major General Dix and commanded the Military District of Northern New York (Albany) until the war ended. The War Department directed October 8 that he be "assigned to duty according to his brevet rank of major general."[31]

James Rice's Second Brigade, Wadsworth's division, fought hard May 5 near the Orange Turnpike and then north of the Orange Plank Road May 6. It suffered heavy casualties both days. The division, commanded now by Lysander Cutler, took up a position at Laurel Hill, west of Spotsylvania, on May 8. Two days later, Rice led another charge at 4:00 p.m. against Richard Anderson's First Corps. A musket ball shattered one of his thighbones. Failing to recover from the amputation, the brigadier died before sunset. The *Philadelphia Inquirer* reported that with his last breath, Rice begged "his attendants to turn him over so that he might die with his face to the enemy." Lyman recorded in his diary that while lying on a stretcher, Rice called out to Meade, "Don't you give up this fight! I am willing to lose my life, if it is to be; but don't you give up this fight!" A volunteer general like Rowley, James Rice's bravery and performance during these two battles were exceptional.[32]

William Hopkins Morris's First Brigade, James Ricketts's Third Division, Sedgwick's Sixth Corps, was not engaged May 5. The following afternoon, Robert E. Lee and Richard Ewell agreed to an evening attack on Sedgwick's exposed right flank. Near sunset, John B. Gordon led the opening assault. Initially, it seemed to be a repeat of Chancellorsville with two Federal brigades swept aside. Neill's command, the third in line, formed a double line that bent but did not break. In reserve, Morris initially collected stragglers then moved his men forward to support Neill. Around 9:00 p.m., Gordon gave up the attack. The Federals moved to Spotsylvania. Here on May 9, enemy musketry killed John Sedgwick and severely wounded William Morris. After his recovery, the War Department assigned Morris to a court of inquiry in late June. He later received a brevet to major general of volunteers.[33]

For two days, Wheaton's brigade saw hard fighting along the Brock Road in the Wilderness. After being wounded in the shoulder May 6, Getty initially gave his division to Frank Wheaton, who was the senior brigade commander present. The next day, Neill assumed and retained divisional command until Grant relieved him June 21. Succeeding Neill, Wheaton resumed brigade command when George Getty returned from medical leave. In early July, Jubal Early moved north and threatened the capital. Leaving

Petersburg, Virginia, the Second Division disembarked at Washington on July 11. Wheaton attacked the enemy lines outside Fort Stevens with a reinforced brigade. Horatio Wright's Sixth Corps chased Early across the Potomac but remained in Maryland. On July 17, Wheaton received temporary command of the Third Division. Two weeks later, Early recrossed the Potomac and burned Chambersburg, Pennsylvania. Following the September 19 victory at Winchester, Frank Wheaton received permanent command of the First Division. Wright later recommended the brigadier for promotion based on his performance at Winchester and Fisher's Hill. Early's final defeat occurred at Cedar Creek on October 19.[34]

Wright's Corps left the Shenandoah Valley and returned to Petersburg on December 6. Wheaton received a brevet to major general in both the regular army and volunteers, and appeared on Lincoln's December 29, 1864, list of officers "hereby assigned to duty according to their brevet rank." Brevet Maj. Gen. Frank Wheaton led the First Division to Appomattox. Like Alexander Webb, he also appeared on Meade's June 6, 1865, list of officers to be promoted as vacancies occurred. Frank Wheaton was the only court member who did not lose his life, a limb, health, or reputation during Grant's Overland campaign. The basis for Rowley's statement in his October 8 letter to Dana, "Wheaton dismissed or asked to resign," could not be found.[35]

The Prosecution

DeWitt C. McCoy commanded the 83rd Pennsylvania from the Wilderness to Petersburg. The regiment's original term of service expired September 18, 1864, and McCoy mustered out October 14. On April 25, 1865, he was brevetted colonel, effective August 1, 1864, "for gallant and distinguished services at the battles of Spotsylvania and North Anna." McCoy resumed his Meadville law practice.[36]

Craig Wadsworth received permission from General Torbert to visit his father in the Wilderness the morning of May 6. Shortly after his son's departure, James Wadsworth was mortally wounded on the Orange Plank Road. The president accepted Craig's July 16 resignation. He was later brevetted lieutenant colonel and colonel of volunteers March 13, 1865, "for gallant courage in the engagements at Cold Harbor and Trevillian Station, Virginia."[37]

Lysander Cutler led his brigade into the Wilderness where a shell fragment struck him in the face May 6. In spite of constant pain from this injury, he succeeded a mortally wounded Wadsworth as Fourth Division commander. On September 19, George Meade sent Stanton a lengthy list of officers recommended for brevet commissions. Cutler received an endorsement for major general based on "constant and faithful services in this campaign and for wound at Globe Tavern [Weldon Railroad]." The secretary of war took no immediate action on the list. Finding himself unable to mount a horse without assistance, the brigadier general requested to be relieved from field duty that fall. Grant sent him "to visit the Middle and Eastern States to hasten the forwarding to the front of regimented and detachments of troops that have recently entered the service." On October 20, the War Department gave him a 25 day leave of absence. The general's aide, 1st Lt. Thomas Miller, remained in New York City. Partially recovered, Cutler took command of the Jackson, Michigan, Draft Rendezvous on November 18, 1864. Lt. Earl M. Rogers, Clayton's brother and former aide to Wadsworth, reported to Jackson on December 2 to be assigned to temporary light duty. In February 1865, Cutler received an appointment to major general by brevet for meritorious service, effective August 14, 1864. His health failing, Lysander Cutler resigned June 30, 1865, returned to Milwaukee, and died there July 29, 1866.[38]

Col. William W. Robinson succeeded Cutler as First Brigade commander, Wadsworth's division. Wounded in the Wilderness, he resigned July 9, 1864, and resumed farming in Wisconsin. Upon Grant's recommendation, Robinson received an honorable discharge September 9. Mark Finnicum led the 7th Wisconsin from Spotsylvania to the siege of Petersburg. The lieutenant colonel was discharged in August 1864. Thomas W. Miller mustered out the day his term of service expired January 4, 1865.[39]

The Defense

G. K. Warren commended Edmund L. Dana for his energy and the courage he displayed during the 1865 siege of Petersburg. Dana never received his star but was brevetted brigadier general July 26, 1865, and mustered out August 23. A Luzerne County judge for over 10 years, he died in Wilkes-Barre on April 25, 1889.[40]

Assigned to Brig. Gen. John F. Hartranft's Ninth Corps Division, Alfred B. McCalmont's 208th Pennsylvania participated in the April 1865 assault and capture of Petersburg. On June 1, the 208th and its colonel mustered out of service. Later that month, President Johnson, in recognition of his gallantry and brilliance on the battlefield, brevetted McCalmont a brigadier general, effective March 13, 1865. Returning home, he resumed a law practice that would bring him before the U. S. Supreme Court. Considered a Democratic gubernatorial candidate in 1872, McCalmont succumbed to cancer May 7, 1874, in Philadelphia.[41]

Horatio N. Warren, 142nd Pennsylvania, survived Grant's Overland campaign from the Wilderness to the siege of Petersburg. At Spotsylvania, he temporarily replaced James Rice as brigade commander. Commissioned lieutenant colonel September 17, 1864, Warren was severely wounded at Five Forks on April 5, 1865. For his gallantry, he later advanced to colonel. Wounded in the Wilderness on May 5 and at Five Forks on April 1, 1865, Frank M. Powell, 142nd Pennsylvania, was discharged by special order June 3, 1865. After Dana's capture in the Wilderness, James Glenn briefly commanded the 143rd Pennsylvania. Promoted to lieutenant colonel February 21, 1865, he was discharged the following August. Glenn returned to Pittsburgh becoming a successful grain and feed merchant. After serving three and a half years in the army, Surgeon W. T. Humphrey mustered out by Special Order on January 17, 1865.[42]

Promoted to major immediately after Rowley's court-martial, George W. Jones led the 150th Pennsylvania into the Wilderness. Jones commanded the regiment at Spotsylvania, Cold Harbor, Petersburg, the Weldon Railroad, and Hatcher's Run. The State of Pennsylvania belatedly recognized his accomplishments and gave Jones a lieutenant colonel's commission May 16, 1865, and a colonel's June 15. For the latter, he was never mustered and left the army late that month. While serving as an aide to Colonel Bragg, Capt. William M. Dalgliesh, 149th Pennsylvania, was shot through both hips May 10, 1864, at Laurel Hill. Like Joshua Chamberlin, he recovered, returned to duty, and was mustered out June 23, 1865. Charles H. Stout, 143rd Pennsylvania, received an honorable discharge November 3, 1864. Fellow officer Charles H. Reilay was killed in action May 10, 1864.[43]

Two of Rowley's commanding officers, the First Brigade flag captured at Gettysburg, and Camp Berry, Maine, will close this chapter.

Abner Doubleday remained loyal to his former subordinate, Thomas Rowley, by what he wrote and said both during and after the war. Given his abolitionist, Republican views, and open hostility toward George Meade, Doubleday's army career suffered as much as Rowley's. In response to Jubal Early's first invasion, Doubleday received a temporary assignment to the Department of Washington. In late July 1864, the major general resumed his position as president of the 18th Street Military Commission "for the trial of such cases as the Chief of the Bureau of Military Justice may present to it." His commission temporarily moved to Baltimore in September, concentrating on the "trial of various persons arrested for furnishing goods to blockade runners." It returned to Washington in late October. Doubleday never saw action after Gettysburg.[44]

He did benefit, however, from the postwar deluge of brevet nominations for the regular army: lieutenant colonel "for gallant and meritorious service at Antietam," colonel for the same at Gettysburg, and finally brigadier general for the same during the war. The ad interim secretary of war, U. S. Grant, submitted Doubleday's name for promotion to full colonel, 35th Infantry, on December 3, 1867. This vacancy resulted from the death of Charles Griffin,

G. K. Warren's successor. During a yellow fever outbreak in Galveston, Major General Griffin refused to leave the city. He contracted the fever and died September 17, 1867. Colonel Doubleday retired from the Army six years later.[45]

Darius Couch passed into and out of Rowley's military life for over two and a half years. At best a supporter of Rowley and at worst neutral on the brigadier general, he deserves a final comment. On November 11, the major general took a one-week leave of absence. He was then relieved from command of the Department of the Susquehanna, which passed into army history December 1, 1864. A week later, Couch reported to George Thomas in Tennessee, who assigned him to Maj. Gen. John Schofield's Twenty-third Corps. Relieving Brig. Gen. Thomas Ruger, he commanded Schofield's Second Division. This unit stayed in reserve throughout the Battle of Nashville. In January 1865, the corps moved from Nashville to Fort Fisher, outside Wilmington, North Carolina. Following the city's capture, they moved north and joined Sherman's army. The division remained in North Carolina while Sherman's men marched in Washington's Grand Review. Maj. Gen. Darius Couch resigned his commission May 25, 1865.[46]

Mr. Howard M. Madaus informed the author that Rowley's (Biddle's) brigade flag was among the captured Union flags found in the "Rebel Archives." In the War Department's "Register of Captured Flags, 1861–65," this white triangular flag with a dark blue disc is listed with the recaptures as "No. 194 — Art. flag of the 1st Brigade, 3rd Division, 1st Army Corps — no history." In 1906, it became Collection No. 2667 in the West Point Museum, where it remains today. Mr. Madaus examined the flag in 1963.[47]

Nothing remains today of Camp Berry either above or below ground. Its exact location is unknown because the original plans did not show waterlines. A large oil tank farm at the end of Lincoln Street has replaced the stockade fence, barracks and drill field. Highway US 1 skirts the northern edge of the former camp site and I-295 is just beyond it. Thomas Rowley is at best a brief footnote to Portland's Civil War history.[48]

Conclusion

Thomas A. Rowley's Place in History Revisited

Thomas Rowley was well known in many Civil War circles before the publication of this book. Infamously known would be a better description. His name usually appears on the various lists of Civil War villains, failures, scoundrels, and the 10 worst generals at Gettysburg. Many historians and writers have chosen to ignore the fact that two highly placed and exceptional lawyers, Lincoln and Stanton, came to a different conclusion than the military court. Lincoln's revocation of the verdict is dismissed as nothing more than softness and political expediency. After all, his plurality in Allegheny County was enough to carry the state. A few examples will define Rowley's current place in history.

Just before the battle's centennial, Edwin Coddington thoroughly denounced the brigadier general's performance at Gettysburg. "Rowley's conduct was questionable in the extreme; it led to charges of drunkenness on duty on the battlefield, conduct prejudicial to good order and military discipline, conduct unbecoming an officer and a gentleman, and disobedience of orders." The author went on to describe an incident involving Chapman Biddle's 121st Pennsylvania Infantry and one of Charles Wainwright's batteries the afternoon of July 1, 1863:

> Although declared guilty by a court-martial of all accusations except the last, at least one colleague, Colonel Wainwright, doubted whether Rowley would have handled his division any better had he been sober. One of his worst blunders occurred just before the final Confederate assault on McPherson's Ridge, when the First brigade of his division under Colonel Chapman Biddle was sent in support of two sections of Lieutenant George Breck's battery and through improper management persisted in getting in front of the guns and obstructing their fire. Whatever mistakes Colonel Biddle may have made, Rowley was in large measure responsible by virtue of his position.

This narrative presented a different explanation for the incident, one favorable to Rowley and unfavorable to Doubleday.[1]

The next critic Coddington cited was Theodore Gates, 20th NYSM. This regiment joined Rowley's First Brigade the evening of June 30, fought on McPherson's Ridge and at the seminary July 1, and helped repulse Pickett's Charge. Gates submitted at least five reports discussing the Gettysburg campaign: July 2, 1863, to Chapman Biddle; July 4 to Thomas Rowley; August 13, September 10, and January 30, 1864, to Abner Doubleday. He did not criticize Thomas Rowley's performance until a February 4, 1864, letter to Doubleday, "During the fighting on the first day the general commanding the division was hardly competent to judge correctly the condition of things, or to know what transpired on the field." A public denouncement of the Pennsylvania brigadier general appeared 15 years later in Gates's regimental history, *The "Ulster Guard."* "Advancing the commander of the First brigade ... to the command of the division ... was detrimental to the efficiency of the division, and left the brigades to act very much upon their own discretion." Critical of how the brigade was handled from its arrival on McPherson Ridge to Pettigrew's afternoon attack, Gates appeared to hold his interim divisional commander responsible for everything that went wrong July 1. He failed to mention, however, Rowley's supposed drinking that day.[2]

One hundred and ten years later, Seward R. Osborne generally reiterated Gates's post-1863 views in *Holding the Left at Gettysburg*. "The brigade's seemingly aimless roving can in part, if not in whole, be attributed to the alleged, inebriated condition of General Rowley, who during this critical time frame functioned mercurially at best." The brigadier did escape censure, however, in Gates's Civil War diaries that Mr. Osborne edited in 1991. The "aimless roving" controversy will be revisited shortly.[3]

Articles in the *Gettysburg Magazine* have thoroughly discussed Rowley's performance and subsequent court-martial. Lance Herdegen, "The Lieutenant who Arrested a General," considered the general to be "a loud, slap-on-the-back, 'how-you-doing-boys' produced by the volunteer system; a man certainly brave and with some military ability, but with one eye on his 'political connections' and the other on military advancement." Herdegen closed the subject with some compassion, "In the end Rowley came off as an officer of limited ability trying to do his best in a bad situation even though befuddled by 'poor commissary.'" Politics and drinking will be considered shortly.[4]

Four and a half years later, J. Michael Miller, "Perrin's Brigade on July 1, 1863," stated, "Rowley did not actually exercise command, choosing instead to drink heavily from his personal supply of alcohol." The footnotes cited Abner Doubleday's Gettysburg report but this report actually praised Thomas Rowley's performance that day. Kevin O'Brien, "'Give Them Another Volley, Boys!' Biddle's Brigade Defends the Union Left on July 1, 1863," questioned history's treatment of General Rowley, "Most Gettysburg historians have concluded that Rowley's poor command performance was due to drunkenness.... The transcript of Rowley's court martial reveals that the evidence of drunkenness was not conclusive, however." O'Brien's observation will now serve as the introduction to revisiting the brigadier's place in history. First, Rowley's July 1, 1863, battlefield performance — the command controversies — will be examined, temporarily ignoring the sobriety issue.[5]

George Meade returned John Reynolds to left wing command June 30, 1863. For the second time in less than a week, Abner Doubleday took over the First Corps and Thomas Rowley its Third Division. Neither individual had led a unit of this size into battle before. Consequently, John Reynolds prudently stayed close to Doubleday. It is reasonable to assume that Doubleday kept a close watch over Rowley, who had limited battlefield experience at the brigade level. On July 1, James Wadsworth and Rowley faced the same command problem. Their two brigades were physically separated. As a result, Wadsworth focused on Cutler's, Rowley on Biddle's, and Doubleday on Meredith's and Stone's. John Robinson's Second Division did not face this problem. His two brigades held the corps's right flank that afternoon.[6]

The first performance controversy, "the aimless wandering of Biddle's Brigade," took place shortly after its arrival on the battlefield around 11:30 a.m. Maj. Alexander Biddle, 121st Pennsylvania, rightfully complained about "the constant changes of positions that the regiment was ordered to make and the seeming uncertainty of which way we were to expect an attack, or what position we were to defend." Thomas Rowley cannot be singled out for sole responsibility. Shortly after reaching the battlefield and taking a position on McPherson Ridge, Captain Slagle rode up carrying Doubleday's orders to close on Meredith's left. Advancing into a ravine, Biddle's command came under fire. Finding itself in an untenable position, the unit returned to McPherson Ridge. An hour later, W. P. Carter's battery on Oak Hill opened fire, enfilading Cutler's, Stone's, and Biddle's infantry. Rowley and Chapman Biddle made several changes in an attempt to minimize casualties. Under orders from Doubleday, Cooper's battery responded to Carter with counter-battery fire, forcing Biddle to change front again. It is hard to accept that Doubleday, watching from the seminary, would not have stopped these "constant changes of positions" immediately, unless he was responsible for them.[7]

The second performance controversy involved Col. Charles Wainwright and Breck's battery. Out of position when Rowley ordered the First Brigade to reform on Middle Ridge, the 121st Pennsylvania passed in front of Lieutenant Bower's four guns. Critics, then and now, hold Rowley responsible for another infantry miscue. Lt. Col. A. B. McCalmont's written affidavit presents a different view of this incident. According to McCalmont, Doubleday had earlier ordered the 121st and 142nd Pennsylvania to move north and sup-

There is no evidence that James Wadsworth played any role in Rowley's arrest and court-martial. Courtesy of James Wadsworth Family Papers and the Library of Congress.

port Roy Stone's brigade at the Chambersburg Pike. Rowley quickly brought back both regiments to meet Pettigrew's coming assault. The 121st passed in front of Bower's guns while moving to their assigned position on the brigade's left.[8]

The *Official Reports*, personal correspondence, and diaries of Rowley's superiors, peers, and subordinates provide another means to evaluate the brigadier general's July 1 performance. As already mentioned, Abner Doubleday's December 1863 report was very favorable. Col. Chapman Biddle did not refer to Rowley's skills or lack thereof at Gettysburg in his report and later writings. His cousin, Maj. Alexander Biddle, expressed displeasure at the way his regiment (121st Pennsylvania) was handled but stopped well short of criticizing Rowley. Lt. Col. George McFarland (151st Pennsylvania) and Alfred B. McCalmont (142nd Pennsylvania) never mentioned their brigade commander. McFarland maintained his positive view of Rowley during and after the war. Col. Theodore B. Gates's diary and his five reports generally agreed with McFarland and Biddle. As time passed, however, Gates became increasingly critical of Rowley's military skills and judgment. This change may have resulted from a desire to enhance Abner Doubleday's role at Gettysburg. The postwar period provided many opportunities to set the record straight on Thomas Rowley. Only three participants — Gates, Rufus Dawes, and Clayton Rogers — chose to do so.

It is time to consider the most challenging question: was Rowley drunk July 1, 1863? The issue is not whether the general ever took a drink but did he drink so much that it affected his performance? Richard Shue wrote, "He [Rowley] drank heavily this day and ended up being court martialed for it. While he probably started drinking early in the morning, whether he was noticeably intoxicated by midday is unclear." James Dougherty observed, "Rowley was in the difficult position of commanding two brigades positioned nearly a quarter of a mile apart.... Rowley made matters worse for himself by becoming drunk during the battle," and was guilty of "an alcohol induced display of bravado." To J. Michael Miller, "Rowley did not actually exercise command, choosing instead to drink heavily from his personal supply of alcohol." Lance Herdegen concluded, "It would appear that the general began drinking early in the day and by late afternoon, the alcohol had left him confused."[9]

During the court-martial, five prosecution witnesses testified about the brigadier general's condition that late afternoon and early evening of July 1. First, Lysander Cutler, commander Second Brigade, Wadsworth's division, at Gettysburg, testified, "I considered him drunk from his appearance and conversation." Second, Col. William W. Robinson, 7th Wisconsin, said, "I thought he was intoxicated." Third, Lt. Thomas W. Miller, 55th Ohio and one of Cutler's aides, thought Rowley drunk because "he appeared very excited

... his pretensions to command all the troops within his reach, his general appearance, language, and action." Fourth, Capt. Craig Wadsworth, aide-de-camp to John Reynolds, saw Rowley "five or six times during the day" and thought "he was drunk at the time I saw him just before we fell back from Seminary Ridge [about 4:30 p.m.]." Fifth, Lt. Col. Mark Finnicum, 7th Wisconsin, said, "I thought from General Rowley's actions and conversations that he was drunk." Two prosecution witnesses, Doubleday and Harney, did not support the charge of drunkenness. None of the seven observed the brigadier taking a drink or reported the smell of liquor on his breath. The evidence provided is at best circumstantial.[10]

Was Rowley drunk July 1, 1863? The author does not think so and will now justify his position. Civil War officers and enlisted men suffered no qualms about criticizing incompetent superiors, particularly those that found their courage in a bottle. For this reason, letters, diaries, and other reminiscences from the 13th, 102nd, 121st, 142nd, 143rd, 150th, and 151st Pennsylvania and 147th New York regiments were examined. Based on this evidence alone, Thomas Rowley never experienced a drinking problem before, at, or after Gettysburg. Several men in the 142nd assumed that Rowley had returned from Maine in April 1864 to command their brigade. Besides Gettysburg, the most intense fighting Rowley experienced was on the peninsula. Three times his superiors cited the colonel for bravery and sound judgment. If Rowley required a bottle to sustain him at Williamsburg, Seven Pines, and Malvern Hill, he hid it well from the 102nd Pennsylvania.

The strongest support of the writer's position comes from the 12 officers who constituted the general's defense at Culpeper. Some of Rowley's critics consider them a trial aberration and accept the prosecution's five witnesses without demur. Edwin Coddington dismissed the defense as nothing but "some of Rowley's friends and aides staunchly [swearing] to his sobriety." Coddington did admit that "Doubleday gave equivocal testimony which proved damaging to the prosecution," reducing the judge advocate's case to six witnesses. James Dougherty viewed Dana's agreement to serve as defense counsel ironic, and strange that "some of the supporting testimony came from the men of Stone's brigade who had no contact with Rowley until the evening supposedly giving the general enough time to sober up." Lance Herdegen correctly pointed out that "all the defense witnesses were officers of Pennsylvania regiments in Rowley's division," and "some admitted long acquaintances back to boyhood days in Allegheny County." Richard Shue went further. "The singular thing about this group [defense witnesses] is that they were all his subordinates, and hence could hardly be considered unbiased." The prosecution's witnesses, however, "did not have to fear reprisal from the accused [and] stated that, in their opinion, Rowley was drunk." Let us consider these points.[11]

Thomas Rowley was never a political power in western Pennsylvania before, during, or after the war. If one of the witnesses called by Edmund Dana later expected a reward for testifying, he was solely disappointed. By April 1864, Rowley's military career had struck rock bottom. No one who participated at the trial was subordinate to the defendant. To even consider that Dana's witnesses feared possible reprisal — political, financial, or militarily — gives the brigadier power far beyond his status and accomplishments. The army did not accept the reprisal view either. Of the eight defense witnesses on active duty, one received a brevet to brigadier general, one a promotion to colonel, one to lieutenant colonel, one to major, and one to captain. Of the three not promoted, Frank Powell was severely wounded in the Wilderness and at Five Forks, Charles Reilay was killed at Spotsylvania, and Surgeon Humphrey served out his enlistment. Ultimately, the nine Culpeper witnesses (including O. K. Moore) received honorable discharges from the service. His defense counsel also received a brevet to brigadier general.

Except for friendship, what could Rowley offer them? Is friendship enough for a military officer to openly perjure himself, to have "willfully misstated both the facts and their opinion?" Two former members of Rowley's staff at Gettysburg were civilians in April 1864. William Wilson traveled at his own expense from New York City to Culpeper, Virginia. Departing Wilkes-Barre, Pennsylvania, Oliver K. Moore arrived too late to testify. The professional and political achievements of A. B. McCalmont and Edmund Dana had and would continue to exceed those of the defendant. Their linkage to Rowley was probably the Masonic Lodge. Most witnesses, including H. N. Warren, James Glenn, and William Wilson, overshadowed Rowley in the postwar years. What could have driven this group of 11 to support the defendant, an unlikely hero figure? The fact that Rowley was not drunk July 1.

Accepting this position, what caused Rowley's erratic behavior that afternoon and evening? Dr. Gerald P. Sherwin, Allentown, Pennsylvania, feels that the answer may be found in Abner Doubleday's testimony at the court-martial. "His [Rowley's] face was very red and he enunciated slowly, brought his words out slowly ... was somewhat inattentive ... spoke slowly with a little effort." The very red face and difficulty in concentrating and speaking are symptomatic of heat stroke. Like many others, Thomas Rowley endured temperatures in the upper 70s, oppressive humidity, a wool uniform, dehydration, and severe stress that day. These factors combined with a general infection as indicated by his boils may have caused severe heat stroke. Depending upon the individual, heat stroke can be accompanied by bizarre behavior, hallucinations, dizziness, and loss of balance. The lack of knowledge regarding heat-related illnesses could easily have led to the erroneous conclusion that Rowley was drunk. Two additional factors support Sherwin's conjecture. First, Doubleday's testimony is the only known instance when

A small flag marks Thomas Rowley's gravesite (left) while nearby Alexander Hays receives full honors on Memorial Day. Author's photographs.

someone described Rowley as having a very red face. He was never the stereotypical hard-drinking Irishman with a red face and bulbous nose. Second, after Gettysburg the brigadier requested and received an extended medical leave. Two and a half months passed before he regained his physical health. The likelihood of heat stroke, the integrity of the defense witnesses, and the administration of the court-martial justify a second look at Thomas Rowley.[12]

The author is not alone in concluding that Thomas Rowley deserves this. Lance Herdegen closed his analysis, "It is hard to censure him [Rowley] with much conviction. By any standard, that Wednesday of July 1, 1863, at Gettysburg was a hard morning for any soldier. Rowley, overweight, suffering from boils, and a veteran of two wars, had been in the thick of it, drunk or sober." Kevin E. O'Brien expressed similar thoughts. "There may be a simpler answer than intoxication for general Rowley's poor deployment of his troops.... Rowley ... may simply not have had the leadership skills and ability to command a division.... Rowley had no time to learn or hone his skills.... Add on the boils, the confusion of the first day of battle and the overwhelming Confederate numbers. General Rowley may have simply been out of his league at Gettysburg." Wounded at Fair Oaks and Gettysburg, Thomas Rowley suffered greater pain at Culpeper.[13]

On Sunday, October 17, 1909, a feature article discussing the local men and regiments that had fought at Gettysburg appeared in *The Pittsburgh Gazette Times*. His brief biography contained many errors but 'Tom' Rowley would have enjoyed the ending. "When he was buried, the old Thirteenth turned out as it never turned out since the war, and the man in worn garment marched side by side with the solid and prosperous business man and touched elbows as when comrades in the old days — their last tribute to their old commander."[14]

Appendix I. Commands of Thomas A. Rowley

First Bull Run—July 1861[1]

GEN. ROBERT A. PATTERSON'S CORPS

First Division
Maj. Gen. George Cadwalader

FOURTH BRIGADE
COL. DIXON S. MILES

Detachments—2nd and 3rd U. S. Infantry
9th Pennsylvania Volunteers, Col. Henry C. Longnecker
13th Pennsylvania Volunteers, Col. Thomas A. Rowley
16th Pennsylvania Volunteers, Col. Thomas A. Zeigle

Washington, D.C.—September, 1861[2]

Brig. Gen. Don Carlos Buell's division
BRIG. GEN. JOHN J. PECK'S BRIGADE

55th New York, Col. Regis DeTrobriand
62nd New York, Col. John L. Riker
93rd Pennsylvania, Col. James M. McCarter
102nd Pennsylvania, Col. Thomas A. Rowley

Peninsular Campaign—May–June 1862[3]

FOURTH CORPS—ARMY OF THE POTOMAC
BRIG. GEN. E D. KEYES

First Division
Brig. Gen. D N. Couch
THIRD BRIGADE
BRIG. GEN. JOHN J. PECK

55th New York, Col. Regis DeTrobriand
62nd New York, Col. John L. Riker
93rd Pennsylvania, Col. James M. McCarter
98th Pennsylvania, Col. John F. Ballier
102nd Pennsylvania, Col. Thomas A. Rowley

Fredericksburg — December 1862[4]

**Left Grand Division
Maj. Gen. William B. Franklin**

SIXTH CORPS, ARMY OF THE POTOMAC
MAJ. GEN. WILLIAM F. SMITH

*Third Division
Brig. Gen. John Newton*

THIRD BRIGADE
COL. THOMAS A. ROWLEY

62nd New York, Col. David J. Nevin
93rd Pennsylvania, Col. John M. Mark
98th Pennsylvania, Lt. Col. Adolph Mehler
102nd Pennsylvania, Col. Thomas A. Rowley
139th Pennsylvania, Col. Frederick H. Collier

Chancellorsville — May 1863[5]

FIRST CORPS, ARMY OF THE POTOMAC
MAJ. GEN. JOHN F. REYNOLDS

*Third Division
Maj. Gen. Abner Doubleday*

FIRST BRIGADE
BRIG. GEN. THOMAS A. ROWLEY

121st Pennsylvania, Col. Chapman Biddle
135th Pennsylvania, Col. James R. Porter
142nd Pennsylvania, Col. Robert P. Cummins
151st Pennsylvania, Col. Harrison Allen

Gettysburg — July 1, 1863[6]

**Left Wing, Army of the Potomac
Maj. Gen. John F. Reynolds**

FIRST CORPS, ARMY OF THE POTOMAC
MAJ. GEN. ABNER DOUBLEDAY

Third Division
Brig. Gen. Thomas A. Rowley

FIRST BRIGADE
COL. CHAPMAN BIDDLE

121st Pennsylvania, Maj. Alexander Biddle
142nd Pennsylvania, Col. R. P. Cummins, Lt. Col. A. B. McCalmont
151st Pennsylvania, Lt. Col. George F. McFarland, Capt. Walter Owens
20th NYSM, Col. Theodore B. Gates

SECOND BRIGADE
COL. ROY STONE, COL. LANGHORNE WISTER, COL. EDMUND DANA

143rd Pennsylvania, Col. Edmund Dana, Maj. John Musser

149th Pennsylvania, Lt. Col. Walton Dwight, Capt. A. J. Sofield, Capt. John Irvin

150th Pennsylvania, Col. L. Wister, Lt. Col. H. S. Huidekoper,
Capt. C. C. Widdis, Capt. G. W. Jones

★★★

Rowley's Staff at Gettysburg[7]

Capt. Charles H. Flagg — acting assistant inspector general
First Lt. William L. T. Wilson, 142nd Pennsylvania — acting assistant adjutant general
First Lt. George A. Heberton, Battery F Pennsylvania Light — assistant aide–de–camp
First Lt. Oliver K. Moore, 143rd Pennsylvania — assistant commissar of musters
Surgeon Thomas J. Kelly, 143rd Pennsylvania — surgeon (absent)

Appendix II.
Court–Martial Participants

Members of the Court— Brigadier Generals

John C. Robinson, president — career army
Henry L. Eustis — West Point 1855
Alexander Hays — West Point 1844
William H. Morris — West Point 1851
Thomas H. Neill — West Point 1847
James C. Rice — civilian volunteer
John H. H. Ward — career army
Alexander S. Webb — West Point 1855
Frank Wheaton — career army

Judge Advocate

Lt. Col. De Witt C. McCoy — 83rd Pennsylvania

Prosecution Witnesses in Order of Appearance

Brig. Gen. Lysander Cutler — 6th Wisconsin
Col. William W. Robinson — 7th Wisconsin
Lt. Thomas W. Miller — 55th Ohio — ADC General Cutler
Lt. Col. George Harney — 147th New York
Capt. Craig Wadsworth — Former ADC John Reynolds
Then ADC Gen. John Fremont
Lt. Col. Mark Finnicum — 7th Wisconsin
Maj. Gen. Abner Doubleday

Defense Council

Col. Edmund L. Dana — 143rd Pennsylvania

Defense Witnesses in Order of Appearance

Maj. Horatio N. Warren — 142nd Pennsylvania
Capt. Frank M. Powell — 142nd Pennsylvania
Maj. James Glenn — 149th Pennsylvania
Maj. W. T. Humphrey, Surgeon — 149th Pennsylvania
Capt. George W. Jones — 150th Pennsylvania
Lt. W. M. Dalgliesh — 149th Pennsylvania
Lt. Charles B. Stout — 143rd Pennsylvania
Lt. Charles W. Reilay — 143rd Pennsylvania
William L. Wilson — New York City, former lieutenant, 142nd Pennsylvania

Written Statements Prepared and Submitted

Lt. Col. Alfred McCalmont — Camp Curtin, Pennsylvania, formerly 142nd Pennsylvania
Oliver K. Moore — Wilkes–Barre, Pennsylvania, former captain, 143rd Pennsylvania

Appendix III. Thomas A. Rowley's Defense Statement

Edmund L. Dana and Thomas A. Rowley prepared the statement. The defendant read it to the court April 29, 1864. It may reflect nothing more than a desperate individual trying to save his military career. At the least, this is Rowley's version of what happened July 1, 1863.

The intelligence and experience of the officers composing this court, their patient and attentive consideration of the testimony as it has been presented, relieve me of the necessity of an extended description of either the law or the facts involved in this case and also of all apprehension that any material point in either will be overlooked or forgotten.

Having been engaged in the service for a period of over three years and participant in the battles of the Peninsula, of Fredericksburg, Chancellorsville, and Gettysburg, besides an experience of nearly two years in the Mexican War, without once falling under the censure of any superior officer or being up to the time of this occurrence for one moment under arrest, and having at much personal inconvenience, endeavored faithfully to discharge my duty, looking forward to the reward of a good name as a patriotic citizen and soldier, this court can well conceive the interest to me now and for life, the determination of this issue.

It is respectfully submitted that the prosecution has wholly failed in establishing the serious charge of disobedience of orders. The testimony of General Doubleday is that he was in doubt as to the propriety of the order given to me, that he did not require its execution, and that given under such circumstances, it was not positive but left discretionary and dependent upon the issue of events and the contingencies of the attack thus impending upon that portion of the line. The result shows that my division so far from being able to admit of the detaching of supports for another brigade was overwhelmed by numbers and although "behaving admirably," according to the admission of General Doubleday, was driven back with fearful loss through the town to Cemetery Hill. The evidence of General Doubleday, the person issuing the order, who knows best its term and tenor, and who is, if anyone be, entitled to complain of the failure of a subordinate to obey, is that he was satisfied with the manner in which his orders were executed, that he had no cause of complaint and that these troops under my command were moved with dispatch and precision to the points he ordered.

This charge of conduct unbecoming an officer and a gentleman, it is respectfully submitted, is merely a reiteration of the first charge, of being drunk: a finding upon that charge disposes of this. The fact of my falling from or being thrown from my horse, except as an incident or rather evidence of drunkenness, especially under the circumstances shown in the testimony, cannot support this or any other charge. Skill horsemanship is an accomplishment of a gentleman and a needful qualification of an officer, but its partial absence, either through physical conformation, corpulence, or sickness, is not militarily a capital offense nor the crime at which the 83rd Article of war is leveled,

This second charge of conduct prejudicial to good order and military discipline is predicated under the specification; first on the claim, said to be a misapprehension, that upon the fall of General Reynolds, General Doubleday succeeded to his command and that temporarily at least, the command of the First Corps devolved upon me; and second, that under that misapprehension and in the honest discharge of a supposed duty, I undertook to post two regiments in a position where I conceived they could best contribute to repel the anticipated attack upon the cemetery; and third that I reprimanded with too much severity the officers of the 7th Wisconsin for having been seen, a portion of them that morning by me, upon the road separated from their regiment.

It is submitted that the version of Colonel Robinson, the person to whom it is claimed by the prosecution the words of censure on the officers of the 7th Wisconsin were addressed, should be taken in preference to the other witness Lieutenant

Colonel Finnicum. The supposed straggling of company officers of the regiment is fully and satisfactorily explained by proof of the occasion and duties by which they had been detained. But that explanation was not known to me.

The real charge, however, the principal out of which the others are mere accessories and either stand or fall with it, is the charge of being drunk.

Whether this be sustained by the process beyond all reasonable doubt is purely a question of fact and without taking up the evidence of each witness and detaining you with an analysis of the "opinion expressed," and the grounds on which they are severally based, and the opportunities of the witnesses either by their former acquaintances with me or their more or less frequently meeting me during the day, none of which I am satisfied will escape your attention or your careful and candid consideration. I beg leave merely to submit two or three suggestions as aids to a correct decision and with them leave my cause and the vindication of my character in your hands.

First, it will be observed that the witnesses of the Prosecution had never seen nor known me before, and based their opinion upon a hasty interview, a few words dropped, an order issued, a single act or position occurring in the excitement and confusion of a retreat after a desperately contacted battle. That the witnesses for the Defense were well acquainted with me, the acquaintance of some of them extending over many years and formed their opinion of my condition upon many concurrent facts upon my acts, conversations, and manner during the entire day.

It will ever be the effort of a court as well as a jury to reconcile testimony when it can be without imparting the crime of perjury to a single witness; much more so when a large and respectable body of witnesses is concerned. Drunkenness is a state or condition of mind and body. Its existence or nonexistence is a matter of opinion. Opinion is of much or little weight according as it is founded upon many concurrent facts or upon few. The witnesses of the prosecution forming their opinion upon few facts may be honestly mistaken. Those of the Defense from their superior opportunities of knowing from their numerous circumstances could not be mistaken in the fact and are correct in the opinion they express, or they have willfully misstated both the facts and their opinion.

It is further submitted that the reasons given for their conclusion of drunkenness by the witnesses of the Prosecution are explained without the imputation of this gross moral and military offense to a commander of a division of brave men. I "sat unsteadily in my saddle." My "singular position in the saddle," say the witnesses. My alleged fall from my horse. Are not these all explained by proof of my condition of health at the time and the serious affections under which I was suffering? And are not these the chief reasons stated by these witnesses for their opinions? Unquestionably had these gentlemen known the facts and my sufferings from the causes explained to you, they would have come to a different conclusion. It is a singular corroborative fact that all the witnesses who saw me on foot thought me perfectly sober.

It is respectfully suggested in conclusion that if under all the evidence there is a reasonable doubt of guilt, it will be the pleasure of this court to relieve me from lifelong disgrace and return me to the post of duty and danger, to my command which is awaiting anxiously and hopefully my return to it. And it is further confidently and respectively submitted that the preponderance of the testimony both in numbers and in the facts, facilities, and means of knowledge of judging correctly is in my favor.

I need not remind the court of the fact that several gentlemen of high position and respectability who were with me all of that eventful day upon my staff or holding command under me have retired from the service, and in emergency of the impending campaign, a postponement of trial to secure their attendance or evidence can neither be asked nor granted.

With these hastily and crudely prepared suggestions, my cause is respectfully entrusted to your disposition

Thomas A. Rowley[1]

Appendix IV. "Transfer from Jail to Pleasanter Quarters": Colonel Edmund Dana, Prisoner of War

The Wilderness

Born in Wilkes–Barre, Pennsylvania, Edmund L. Dana graduated from Yale College in 1838 and was admitted to the Luzerne County bar three years later. After fighting broke out in Texas, Dana brought an artillery company to Pittsburgh in December 1846. It was redesignated Company I and assigned to the First Pennsylvania Infantry where he met 2nd Lt. Thomas Rowley. Dana accompanied Scott's army to Mexico City, fought at Cerro Gordo, and mustered out in July 1848. Subsequent campaigns for U. S. House and Pennsylvania Senate seats failed. In the summer of 1862, Governor Curtin placed Dana in charge of Camp Luzerne, outside Harrisburg. Recruited and organized there, the 143rd Regiment elected the camp commandant their colonel. On February 19, 1863, John Reynolds assigned the regiment to Roy Stone's brigade. Dana assumed brigade command July 1 after Stone was seriously wounded near McPherson's farm. He retained this position until relieved by Langhorne Wister on August 22. The First Corps passed into history March 26, 1864, and Dana's 143rd became part of Stone's Third Brigade, Wadsworth's Fourth Division, Warren's Fifth Corps.[1]

Rowley's court–martial ended unfavorably that spring and Dana gave his full attention to the coming Overland campaign. On a pleasant but cloudy April 30 he mustered the regiment for pay. Weeks of drilling and preparation ended three days later. At 1:00 a.m. May 4, Warren's Fifth Corps departed their Culpeper camps. The 143rd Pennsylvania crossed the Rapidan River at Germanna Ford, marched five or six miles, and camped near the Wilderness Tavern. Next morning, Wadsworth's division followed Crawford's southward on the Parker Store Road. Before long, the men heard firing behind them on the Orange Turnpike and then up ahead on the Orange Plank Road. The brigade stopped and formed a line of battle but remained in place for several hours. About 11:00 a.m., Wadsworth ordered a general advance to the northwest; their objective was General Griffin's left flank near the Orange Turnpike. While pushing through the Wilderness tangle, the Pennsylvanians came under heavy frontal and flank fire from an invisible enemy. Enemy musketry wounded Dana then killed his horse. Unable to fall back, he was captured 30 minutes later and taken to the Confederate rear.[2]

Near dusk, guards started the large group of Fifth Corps prisoners toward Orange

Court House, about 15 miles away. Dana rode part of the time on a horse. The march finally ended after midnight. Exhausted and ill, he slept in the courthouse yard, sharing a blanket with Col. Ira G. Grover, 7th Indiana. The next morning, those prisoners able to walk set out on foot for Gordonsville, Virginia. Unable to move, guards took both colonels to a nearby church, already full of Federal wounded. Placed in a pew, Dana received rations from members of the congregation who "were quite rude to us in language." Wounded Yankees continued to arrive and Confederate officers made arrangements to send a trainload to Gordonsville that evening. Nothing happened, however, and Dana spent the night in a pew, loaning his blanket to another prisoner.[3]

At dawn May 7, the Confederates moved several wounded prisoners from the church to a nearby train siding. Dana first found himself in a crowded boxcar then a platform car with an overhead awning. The train left at 6:00 a.m. and after a "quite comfortable" ride of six miles reached Gordonsville. Federal officers in the original prisoner group had already departed for Lynchburg, Virginia. A very sick Edmund Dana spent another night sleeping on the ground.[4]

Lynchburg, Virginia

The prisoners reboarded and the train left Gordonsville at 1:00 p.m. Very hot temperatures and several mechanical breakdowns made it "a tedious ride ... through a lovely way and country." Passing through Monticello and Charlottesville, the train finally reached Lynchburg, a journey of 85 miles on the Orange and Alexandria Railroad. About 6:00 a.m., May 9, 79 officer prisoners were marched through town to a prison building and placed in hot and crowded rooms. The guards issued "tolerably good rations comprising soft bread and boiled ham." The enlisted men camped in a nearby field.[5]

Thirty additional Federal officers, including Brig. Gens. Truman Seymour and Alexander Shaler, arrived the next day. Both brigadier generals had been captured May 7 during John Gordon's evening attack on the Sixth Corps. Unable to lie down and very hot, the prisoners passed the day by singing. A couple verses of "We'll Hang Jeff Davis on a Sour Apple Tree" brought in armed guards who made them stop. May 11, the Confederates transferred five colonels, including Dana, to rooms occupied by generals and their staffs. It turned out to be "a pleasant change." Dana and Truman Seymour spent considerable time reliving their Mexican War experiences.[6]

To augment his group's soft bread and bacon fare, Dana bought some onions and radishes for $5. He passed the day watching Seymour make sketches of prison life in Lynchburg. The camp commandant, Brig. Gen. Francis Nicholls, visited them May 12. He had lost his left arm during Stonewall Jackson's 1862 Valley campaign, then his left foot while commanding a Louisiana brigade at Chancellorsville. All enlisted prisoners departed for Danville. Rainstorms broke the hot spell but Dana spent the next few days trying to recover from a bad cold and cough. About the time he succeeded, word came that they were also going to Danville, Virginia. The prisoners packed and boarded the cars at 6:00 p.m.

Near sunrise, the train stopped in Burksville. It left shortly after lunch and crossed the Staunton River at sunset. Guards placed two Confederate soldiers recently killed in Dana's car at Lynchburg. By late evening, the smell became very bad. Without any objections, the prisoners threw both bodies out of the car. Sixty-five miles later, the train reached Danville, close to the North Carolina state line. Here, the prisoners were marched to a tobacco warehouse. They returned to the cars at sunrise May 20 and the journey resumed. Around 9:00 p.m., Dana got off in Charlotte, North Carolina, 140 miles from Danville, and slept "in a sunken lot." The Federals boarded a different train at 2:00 p.m. Assigned to two "quite comfortable" passenger cars, the officers received two days rations of bacon and hard bread.[7]

Daylight found them 90 miles farther south, passing through Columbia, South Carolina. Three miles beyond the state capital, two cars ran off the tracks. Considerable confusion followed with the prisoners climbing out windows and doors. The guards drew their rifles but no one fired. After pushing the damaged cars out of the way, the Federals reboarded those that had remained on the tracks. They traveled all night with Dana sleeping again on the floor.[8]

At 5:00 a.m. May 23 and 68 miles from Columbia, the train stopped in Augusta, Georgia. Rations were issued but the prisoners remained on board. Dana considered the town to be "exceedingly pleasant, the streets broad with rows of trees in the middle." The Lynchburg guards were "to our sorrow replaced by a 'new issue' of city or home guards." That afternoon, they "started a pleasant journey through wooded country, new foliage, and rice fields." Macon, their final destination, came into sight before daylight. Dana had now traveled over 500 miles since his capture in the Wilderness.[9]

Macon, Georgia

Confederate officials concluded in late 1863 that the growing number of Federal prisoners in the Richmond area was not only a security threat but also a major consumer of local food supplies. Consequently, they sent noncommissioned officers and enlisted men to Andersonville, Georgia, leaving only the officers in Libby Prison. Federal cavalry raids the following winter and spring made this arrangement impractical. By mid–May 1864, the remaining prisoners left Libby for a new facility in Macon, Georgia.[10]

After sunrise May 24, Dana's group departed the train and a strong guard marched them to a prison camp in Macon's suburbs. Here, they were searched and interviewed by Captain Tabb, camp commandant, who confiscated their money. Released briefly into an adjoining field, the Federal officers later moved into the prison yard. The surrounding walls enclosed a main building, several rough sheds used as barracks, and about three acres of open ground. There were now over 1,100 confined in this camp. Experienced inmates explained "dead line" rules to the new arrivals or "fresh fish."[11]

Outside in the yard, the prisoners formed squads of 100 and received barrack assignments. Lt. Col. H. C. Bolinger, 7th Pennsylvania Reserves, commanded Dana's squad or unit. The new arrivals found "many pleasant and intelligent officers" at Macon. Several captured earlier at Gettysburg, however, appeared to be demoralized. Generals and colonels "without covering were admitted into the building and slept on the floor."[12]

In each barrack, the squad divided into small groups with five men allocated per room. Placed in room command, Dana assigned quarters and duties for his small group. They took turns cooking. Guards permitted writing paper "to be brought in at $0.60 per half sheet" and chaplains gave sermons on Sundays. In spite of having to wash clothes in cold water, he found "the condition of things better than we had expected." Each day, two or three newcomers joined Bolinger's squad. The crowding that resulted was offset somewhat by those taken to the camp hospital. Dana became ill May 28 but remained in the room. His efforts to recover were helped by pleasant weather, reading *Pilgrim's Progress*, and a chaplain's visit.[13]

Captain Tabb took roll call daily at 7:00 a.m. and 6:00 p.m. When the counts did not agree, usually because of his mistakes, Tabb verbally abused the prisoners and threatened them with punishment. On May 31, the guards placed a cannon at each corner of the enclosure. The next day, Captain Hirsch, a prisoner, was bucked and gagged "for refusing to get up and take a shovel from a negro and fill up a hole which Tabb supposed was intended for a tunnel." Captain Gibbs became commandant June 3 and the situation improved.[14]

Rations consisted of corn bread, corn flour, bacon, rice, salt, beans, and vinegar made out of fermented meal. It was "fairly good when the worms were not too plenty." There were opportunities to buy food. May 30, Dana bought three onions for $1.50, a pint of molasses for $6, loaf of bread for $1, and a tin plate for $5. His first "tour of duty as cook" began June 2. Breakfast at 8 consisted of corn cakes, bacon, and fried onions. Corn bread baked in a dutch oven, fried fish, onions, and cold water were served for dinner. Except for burning his hand, Dana seemed pleased with his culinary skills.[15]

Extreme heat and humidity replaced the pleasant weather of late May. With no trees for shade, living conditions at Macon deteriorated rapidly. News of Grant's inability to defeat Lee depressed everyone. To avoid being either physically or mentally overwhelmed by imprisonment, Dana actively practiced his religious convictions and established an ongoing program to improve his intellect. Within the building, a "circulating library" was established. Besides *Pilgrim's Progress*, he read books on geology, philosophy, and art, and novels, several of them written in German.[16]

Savannah, Georgia

For several months, Federal batteries on Morris Island had been firing shells into Charleston, South Carolina, destroying property and threatening the inhabitants. Maj. Gen. Samuel Jones, Confederate commander of the Department of South Carolina, Georgia, and Florida, sought permission to place Federal prisoners in the exposed parts of the city and, possibly, stop the shelling. Secretary of War James Seddon approved and issued orders June 9 to furnish Jones the prisoners requested.[17]

Captain Gibbs posted the next day "a list of officers to be moved from Macon: 5 Brigadier Generals, 11 Colonels, 25 Lieutenant Colonels, and 9 Majors." Dana found his name on the list. The 50 prisoners boarded a passenger car about 3:30 p.m. and departed Macon in the rain, destination unknown. After receiving cooked rations, they began speculating about the future. Many had opinions as to what would happen next, the most popular being an exchange. Supporting this optimistic but unfounded view, the guards requested mementos, such as knives, from the officers. Later in the darkness, Confederates cut off all of the buttons on General Seymour's coat. Just after daybreak, the train pulled into Savannah, Georgia, 171 miles from Macon. Stopping in a seaport started more rumors about an immediate exchange.[18]

The group disembarked, marched to the "old United States Barracks," and stayed in the guard house. Generals and colonels later moved to the barracks's officer quarters. Granted a temporary parole, all but three spent "a pleasant day" taking liberty in the yard. Here, they could "purchase onions, gingerbread, new potatoes, plums, and cucumbers." Dana secured a much–needed pair of shoes for Brig. Gen. Eliakim Scammon, captured by West Virginia guerrillas in February. The price was $130, "either Confederate or greenback money." The three prisoners who refused parole remained locked up. This pleasant interlude abruptly ended at 5:00 a.m. June 12, when the group boarded boxcars and left Savannah.[19]

Charleston, South Carolina

Nine hours and 105 miles later, the train pulled into Charleston during a heavy rainstorm. The 50 prisoners left the cars and marched a mile and a half in "knee––deep water" to the city jail. Federal siege guns fired to the southeast. At the jail, they were quartered, four or five to a cell, and locked up until morning. The rooms "were filthy, abounding in lice [and containing] nothing but a floor." Those who lost their blankets at the depot suffered through a cold and wet night.[20]

A prison routine was quickly established. At 6:00 a.m., guards opened the doors and "colored prisoners" from the 54th Massachusetts swept out the rooms. "Afterwards [we were] allowed to go down to [the] Prison yard to wash then locked up again." Around 10:00 a.m., guards unlocked and left open the third–floor cell doors, making it possible to visit the other rooms. Moving around, Dana saw that an adjoining building had been "partly burned by shells." All freedom of movement ceased at sunset. "The grating of the locks as the doors are closed at night is most disagreeable and seems unnecessary when there is a guard." Primitive sanitary facilities generated foul odors that some found very offensive.[21]

Brought in around 3:00 p.m., dinner usually consisted of bacon and rice. A mixture of rice and beans cooked together, Hopping Johnny, was also served with a small piece of bacon. For variety, Dana bought molasses at $40 a quart. Another day the guards served "greasy soup in which there is a tough dumpling [which] was a severe test of taste and digestion." The prisoners deluged a Confederate officer and his staff inspecting the cells with complaints about the jail food and their treatment. Two days later, security was relaxed. During daylight, they could now walk downstairs without a guard. That night Dana "heartily" ate fresh beef and soup.[22]

On June 13, General Jones sent a letter to Maj. Gen. John G. Foster, commander of the Department of the South, informing him that "5 generals and 45 field officers of the Federal army have been ordered to be confined in Charleston ... [they] will be provided with commodious quarters in a part of the city occupied by non–combatants ... it is a part of the city which has been for many months exposed day and night to the fire of your guns."[23]

Every night Federal guns fired on the city. Many shells burst overhead, usually to the northeast. Dana's squad shared the *Charleston Mercury*. Its June 15 edition reported that their imprisonment in the jail was to discourage and hopefully stop the bombardment. A list of prisoner names appeared in the June 14 issue. The next day Dana first heard of a proposal "to remove us from our present place of confinement on condition of giving our parole." Five brigadiers and 39 field officers received and signed a written parole June 17. This was required for "transfer from jail to pleasanter quarters." Six Federal prisoners refused to sign. After eating a final meal of boiled mutton soup, those who had accepted the terms moved that afternoon "to a pleasanter house near the Ashley River."[24]

General Foster formally protested Jones's intentions June 16 and said that shelling to destroy military targets in Charleston would continue. "You [Jones] seek to defeat this effort, not by means known to honorable warfare, but by placing unarmed and helpless prisoners under our fire." Foster closed his letter with a threat, already suggested to President Lincoln and Army Chief of Staff Henry Halleck, that the North should retaliate by sending "an equal number of [Confederate] prisoners of the like grades, to be kept by me [Foster] in positions exposed to the fire of your [Jones's] guns."[25]

Forty–four Federal prisoners relocated June 19 to Colonel O'Connor's private home at the corner of Broad and Rutledge Streets near Chisolm's Mill on Charleston's south side. The six who refused parole remained in the city jail. Firing at irregular intervals, the Morris Island batteries averaged 50 shots per day into the city.[26]

Edmund Dana and seven others occupied a first–floor parlor room. Initially, cool breezes off the river kept temperatures comfortable but soon it became "intensely hot in the sun." Mosquitoes were "a little troublesome at night" but soon became "very troublesome." Visitors were a pleasant change from the city jail. A Confederate officer whom Dana knew at Yale, Captain Raymond, stopped in and promised "the loan of his library." True to his word, several books arrived the next day. Dana selected one by Herman Melville, later concluding that it was not remarkable. He then read some editions on classic art and artists in a second lot from Raymond. Local citizens walked by daily on Broad Street "to get a view of the Yankees."[27]

The group of eight officers shared cooking duties. Even though rations improved, efforts to locate and buy additional provisions continued. Milk cost a dollar a quart and four squashes 50 cents. Fifteen dollars bought a half–gallon of molasses and a quart of vinegar. They subscribed again to the *Mercury*, paying $3.25 monthly. Dana tried but failed to have church services held at the house.[28]

Secretary of War Stanton approved General Foster's recommendation June 21 with the admonishment that "you will exercise great vigilance and that the rebel officers will be treated with the same severity that they treat ours." The next day, Foster sent a list of the 44 prisoners in Dana's group to Halleck. After confirming their move to 180 Broad Street, he notified the commanding artillery officer on Morris Island.[29]

Earlier, Confederate authorities had refused requests from the city jail to contact a Federal ship and the base at Hilton Head. After moving to Broad Street, Dana prepared a list of items needed and asked a Confederate officer to send it to Hilton Head. On June 24, Dana celebrated St. John's Day with other members of the Masonic Rite. He remembered that a year earlier, the 143rd Pennsylvania was camped along Broad Run on their northward march to Gettysburg. Later that evening, Raymond sent over a bottle of brandy wine. To escape the heat inside, they moved cots to the porch.[30]

Afternoon and nighttime shelling by Federal batteries continued. It seemed that the guns aimed for St. Michael's Church but "never hit it." One fragment from a bursting shell fell near the house's front door. Besides reading, Dana wrote letters and sketched "the burnt district." He studied and practiced Spanish, French, and German with other prisoners. The first week on Broad Street passed "fast and rather pleasantly but a dearth of news." Dana heard nothing of Grant's fighting outside Richmond and Petersburg. Federal District Headquarters at Hilton Head received word June 27 that 35 Confederate field and general officers then in transit would be interned on Morris Island.[31]

On the edge of Charleston Bay, the Confederates built a bathhouse for the Broad Street prisoners. They first tried it the afternoon of June 27. "Six of us [were] permitted out at a time." The tide came in at 4:00 p.m. and the water was warm. That

Col. Edmund Dana spent over six weeks at 180 Broad Street, the "pleasanter quarters" in Charleston. Courtesy of Mass. MOLLUS and USAMHI.

week one room of prisoners challenged another to games of chip and wicket, the latter a competitive team sport combining features of baseball and cricket. Requiring minimal equipment, the game was popular in Civil War prison camps.[32]

On July 1, Samuel Jones sent Foster "a letter addressed by 5 general officers of the U. S. Army now prisoners of war in this city to Brig. Gen. L. [Lorenzo] Thomas, Adjutant–general . . . recommending and asking an exchange of prisoners of war." The five brigadiers, staying on Broad Street, strongly disagreed with the recent decision to subject enemy field officers to similar treatment. Jones liked the exchange recommendation and suggested to Foster that both generals inform their respective governments and, if approved, proceed with negotiations. Dana was either unaware of the generals's letter to Thomas or chose not to discuss it in his diary.[33]

Dana rose to cook breakfast June 30 and found "the hot sun looking like a heated globe of iron." He served boiled eggs, fried mush, hot bread, molasses, sliced cucumbers and tomatoes. Captain Raymond loaned him a copy of Blackstone. The colonel took a bath, played wicket, and sketched the house. Living conditions deteriorated in July as temperatures climbed and mosquitoes turned "voracious." The nights became "a struggle between suffocation and being eaten up."[34]

By mid–May 1864, the Confederates had stripped their garrisons in South Carolina, sending the troops to Virginia. John Foster, present when Fort Sumter surrendered April 13, 1861, assured Halleck on June 15 that "Fort Sumter could be taken with 5,000 men." General Grant wanted these troops to make raids along the coast and tie up southern forces. Irritated by the continued exposure of the prisoners on Broad Street, Halleck and Grant reluctantly approved Foster's plan to launch five separate and concurrent attacks in and around Charleston.[35]

At daybreak July 2, Dana heard the "heavy fire of both artillery and musketry towards Morris Island and Stono River." The next day, "the prison guard, Captain Molby's company of Colonel Harrison's 32nd Georgia, were ordered to the scene of hostilities." A detachment from the city's fire brigade served as temporary replacements. Firing continued all night and into the early afternoon of July 3. Near sunset, Dana watched over a hundred Federal prisoners, including two colonels from the 52nd Pennsylvania, march down Broad Street on their way to the city jail. July 4 saw more fighting at Stono River with "unfavorable reports of the results of our attack." Cadets from the Citadel assisted the firemen in guarding the house. Fighting at Stono River resumed July 8 with long columns of white and black smoke visible. The next day, the forts were engaged but no one knew the outcome. The fighting ceased July 11. "A report of a reverse on our part and a withdrawal from the islands [Johns and James]" reached Dana.[36]

During this fighting, Foster and Jones continued their correspondence. Even though Foster also desired an exchange, he felt that negotiations could not begin until "you [Jones] withdraw from exposure to our fire those officers now confined in Charleston. I have not yet placed your prisoners in a similar position...." Jones replied that he had already provided sufficient information on prisoner location so as to minimize their danger. In spite of this impasse, negotiations began July 13 with the approval of both governments.[37]

Unable to secure a chaplain or preacher, Dana spent most of Sunday, July 10, playing ball. Late that afternoon, he joined "a party of officers [who] met to organize a Bible class." He was elected the group leader and they would "meet on Sundays and Wednesdays at 9:00 ... twelve officers in the class." Captain Molby's Company H returned to Broad Street on July 13. Their casualties in the recent fighting included five killed and 10 wounded. Federal shelling of the city stopped. News came of Jubal Early's raid into Maryland and Pennsylvania. Two days later, Dana served a dinner of "mashed potatoes, milk, hash, and stewed tomatoes." July 16, he bought a watermelon for $4, two quarts of tomatoes $1, and six cans of corn $1. "The price of $120 per gallon for whiskey checked the frequent purchase...."[38]

The Bible class met at 9:00 a.m. Sunday, July 17. Confederate batteries fired on Federal positions but Charleston enjoyed the fifth consecutive day free of enemy shelling. The officers met Monday and agreed to send a list of needed articles to the Sanitary Commission. Next, they passed a resolution that "a conspiracy [had been] discovered and [the] proceedings annulled." Dana offered no explanation except "misconstruction of the meeting held yesterday."[39]

Federal firing on the city resumed July 20. Even though the house shook, Dana's "Bible class met at 9:00 A.M. with good attendance and much interest felt on the lesson." They held a house meeting July 22 to clarify wicket rules. Earlier that day, an "altercation between Col. [Richard] White [55th Pennsylvania] and Lt. Col. [E.]

Olcott [121st New York]—charge of conduct unbecoming an officer and a gentleman," had taken place. Dana never recorded whether wicket caused the fight or who was charged. The incident was soon forgotten when three boxes from the U. S. Quartermaster and Sanitary Commission on Hilton Head Island arrived the next day. "Pants, shirts, shoes, socks, caps, blouses, haversacks and canteens in the former and shirts, drawers, towels, pillow cases, slippers, lemon juice, and six bottles spirits (appropriated by the generals)" from the commission. Financially able to buy items privately, Dana divided his share among those who could not.[40]

Sunday, July 24, Reverend Gladsden, "the eloquent rector of St. Luke's Episcopal Church preached to the prisoners." A week later, Reverend Porter, "also an Episcopalian [and] an ardent advocate for secession," offered to do the same. "But thinks he [Porter] must use the Confederate Prayer Book and prayers including that for the Confederate President." After some thought, Porter's offer was declined.[41]

John Foster received Washington's approval July 29 to proceed and exchange Confederate prisoners currently in his district for Federal officers confined in Charleston. He requested Adm. J. A. Dahlgren's assistance to conduct the exchange and transport the group to Port Royal.[42]

Six hundred additional officer prisoners arrived in Charleston on July 29 from Macon. Supposedly, 78 Federals had escaped en route. "A few shells fired at the city [today], one fell close to our quarters." The mosquitoes, shelling, and hot weather were quickly forgotten when news came that Dana's group would be exchanged in two days. They spent the day collecting autographs and giving personal articles to those not eligible for exchange. Edmund Dana returned to the city jail and gave $100 Confederate to Lt. Col. John B. Conyngham (52nd Pennsylvania), and Capt. C. C. Widdis (150th Pennsylvania).[43]

The prisoners left the Broad Street house at 7:00 a.m. August 3 and walked to a nearby wharf. Accompanied by Reverend Porter, "they were taken on board a steamer and moved off down the bay." The Federals were kept below "until we had passed Sumter" and other Confederate works. Their steamer then stopped and the U.S.S. *Cosmopolitan*, carrying 50 Confederate prisoners, came up and anchored nearby. "The roll of fifty Federals was called, their names checked, and they hurried on board the *Cosmopolitan*." For a few minutes the two prisoner groups conversed, each one convinced that "they and their respective governments were the gainers...." By 11:30 the Confederates completed their transfer and the steamer departed for Charleston. "The exchange so earnestly hoped for was accomplished."[44]

The actual exchange began at 10:00 a.m. in the North Channel between Fort Moultrie and Battery Putnam. Federal guns ceased firing as soon as the "rebel steamer was seen coming out of the harbor." U.S.S. *Pawnee* fired a salute as the released officers came on board the *Cosmopolitan*.[45]

Enjoying their new freedom, the officers visited the U.S.S. *Philadelphia*. Here Gens. John Foster and Daniel Sickles and Adm. John Dahlgren welcomed the group. They "were kindly received and treated, lustily cheering the American Flag ... until we became hoarse ... then came back and got on the *Cosmopolitan*." The ship reached Hilton Head at daybreak. Dana "went on shore, took breakfast, and found a valise," and then "drew my payment [back pay] of $763.35, $600 in check [government bonds or certificates] and $163.35 in cash." After calling on General Foster, Dana severely injured his left knee, leg, and ankle while boarding the steamer *Fulton*.[46]

"With the aid of two men and a pair of crutches," Dana was on deck when the Fulton weighed anchor at 6:00 a.m. August 5. Taken below deck to Stateroom No. 26, an examining doctor found no broken bones. Dana applied water to his leg all day. In addition to enduring the most intense pain since being wounded, he became seasick. In spite of it all, the 50 were free and on their way home. The next morning, the ship reached Fortress Monroe and "just before sunset, started for New York."[47]

Even though August 8, 1864, began with a beautiful sunrise, the steamer U. S. S. *Fulton made* little progress toward its final destination, New York City. In his stateroom, Edmund Dana spent the daylight hours writing out leaves of absence for the 50 officers. The tedious assignment helped Dana to ignore his swollen left leg. After sunset, heavy fog rolled in, forcing the ship to slow even more and blow its whistle throughout the night.[48]

At dawn, conditions improved and the *Fulton* resumed normal speed. Standing on deck as they entered New York Harbor, Dana thought about the past three months spent in Confederate prisons. The price of freedom had no limit that morning, particularly to those left behind in Charleston.[49]

Wilkes–Barre, Pennsylvania, August 12, 1864

The *Fulton* docked at Staten Island at 9:00 a.m. August 9. Taking his few possessions, Dana went first to the Metropolitan Hotel then to the home of Col. D. W. Lee, (27th Massachusetts). He spent most of the next two days helping fellow officers from midwestern states redeem or cash the certificates received at Hilton Head. Dana departed New York on August 12 on a 7:00 a.m. train and reached Wilkes–Barre 12 hours later. His journey was over. "The expedient of defending a city against bombardment by the exposure of prisoners remain[ed] alone, a memory of the war."[50]

Chapter Notes

Preface

1. Coddington, The Gettysburg Campaign, pp. 309, 707, fn #127.
2. Rufus R. Dawes, "A Gallant Officer," Chippewa Herald, Jan. 4, 1884.
3. Coddington, Gettysburg, p. 706 fn #121.

1. Pittsburgh, Pennsylvania

1. Niebaum, History of the Pittsburgh Washington Infantry, p. 31.
2. Memoirs of Allegheny County, Pennsylvania, Vol. 1, pp. 83–4; Thomas A. Rowley obituary, New York Times, May 15, 1892, p. 4; James Onslow, "Sketch of Brigadier General Thomas A, Rowley," George McFarland Papers, J. Horace McFarland Collection, Pennsylvania State Archives (hereafter PSA), p. 1.
3. Onslow, "Sketch," p. 1; Memoirs Allegheny County, p. 83; Niebaum, History Washington Infantry, p. 31.
4. Niebaum, History Washington Infantry, p. 31 ; Memoirs Allegheny County, p. 83.
5. Niebaum, History Washington Infantry, pp. 32, 36.
6. Ibid., p. 36.
7. Ibid., pp. 36–7.
8. Ibid., p. 38.
9. Ibid., pp. 38–40; Bates, Martial Deeds of Pennsylvania, p. 791.
10. Niebaum, History Washington Infantry, pp. 50–1.
11. Niebaum, History Washington Infantry, p. 56; History of the Washington Infantry of Pittsburgh, Pennsylvania, Pittsburgh, 1891, pp. 21, 23; Obituary, New York Times; "General Rowley's Death," Pittsburgh Commercial Gazette, May 16, 1892; Allegheny Cemetery Interments, Allegheny Cemetery Historical Association, Section 7, Lot 110, p. 37; "Declaration for Original Invalid Pension," February 1, 1878, Thomas A. Rowley Pension File, National Archives (hereafter NA); History of Allegheny County, Pennsylvania, Vol. 1, pp. 180–1.
12. Fox, Pittsburgh During the American Civil War, p. 13; Niebaum, History Washington Infantry, pp. 64–5; History Washington Infantry Pittsburgh, pp. 25, 27.
13. Miners, Lincoln Day by Day, Vol 3, pp. 11–13; Dahlinger, "Abraham Lincoln in Pittsburgh," pp. 160–1.
14. Dahlinger, "Abraham Lincoln in Pittsburgh," pp. 162–3.
15. Ibid., pp. 162–5.
16. Ibid., pp. 165–6; Fox, Pittsburgh During the Civil War, p. 14; Under the Maltese Cross, p. 2.
17. Dahlinger, "Abraham Lincoln in Pittsburgh," pp. 165–6.
18. Ibid., pp. 167–8; Under the Maltese Cross, p. 2; Niebaum, History Washington Infantry, p. 63; Miners, Lincoln Day by Day, Vol 3, p. 14.

2. The War Begins

1. The Pennsylvania Thirteenth, July 4, 1861.
2. Ibid.; Fox, Pittsburgh During the Civil War, pp. 24, 31; Historical Society of Western Pennsylvania (hereafter HSWP), Washington Infantry Correspondence, Box 1, Folder 4; Bates, History of Pennsylvania Volunteers, Vol 1, p. 125; Niebaum, History Washington Infantry, pp. 65, 69; Miller, The Training of An Army, p. 248; Pennsylvania Department of Military Affairs, "Index of Civil War Soldiers, 1861–6," RG-19 Records, U.S. Army Military History Institute Library (hereafter MHI).
3. Patterson, letter to Wife Almira, June 6, 1861, William Phillis Collection.

4. Boatner, *The Civil War Dictionary*, p. 640; Cleaves, *Rock of Chickamauga*, pp. 68, 72–3; U. S. War Department, *The War of the Rebellion: A Compilation of the Official Records of the Union and Confederate Armies*, Washington DC: Govt. Printing Office, 1880–1901, (hereafter cited as *OR*; unless otherwise noted, all subsequent references are from Series 1), Vol. 51, Part 1, p. 398; *History Washington Infantry Pittsburgh*, p. 29.

5. Malone, *Dictionary of American Biography*, Vol 7, pp. 306–7; Leech, *Reveille in Washington,* p. 90.

6. *History Washington Infantry Pittsburgh*, p. 29; Nevins, *War for the Union*, Vol 1, pp. 214–6.

7. Miller, *The Training of An Army*, p. 248; Bates, History *of Pennsylvania Volunteers*, Vol 1, p. 126; Cleaves, *Rock of Chickamauga*, pp. 72–3; *Pennsylvania Thirteenth*, July 4, 1861, p. 1.

8. Niebaum, *History Washington Infantry*, p. 75.

9. Niebaum, *History Washington Infantry*, p. 75; *Dictionary of American Biography*, Vol 7, p. 307; Cleaves, *Rock of Chickamauga*, p. 75; Warner, *Generals in Gray*, pp. 22, 161; Boatner, *Civil War Dictionary*, p. 623; *OR*, Vol. 51, Part 1, p. 398 and Series III, Vol. 1, p. 360.

10. *Pennsylvania Thirteenth*, February 22, 1862.

11. *Ibid.*, Nov. 16, 1861; *History Washington Infantry Pittsburgh*, p. 29; Niebaum, *History Washington Infantry*, pp. 77, 86; Bates, *History of Pennsylvania Volunteers*, Vol 1, p. 127 and Vol 4, p. 647; Phillis, "John Williams Patterson," pp. 40–1; Fox, *Pittsburgh During the Civil War*, p. 27; Thomas A. Rowley, Military File NA; *History of Allegheny County*, p. 212; *Memoirs Allegheny County*, p. 84; Davis, Perry, and Kirkley, *The Official Military Atlas of the Civil War*, plate #7.

12. De Trobriand, *Four Years with the Army of the Potomac*, pp. 85, 87; Warner, *Generals in Blue*, pp. 364–5.

13. Warner, *Generals in Blue*, p. 122; Faust, *Historical Times Illustrated Encyclopedia*, p. 217; De Trobriand, *Four Years with the Army*, pp. 72–3, 86–7.

14. De Trobriand, *Four Years with the Army*, p. 95; Matthews, "Colonel McCarter, the Fighting Parson," pp. 1–2; Joseph King, Letter to Adam Rumbaugh, Feb. 2, 1862, in Sandow, *"Remember Your Friend Until Death,"* p. 18; Niebaum, *History Washington Infantry*, p. 86.

15. Niebaum, *History Washington Infantry,* Warner, *Generals in Blue*, p. 264; Dyer, *A Compendium of the War of the Rebellion*, Part 1, p. 274.

16. Joseph King Letter to Adam Rumbaugh, December 19, 1861, in Sandow, *"Remember Your Friend Until Death,"* pp. 16, 21; De Trobriand, *Four Years with the Army*, pp. 98–9, 107, 109, 141; *Pennsylvania Thirteenth*, Nov. 9 and 16, 1861.

17. *Pennsylvania Thirteenth*, Nov. 9 and 16, Dec. 7, 1861; Boatner, *Civil War Dictionary*, p.

96; Warner, *Generals in Blue*, p. 51; De Trobriand, *Four Years with the Army*, pp. 112, 119, 121.

18. De Trobriand, *Four Years with the Army*, p. 128; Large, *One Man's War*, p. 61; John Larkin Richards, Letter to Almira Patterson, Dec. 15, 1861, William Phillis Collection; *Pennsylvania Thirteenth*, Dec. 28, 1861.

19. *Pennsylvania Thirteenth*, Dec. 28, 1861; Patterson letter to Wife Almira, Feb. 20, 1862, William Phillis Collection; Joseph B. Martin, 1862 Diary, 102nd Pennsylvania Web site.

20. Martin diary, December 29, 1861; De Trobriand, *Four Years with the Army*, p. 128.

21. Samuel Myers, letter to George Kniess, Jan. 3, 1862, Lynn K. Lepley, 102nd PA Website; Martin Diary.

22. Warner, *Generals in Blue*, p. 95; Niebaum, *History Washington Infantry*, p. 97; *Pennsylvania Thirteenth*, January 4, 16, and 25, 1862

23. *Pennsylvania Thirteenth*, Feb. 1, 8, and 15, 1862; Joseph King, letter to Adam Rumbaugh, Feb. 2, 1862, p. 22.

24. Patterson, Letters to Wife, Feb. 20, 1862; Martin diary; *Pennsylvania Thirteenth*, Feb. 15 and 22, 1862.

25. *Pennsylvania Thirteenth*, Feb. 8, 1862; Niebaum, *History Washington Infantry*, p. 86; Lord, "Diary of Edward Lewis Hoon," p. 28; Martin diary; De Trobriand, *Four Years with the Army*, pp. 155–8.

26. De Trobriand, *Four Years with the Army*, pp. 158–9; *OR*, Vol. 5, p. 18; Sears, *To the Gates of Richmond*, pp. 8, 361–2; Gambone, *Major General Darius Nash Couch*, p. 67; Martin diary.

3. The Peninsula Campaign

1. Martin diary.

2. Dyer, *A Compendium*, Part 1, pp. 274, 276, 298; *OR*, Vol 11, Part 1, p. 282.

3. De Trobriand, *Four Years with the Army*, pp. 159–60; Sears, *To the Gates of Richmond*, p. 396 fn #2; *Historical Times Illustrated Encyclopedia*, pp. 276, 842; Martin diary; Niebaum, *History Washington Infantry*, p. 86.

4. Niebaum, *History Washington Infantry*, p. 86; Dyer, *A Compendium*, Part 1, pp. 298–9; De Trobriand, *Four Years with the Army*, pp. 163, 165; Patterson, Letter to Wife, April 2, 1862; Gambone, *Major General Darius Nash Couch*, p. 70; Bates, *History of Pennsylvania Volunteers*, Vol 4, p. 647; Boatner, *Civil War Dictionary*, p. 561; Hays, *Life and Letters of Alexander Hays*, p. 200; Martin diary; Large, *One Man's War*, pp. 109–10.

5. Large, *One Man's War*, pp. 112–3; De Trobriand, *Four Years with the Army*, pp. 174–5; Gambone, *Major General Darius Nash Couch*, p. 70; Niebaum, *History Washington Infantry*, p. 86;

Martin diary; Sears, *To the Gates of Richmond,* pp. 35, 37, map p. 51.

6. Sears, *To the Gates of Richmond,* p. 61; Large, *One Man's War,* pp. 113, 115; Martin diary; Patterson, letter to wife, April 6 and 13, 1862.

7. Patterson, letter of wife, May 6, 1862; De Trobriand, *Four Years with the Army,* pp. 188–91; Sears, *To the Gates of Richmond,* pp. 61, 70; *Historical Times Illustrated Encyclopedia,* p. 370; Boatner, *Civil War Dictionary,* pp. 775, 929.

8. *OR,* Vol. 11, Part 1, pp. 522.

9. Boatner, *Civil War Dictionary,* p. 929; Sears, *To the Gates of Richmond,* pp. 72–7, map p. 76.

10. Sears, *To the Gates of Richmond,* pp. 70–1, 73; *OR,* Vol. 11, Part 1, pp. 517; Niebaum, *History Washington Infantry,* p. 87; De Trobriand, *Four Years with the Army,* p. 194.

11. De Trobriand, *Four Years with the Army,* pp. 194–5; Large, *One Man's War,* p. 118; Martin diary; *OR,* Vol. 11, Part 1, pp. 513, 517–8, 522–3.

12. *OR,* Vol. 11, Part 1, pp. 513, 517, 524; Patterson, letter to wife, May 6, 1862.

13. *OR,* Vol. 11, Part 1, pp. 881.

14. Large, *One Man's War,* p. 121; De Trobriand, *Four Years with the Army,* pp. 222, 229–30; Niebaum, *History Washington Infantry,* p. 87; Sears, *To the Gates of Richmond,* pp. 109–10, 113, 117–9, 371, 380–1, map p. 122.

15. Sears, *To the Gates of Richmond,* p. 8, 117,124; Warner, *Generals in Blue,* pp. 74–5.

16. Sears, *To the Gates of Richmond,* pp. 110, 119, 123, 125–6, 370–1, 386, map p. 122; Boatner, *Civil War Dictionary,* p. 272; Niebaum, *History Washington Infantry,* p. 87.

17. Niebaum, *History Washington Infantry,* p. 87; Sears, *To the Gates of Richmond,* p. 131, map p.139; *OR,* Vol. 11, Part 1, pp. 879–80; Niebaum, *History Washington Infantry,* p. 87.

18. Niebaum, *History Washington Infantry,* p. 87; Sears, *To the Gates of Richmond,* pp. 138, 386, map p. 139; *OR,* Vol. 11, Part 1, pp. 888–90, 894–5; Boatner, *Civil War Dictionary,* p. 273; Thomas A. Rowley Military File, NA; Bates, *History of Pennsylvania Volunteers,* Vol 4, p. 648; M. P. Morrison, "Officer's Certificate of Disability," January 30, 1878, Thomas A. Rowley Pension File, NA.

19. Thomas A. Rowley Pension File, NA; De Trobriand, *Four Years with the Army,* p. 231; Large, *One Man's War,* p. 125; Patterson, letter to wife, Aug. 31, 1862; Phillis, "The Death of Colonel John Williams Patterson in the Wilderness," p. 1.

20. *OR,* Vol. 11, Part 1, p. 761.

21. *Ibid.,* p. 890.

22. Almira Patterson, letter to husband, May 28, 1862.

23. "Charges and Specifications preferred against Joseph M. Kinkead of One Hundred and Second Regiment Pennsylvania Volunteers,"

Joseph M. Kinkead Military File, NA, William Phillis Collection.

24. Sears, *To the Gates of Richmond,* pp. 149, 158–60; Warner, *Generals in Blue,* p. 357; Boatner, *Civil War Dictionary,* p. 414; Martin Diary; *OR,* Vol. 11, Part 1, p. 761; Part 2, pp. 28–9.

25. *OR,* Vol. 11, Part 2, pp. 201–2; Gambone, *Major General Darius Nash Couch,* p. 89; Sears, *To the Gates of Richmond,* pp. 145, 184, 189, maps p. 185.

26. Sears, *To the Gates of Richmond,* pp. 145, 184, 189, map p. 198; *OR,* Vol. 11, Part 2, p. 192, 202.

27. *OR,* Vol. 11, Part 2, p. 192, 202; Sears, *To the Gates of Richmond,* p. 256, map p. 273.

28. Sears, *To the Gates of Richmond,* pp. 272, 274, 276, map p. 273; *OR,* Vol. 11, Part 2, pp. 193.

29. *OR,* Vol. 11, Part 2, pp. 193, 202; Sears, *To the Gates of Richmond,* p. 276.

30. *OR,* Vol. 11, Part 2, pp. 193, 202.

31. *Ibid.;* Martin Diary; Sears, *To the Gates of Richmond,* pp. 278, 280–1, map pp. 273, 297.

32. Sears, *To the Gates of Richmond,* pp. 294–5, map p. 297; Alexander, *Military Memoirs of a Confederate,* p. 155.

33. Martin diary; *OR,* Vol. 11, Part 2, p. 202, 210.

34. *OR,* Vol. 11, Part 2, pp. 202–3; Sears, *To the Gates of Richmond,* pp. 310–2, map p. 328.

35. Sears, *To the Gates of Richmond,* pp. 313–4.

36. *Ibid.,* pp. 315, 317–8, 321.

37. *OR,* Vol. 11, Part 2, pp. 208, 211.

38. *Ibid.,* pp. 203, 275, 314; Sears, *To the Gates of Richmond,* pp. 322, 324, map p. 328.

39. Sears, *To the Gates of Richmond,* pp. 326–7, map 328; *OR,* Vol. 11, Part 2, p. 213.

40. *OR,* Vol. 11, Part 2, pp. 207–10; Sears, *To the Gates of Richmond,* p. 326.

41. Sears, *To the Gates of Richmond,* p. 327; *OR,* Vol. 11, Part 2, pp. 209, 214, 275, 314.

42. *Ibid., OR,* pp. 28–9, 210.

43. Niebaum, *History Washington Infantry,* pp. 92, 118; Bates, *History of Pennsylvania Volunteers,* Vol 4, p. 648; Sears, *To the Gates of Richmond,* pp. 347–8.

4. Second Bull Run, Antietam, and Fredericksburg

1. Thomas A. Rowley, Staff Officer File, Box 1158, NA.

2. Sears, *To the Gates of Richmond,* pp. 350–3; Boatner, *Civil War Dictionary,* p. 879; Martin diary; *Historical Times Illustrated Encyclopedia,* pp. 787–8.

3. *Historical Times Illustrated Encyclopedia,* 121; Dyer, *A Compendium,* Part 1, p. 298; *The*

Civil War Day by Day, John S. Bowman ed., Barnes & Noble, 1993, p. 77; Niebaum, *History Washington Infantry*, p. 92.

4. Niebaum, *History Washington Infantry*, pp. 92, 94; Hennessy, *Return to Bull Run*, pp. 31, 33, 35, map p. 36.

5. Hennessy, *Return to Bull Run*, pp. 419, 422, map p. 417; Niebaum, *History Washington Infantry*, pp. 92, 94; *Historical Times Illustrated Encyclopedia*, pp. 92–3; Boatner, *Civil War Dictionary*, pp. 104–5.

6. Boatner, *Civil War Dictionary*, p. 797; Warner, *Generals in Blue*, p. 95; *OR* Vol. 19, Part 1, p. 174; Stackpole, *From Cedar Mountain to Antietam*, pp. 218–9, 239, 390.

7. Sears, *Landscape Turned Red*, p. 81; *OR*, Vol. 19, Part 1, pp. 25, 38–39, Part 2, pp. 171, 209; Gambone, *Major General Darius Nash Couch*, p. 102.

8. Lord, "Diary of Edward Lewis Hoon," p. 28; Lewis C. White, "Sergeant's Memoir 1862–4," 102nd PA Infantry, PA "Save the Flags" Collection, MHI Archives, p. 8; Niebaum, *History Washington Infantry*, p. 94.

9. Niebaum, *History Washington Infantry*, p. 94; *OR*, Vol. 19, Part 1, p. 174, Part 2, p. 271.

10. Sears, *Landscape Turned Red*, pp. 87, 90–91, 93, 109–110.

11. *Ibid.*, pp. 113, 116–117, 124.

12. Phillis, "The Death of Colonel John Williams Patterson," p. 1; Niebaum, *History Washington Infantry*, p. 94; Gambone, *Major General Darius Nash Couch*, p.101.

13. Gambone, *Major General Darius Nash Couch*, p. 101; Sears, *Landscape Turned Red*, pp. 145, 148; *OR*, Vol. 19, Part 1, p. 48, 374, Part 2, p. 271.

14. *OR*, Vol. 19, Part 1, p. 48, 55; Sears, *Landscape Turned Red*, pp. 153, 156.

15. Sears, *Landscape Turned Red*, p. 257; Gambone, *Major General Darius Nash Couch*, pp. 106–7; *OR*, Vol. 19, Part 1, pp. 48, 376.

16. *OR*, Vol. 19, Part 1, pp. 66–67; Gambone, *Major General Darius Nash Couch*, pp. 106–9; Sears, *Landscape Turned Red*, pp. 257, 301, 307, 364; Niebaum, *History Washington Infantry*, p. 94; Stackpole, *From Cedar Mountain to Antietam*, pp. 308, 399, 439.

17. *OR*, Vol. 19, Part 1, pp. 68, 820–821, Part 2, pp. 339, 343.

18. Large, *One Man's War*, p. 14; Patterson, letter to wife, October 14, 1862.

19. Sears, *Landscape Turned Red*, p. 327; Dyer, *A Compendium*, Part 1, p. 311, Part 2, pp. 400, 446; Boatner, *Civil War Dictionary*, pp. 190, 204, 818; *OR*, Vol. 19, Part 1, p. 27,174.

20. Patterson, letter to wife, October 14, 1862; Niebaum, *History Washington Infantry*, p. 94.

21. Rowley, Staff Officer File, NA; *History of Allegheny County*, Vol 1 p. 239, Vol 2, pp. 231, 241.

22. Warner, *Generals in Blue*, p. 239; Patterson, letter to wife, November 10, 1862; *OR*, Vol. 21, pp. 60; Niebaum, *History Washington Infantry*, pp. 94, 96.

23. Matthews, "Colonel McCarter, the Fighting Parson," pp. 2–3.

24. *Ibid.*, p. 96; *OR*, Vol 30, Part 3, pp. 394–6.

25. Niebaum, *History Washington Infantry*, p. 96; Patterson, letter to wife, December 14, 1862.

26. Patterson, letter to wife, December 14, 1862; Niebaum, *History Washington Infantry*, p. 96; *Historical Times Illustrated Encyclopedia*, p. 289.

27. Patterson, letter to wife, December 24, 1862.

28. Warner, *Generals in Blue*, p. 414; Rowley, Staff Officer File, NA; Dyer, *A Compendium*, Part 1, pp. 311–2; White, "Sergeant's Memoir 1862–4," p. 5; Catton, *Glory Road*, p. 69; *OR*, Vol. 21, pp. 60, 142, 934–5; Niebaum, *History Washington Infantry*, p. 96.

29. Niebaum, *History Washington Infantry*, p. 96; Rowley, Staff Officer File, NA; Large, *One Man's War*, p. 172; John Porter, 102nd PA Infantry, Civil War Diary, PSA, MG–6; Patterson, letter to wife, January 26, 1863.

5. First Corps Brigadier

1. George F. McFarland, letter to wife, April 30, 1863, J. Horace McFarland Papers, PSA.

2. *Journal of the Executive Proceedings of the Senate of the United States of America,* Library of Congress (hereafter LC), Vol 13, pp. 92–4, 97, 128; Leech, *Reveille in Washington*, pp. 457–8.

3. Rowley, Military File NA; Rowley, Staff Officer File, NA.

4. Patterson, letters to wife, November 10, 1862, March 2 and 24, 1863.

5. *Executive Proceedings of the Senate*, Vol 13, pp. 212–5, 221, 225, 261–2; General Orders of the War, Part III, pp. 1–100.

6. *OR*, Vol. 51, Part 1, pp. 995, 996, 998; Porter, Civil War Diary; SO No. 142, *Special Orders of the War Department*; Dyer, *A Compendium*, Part 1, 284, 286; NA, RG 393, V0111, Part 1, 3984, p. 221; Bates, *History of Pennsylvania Volunteers*, Vol. 7, p. 465; *History of the 121st Regiment Pennsylvania Volunteers*, p. 35.

7. *Executive Proceedings of the Senate*, Vol 13, pp. 102, 211, 274; Leech, *Reveille in Washington*, p. 281.

8. Edmund L. Dana, Personal Diary Recopied 1867–69, Wyoming Historical and Genealogical Society (hereafter WHGS), Wilkes–Barre, PA, Box 4S40; Edmund L. Dana obituary, *New York Times*, April 26, 1889, p. 5;

Kulp, *Families of the Wyoming Valley*, Vol. 1, pp. 33–4, 41; H. T. Lee, letter to Edmund Dana, February 19, 1863, Edmund L. Dana Papers, WHGS, Folder 1863–C.

9. McCalmont, *Extracts from the Letters,* pp. 5, 7; "*Alfred B. McCalmont Biography*," Venango County Genealogical Club (hereafter VCGC), Oil City, Pa.: 1997; Hunt and Brown, *Brevet Brigadier Generals in Blue*, p. 391; Bates, *Martial Deeds*, p. 623.

10. Bates, *History of Pennsylvania Volunteers*, Vol 6, p. 30; Ashhurst, "Address Delivered at the Meeting of the Philadelphia Bar," pp. 14–5; O'Brien, "'Give Them Another Volley, Boys,'" pp. 37–8; *Pennsylvania at Gettysburg*, Vol 2, p. 664.

11. *Pennsylvania at Gettysburg*, Vol. 2, p. 665; Rosengarten, "Upon the Occasion of the Death of Chapman Biddle," pp. 17–8; *History of the 121st Regiment*, pp. 10, 13, 30.

12. Bates, *History of Pennsylvania Volunteers*, Vol 7, pp. 464–5; Heffley and Heffley, *Civil War Diaries,* p. 1; Warren, *Declaration of Independence*, pp. 14–6.

13. Warren, *Declaration of Independence and War History,* pp. 16, 18–9; O'Brien, "Give Them Another Volley, Boys," p. 38; Heffley, *Civil War Diaries*, p. 19.

14. Dreese, *The 151st Pennsylvania Volunteers at Gettysburg*, p. 5; Dreese, *An Imperishable Fame*, pp. 7–8.

15. Dreese, *An Imperishable Fame*, pp. 6–8, 12; "Diary of Alfred D. Staudt," p. 15.

16. "Diary of Alfred D. Staudt," p.15; Dreese, *An Imperishable Fame*, pp. 81, 87, 89; McFarland, letter to wife, March 1, 1863.

17. "Diary of Alfred D. Staudt," p. 15; Heffley, *Civil War Diaries*, p. 2; Zorn, *A Sergeant's Story*, pp. 55–6; Henry A. Cornwell, letter to Lucy Cornwell April 8, 1863, Henry A. Cornwell Correspondence (MMS 1401), Center for Archival Collections, Bowling Green State University (hereafter BGSU), Bowling Green, Ohio, p. 1.

18. Cornwell, letter to Lucy Cornwell, April 8, 1863, pp. 1–2.

19. Dreese, *An Imperishable Fame*, p. 96.

20. *Ibid.*, p. 89; Heffley, *Civil War Diaries*, p. 43; "Diary of Alfred D. Staudt," p. 15; *OR*, Vol 25, Part 2, p. 234, Part 1, pp. 137, 256; McFarland, letter to wife, April 23, 1863, pp. 1–2.

21. McFarland, letter to wife, April 23, 1863, p. 3; "Diary of Alfred D. Staudt," p. 15; Dreese, *An Imperishable Fame*, p. 89; Chamberlin, *History of the One Hundred and Fiftieth*, pp. 79–81.

22. McFarland, letter to wife, April 23, 1863, pp. 3–4.

23. *Ibid.*, pp. 4–5; Chamberlin, *History of the One Hundred and Fiftieth*, pp. 81, 83; Zorn, *A Sergeant's Story*, p. 57; Doubleday, *Chancellorsville and Gettysburg*, p. 5; MOLLUS, Commandry of the State of Pennsylvania, Circular No. 7,

Philadelphia, April 20, 1888, p. 1; Tevis and Marquis, *The History of the Fighting Fourteenth*, pp. 64–5; Sears, *Chancellorsville*, p. 134.

24. Sears, *Chancellorsville*, p. 136.

25. Heffley, *Civil War Diaries*, p. 45; McFarland, letter to wife, May 8, 1863, pp. 1–2.

26. McFarland, letter to wife, May 8, 1863, pp. 12–3; "Diary of Alfred D. Staudt," p. 15; Heffley, *Civil War Diaries*, p. 45; Sears, *Chancellorsville*, p. 136.

27. Dreese, *An Imperishable Fame*, p. 96; Zorn, *A Sergeant's Story*, p. 58; Dana, *Personal Diary*, McFarland, letter to wife, May 8, 1863, pp. 3–4, Apr. 30, 1863, pp. 1–2.

28. Sears, *Chancellorsville*, pp. 228–9, 237.

29. Zorn, *A Sergeant's Story*, p. 58; "Diary of Alfred D. Staudt," p. 15; Bigelow, *The Campaign of Chancellorsville*, pp. 273, 301, map #19; McFarland, letter to wife, May 8, 1863, pp. 4–5.

30. McFarland, letter to wife, May 8, 1863, p. 6; "Partial History of the 121st Pennsylvania Regiment," n. d., n. s., J. Horace McFarland Papers, PSA, Copy GNMP Library, p. 3.

31. McFarland, letter to wife, May 8, 1863, p. 6; Bigelow, *The Campaign of Chancellorsville*, map #24 and #39; Heffley, *Civil War Diaries*, p. 47; Dreese, *An Imperishable Fame*, p. 102; Dana, *Personal Diary*; Warner, *Generals in Blue*, p. 493; Nesbit, *General History of Company D*, p. 10; *OR*, Vol. 25, Part 1, pp. 158, 255–6, 287–90.

32. Patterson, letter to wife, May 25, 1863; Sears, *Chancellorsville*, pp. 424–5, map p. 413; Niebaum, *History Washington Infantry*, p. 79; Frank Wheaton, letter to Lt. Col. McMahan, May 23, 1863 and "Charges and Specifications preferred against Joseph M. Kinkead of One Hundred and Second Regiment Pennsylvania Volunteers," Joseph M. Kinkead Military File, NA, Copy William Phillis Collection.

33. "*Diary of Alfred D. Staudt*," p. 16; Chapman Biddle, letter to Alexander Biddle, May 17, 1863, University of Delaware; "*Annual Report of the Adjutant General*," Vol. 2, p. 558; Dyer, *A Compendium*, Part 1, p. 225; *OR*, Vol. 25, Part 2, p. 576.

34. *OR*, Vol. 25, Part 2, p. 576; Dana, *Personal Diary*; NA, RG 393, Part 2, #3605; Hewett, Trudeau, and Suderow, *Supplement to the Official Records of the Union and Confederate Armies*, (hereafter *SOR*), Vol 5, Addendum {Reports} Vol. 27, Serial Nos. 43–44, p. 114; Weld, *War Diary and Letters*, p. 289.

35. McFarland, letter to wife, June 5, 1863, Typed Copy GNMP Library.

36. Wheeler, *Witness to Gettysburg*, pp. 1–3; Longstreet, *From Manassas to Appomattox*, p. 334.

6. The Gettysburg Campaign

1. Longstreet, *From Manassas to Appomattox*, pp. 334–8; Wheeler, *Witness to Gettysburg*, pp. 19, 33.

2. *OR*, Vol. 27, Part 3, p. 81; Weld, *War Diary and Letters*, p. 213.

3. NA, RG 393, Part 2, #3605; Zorn, *A Sergeant's Story*, p. 64; Dreese, *An Imperishable Fame*, p. 118; Nesbit, *General History of Company D*, p. 11; *The Official Military Atlas of the Civil War*, Plate 8, Sheet 2.

4. *OR*, Vol 27, Part 3, pp. 89, 91.

5. *The Official Military Atlas of the Civil War*, Plate 8, Sheet 2; Dreese, *An Imperishable Fame*, p. 119; Chamberlin, *History of the One Hundred and Fiftieth*, p. 109; Zorn, *A Sergeant's Story*, p. 64.

6. Zorn, *A Sergeant's Story*, p. 65; Boatner, *Civil War Dictionary*, p. 650; *OR*, Vol. 27, Part 3, pp. 148–9, 151; Dreese, *An Imperishable Fame*, p. 120.

7. Dreese, *An Imperishable Fame*, p. 120; Weld, *War Diary and Letters*, pp. 217, 220; *Official Military Atlas*, Plate 7, Sheet 1; *"Diary of Alfred D. Staudt,"* p. 16.

8. Large, *One Man's War*, pp. 339–40; J. K. Moorhead, telegram to A. Lincoln, June 17, 1863, LC; Wheeler, *Witness to Gettysburg*, p. 61.

9. NA, RG 393, Part 2, #3605; *SOR*, Vol 5, Addendum {Reports} Vol. 27, Serial Nos. 43–44, p. 111.

10. *"Diary of Alfred D. Staudt,"* p. 16; Dana, *Personal Diary*; McCalmont, *Extracts from the Letters*, pp. 42–3, 46.

11. *OR*, Vol 27, Part 3, pp. 308, 329, 333–4; Dreese, *An Imperishable Fame*, pp. 120–1.

12. Dreese, *An Imperishable Fame*, p. 121; Dana, *Personal Diary*; Weld, *War Diary and Letters*, p. 224; *OR*, Vol. 27, Part 3, pp. 305–6.

13. Dreese, *An Imperishable Fame*, pp. 121–2.

14. *Ibid.*, p. 123; Weld, *War Diary and Letters*, p. 226; Nesbit, *General History of Company D*, p. 13; Zorn, *A Sergeant's Story*, p. 66; Locke, *The Story of the Regiment*, p. 222; *OR*, Series 1, Vol. 27, Part 3, pp. 373, 375–6.

15. *OR*, Series 1, Vol. 27, Part 3, pp. 374, 376, 418–9; *History of the 121st Regiment*, p. 41; Krumwiede, "A July Afternoon on McPherson's Ridge," p. 44.

16. *OR*, Vol 27, Part 3, pp. 415–7, Part I, pp. 243–4.

17. *OR*, Vol 21, pp. 1, 777, 860, 876, 965.

18. *OR*, Vol 21, p. 2, Vol 51, Part I, pp. 943–944, 951, 965, 974, 991, Vol 19, Part 2, pp. 542, 550, 569; Dyer, *A Compendium*, Part 1, pp. 284.

19. Longstreet, *From Manassas to Appomattox*, pp. 333, 347–8.

20. *OR*, Vol 27, Part I, pp. 243–4, Part 3, pp. 415–7.

21. J. W. Hofmann, "Remarks on the Battle of Gettysburg," p. 3; *1858 Map of Adams County*, Adams County Historical Society, Drawn from Actual Survey by G. M. Hopkins, Traced by J. R. Hershey May 5, 1980; Cooke, "The First Day of Gettysburg," p. 4; "Partial History of the 121st Pennsylvania Regiment," p. 3; Marsh, *The Nineteenth Indiana at Gettysburg*; *History of the 121st Regiment*, p. 44; Nesbit, *General History of Company D*, p. 13; Krumwiede, "A July Afternoon on McPherson's Ridge," p. 44; *OR*, Vol. 27, Part III, pp. 334–6, 417.

22. Gates, *Civil War Diaries*, pp. 89, 91; Gates, *The 'Ulster Guard*,*"* p. 421; 20 NYSM Vertical File, GNMP Library.

23. Coddington, *The Gettysburg Campaign*, pp. 266–7, 272–3.

24. Thomas A. Rowley, Court–Martial File, Box 1002, 118 pages, NA; H. N. Warren Testimony, p. 55, *Ibid.*, W. T. Humphrey Testimony, pp. 69–70; Bates, *History of Pennsylvania Volunteers*, Vol 7, p. 469; Barnes, *Medical and Surgical History of the Civil War*, Vol 1, pp. 179, 181; PA Dept. Military Affairs Index.

25. *OR*, Vol. 27, Part 1, p. 256.

26. Coddington, *The Gettysburg Campaign*, fn #7, p. 681; Martin, *Gettysburg July 1*, p. 91.

27. Martin, *Gettysburg July 1*, p. 92; Shue, *Morning at Willoughby Run*, p. 53; Doubleday, *Chancellorsville and Gettysburg*, pp. 124–5; Pearson, *James S. Wadsworth of Geneseo*, p. 204.

28. Coddington, *The Gettysburg Campaign*, pp. 237, 240.

29. W. T. Humphrey Testimony, Rowley Court–Martial File NA, pp. 70–1; Krumwiede, "A July Afternoon on McPherson's Ridge," p. 44; *OR*, Vol. 27, Part 1, pp. 315, 324, 326.

30. *OR*, Vol. 27, Part 1, p. 897; Biddle, "The First Day of the Battle of Gettysburg," pp. 23, 30; *Pennsylvania at Gettysburg*, Vol 2, p. 897; *History of the 121st Regiment*, pp. 44, 119–20; Busey and Martin, *Regimental Strengths and Losses at Gettysburg*, p. 22; Edwin R. Gearhart, "In the Years '62 to '65: Personal Recollections of Edwin R. Gearhart, A Veteran," Stroudsburg, PA: *The Daily Times*, Mar. 19 — Aug. 6, 1900, Copy GNMP, p. 33; Jacob F. Slagle, Letter about his experiences July 1st to 4th, 1863, Civil War Misc. Collection, MHI, copy Richard Matthews Collection, pp. 1–2; Osborne, *Holding the Left at Gettysburg*, pp. 4–5.

31. Osborne, *Holding the Left*, map p. 2, p. 6; Biddle, "The First Day of the Battle of Gettysburg," p. 31; *History of the 121st Regiment*, pp. 45, 120; Theodore B. Gates, letter to J. P. Bachelder, January 30, 1864, *The Bachelder Papers*, Vol I, p. 81; George F. McFarland, "Report of the 151st Regiment Pennsylvania Volunteers, March 16, 1864," *The Bachelder Papers*, Vol I, p. 88; John D. S. Cook, "Personal Reminiscences of Gettysburg," *The Gettysburg Papers*, Vol. 2, Brandy and Freeland, p. 917; J. P. Bachelder, Conversation with George F. McFarland (n. d.), *The Bachelder Papers*, Vol I, p. 271; *OR*, Vol. 27, Part 1, pp. 315, 320, 323, 327.

32. H. N. Warren Testimony, Rowley

Court–Martial File NA, p. 55; NA, RG 393, Part 2, #3614; George F. McFarland, handwritten notes, J. Horace McFarland Papers, PSA, Copy GNMP; Oliver K. Moore, letter to Edmund L. Dana, April 21, 1864, Edmund L. Dana Papers, WH&GS, Folder 1864–C; *SOR*, Vol. 5, Part 1, p. 115.

33. *SOR*, Vol. 5, Part 1, p. 95; Abner Doubleday Testimony, Rowley Court–Martial File, p. 43; Slagle, letter about his experiences, p. 2; McFarland, "Report of the 151st Regiment," p. 88; Gates, letter to J. P. Bachelder, January 30, 1864, p. 81; Zorn, *A Sergeant's Story*, p. 67; *Pennsylvania at Gettysburg*, Vol 2, p. 897; *History of the 121st Regiment*, p. 162; *OR*, Vol. 27, Part 1, pp. 320, 364, 897.

34. *OR*, Vol. 27, Part 1, pp. 330, 355; Scott, *The Story of the Battle of Gettysburg*, p. 144; Testimony of Brigadier General James S. Wadsworth, Washington, March 23, 1864, Joint Congressional Committee on the Conduct of the War, Report of 1865, Vol 1, p. 413, GNMP; Harrison, *Edward McPherson Farm*, p. 37; A. S. Coe, letter to J. B. Bachelder, Dec. 28, 1888, *The Bachelder Papers*, p. 1564.

35. Chamberlin, *History of the One Hundred and Fiftieth*, p. 118; Nesbit, *General History of Company D*, p. 14; Matthews, *149th Pennsylvania Volunteer Infantry Unit*, p. 80; Chamberlin, "Address at the Dedication of the Monument," *Pennsylvania at Gettysburg*, Vol. 2, p. 745; *OR*, Vol. 27, Part 1, pp. 360–1.

36. Gates, letter to Bachelder, January 30, 1864, p. 81; Gates, *The 'Ulster Guard*,'' pp. 433, 436; Biddle; "The First Day of the Battle of Gettysburg," p. 31; New York Monuments Commission for the Battlefields of Gettysburg, Chattanooga, and Antietam, *Final Report on the Battle of Gettysburg* (hereafter New York at Gettysburg), Vol 3, p. 643; *OR* , Vol. 27, Part 1, p. 317.

37. Howard, *Autobiography*, pp. 412–3; Harry W. Pfanz, *Gettysburg—The First Day*, Chapel Hill, NC: Univ. of North Carolina Press, 2001, pp. 137–8, fn #16 p. 402; Gates, *The 'Ulster Guard,'* pp. 436; Abner Doubleday, letters to Samuel P. Bates, April 24, 1874, and October 18, 1875, Samuel P. Bates Papers, PSA, copy GNMP.

38. Martin, *Gettysburg July 1*, p. 98.

39. Pfanz, *Gettysburg—The First Day*, pp. 137–8, 140–1; Coddington, *The Gettysburg Campaign*, pp. 282.

40. Coddington, *The Gettysburg Campaign*, pp. 215–7, 284–5.

41. *OR*, Series 1, Vol. 27, Part 1, p. 897.

42. Abner Doubleday Testimony, Rowley Court–Martial File, p. 44; W. W. Robinson Testimony, *Ibid.*, p. 19.

43. *SOR*, Vol. 5, Part 1, p. 97; *Pennsylvania at Gettysburg*, Vol 2, p. 89; O'Brien, "Give Them Another Volley, Boys," p. 43; *OR*, Vol. 27, Part 1, pp. 327, 362.

44. *OR*, Vol. 24, Part 1, p. 362; Gates, letter to Bachelder, January 30, 1864, p. 81; New York at Gettysburg, Vol 3, p. 1260; *Pennsylvania at Gettysburg*, Vol 2, p. 898; Bachelder, conversation with George F. McFarland, p. 271; McFarland, "Report of the 151st Regiment," p. 88.

45. McFarland, "Report of the 151st Regiment," p. 89; Bachelder, Conversation with George F. McFarland, p. 271; Locke, *Story of the Regiment*, p. 229; Kress, *Memoirs of Brigadier General John Alexander Kress*, p. 18.

46. J. Glenn Testimony, Rowley Court–Martial File, p. 65.

47. Howard, "Campaign and Battle of Gettysburg," p. 56; Testimony of James S. Wadsworth, p. 413; Doubleday, *Chancellorsville and Gettysburg*, p. 141; Martin, *Gettysburg July 1*, p. 270; *OR*, Vol 27, Part 1, pp. 266, 360; Abner Doubleday, letter to Bates, October 18, 1875; Coddington, *Gettysburg*, p. 282, fn # 107, p. 693; Pfanz, *Gettysburg—The First Day*, p. 142, 323.

48. Coddington, *Gettysburg*, pp. 282–3; 310–3, 315; Doubleday, letter to Bates, April 24, 1874.

49. Martin, *Gettysburg July 1*, p. 346; Busey and Martin, *Regimental Strengths and Losses*, pp. 21, 163, 173–4.

50. Busey and Martin, *Regimental Strengths and Losses*, p. 174; Andrew Cross, *The War*, 1865, "Account of Captain Benjamin F. Little, Co. F, 52nd North Carolina," typescript by K. G. Harrison, March, 1987, copy GNMP, p. 25; Wainwright, *A Diary of Battle*, p. 235; O'Brien, "Give Them Another Volley, Boys," p. 43; Jordan, *North Carolina Troops 1861–1865,* Vol. 12 Infantry, p. 400; Clark, *Histories of the Several Regiments*, Vol 3, pp. 105–6; *OR*, Vol. 27, Part 1, p. 313, 320, 356, Part 2, pp. 638, 643.

51. *OR*, Vol. 27, Part 1, p. 313, 356, Part 2, pp. 638–9; *Pennsylvania at Gettysburg*, Vol 1, p. 671, 898; Bates, *History of Pennsylvania Volunteers*, Vol 7, p. 466; Alfred B. McCalmont, Sworn Statement, May 4, 1864, NA, Box 1002; *History of the 121st Regiment*, p. 161; F. M. Powell Testimony, Rowley Court–Martial File, pp. 57–8.

52. Powell Testimony, p. 58; Gates, letter to Bachelder, January 30, 1864, pp. 81–2, 236; Clark, *Histories of the Several Regiments*, Vol 5, p. 119; Cross, "Account of Captain Benjamin F. Little," p. 25; *OR*, Vol. 27, Part 1, pp. 362–3.

53. *OR*, Vol. 27, Part 1, pp. 313, 315, 323, 356, 362–3; Wainwright, *A Diary of Battle*, p. 235; *History of the 121st Regiment*, pp. 121, 161; Gates, *The 'Ulster Guard,'* p. 440.

54. H. N. Warren Testimony, Rowley Court–Martial File, pp. 51–3; F. M. Powell Testimony, *Ibid.*, p. 57; McCalmont, Sworn Statement; Gearhart, "*In the Years '62 to '65*," p. 35.

55. Gearhart, "In the Years '62 to '65," p. 35; New York at Gettysburg, Vol 3, p. 1257; Wainwright, *A Diary of Battle*, p. 235; *OR*, Vol. 27, Part 1, pp. 313, 315, 356, Part 2, p. 643.

56. *OR*, Vol. 27, Part 2, p. 643; Gates, letter to Bachelder, January 30, 1864, pp. 81–2; *History of the 121st Regiment*, pp. 121,161; Cook, "Personal Reminiscences of Gettysburg," p. 919; Frank J. Sterling, letter to father, July 10, 1863, Rutgers University Special Collections and Archives, Copy GNMP, p. 1.

57. McFarland, "Report of the 151st Regiment," p. 89; Bachelder, conversation with George F. McFarland, p. 271; McFarland, "Report of Movements of 151st Pennsylvania," p. 300; Dreese, *The Hospital on Seminary Ridge*, p. 77; *OR*, Vol. 27, Part 1, p. 313, 327; Bates, *History of Pennsylvania Volunteers*, Vol 7, p. 466.

58. Bates, *History of Pennsylvania Volunteers*, Vol. 7, p. 466; Gearhart, "*In the Years '62 to '65*," p. 35; McCalmont, *Extracts from the Letters*, p. 53; *History of the 121st Regiment*, p. 46; Dreese, *The Hospital on Seminary Ridge*, p. 78; *Pennsylvania at Gettysburg*, Vol 2, p. 691; Wilkins, "A Personal War History," in *"Remember Your Friend Until Death*," p. 65; Clark, *Histories of the Several Regiments*, Vol 3, pp. 106–7; Warren, *The Declaration of Independence*, p. 30.

59. McFarland, "Report of Movements of 151st Pennsylvania," pp. 300–1; Sterling, letter to father, July 10, 1863, p. 1; O'Brien, "Give Them Another Volley, Boys," p. 47; Osborne, *Holding the Left*, p. 23, fn #52; Bates, *History of Pennsylvania Volunteers*, Vol 6, p. 32; *History of the 121st Regiment*, pp. 48, 161; McFarland, "Report of the 151st Regiment," p. 89; *OR*, Vol. 27, Part 1, pp. 313, 327, Part 2, pp. 638, 643.

60. Coddington, *Gettysburg*, fn #149, p. 708; Pfanz, *Gettysburg—The First Day*, pp. 142–3, 339; Spencer G. Welch, letter to wife, August 2, 1863, Joyner Library, Eastern Carolina Library, typed copy GNMP, pp. 1–2.

61. Welch, letter to wife, August 2, 1863, p. 3; Warren, and Bachelder, "First Days Battle," *Maps of the Battle Field of Gettysburg*; Shue, *Morning at Willoughby Run*, p. 77, map p. 60; *1858 Map of Adams County*, Adams County Historical Society; Caldwell, *The History of a Brigade of South Carolinians*, p. 96.

62. Caldwell, *The History of a Brigade of South Carolinians*, p. 96; Warren and Bachelder, "First Days Battle"; Welch, letter to wife, August 2, 1863, p. 3; Washington P. Shooter, letter to George A. McIntyre, July 20, 1863, Charleston, SC CWRT *Drumbeat*, June 1989, copy GNMP, pp. 2–3; Brooks, *Stories of the Confederacy*, excerpt GNMP, p. 35; Brown, *A Colonel at Gettysburg and Spotsylvania*, p. 77.

63. Caldwell, *The History of a Brigade of South Carolinians*, p. 97; Dawes, *Service with the Sixth Wisconsin Volunteers*, p. 175; *OR*, Vol. 27, Part 2, pp. 639, 656–7, 661.

64. *OR*, Vol. 27, Part 1, p. 313, 927, 934; Miller, "Perrin's Brigade on July 1, 1863," pp. 25, 28.

65. Caldwell, *The History of a Brigade of South Carolinians*, p. 97; Shooter, letter to George A. McIntyre July 20, 1863, p. 3.

66. Tompkins and Tompkins, *Company K, Fourteenth South Carolina Volunteers*, copy GNMP, pp. 19–20.

67. Brown, *A Colonel at Gettysburg and Spotsylvania*, pp. 81, 214; Shooter, letter to George A. McIntyre July 20, 1863, p. 3; Welch, letter to wife, August 2, 1863, pp. 3–4; Bonham, "A Little More Light on Gettysburg," GNMP Library, p. 522; *OR*, Vol. 27, Part 1, p. 313, Part 2, pp. 661–2; 214.

68. H. N. Warren Testimony, Rowley Court–Martial File, p. 53; F. M. Powell Testimony, *Ibid.*, p. 58.

69. Caldwell, *The History of a Brigade of South Carolinians*, p. 97; Shooter, letter to George A. McIntyre, July 20, 1863, p. 3.

70. Brown, *A Colonel at Gettysburg and Spotsylvania*, pp. 81, 214–5, 231; Miller, "Perrin's Brigade on July 1, 1863," pp. 25, 28; *Pennsylvania at Gettysburg*, Vol. 2, p. 763; *OR*, Vol. 27, Part 1, pp. 313, 821, 927, 934, Part 2 pp. 661–2.

71. Coddington, *Gettysburg*, fn #125 p. 706; Pfanz, *Gettysburg—The First Day*, p. 143; Doubleday, letters to Bates, April 3, 1874 and October 4, 1875; Pearson, *Wadsworth of Geneseo*, p. 221.

72. Howard M. Madaus, e–mail to author, August 11, 2002; Bonham, "A Little More Light on Gettysburg," p. 522; Shooter, letter to George A. McIntyre, July 20, 1863, p. 3; Holabird, *Flags of the Army of the United States*, "1st Army Corps"; Todd, *American Military Equipage*, p. 321.

73. Sword, "Capt. James Glenn's Sword and Pvt. J. Marshall Hill's Enfield," p. 11; C. W. Wadsworth Testimony, Rowley Court–Martial File, pp. 30–2; J. Glenn Testimony, *Ibid.*, p. 65.

74. Dreese, *The Hospital on Seminary Ridge*, p. 85; Wilkins, "A Personal War History," pp. 65–6; *New York at Gettysburg*, Vol 3, p. 64; Miller, "Perrin's Brigade on July 1, 1863," pp. 25, 26; *Pennsylvania at Gettysburg*, Vol 2, pp. 662, 691, 699; McFarland, "Report of Movements of 151st Pennsylvania," p. 302; Gates, letter to Bachelder, January 30, 1864, p. 83; Gates, *The 'Ulster Guard*," p. 443; *OR*, Vol. 27, Part 1, p. 313, Part 2, p. 662; Brown, *A Colonel at Gettysburg and Spotsylvania*, p. 81.

75. "After the Battle #2, Introduction — The Killed and Wounded Heroes, 1, General Reynolds," J. Horace McFarland Papers, PSA, Copy GNMP, p. 1; Matthews, *The 149th Pennsylvania*, p. 238; Nesbit, *General History of Company D*, p. 15.

76. Nesbit, *General History of Company D*, p. 15; Bonham, "A Little More Light on Gettysburg," p. 522; Brown, *A Colonel at Gettysburg and Spotsylvania*, pp. 223–4; Slagle, letter about his experiences, p. 248.

77. Slagle, letter about his experiences, p. 227; Locke, *The Story of the Regiment*, p. 231; McLean, *Cutler's Brigade at Gettysburg*, p. 143.

78. Zorn, *A Sergeant's Story*, pp. 67, 82.

79. C. W. Wadsworth Testimony, Rowley Court–Martial File, pp. 30–1; W. L. T. Wilson Testimony, *Ibid.*, pp. 80–1; Oliver K. Moore, Sworn Statement, May 2, 1864, NA, Box 1002.

80. F. M. Powell Testimony, Rowley Court–Martial File, p. 59; McLean, *Cutler's Brigade at Gettysburg*, p. 141.

81. McLean, *Cutler's Brigade at Gettysburg*, p. 143; T. W. Miller Testimony, Rowley Court–Martial File, p. 21; Cook, "Personal Reminiscences of Gettysburg," p. 917; Wainwright, *A Diary of Battle*, p. 237; Bates, *History of Pennsylvania Volunteers*, Vol 7, p. 467.

82. Cutler Testimony, Rowley Court–Martial File, p. 12; T. W. Miller Testimony, *Ibid.*, pp. 21, 23; W. L. T. Wilson Testimony, *Ibid.*, pp. 81–2.

83. McLean, *Cutler's Brigade at Gettysburg*, p. 141; Warner, *Generals in Blue*, p. 110; Dennis B. Dailey Affidavit, Lysander Cutler, Pension File, NA.

84. W. L. T. Wilson Testimony, Rowley Court–Martial File, p. 81; Wainwright, *A Diary of Battle*, p. 237; Slagle, letter about his experiences, pp. 248–9.

85. *Official Army Register of the Volunteer Force*, Vol 3, p. 989; W. N. Dalgliesh Testimony, Rowley Court–Martial File, pp. 74–5; McCalmont, Sworn Statement.

86. *OR*, Vol 27, Part 1, pp. 336–7.

87. W. W. Robinson Testimony, Rowley Court–Martial File, pp. 17–8; M. Finnicum Testimony, *Ibid.*, pp. 36, 38.

88. M. Finnicum Testimony, Rowley Court–Martial File, pp. 35–9; F. M. Powell Testimony, *Ibid.*, pp. 59–60.

89. Pfanz, *Gettysburg—The First Day*, pp. 337–8; Howard, *Autobiography*, p. 418; Howard, "Campaign and Battle of Gettysburg," p. 58; Hancock, "Gettysburg, A Reply to General Howard," pp. 823–5.

90. Hancock, "Gettysburg, A Reply to General Howard," pp. 825, 830; Doubleday, *Chancellorsville and Gettysburg*, pp. 147–8; Charles H. Morgan, "Report of Lieutenant Colonel Charles H. Morgan," *The Bachelder Papers*, Vol. III, pp. 1351–2; *Maine at Gettysburg*, pp. 89–90; *OR*, Vol. 27, Part 1, p. 252.

91. Dawes, *Service with the Sixth Wisconsin*, p. 179; Dawes, "With the Sixth Wisconsin at Gettysburg," *The Gettysburg Papers*, Vol. 1, p. 233; W. W. Robinson Testimony, Rowley Court–Martial File, p. 18; M. Finnicum Testimony, *Ibid.*, p. 38; Clayton E. Rogers, "Gettysburg Scenes," *Milwaukee Sunday Telegraph*, February 13, 1887, State Historical Society of Wisconsin (hereafter SHSW), p. 3.

92. Thompson, *Narrative of the Service of the Seventh Indiana Infantry*, pp. 162–4; Snyder, "The One Hundred Forty–Seventh Infantry; Immortality at Gettysburg," p. 61; J. W. Hofmann, "Remarks on the Battle of Gettysburg," Presentation to the Historical Society of Pennsylvania (hereafter HSP), March 8, 1880, Philadelphia: A. W. Auner, 1880, Manuscript Collection, Gettysburg College, pp. 6–7.

93. T. W. Miller Testimony, Rowley Court–Martial File, pp. 121–2; Cutler Testimony, *Ibid.*, p. 12.

94. Cutler Testimony, Rowley Court–Martial File, pp. 12–3.

95. Rogers, "Gettysburg Scenes"; Thomas A. Rowley, letter to Edmund L. Dana, October 8, 1864, Edmund L. Dana Papers, WH&GS, Folder 1864–D, p. 3; Rufus R. Dawes, "A Gallant Officer," *Chippewa Herald*, January 4, 1884.

96. Benet, *A Treatise on Military Law*, p. 46; "General Courts–Martial," *Army and Navy Journal*, March 19, 1864, p. 507.

97. "General Courts–Martial," p. 507; Rogers, "Gettysburg Scenes"; Dawes, *Service with the Sixth Wisconsin*, p. 179; Weld, *War Diary and Letters*, p. 231.

98. Coddington, *Gettysburg*, pp. 313–5, fn.'s 148–151 pp. 708–9.

99. "General Courts–Martial," p. 507; Benet, *A Treatise on Military Law*, pp. 47–9.

100. Thomas A. Rowley Pension File, NA; *OR*, Vol. 27, Part 1, pp. 156, 316.

101. *OR*, Vol. 27, Part 1, pp. 156, 313, 316, 323; Cook, "Personal Reminiscences of Gettysburg," p. 922; Moore, letter to Dana, April 21, 1864; *History of the 121st Regiment*, pp. 121, 123; *Pennsylvania at Gettysburg*, Vol 2, p. 691; Bates, *History of Pennsylvania Volunteers*, Vol 7, p. 467; Walter L. Owens, letter to J. P. Bachelder August 6, 1866, *The Bachelder Papers*, Vol I, p. 268.

102. Coddington, *Gettysburg*, pp. 97–8; Benedict, *Army Life in Virginia*, pp. 159, 161–3.

103. Benedict, *Army Life in Virginia*, pp. 163–5; Slagle, letter about his experiences, p. 249.

104. *OR*, Vol. 27, Part 1, p. 256.

105. *Ibid.*, p. 316; NA, RG 393, Part 1, #3605; *SOR*, Vol 5, Addendum Reports, Vol 27, Serial Nos. 43–44, p. 116.

106. Owens, letter to Bachelder, August 6, 1866; *OR*, Vol. 27, Part 1, p. 316.

107. *OR*, Vol. 27, Part 1, pp. 316, 325; Rowley Pension File; Bates, *History of Pennsylvania Volunteers*, Vol 7, p. 467; Dana, *Personal Diary*.

108. Dana, *Personal Diary*, p. 102; *SOR*, Vol. 5, Part 1, p. 120; Dyer, *A Compendium*, Part 1, p. 286; "Partial History of the 121st Pennsylvania Regiment," p. 4; Matthews, *The 149th Pennsylvania*, pp. 101, fn #84 p. 108.

109. Matthews, *The 149th Pennsylvania*, p. 101; NA, RG 393, Part 2, #3614, p. 141; *Ibid.*, #3605; Dana, *Personal Diary*, p. 102; "Army Personal," *Army and Navy Journal*, September 12, 1863, p.

38; Weld, *War Diary and Letters*, p. 240; J. C. McGee, "Certificate of Sick Leave," October 2, 1863, Rowley Military File; Rowley Court–Martial File; U. S. War Department, Adjutant General's Office, Report on Thomas A. Rowley, July 11, 1878, Rowley Pension File; S O #365, Special Orders War Department, 1863.
110. NA, RG 393, Part 2, #3614, p. 369; Dyer, *A Compendium*, Part 1, p. 286; Ibid., Part 3, pp. 1653–4; *The Civil War Diaries of Col. Theodore B. Gates*, p. 97; "Diary of Alfred D. Staudt," p. 33; McCalmont, *Extracts from the Letters*, p. 59; *History of the 121st Regiment*, pp. 52, 58, 68.
111. W. T. L. Wilson, letter to E. L. Dana Aug. 4, 1863, Edmund L. Dana Papers, WH&GS, Folder 1863–B.
112. Dana, *Personal Diary*; Rowley, Staff Officer File, NA; *OR*, Vol. 27, Part 1, pp. 312–4.
113. *OR*, Vol. 27, Part 1, pp. 253, 256; *Historical Times Illustrated Encyclopedia*, p. 224; Report on Thomas A. Rowley, July 11, 1878, Rowley, Staff Officer File, NA.
114. General Orders War Department, 1863, Part III, pp. 1, 32–39, 100.
115. Benet, *A Treatise on Military Law*, pp. 50–1.
116. "General Courts–Martial," p. 507.

7. Camp Berry, Maine

1. Moore, letter to Dana, April 21, 1864.
2. *Memoirs Allegheny County*, p. 83; *OR*, Vol. 26, Part 2, p. 322; S O #460, Special Orders War Department, 1863.
3. S O #296, 305, 318, 335, 346, *Ibid.*, Vol 2.
4. *War for the Union*, Vol 2, pp. 143–4; Phone conversation with Kenneth E. Thompson Jr., July 9, 2002; Whitman and True, *Maine in the War for the Union*, pp. 7, 9; Kenneth E. Thompson Jr., e–mail to the author August 20, 2002.
5. Thompson e–mail, August 20, 2002; *Civil War Day by Day*, pp. 99, 121–2.
6. Thompson e–mail August 20 and Sept. 6, 2002; Thompson, *Civil War Maine Hall of Fame*, pp. 50–1, 63–4; Whitman and True, *Maine in the War for the Union*, p. 11; Camp Berry Post Records September 1863 through March 1864, NA, M617 Roll 1495.
7. Camp Berry Post Records.
8. McCalmont, *Extracts from the Letters*, pp. 66–7; Rowley, Staff Officer File, NA.
9. NA, RG 393, Vol 29/30, p. 586; *Under the Maltese Cross*, p. 119; Thompson, *Civil War Maine Hall of Fame*, pp. 65–6; Camp Berry Post Records.

10. Camp Berry Post Records; Thompson, e–mail, August 20, 2002.
11. *Journal of the Executive Proceedings*, Vol 13, pp. 335, 342.
12. Thompson, *Civil War Maine Hall of Fame*, p. 66; Camp Berry Post Records; NA, RG 393, Vol II, Part 1, 3944, Vol 29/30, pp. 586, 692, 703.
13. "General Officers without Commands," *Army and Navy Journal*, January 23, 1864, pp. 347–8.
14. Ibid., p. 348.
15. Porter, *Campaigning with Grant*, p. 24; Grant, *Personal Memoirs*, pp. 403–4, 407–8.
16. "Army Personal," *Army and Navy Journal*, March 19, 1864, p. 503 .
17. Zorn, *A Sergeant's Story*, p. 106; Dana, *Personal Diary*; Warner, *Generals in Blue*, pp. 262, 345; S O No. 126, *Special Orders of the War Department*, January through April 1864, Part 1, 1864; General Orders No. 3, April 16, 1864, Edmund L. Dana Papers, WH&GS, Folder 1864–A.
18. Camp Berry Post Records; Thompson, *Civil War Maine Hall of Fame*, p. 66.

8. The Culpeper Court–Martial

1. Zorn, *A Sergeant's Story*, p. 109.
2. "Appointments by the President," *Army and Navy Journal*, April 9, 1864, p. 556; *Special Orders of the War Department*, May through August 1864, Part 2, 1864.
3. John W. Patterson, Regimental Circular, Mar. 17, 1864, William Phillis Collection; Ronn Palm photo; William Phillis correspondence and e–mails, December 2–5, 2003.
4. Zorn, *A Sergeant's Story*, p. 109; Dana, *Personal Diary*.
5. NA, RG 393, Vol II, Part 1, 3985, Vol 91, pp. 65, 66; Rhodes, *All for the Union*, p. 133; Extract from Diary of Captain George Meade, HSP; Rowley, Staff Officer File, NA.
6. Dana, *Personal Diary*; p. 154; NA, RG 393, Vol II, Part 1, 3984, Index No. 30, p. 109.
7. Benet, *A Treatise on Military Law*, pp. 28, 37, 41, 42; "General Courts–Martial, " p. 507.
8. McCalmont, Sworn Statement, p. 2.
9. "General Courts–Martial, " p. 507; Benet, *A Treatise on Military Law*, pp. 17, 25.
10. Exhibit A, Request for Extension, Rowley Court–Martial File, NA; NA, RG 393, Vol II, Part 1, 3985, Vol 91, p. 75; *Ibid.*, 3984, Index No. 30, p. 1118; *OR*, Vol. 33, p. 468, Vol. 36, Part 1, p. 202; Rhodes, *All for the Union*, p. 134; Wainwright, *A Diary of Battle*, p. 342; "Annual

Report of the Adjutant General," p. 445; *Special Orders War Department,* January through April 1864; Bates, *Martial Deeds,* p. 655; DeWitt Clinton McCoy obituary, *Meadville Evening Republican,* Dec. 1, 1902, p. 3; *History of Crawford County, 1885,* Meadville, PA: Crawford County Historical Society (hereafter CCHS), 1975, p. 356; Clark B. Hall, e–mail to author, Nov. 11, 2002.

11. "General Courts–Martial, " p. 507; Rowley Court–Martial File, NA, pp. 5–6; Coppee, *Field Manual of Courts Martial,* MHI, pp. 20, 57–59.

12. Coppee, *Field Manual of Courts Martial,* pp. 15, 48–9; *OR,* Vol. 33, p. 468.

13. Dana, *Personal Diary;* p. 154; Zorn, *A Sergeant's Story,* p. 110; *History of the 121st Regiment,* pp. 73–5; *Special Orders War Department,* January through April 1864; Warren, *The Declaration of Independence,* p. 27.

14. NA, RG 393, Vol II, Part 1, 3985, Vol 91, p. 80.

15. *"Annual Report of the Adjutant General,"* p. 745; Dana, *Personal Diary;* p. 154; Bates, *History of Pennsylvania Volunteers,* Vol 7, p. 469; *Official Army Register* , pp. 981–2; D. C. McCoy, telegram to O. K. Moore, April 21, 1864, Dana Papers, WH&GS, Folder 1864–B; McCalmont, Sworn Statement, p. 2.

16. Benet, *A Treatise on Military Law,* pp. 17, 25; Rowley Court–Martial File, NA, pp. 1–2; "General Courts–Martial, " p. 507.

17. "General Courts–Martial," pp. 507–8; Benet, *A Treatise on Military Law,* pp. 59, 61–2, 83–4.

18. "General Courts–Martial," p. 507.

19. Rowley Court–Martial File, NA, p. 3.

20. *Ibid.,* pp. 3–5; Benet, *A Treatise on Military Law,* pp. 65, 112; "General Courts–Martial," p. 508; Dana, Personal Notes.

21. Dana, *Personal Diary;* p. 154; Mattocks, *"The Unspoiled Heart,"* p. 127; Zorn, *A Sergeant's Story,* p. 111.

22. Rowley Court–Martial File, NA, p. 6.

23. *Ibid.,* pp. 3–5.

24. *Ibid.,* pp. 5–6, Exhibit A Request for Extension; Coppee, *Field Manual of Courts Martial,* pp. 22–23.

25. Coppee, *Field Manual of Courts* Martial, p. 50; Benet, *A Treatise on Military Law,* pp. 84, 87, 112–3.

26. Rowley Court–Martial File, NA, pp. 6–8.

27. *Ibid.,* pp. 8–9.

28. Benet, *A Treatise on Military Law,* pp. 57, 63, 65, 194.

29. *Ibid.,* pp. 208, 217, 221; Alotta, *Military Executions,* pp. 2, 116.

30. O'Brien and Oliver Diefendorf, *General Orders of the War Department 1861, 1862, & 1863,* Vol II, G O #18, p. 10; Sears, *Chancellorsville,* pp. 22–3.

31. Sears, Chancellorsville, pp. 325, 457–6; Bigelow, *The Campaign of Chancellorsville,* pp. 351, 354–5.

32. Bigelow, *The Campaign of Chancellorsville,* fn #1 p. 355; Sears, *Chancellorsville,* p. 326; O'Brien and Diefendorf, *General Orders of the War Department,* G O #282, pp. 355–6; *A Statement of the Case of Brigadier General Joseph W. Revere,* New York: C. A. Alford, 1863, MHI, pp. 40–1.

33. Coppee, *Field Manual of Courts Martial,* p. 21; Cutler Testimony, Rowley Court–Martial File, NA, pp. 10–3.

34. Cutler Testimony, pp. 13–4.

35. W. W. Robinson Testimony, *Ibid.,* pp. 15–9; Rhea, *The Battle of the Wilderness,* Order of Battle.

36. *Official Army Register,* Vol 5, p. 137; T. W. Miller Testimony, Rowley Court–Martial File, pp. 120–3.

37. Miller Testimony, pp. 123–4.

38. Hays, *Life and Letters of Alexander Hays,* pp. 585–7, 589; *Under the Maltese Cross,* p. 257.

39. Edmund L. Dana, letter to friend, April 24, 1864, WH&GS, Box 4S40.

40. *Ibid.*

41. *OR,* Vol 19, Part 1, p. 174.

42. *Ibid.,* Vol 2, p. 400; *Historical Times Illustrated Encyclopedia,* pp. 522–3; Warner, *Generals in Blue,* pp. 342, 558.

43. Warner, *Generals in Blue,* pp. 342,558.

44. *Ibid.,* p. 144; *Dictionary of American Biography,* Vol 3, p. 192; *Official Army Register* , Vol 1, p. 161.

45. *OR,* Vol 19, Part 1, p. 174; Vol 33, p. 738, 786, 1042; Bates, *History of Pennsylvania Volunteers,* Vol. 4, p. 651; Warner, *Generals in Blue,* p. 558.

46. Warner, *Generals in Blue,* pp. 407–8; *OR,* Vol 12, Part 3, p. 586; Vol 14, p. 222; Vol 21, p. 899; Vol 27, p. 156; Vol 33, pp. 784–5.

47. *OR,* Vol 25, Part 2, pp. 589–90; Vol. 11, Part 1, pp. 52, 524, 890, 896; Vol. 19, Part 2, p. 338; Vol. 21, p. 963; Vol. 29, Part 1, p. 220; Vol. 33, p. 1037; Warner, *Generals in Blue,* p. 335.

48. Warner, *Generals in Blue,* p. 400; *OR,* Vol. 11, Part 1, p. 729; Part 2, p. 337; Vol. 27, Part 1, p. 161; Vol. 29, Part 1, p. 217; Vol. 33, p. 738.

49. *OR,* Vol. 11, pp. 493–4, 815, 841; Vol. 51, Part 1, p. 951; Vol. 21, p. 53; Vol. 33, pp. 736–7; Warner, *Generals in Blue,* p. 537; "Army Personal," *Army and Navy Journal,* August 29 and September 12, 1863, p. 556.

50. Hays, *Life and Letters of Alexander Hays,* p. 476; Parke, *Recollections of Seventy Years,* p. 321.

51. Parke, *Recollections of Seventy Years,* p. 323; Sears, *To the Gates of Richmond,* pp. 370, 380; *Dictionary of American Biography,* Vol. 4, p. 461; Hennessy, *Return to Bull Run,* pp. 274–5.

52. Jordan, *Genealogical and Personal History,* Vol. 2, p. 852; *New York at Gettysburg,* Vol. 3,

p. 905; Dreese, *An Imperishable Fame*, pp. 58, 63–4; Coddington, *Gettysburg*, pp. 97–8.

53. Hays, *Life and Letters of Alexander Hays*, pp. 585–7, 589; *OR*, Vol. 33, p. 691.

54. Warner, *Generals in Blue*, p. 544; Alexander S. Webb Vertical File, GNMP; Dyer, *A Compendium*, Part 1, p. 290.

55. Hays, *Life and Letters of Alexander Hays*, pp. 460, 462.

56. *Ibid.*, pp. 458–9, 463.

57. *Ibid.*, pp. 463–4.

58. *Ibid.*, p. 559; Alexander Webb, letter to wife Aug. 8, 1863, Yale Univ. Library, Copy GNMP; *OR*, Vol. 29, Part 1, pp. 218, 669; Part 2, p. 601.

59. *OR*, Vol. 33, Part 1, pp.1037–44; Rowley Court–Martial File, NA, p. 2.

60. G. Harney Testimony, Rowley Court–Martial File, NA, p. 27.

61. *Ibid.*, pp. 25–7, C. W. Wadsworth Testimony, p. 28; *New York at Gettysburg*, Vol. 3, pp. 1001–2; *OR*, Vol. 36, Part 1, p. 811.

62. C. W. Wadsworth Testimony, Rowley Court–Martial File, NA, pp. 28–34.

63. M. Finnicum Testimony, *Ibid.*, pp. 35–9.

64. NA, RG 393, Vol II, Part 1, 3985; Vol 91, p. 104.

65. Rowley Court–Martial File, NA, p. 39.

66. "General Courts–Martial," p. 507; "Army Personal," *Ibid.*, p. 567.

67. A. Doubleday testimony, *Ibid.*, pp. 48–9.

68. "General Courts–Martial," p. 507; Rowley Court–Martial File, NA, p. 39.

69. A. Doubleday testimony, *Ibid.*, pp. 40–1, 47.

70. *Ibid.*, pp. 42–3, 45–6, 48.

71. *Ibid.*, pp. 44–5.

72. *Ibid.*, pp. 45–7.

73. *Ibid.*, pp. 48–9.

74. *Ibid.*, pp. 49–50.

75. NA, RG 393, Part 2, #3699; *Roster of Wisconsin Volunteers, War of the Rebellion, 1862–1865*, SHSW, pp. 529, 871; Rowley Court–Martial File NA, p. 50.

76. Benet, *A Treatise on Military Law*, pp. 115, 117.

77. Oliver K. Moore, letter to Edmund L. Dana, April 21, 1864, Dana Papers, WH&GS, Folder 1864–C; D. C. McCoy, telegram to O. K. Moore, April 21, 1864, Dana Papers, WH&GS, Folder 1864–B.

78. W. T. Humphrey Testimony, Rowley Court–Martial File NA pp. 70–1.

79. Bates, *Martial Deeds*, p. 689; Coppee, *Field Manual of Courts Martial*, p. 22; H. N. Warren Testimony, Rowley Court–Martial File NA, p. 55.

80. Warren Testimony, pp. 51, 53–6.

81. Warren, *The Declaration of Independence*, p. 31; Pennsylvania Executive Office, Military Department, *Roster of Commissions*, p. 152; White, *History of Mercer County, Pennsylvania*, Vol. 1, p. 188.

82. F. M. Powell Testimony, Rowley Court–Martial File NA pp. 60–3.

83. Bates, *History of Pennsylvania Volunteers*, Vol 7, p. 617; J. Glenn Testimony, Rowley Court–Martial File NA pp. 65–6.

84. Glenn Testimony, pp. 67–8.

85. PA Dept. Military Affairs Index; W. T. Humphrey Testimony, Rowley Court–Martial File NA pp. 69–70.

86. Humphrey Testimony, p. 71.

87. G. W. Jones Testimony, *Ibid.*, pp. 72–3; Bates, *History of Pennsylvania Volunteers*, Vol. 8, p. 658; *Roster of Commissions Issued to Officers*, p. 162.

88. *Ibid.*, p. 160; *Official Army Register*, Part 3, p. 989; *SOR*, Vol 5, Part 1, p. 95; W. N. Dalgliesh Testimony, Ibid., p. 73.

89. *Ibid.*, pp. 74–6.

90. Rowley Court–Martial File NA p. 75; Dana, *Personal Diary*, p. 155.

91. Moore, Letter to Edmund L. Dana, April 21, 1864.

92. *Ibid.*, p. 156.

93. Dana, *Personal Diary*, p. 155.

94. *Official Army Register*, Part 3, p. 982; *Roster of Commissions*, p. 154; C. B. Stout Testimony, Rowley Court–Martial File NA pp. 76–7; C. H. Reilay Testimony, *Ibid.*, pp. 78–9.

95. W. L. T. Wilson Testimony, *Ibid.*, pp. 79–83.

96. Dana, *Personal Diary*; Edmund L. Dana, Personal Notes Brig. General Thomas A. Rowley's Court–Martial, WH&GS, Folder 1864–B; Rowley Court–Martial File NA, Box 1002, Exhibit B.

97. Rowley Court–Martial File NA, Box 1002, Exhibit B; Dana, Personal Notes; Kathleen Georg Harrison, Transcript of Edmund L. Dana's Personal Notes, Court–Martial of Brig. General Thomas A. Rowley, 1981, Typed Copy GNMP.

98. Benet, *A Treatise on Military Law*, pp. 126–7, 136; "General Courts–Martial," p. 508.

99. Benet, *A Treatise on Military Law*, pp. 137–9.

100. Rowley Court–Martial File NA, p. 85; *OR*, Vol. 36, Part 2, p. 330; U. S. War Department, Adjutant General's Office, Cover Page, MM 1416, Box 1002, NA.

101. Hays, *Life and Letters of Alexander Hays*, p. 593; Dana, *Personal Diary*; pp. 156, 158; Moore, "Sworn Statement"; "General Courts--Martial," p. 508.

102. *Journal of the Executive Proceedings*, Vol 13, pp. 514, 519.

103. "General Courts–Martial," p. 508; Benet, *A Treatise on Military Law*, pp. 152–3, 158.

104. Donald, *Lincoln*, p. 313; E. R. Platt, letter to Joseph Holt, May 1, 1864, NA, Box 1002.

105. Dana, *Personal Diary*; GCMO #120,

Index of General Court–Martial Orders, Adjutant General's Office, 1864, Washington: GPO, 1865, pp. 1–3.

9. The Defendant Reacts

1. Matthews, "Colonel McCarter, the Fighting Parson," p. 3.
2. Official Army of the Potomac Correspondence, Letters, etc., Sent by General Meade, April 16, 1864 to Aug. 19, 1864, George Meade Papers, HSP; *OR*, Vol. 36, Part 2, p. 330.
3. Miller, *The Training of An Army*, p. 217; McCalmont, Sworn Statement; Ness, "Excerpts from the Civil War Diary of George Randolph Snowden," pp. 158, 162.
4. Thomas A. Rowley, letter to James K. Moorhead, May 5, 1864, NA, Box 1002, pp. 1–2; *History of Allegheny County*, p. 239.
5. Phillis, "John Williams Patterson" p. 41; Phillis, "The Death of Colonel John Williams Patterson," p. 2; Rhea, *The Battle of the Wilderness*, pp. 133–5, 190–1, 202–3.
6. Matthews, *The 149th Pennsylvania*, pp. 150, 168; OR, Vol. 40, Part 1, p. 520.
7. Dreese, *An Imperishable Fame*, p. 164; Conversation with Michael A. Dreese, Feb. 26, 1999.
8. Joseph Holt, Report to President Lincoln, May 6 and 11, 1864, MM 1416, Box 1002, NA, pp. 1–11.
9. *Ibid.*, pp. 11–14.
10. E. D. Townsend, General Court–Martial Orders No. 120, May 27, 1864, MM 1416, Box 1002, NA; Adjutant General's Office, Cover Page, *Ibid.*
11. The Major General Gouverneur K. Warren Papers, New York State Library (hereafter NYSL), Manuscripts and Special Collections, Box 26, SC10668.
12. General Court–Martial Orders No. 120, pp. 1–3.
13. Major General Gouverneur K. Warren Papers.
14. Rhea, *The Battle of the Wilderness*, pp. 95, 439; Meade, *Life and Letters of George Gordon Meade*, Vol. 2, pp. 157–8, 185, 375–6; Grant, *Personal Memoirs*, p. 604; Porter, *Campaigning with Grant*, pp. 107–8; Nevins, *War for the Union*, Vol 4, p. 284.
15. Wheeler, *On Fields of Fury*, pp. 264–5; Nevins, *War for the Union*, Vol 4, fn #30, p. 45; *Historical Times Illustrated Encyclopedia*, p. 577; *Civil War Day by Day*, pp. 45, 167; Alexander, *Military Memoirs*, pp. 546–7.
16. Stine, *History of the Army of the Potomac*, pp. 660–1.
17. *Ibid.*, p. 662; Wheeler, *On Fields of Fury*,

p. 265, map p. 76; Alexander, *Military Memoirs*, pp. 548–9; Catton, *A Stillness at Appomattox*, p. 187; *OR*, Vol. 40, Part 1, p. 20.
18. Stine, *History of the Army of the Potomac*, pp. 660–1.
19. *Ibid.*, p. 662; Boatner, *Civil War Dictionary*, pp. 644–5, 777; *Official Military Atlas*, plates 64 and 65; *Historical Times Illustrated Encyclopedia*, p. 577; Catton, *A Stillness at Appomattox*, pp. 187–8, 191; Alexander, *Military Memoirs*, pp. 547, 550, 552–3.
20. Alexander, *Military Memoirs*, p. 549; Dawes, *Service with the Sixth Wisconsin*, p. 290; Matthews, *The 149th Pennsylvania*, p. 179: Chamberlin, *History of the One Hundred and Fiftieth*, pp. 259–60.
21. Alexander, *Military Memoirs*, pp. 549, 554; *OR*, Vol. 40, Part 2, pp. 86, 94.
22. *OR*, Vol. 40, Part 2, p. 94; Alexander, *Military Memoirs*, p. 550; *Civil War Day by Day*, p. 167; Catton, *A Stillness at Appomattox*, pp. 192–4.
23. Catton, *A Stillness at Appomattox*, pp. 193–5; *OR*, Vol. 40, Part 2, p. 125.
24. *OR*, Vol. 40, Part 2, pp. 118, 172, 174; Catton, *A Stillness at Appomattox*, p. 196; Alexander, *Military Memoirs*, pp. 550–2, 554; Wheeler, *On Fields of Fury*, p. 267.
25. Wheeler, *On Fields of Fury*, pp. 196–7; Alexander, *Military Memoirs*, pp. 554–5; *OR*, Vol. 40, Part 2, pp. 172, 174–6.
26. *OR*, Vol. 40, Part 2, pp. 176–7, 179, Part 1, p. 25.
27. *OR*, Vol. 40, Part 2, pp. 167,179.
28. *Ibid.*, p. 157; Chamberlin, *History of the One Hundred and Fiftieth*, pp. 261, 263.
29. Wheeler, *On Fields of Fury*, p. 269; Catton, *A Stillness at Appomattox*, p. 199; Stine, *History of the Army of the Potomac*, p. 669; *OR*, Vol. 40, Part 2, pp. 155–7, 180–1; Part 1, pp. 24–5; Alexander, *Military Memoirs*, pp. 555–7.
30. Alexander, *Military Memoirs*, pp. 547, 577; *Historical Times Illustrated Encyclopedia*, p. 578; Nevins, *War for the Union*, Vol 4, fn #39, p. 49; Wheeler, *On Fields of Fury*, p. 269; Catton, *A Stillness at Appomattox*, p. 199.
31. *OR*, Vol 40, Part 2, p. 216.
32. *Ibid.*, Part 3, p. 393; *Pittsburgh Commercial*, July 14, 1864, p. 1.
33. *OR*, Vol 40, Part 3, pp. 393–4.
34. Flanagan, *The Life of General Gouverneur Kemble Warren*, fn #29, p. 181; G. K. Warren Papers, Box 26, SC10668.
35. G.K. Warren Papers, Box 26, SC10668.
36. *Ibid.*; NA, RG 393, Vol II, Part 1, 3964, Vol 5, pp. 276, 284; *OR*, Vol. 40, Part 1, p. 26; Letters, etc., Sent by General Meade.
37. McPherson, *Battle Cry of Freedom*, pp. 588–9; Kevin Anderson, "Grant's Lifelong Struggle with Alcohol," p. 23; Perret, *Ulysses S. Grant*, p. 262.

38. Perret, *Ulysses S. Grant*, pp. 269–70; Catton, *A Stillness at Appomattox*, pp. 23, 25; Anderson, "Grant's Lifelong Struggle with Alcohol," pp. 23–4.

39. G. K. Warren Papers, Box 26, SC10668; Boatner, *Civil War Dictionary*, p. 822; Dyer, *A Compendium*, Part 1, p. 257; NA, RG 393, Vol II, Part 1, 3964, Vol. 5, pp. 287, 296; *OR*, Vol. 40, Part 2, p. 270, p. 375.

40. *OR*, Vol. 40, Part 2, p. 270; De Trobriand, *Four Years with the Army*, pp. 593, 598–9.

41. *OR*, Vol 40, Part 1, pp. 26, 28; Flanagan, *The Life of General Gouverneur Kemble Warren*, p. 182.

42. Flanagan, *The Life of General Gouverneur Kemble Warren*, p. 283; Matthews, *The 149th Pennsylvania*, pp. 193–4; Bates, *History of Pennsylvania Volunteers*, Vol 6, p. 36.

10. Jubal Early's Invasions of Pennsylvania

1. "The Late Invasion of Pennsylvania," *Philadelphia Inquirer*, Aug. 3, 1864, p. 1.

2. Boatner, *Civil War Dictionary*, p. 822; S O #218, *Special Orders War Department, May thru Aug. 1864*; Warner, *Generals in Blue*, p. 47, fn #446, pp. 647–8; *OR*, Vol. 37, Part 1, p. 683, Vol. 40, Part 2, p. 375.

3. "Army and Navy Personal," July 9, 1864, *Army and Navy Journal*, p. 759; *Ibid.*, "General Officers without Commands," Jan. 23, 1864, pp. 347–8; *Ibid.*, "Army Personal," April 16, 1864, p. 567; Department of the Monongahela," *Army and Navy Official Gazette*, Oct. 29, 1864, p. 670.

4. *Pittsburgh Gazette*, Aug. 2, 1864, p. 2; Boatner, *Civil War Dictionary*, pp. 423, 497, 588; Nevins, *War for the Union*, Vol 4, p. 51; *Historical Times Illustrated Encyclopedia*, pp. 454, 711.

5. *Historical Times Illustrated Encyclopedia*, p. 527; Boatner, *Civil War Dictionary*, pp. 419, 423; Gambone, *Major General Darius Nash Couch*, p. 189.

6. Gambone, *Major General Darius Nash Couch*, pp. 191, 198; *Civil War Dictionary*, p. 255; *Historical Times Illustrated Encyclopedia*, p. 454; "The Raid — Another Account," *Philadelphia Inquirer*, July 5, 1864, p. 1; "Proclamation by Governor Curtin," *Ibid.*, July 6, 1864, p. 1; *OR*, Vol. 37, Part 1, p. 705.

7. *Pittsburgh Gazette*, July 6, 1864, p. 1.

8. *Ibid.*, July 8, 1864, p. 3; *Ibid.*, July 9, 1864, p. "Composition of the Invading Rebel Force," *Philadelphia Inquirer*, July 6, 1864, p. 4; "The Excitement in Harrisburg," *Ibid.*, July 7, 1864, p. 1; *Civil War Day by Day*, p. 168.

9. S O #225, *Special Orders War Department*, May through August 1864.

10. G C M O #239, *General Court-Martial Orders*, pp. 1–3; *Pittsburgh Commercial*, July 9, 1864, p. 1.

11. S O #230, *Special Orders War Department*, May through Aug. 1864.

12. *Civil War Dictionary*, p. 256; *Pittsburgh Commercial*, July 11, 1864, p. 1; *Historical Times Illustrated Encyclopedia*, pp. 233–4; "Harrisburg," *Philadelphia Inquirer*, July 9, 1864, p. 1; William Acheson, "Civil War Reminiscences of William Acheson," n. p., Feb. 3, 1914, WRHS Archives/Library, p. 7; Gambone, *Major General Darius Nash Couch*, p. 197; *OR*, Vol. 37, Part 1, pp. 272–3, 336, Part 2, p. 132, 185; *Pittsburgh Gazette*, July 12, 1864, p. 2.

13. *Pittsburgh Gazette*, July 11, 1864, p. 2; *Pittsburgh Commercial*, July 11, 1864, p. 1; Leech, *Reveille in Washington*, pp. 338–9.

14. Leech, *Reveille in Washington*, pp. 338–9; Acheson, "Civil War Reminiscences of William Acheson," p. 7; *OR*, Vol. 37, Part 1, pp. 272–3, 275–6; 342.

15. *OR*, Vol. 37, Part 1, pp. 232, 276, 336, Vol 51, Part 1, p. 228; Leech, *Reveille in Washington*, pp. 342–3.

16. *Civil War Day by Day*, p. 168; *Historical Times Illustrated Encyclopedia*, p. 234; *Civil War Dictionary*, p. 256; Gambone, *Major General Darius Nash Couch*, p. 188; Alvord, "Early's Attack on Washington," pp. 481–2; *OR*, Vol. 37, Part 1, p. 336, *Ibid.*, Part 2, pp. 300, 554.

17. *Pittsburgh Gazette*, July 14, 1864, pp. 1 and 2; *Pittsburgh Commercial*, July 6, p. 1, July 9, p. 3, July 11, p. 1, July 13, p. 1, and July 14, 1864, p. 1.

18. *Civil War Day by Day*, p. 171; "General Couch and Mr. Cameron," *Army and Navy Journal*, Aug. 13, 1864, p. 840; Warner, *Generals in Blue*, pp. 13, 103; *Civil War Dictionary*, pp. 677, 893.

19. *Civil War Dictionary*, pp. 34, 256–7, 677; *Civil War Day by Day*, p. 172; *OR*, Vol. 37, Part 1, pp. 328–330.

20. *OR*, Vol. 37, Part 1, pp. 354–5; Warner, *Generals in Gray*, pp. 157, 198; Gambone, *Major General Darius Nash Couch*, p. 189; *Historical Times Illustrated Encyclopedia*, p. 311; *Pittsburgh Commercial*, July 2, 1864, p. 1.

21. *OR*, Vol. 37, Part 1, pp. 331–2, 341.

22. *Ibid.*, pp. 328–329, 341–2, 355.

23. *Ibid.*, p. 333–4; Gambone, *Major General Darius Nash Couch*, p. 208.

24. Gambone, *Major General Darius Nash Couch*, p. 208–9; *Generals in Gray*, p. 198; "Army and Navy Personal," *Army and Navy Journal*, July 30, 1864, p. 807; *OR*, Vol. 37, Part 1, pp. 333–4, 355; "The Rebel Invasion," *Philadelphia Inquirer*, August 1, 1864, p. 8.

25. *Philadelphia Inquirer*, August 1, 1864, p. 8; *Civil War Day by Day*, pp. 172–3; *OR*, Vol. 37, Part 2, pp. 455, 473, 535, 572.

26. *OR*, Vol. 37, Part 2, pp. 524, 527; "The Late Invasion of Pennsylvania," *Philadelphia Inquirer*, August 3, 1864, p. 1.

27. *Philadelphia Inquirer*, August 3, 1864, p. 1; *Under the Maltese Cross*, p. 8; *Pittsburgh Gazette*, August 1, 1864, pp. 1–2.

28. *Pittsburgh Gazette*, August 1, 1864, pp. 1–2.

29. *Ibid.*, p. 1.

30. *Ibid.*, p. 2; *Pittsburgh Commercial*, Aug. 1, 1864, p. 1.

31. Warner, *Generals in Blue*, p. 63; *Army and Navy Journal*, August 13, 1864, p. 841; *Philadelphia Inquirer*, July 9, 1864, p. 8.

32. *Philadelphia Inquirer*, July 9, 1864, p. 8; *OR*, Vol. 37, Part 2, p. 541.

33. *Pittsburgh Gazette*, Aug. 1, 1864, p. 2, Aug. 2, 1864, p. 1.

34. *Philadelphia Inquirer*, July 5, 1864, p. 1; "From the Middle Division;" *Ibid.*, Aug. 8, 1864, p. 1; *Pittsburgh Gazette*, August 3, 1864, p. 3.

35. *Pittsburgh Gazette*, August 3, 1864, p. 3.

36. *Army and Navy Journal*, Aug. 13, 1864, p. 841; *Philadelphia Inquirer*, Aug. 3, 1864, p. 1; *OR*, Vol. 43, Part 1, p. 706, Vol. 37, Part 2, pp. 540–1.

37. "Early's Second Invasion," *Army and Navy Journal*, Aug. 13, 1864, p. 840; *Pittsburgh Gazette*, Aug. 6, 1864, pp. 1–2.

38. *Pittsburgh Gazette*, August 1, 1864, p. 2, August 10, 1864, p. 3.

39. *Pittsburgh Commercial*, August 6, 1864, p. 2.

40. Warner, *Generals in Blue*, pp. 438–9; *Civil War Day by Day*, p. 173; Porter, *Campaigning with Grant*, pp. 270–1.

41. Porter, *Campaigning with Grant*, p. 270–2, 273; *Lincoln Day by Day*, p. 277; "Other Accounts by Associated Press," *Philadelphia Inquirer*, August 8, 1864, p. 1; "Reports from Harper's Ferry," *Ibid.*, August 8, 1864, p. 1; "Lieutenant–General Perpetrated a Joke," *Ibid.*, August 9, 1864, p. 1; *Pittsburgh Gazette*, August 10, 1864, p. 3; Alvord, "Early's Attack on Washington," p. 485.

42. Alvord, "Early's Attack on Washington," p. 485; "From the Middle Division," *Philadelphia Inquirer*, Aug. 8, 1864, p. 1; *Civil War Dictionary*, p. 549.

43. James Onslow, "Sketch of Brigadier General Thomas A. Rowley," George McFarland Papers, PSA, Copy Michael Dreese.

44. *History of Allegheny County*, Vol. 2, p. 232; *OR*, Vol. 43, Part 1, pp. 306, 409, 523–5, 590, 830, 852.

45. Edward H. Chase, letter to Edmund Dana, July 20, 1864, Edmund L. Dana Papers, WH&GS, Folder 1864–C; Rowley, letter to Dana, Oct. 8, 1864, pp. 1–3; Kulp, *Families of the Wyoming Valley*, pp. 36–7.

46. McCalmont, *Extracts from the Letters*, p. 99; Thomas A. Rowley, letter to Edmund L. Dana, Dec. 15, 1864, Edmund L. Dana Papers,

WH&GS, Folder 1864–D; pp. 1–3; Miller, *The Training of An Army*, p. 271.

47. *OR*, Vol. 43, Part 1, pp. 502, 506–7.

48. Boatner, *Civil War Dictionary*, pp. 640, 822; Dyer, *A Compendium*, Part 1, pp. 257, 531; Rowley, Staff Officer File, NA.

49. *Pittsburgh Gazette*, Dec. 21, 1864, p. 1; NA, RG 393, Part 2, #1409, pp. 11–2, 201.

50. S O's #473 and #476, *Special Orders of the War Department and Headquarters of the Army, For the Months of Sept. thru Dec. 1864*, Part 3; NA, RG 393, Part 2, #1409, p. 13; *History of Allegheny County*, Vol. 2, p. 232; Bates, *History of Pennsylvania Volunteers*, Vol. 8, pp. 812, 817, 1009; Rowley, Staff Officer File, NA; *Journal of the Executive Proceedings*, Vol. 14, p. 109; *Official Army Register*, Vol. 3, pp. 946, 994.

11. Aftermath

1. Rowley obituary, *New York Times*.

2. Thomas A. Rowley, letter to George McFarland, July 23, 1865, J. Horace McFarland Papers, PSA; Onslow, "Sketch of Brigadier General Thomas A, Rowley," p. 7; Bates, *Martial Deeds*, p. 792; *Memoirs Allegheny County*, pp. 83–4; George F. McFarland, letter to "The Officers and Enlisted Men of the Old Third Division of the First Corps," n. d., J. Horace McFarland Papers, PSA, pp. 1–2.

3. George F. McFarland, letter to "The Officers and Enlisted Men of the Old Third Division of the First Corps," n. d., J. Horace McFarland Papers, PSA, pp. 1–3.

4. *Journal of the Executive Proceedings*, Vol 15, Part 1, pp. 79, 214, 267, 327–8; Leech, *Reveille in Washington*, p. 456.

5. Leech, *Reveille in Washington*, p. 456; *Journal of the Executive Proceedings*, Vol 15, pp. 159, 161, 312, 316, 361, 364, 366; 382; *Ibid.*, Vol. 16, pp. 79, 115; *Historical Times Illustrated Encyclopedia*, p. 159.

6. *Memoirs Allegheny County*, pp. 83–4; Niebaum, *History Washington Infantry*, p. 194, 197; Morrison, "Officer's Certificate of Disability."

7. Morrison, "Officer's Certificate of Disability"; "Declaration for Original Invalid Pension," Feb. 1, 1878, Rowley Pension File, July 11, 1878, NA; "Examining Surgeon's Certificate," April 3, 1878, Rowley Pension File, NA; Report on Thomas A. Rowley, NA.

8. Report on Thomas A. Rowley, NA; "Examining Surgeon's Certificate," March 19, 1884, Rowley Pension File, NA; "Declaration for the Increase of an Invalid Pension," Feb. 18, 1884, *Ibid.*; "Private — No. 422, An Act to Increase the Pension of Thomas A. Rowley," *Ibid.*; Rowley obituary, *New York Times*.

9. *Pittsburgh Post* , Aug. 17, 1889, p. 1; Niebaum, *History Washington Infantry*, p. 216.

10. Niebaum, *History Washington Infantry*, p. 216; *Pittsburgh Post* , Aug. 17, 1889, p. 1.

11. George W. Perkins, *Minutes Veteran's Corps Washington Infantry*, Tim Perkins, e–mail to the author, September 10, 2002.

12. Rowley obituary, *New York Times*; Niebaum, *History Washington Infantry*, pp. 219–20; Rowley Obituary, *Pittsburgh Commercial Gazette*; Mary Ann Rowley Death Notice, *Ibid.*, Oct. 17, 1887, p. 5; Thomas A. Rowley obituary, *Pittsburgh Post*, May 16, 1892, p. 2; Allegheny Cemetery Interments, Allegheny Cemetery Historical Assoc., Section 7, Lot 110, p. 37.

13. Stanley E. Lathrop, *A Brief Memorial Tribute to Captain Clayton E. Rogers*, Hayward, Wisconsin, June 1900, pp. 5–6, SHSW; *Roster of Wisconsin Volunteers, War of the Rebellion, 1862–1865*, p. 871, SHSW; NA, RG 393, Vol II, Part 1, 3944, Vol 29/30, p. 416.

14. Dawes, *Service with the Sixth Wisconsin*, pp. 264, 274,279, 283, 291, 298, 300.

15. *Ibid.*, pp. 303–4; Brown, *Brevet Brigadier Generals*, p. 151; Nolan, *The Iron Brigade*, pp. 276–7, fn #48, p. 376.

16. Rufus R. Dawes, "A Gallant Officer," *Milwaukee Sunday Telegraph*, Feb. 3, 1884, p. 3, SHSW.

17. Roe, "A Memoir of Rufus R. Dawes," p. 23.

18. Matthews, "Colonel McCarter, the Fighting Parson," p. 6.

19. Porter, *Campaigning with Grant*, p. 52; *Under the Maltese Cross*, p. 257; Rhea, *The Battle of the Wilderness*, pp. 190–1, 202–3.

20. Rhea, *The Battle of the Wilderness*, p. 205; *In Memoriam, Alexander Stewart Webb 1835–1911*, New York Monuments Commission for the Battlefields of Gettysburg, Chattanooga, and Antietam, Albany: J. B. Lyon Co., 1916, p. 105; *OR*, Vol. 36, Part 1, p. 192, Series 3, Vol 4, p. 438.

21. *OR*, Vol 42, Part 2, p. 886; Vol. 51, Part 1, p. 1181, Vol. 42, Part 2, pp. 482–3, Vol. 46, Part 2, pp. 93–4, Vol. 46, Part 3, pp. 1240, 1259; S O #464, *Special Orders of the War Department* September through December 1864; "Army and Navy Personal," *Army and Navy Journal,* November 12, 1864, p. 179; *New York at Gettysburg*, p. 105.

22. Webb, "An Address Delivered at Gettysburg," p. 12, GNMP.

23. *OR*, Vol. 36, Part 1, p. 96; Part 3 p. 758; Vol. 51, Part 1, p. 1167; Warner, *Generals in Blue*, p. 144.

24. Rhea, *The Battle of the Wilderness*, pp. 197, 199, 269, 394.

25. *Ibid.*, p. 394, fn #73; Colonel Charles Morgan Statement, May 26, 1864, Captain W. S. W. Miller Statement, May 11, 1864, Captain

Charles Noble Jr. Statement, May 7, 1864, Major General David Birney Statement, May 10, 1864, "Papers Relative to the Mustering out of Brig J. H. Hobart Ward," Vertical Files, Fredericksburg and Spotsylvania National Military Park Library (hereafter FSNMP).

26. David Birney, letter to Colonel Walker, June 4, 1864, Major General Winfield Scott Hancock Statement, June 5, 1864, "Papers Relative to the Mustering out of Brig J. H. H. Ward," FSNMP.

27. U. S. Grant's Comments, June 12, 1864, "Papers Relative to the Mustering out of Brig J. H. Hobart Ward," FSNMP; *Generals in Blue*, pp. 144, 537–8; S O #241, *Special Orders War Department,* May through August 1864; Dyer, *A Compendium*, Part 1, pp. 292, 295, 310.

28. Dyer, *A Compendium*, Part 1, p. 310; Warner, *Generals in Blue*, p. 342; Rhea, *The Battle of the Wilderness*, pp. 178, 310, 418, 422; *OR*, Vol 33, p. 1042; Vol. 40, Part 2, p. 270.

29. *OR*, Vol. 42, Part 2, p. 795; Vol. 43, Part 1, pp. 118, 262, 267; "Army and Navy Personal," *Army and Navy Journal*, October 1, 1864, p. 87; "Army and Navy Personal," *Ibid.*, October 8, 1864, p. 102; "Army and Navy Personal," *Ibid.*, November 26, 1864, p. 219; S O #330, #358, *Special Orders of the War Department* September through December 1864; Warner, *Generals in Blue*, p. 476.

30. Warner, *Generals in Blue*, p. 342; *Historical Times Illustrated Encyclopedia*, p. 523; *OR*, Vol. 43, Part 1, pp. 436, 475.

31. *OR*, Vol. 46, Part 3, p. 1053; Vol 43, Part 1, pp. 170, 518, 859; S O's #338 and 350, *Special Orders of the War Department* September through December 1864; *Historical Times Illustrated Encyclopedia*, pp. 638–9; Warner, *Generals in Blue*, pp. 407–8; Rhea, *The Battle of the Wilderness*, pp. 243, 317, 390; "Army and Navy Personal," October 1, 1864; Lyman, *With Grant and Meade*, p. 104.

32. Lyman, *With Grant and Meade*, p. 109; "Our Fallen Heroes, Brigadier General James C. Rice," *Philadelphia Inquirer*, May 14, 1864, p. 2; Boatner, *Civil War Dictionary*, p. 785; Warner, *Generals in Blue*, p. 401.

33. Warner, *Generals in Blue*, p. 335; Rhea, *The Battle of the Wilderness*, pp. 415–8, 422–4; S O #214, *Special Orders War Department,* May through August 1864; *OR*, Vol. 36, Part 1, pp. 721, 724.

34. *OR*, Vol. 36, Part 1, pp. 678; Vol 37, Part 1, p. 272; Part 2, p. 369; Vol. 43, Part 1, p. 134, 459–60.

35. *OR*, Vol 42, Part 3, p. 1095; Vol 46, Part 1, p. 916; Part 3, p. 1259; Boatner, *Civil War Dictionary*, p. 191; S O #473, *Special Orders of the War Department* September through December 1864.

36. Bates, *Martial Deeds*, p. 656; Bates, *History of Pennsylvania Volunteers*, Vol. 4, pp. 1258–9;

DeWitt Clinton McCoy obituary, *Meadville Evening Republican*, December 1, 1902, p. 3.

37. Pearson, *Wadsworth of Geneseo*, p. 282; Francis B. Heitman, *Historical Register and Dictionary of the United States Army*, Washington: GPO, 1903, Vol. 1, p. 991; S O #242, *Special Orders War Department*, May through August 1864.

38. Warner, *Generals in Blue*, pp. 110–1; "Army and Navy Personal," October 1, 1864; S O's #356, #427, *Special Orders of the War Department* September through December 1864; Lysander Cutler, Staff Officer File, NA; Dailey Affidavit, Cutler Pension File, NA; Wolcott Affidavit, *Ibid.*; *OR*, Vol. 51, Part 1, pp. 1181, 1183.

39. S O #232, *Special Orders War Department*, May through August 1864; *OR*, Vol. 36, Part 1, pp. 202–3; Vol. 42, Part 1, p. 470; Vol. 40, Part 3, p. 732; Marsena R. Patrick, *Inside Lincoln's Army*, p. 368; Dyer, *A Compendium*, Part 1, p. 307; *Official Army Register*, Vol. 5, p. 137; Nolan, *The Iron Brigade*, fn #47, p. 376.

40. Dana obituary; Kulp, *Families of the Wyoming Valley*, p. 38; Bates, *History of Pennsylvania Volunteers*, Vol. 7, p. 624.

41. Bates, *History of Pennsylvania Volunteers*, Vol. 7, p. 808; *Official Army Register*, Vol 7, p. 1035; Alfred B. McCalmont obituary, *New York Times*, May 10, 1874, p. 7; *McCalmont Biography*; McCalmont, *Extracts from the Letters*, p. 134.

42. McCalmont, *Extracts from the Letters*, p. 87; *The Mercer Dispatch and Republican*, Mar 2, 1923, p. 1, Mercer County Historical Society; Sword, "Capt. James Glenn's Sword," p. 14; Bates, *History of Pennsylvania Volunteers*, Vol. 7, p. 469–70, 617; 690.

43. Bates, *History of Pennsylvania Volunteers*, Vol. 8, pp. 624, 658; Chamberlin, *History of the One Hundred and Fiftieth*, pp. 307, 318; *Official Army Register*, Vol. 7, p. 982; *Annual Report of the Adjutant General*," pp. 751, 774; McFarland, handwritten notes; Matthews, *The 149th Pennsylvania*, pp. 150, 154; PA Dept. Military Affairs Index.

44. "Army and Navy Personal," *Army and Navy Journal*, July 23, 1864, p. 791; "Army and Navy Personal," *Ibid.*, October 29, 1864, p. 151; S O's #366, #374, *Special Orders of the War Department* September through December 1864.

45. *Journal of the Executive Proceedings*, Vol. 14, pp. 286, 296, 914, 1113; *Ibid.*, Vol 15, Part 1 p. 16; Warner, *Generals in Blue*, pp. 130, 191.

46. S O's #394, #414, *Special Orders of the War Department* September through December 1864; Fox, *Regimental Losses in the American Civil War*, Chap. 8, p. 107; Dyer, *A Compendium*, Part 1, pp. 257, 531; *OR*, Vol. 47, Part 3, pp. 578; Vol 45, Part 1, p. 369.

47. Howard M. Madaus, e–mail to author, August 10 and September 9, 2002; Michael J. McAfee, email to the author, September 13, 2002.

48. Kenneth E. Thompson Jr., e–mail to the author, September 21, 2002; Conversation with Thompson, July 9, 2002.

Conclusion. Thomas A. Rowley's Place in History Revisited

1. Coddington, *The Gettysburg Campaign*, pp. 306–7; Wainwright, *A Diary of Battle*, pp. 235, 237.

2. Gates, *The 'Ulster Guard'* p. 430; *OR*, Vol. 27, Part 1, pp. 317–23; Osborne, *Holding the Left*, pp. 22–23 fn #44; *SOR*, Vol. 5, Addendum, Vol. 27, Serial 43–4, p. 143.

3. Coddington, *The Gettysburg Campaign*, p. 706, fn #123; Osborne, *Holding the Left*, p. 7; *The Civil War Diaries of Col. Theodore B. Gates*, pp. 90–4.

4. Lance J. Herdegen, "The Lieutenant who Arrested a General," p. 30.

5. Miller, "Perrin's Brigade on July 1, 1863," p. 25; O'Brien, "Give Them Another Volley, Boys," p. 40.

6. Martin, *Gettysburg July 1*, p. 343.

7. Slagle, letter about his experiences, p. 2; *OR*, Vol. 27, Part 1, pp. 247, 324; Hassler, *Crisis at the Crossroads*, pp. 57–8.

8. Coddington, *Gettysburg*, p. 308; McCalmont, Sworn Statement; Wainwright, *A Diary of Battle*, p. 235; Martin, *Gettysburg July 1*, p. 356; *OR*, Vol. 27, Part 1, p. 356.

9. Shue, *Morning at Willoughby Run*, p. 175; Dougherty, *Stone's Brigade and the Fight for the McPherson Farm*, pp. 39, 73; Miller, "Perrin's Brigade on July 1, 1863," p. 25; Herdegen, "The Lieutenant who Arrested a General," p. 30.

10. Herdegen, "The Lieutenant who Arrested a General," p. 30, p. 29, fn #30; Rowley Court–Martial File, NA, pp. 11, 17, 22–3, 29, 35.

11. Coddington, *Gettysburg*, pp. 706, fn's #121 and 124; Dougherty, *Stone's Brigade*, pp. 151–3; Herdegen, "The Lieutenant who Arrested a General," p. 30; Shue, *Morning at Willoughby Run*, p. 230.

12. Gerald Sherwin, phone conversations with the author, June 27, July 1, and September 6, 2003; Doubleday testimony, Rowley Court–Martial, NA, pp. 41, 44, 47; Thomas L. Elmore, "A Meteorological and Astronomical Chronology of the Gettysburg Campaign," pp. 10–1.

13. Herdegen, "The Lieutenant who Arrested a General," p. 30; O'Brien, "Give Them Another Volley, Boys," p. 42.

14. "Pittsburgh Men at Gettysburg," *The Pittsburgh Gazette Times*, October 17, 1909, p. 4, Clarence McAllister ed., 102nd PA Web site.

Appendix I. Commands of Thomas A. Rowley

1. Bates, *History of Pennsylvania Volunteers*, Vol 1, p. 125.

2. *Ibid.*, Vol 5, p. 294; De Trobriand, *Four Years with the Army of the Potomac*, p. 85, 87; *Official Army Register of the Volunteer Force of the United Sates Army 1861–5*, Part II, p. 519.

3. Bates, Vol 4, p. 647; Dyer, *A Compendium of the War of the Rebellion*, Part 1, pp. 298–9.

4. *Ibid.*, p. 312; Niebaum, *History of the Pittsburgh Washington Infantry*, pp. 94, 96; Boatner, *The Civil War Dictionary*, pp. 304, 775; Bates, Vol. 5, pp. 294, 469; *Ibid.*, Vol 7, pp. 383; *Official Army Register*, Part II, pp. 518–9.

5. Sears, *Chancellorsville*, p. 454.

6. Doubleday, *Chancellorsville and Gettysburg*, p. 212.

7. Bates, Vol 10, p. 647, p. 897; *Supplement to the Official Records of the Union and Confederate Armies*, Vol. 5, Part 1, p. 115.

Appendix III. Thomas A. Rowley's Defense Statement

1. Edmund L. Dana, Personal Notes of Brig. General Thomas A. Rowley's Court–Martial, Wyoming Historical and Genealogical Society, Wilkes–Barre, PA, Folder 1864 — B; Thomas A. Rowley, Court–Martial File, Box 1002, Exhibit B, 7 pages, NA; Kathleen Georg Harrison, Transcript of Edmund L. Dana's Notes, Court–Martial of Brig. General Thomas A. Rowley, 1981, Typed Copy GNMP Library, Original Wyoming Historical and Genealogical Society.

Appendix IV. "Transfer from Jail to Pleasanter Quarters"

1. Kulp, *Families of the Wyoming Valley*, pp. 33–4, 41; Lee, Letter to Edmund Dana; Dana obituary; Dana, *Personal Diary*; Dyer, *A Compendium*, pp. 284, 294; Warner, *Generals in Blue*, p. 108; Matthews, *The 149th Pennsylvania*, p. 274.

2. Dana, *Personal Diary*, pp. 156–7.

3. *Ibid.*, pp. 157–8; *Official Military Atlas*, Plates 50–1.

4. *Ibid.*; Dana, *Personal Diary*, p. 159.

5. *Ibid.*, pp. 159–60.

6. *Ibid.*, p. 160; Warner, *Generals in Blue*, pp. 432, 434.

7. Dana, *Personal Diary*, pp. 162–3.

8. *Ibid.*, p. 163.

9. *Ibid.*, p. 164.

10. Hesseltine, *Civil War Prisons*, p. 159; Boatner, *Civil War Dictionary*, pp. 15, 482.

11. Dana, *Personal Diary*, p. 164.

12. *Ibid.*, p. 165.

13. *Ibid.*, pp. 165–6.

14. *Ibid.*, pp. 166–8.

15. *Ibid.*, pp. 165, 167–9.

16. *Ibid.*, pp. 167–8.

17. Hesseltine, *Civil War Prisons*, p. 163; Burton, *The Siege of Charleston 1861–1865*, p. 281; Warner, *Generals in Gray*, p. 166.

18. Dana, *Personal Diary*, p. 169.

19. *Ibid.*, p. 170; Warner, *Generals in Blue*, p. 422.

20. Dana, *Personal Diary*, p. 170.

21. *Ibid.*, p. 171.

22. *Ibid.*, pp. 171–2.

23. *OR*, Vol. 35, Part 2, pp. 132–3.

24. Dana, *Personal Diary*, pp. 171–3.

25. *OR*, Vol. 35, Part 2, pp. 132–5.

26. Speer, *Portals to Hell*, p. 213; *OR*, Vol. 35, Part 1, pp. 12–3; *Ibid.*, Part 2, p. 197.

27. Dana, *Personal Diary*, pp. 173–5.

28. *Ibid.*, pp. 174–6.

29. *OR*, Vol. 35, Part 2, pp. 143–4.

30. Dana, *Personal Diary*, pp. 172, 174–5.

31. *Ibid.*, pp. 174–5; *OR*, Vol. 35, Part 2, p. 151.

32. Dana, *Personal Diary*, p. 176; Richard E. Matthews, phone conversation with author, Jan. 19, 2001.

33. *OR*, Vol. 35, Part 2, p. 161.

34. *Ibid.*, pp. 177–8.

35. Burton, *The Siege of Charleston*, pp. 280–6.

36. Dana, *Personal Diary*, pp. 177–81; Edmund L. Dana, Report on his Prison Confinement at Macon and Charleston, Undated, Unpublished, WHGS, Box 4S40, pp. 7–8.

37. *OR*, Vol. 35, Part 2, pp. 164, 174.

38. Dana, *Personal Diary*, pp. 180–2; Dana, Report on Prison Confinement, p. 10.

39. Dana, *Personal Diary*, pp. 182–4.

40. *Ibid.*, pp. 184–5; Dana, Report on Prison Confinement, p. 4.

41. *Ibid.*, p. 9; Dana, *Personal Diary*, pp. 184–5.

42. *OR*, Vol. 35, Part 2, pp. 164, 174, 197, 207.

43. Dana, *Personal Diary*, pp. 185–8.

44. *Ibid.*, p. 188; Dana, Report on Prison Confinement, p. 11.

45. *OR*, Vol. 35, Part 1, p. 70; *Ibid.*, Part 2, pp. 207, 210.

46. Dana, *Personal Diary*, p. 188.

47. *Ibid.*, pp. 1898–90.

48. *Ibid.*, p. 190.

49. *Ibid.*

50. *Ibid.*; Dana, Report on Prison Confinement, p. 12.

Bibliography

Books, Pamphlets, and Addresses

Alexander, E. P. *Military Memoirs of a Confederate.* Dayton, OH: Morningside Press, 1990. First published 1907 by Scribner's.

Alotta, Robert I. Military Executions of the Union Army, 1861–1865. Ph.D. thesis. Temple University, Ann Arbor, MI, 1984, UMI.

Alvord, Henry E. "Early's Attack on Washington." MOLLUS War Papers. Commandery District of Columbia, Vol. 1, Wilmington, NC: Broadfoot Publishing, 1993.

Army Register of the Volunteer Force of the United States, 1861–5. 9 Vols. U. S. War Department. Gaithersburg, MD: Olde Soldier Books, 1987. First published 1867 by Government Printing Office.

Ashhurst, Richard L. "Address Delivered at the Meeting of the Philadelphia Bar, December 11, 1880, Upon the Occasion of the Death of Chapman Biddle." Philadelphia: J. M. Power Wallace, 1880, WRHS Archives/Library.

Barnes, Joseph K. *The Medical and Surgical History of the Civil War,* 15 vols. Wilmington, NC: Broadfoot Publishing, 1990. First published 1870 by Government Printing Office.

Bates, Samuel P. *History of Pennsylvania Volunteers, 1861–5.* 10 Vols. Wilmington, NC: Broadfoot Publishing, 1994. First published 1870 by Singerly.

_____. *Martial Deeds of Pennsylvania.* Philadelphia: T. H. Davis, 1876.

Benedict, George G. *Army Life in Virginia.* Burlington, VT: The Free Press, 1895.

Benet, S. V. *A Treatise on Military Law and the Practice of Courts–Martial.* 4th ed. New York: Van Nostrand, 1864.

Biddle, Chapman. "The First Day of the Battle of Gettysburg." An Address Delivered before the Historical Society of Pennsylvania, March 8, 1880. Philadelphia: J. B. Lippincott & Co., 1880.

Bigelow, John Jr. *The Campaign of Chancellorsville.* New Haven: Yale University Press, 1910, Morningside Edition.

Boatner, Mark Mayo. *The Civil War Dictionary.* Rev. ed. New York: Vintage Books, 1991.

Bowman, John S., ed. *The Civil War Day by Day.* New York: Barnes and Noble, 1993.

Brooks, U. R., ed. *Stories of the Confederacy.* Columbia, SC: State, 1912. excerpt in V7–SC13, GNMP Library.

Brandy, Ken, and Florence Freeland, Compilers. *The Gettysburg Papers.* Dayton, OH: Morningside, 1986.

Brown, Varina D. *A Colonel at Gettysburg and Spotsylvania.* Columbia, SC: State, 1931.

Burton, E. Milby. *The Siege of Charleston 1861–1865.* Columbia: University of South Carolina Press, 1970.

Busey, John W. *These Honored Dead.* Hightstown, NJ: Longstreet House, 1996.

_____. and David G. Martin. *Regimental Strengths and Losses at Gettysburg.* Hightstown, NJ: Longstreet House, 1982.

Caldwell, J.F.J. *The History of a Brigade of South Carolinians.* Dayton, OH: Morningside Press, 1984.

Catton, Bruce. *A Stillness at Appomattox.* Garden City, NY: Doubleday, 1957.

_____. *Glory Road.* New York: Doubleday, 1990.

_____. *Grant Takes Command.* Boston: Little, Brown, 1968.

Chamberlin, Thomas. *History of the 150th Regiment Pennsylvania Volunteers.* Baltimore: Butternut and Blue Reprints, 1986. First published 1905 by McManus.

_____. "Address at the Dedication of the Monument, 150th Regiment Infantry." *Pennsylvania at Gettysburg.* Vol. 2, Edited by John P. Nicholson. Harrisburg, PA: State Printer, 1904.

Clark, Walter. *Histories of the Several Regiments and Battalions from North Carolina in the Great War 1861–5.* 5 Vols. Wendell, N.C.: Broadfoot's Bookmark, 1982. First published 1901 by Nash Bros.

Cleaves, Freeman. *Rock of Chickamauga: The Life of General George H. Thomas.* Norman, OK: University of Oklahoma Press, 1948.

Coddington, Edwin. *The Gettysburg Campaign.* Dayton, OH: Morningside, 1979. First published 1963 by Scribner's.

Cooke, Sidney G. "The First Day of Gettysburg." Read before the Kansas Commandry MOLLUS November 4, 1897. War Paper #17. Kansas State Historical Society.

Coppee, Henry. *Field Manuel of Courts Martial.* Philadelphia: Lippincott, 1863.

Cross, Andrew. *The War — Battle of Gettysburg and the Christian Commission.* "Account of Captain Benjamin F. Little, Co. F, 52nd North Carolina." 1865. pp. 26–7. typescript by K. G. Harrison, March 1987, copy GNMP Library.

Dana, Edmund. "Transcript of the Court–Martial of Brig. General Thomas A. Rowley." Edited by Kathleen Georg Harrison. Unpublished. GNMP Library.

Davis, Maj. George B., Leslie J. Perry, and Joseph W. Kirkley. *The Official Military Atlas of the Civil War.* New York: Gramercy Books, 1983. First published 1891–95 by Government Printing Office.

Dawes, Rufus R. *Service with the Sixth Wisconsin Volunteers.* Dayton, OH: Morningside House, 1996. Reprint.

DeTrobriand, Regis. *Four Years with the Army of the Potomac.* Gaithersburg, MD: Van Sickle Military Books, 1988. First published 1889 by Ticknor.

Donald, David H. *Lincoln.* New York: Simon & Schuster, 1995.

Doubleday, Abner. *Chancellorsville and Gettysburg.* New York: Da Capo Press, 1994.

Dougherty, James J. *Stone's Brigade and the Fight for the McPherson Farm.* Conshocken, PA: Combined, 2001.

Dreese, Michael A. *An Imperishable Fame: The Civil War Experience of George Fisher McFarland.* Mifflintown, PA: Juniata County Historical Society, 1997.

_____. *The 151st Pennsylvania Volunteers at Gettysburg: Like Ripe Apples in a Storm.* Jefferson, NC: McFarland, 2000.

_____. *The Hospital on Seminary Ridge at the Battle of Gettysburg.* Jefferson, NC: McFarland, 2001.

Dyer, Frederick H. *A Compendium of the War of the Rebellion.* Indianapolis: Guild Press of Indiana, 1996. First published 1908 by Dyer.

Faust, P.L., ed. *Historical Times Encyclopedia of the Civil War.* New York: Harper & Row, 1986.

Flanagan, Vincent J. *The Life of General Gouverneur Kemble Warren.* Doctoral thesis. New York: City University of New York, 1969.

Fox, Arthur B. *Pittsburgh During the American Civil War 1860–1865.* Chicora, PA: Mechling Bookbindery, 2002.

Fox, William F. *Regimental Losses in the American Civil War.* Indianapolis: Guild Press of Indiana, 1997.

Gambone, A. M. *Major General Darius Nash Couch — Enigmatic Valor.* Baltimore: Butternut & Blue, 2000.

Gates, Theodore B. *The Civil War Diaries of Col. Theodore B. Gates, 20th NYSM.* Edited by Seward R. Osborne. Hightown, NJ: Longstreet House, 1991.

_____. *The 'Ulster Guard' (20th N. Y. State Militia) and the War of the Rebellion.* New York: Tyrrel, 1879.

General Court–Martial Orders. U. S. War Department, Adjutant General's Office, Washington: GPO, 1865, MHI.

General Orders of the War Department and Headquarters of the Army. Washington: Printing Bureau, Adjutant General's Office, War Department., 1864, MHI.

Grant, Ulysses S. *Personal Memoirs of U. S. Grant.* Reprinted, New York: Konecky & Konecky, 1992.

Harrison, Kathleen Georg. *Edward McPherson Farm: Historical Study.* Unpublished. GNMP.

Hassler, Warren W. Jr. *Crisis at the Crossroads.* Gettysburg, PA: Stan Clark Military Books, 1991.

Hays, Alexander. *Life and Letters of Alexander Hays.* Edited by George Fleming, compiled by Gilbert A. Hays. Pittsburgh, 1919.

Heffley, Albert, and Cyrus P. Heffley. *Civil War Diaries of Capt. Albert Heffley and Lt. Cyrus P. Heffley,* Apollo, PA: Closson Press, 2000.

Heitman, Francis B. *Historical Register and Dictionary of the United States Army.* Washington, DC: Government Printing Office, 1903.

Hennessy, John J. *Return to Bull Run.* New York: Simon & Schuster, 1993.

Hesseltine, William Best. *Civil War Prisons.* New York: Ungar, 1964. First published 1930 by Ohio State University Press.

Hewett, J. B., N. A. Trudeau, and B. A. Suderow, eds. *Supplement to the Official Records of the Union and Confederate Armies.* Wilmington, NC: Broadfoot, 1995.

History of Allegheny County, Pennsylvania. Vol. 1. Chicago: Warner, 1889.

History of Crawford County, 1885. Meadville, PA: Crawford County Historical Society, 1975.

History of the 121st Regiment Pennsylvania Volunteers. Survivors Association. Philadelphia: Burk & McFethridge, 1893.

History of the Washington Infantry of Pittsburgh, Pennsylvania. Pittsburgh, 1891.

Hofmann, J. W. "Remarks on the Battle of Gettysburg." Presentation to the Historical Society of Pennsylvania, March 8, 1880. Philadelphia: Auner, 1880. Manuscript Collection, Gettysburg College.

Holabird, S. B. *Flags of the Army of the United States carried during the War of the Rebellion 1861–1865.* Philadelphia: Burk & McFerridy, 1888.

Howard, Oliver O. *Autobiography of Oliver O. Howard.* New York: Baker & Taylor, 1907.

Hunt, Roger D., and Jack R. Brown. *Brevet Brigadier Generals in Blue.* Gaithersburg, MD: Olde Soldier Books, 1990.

Index of General Court–Martial Orders, Adjutant General's Office, 1864. Washington: Government Printing Office, 1865, MHI.

Jordan, John W., ed. *Genealogical and Personal History of Western Pennsylvania.* New York: Lewis, 1915.

Jordan, Weymouth T. Jr. *North Carolina Troops 1861–1865, A Roster.* Vol. 12, Infantry. Raleigh, NC: North Carolina Division of Archives and History, 1990.

Kulp, George B. *Families of the Wyoming Valley.* Vol. 1. Wilkes–Barre, PA: Wyoming Historical and Geological Society, 1885.

Ladd, David L. and Audrey J. Ladd, eds. *The Bachelder Papers.* 3 vols. Dayton, OH: Morningside Press, 1994.

Large, John. *One Man's War, The Civil War Letters of John Large.* Edited by Angus M. Gunn Jr. Vancouver, BC: Legacy Press, 1985.

Lathrop, Stanley E. *A Brief Memorial Tribute to Captain Clayton E. Rogers.* Hayward, Wisconsin, June 1900, SHSW.

Leech, Margaret. *Reveille in Washington, 1860–1865.* New York: Harper & Brothers, 1941.

Locke, William Henry. *The Story of the Regiment.* New York: Miller, 1872.

Longstreet, James. *From Manassas to Appomattox.* Reprint, New York: Konecky, 1992.

Lyman, Theodore. *Meade's Headquarters 1863–1865, Letters of Colonel Theodore Lyman from the Wilderness to Appomattox.* Edited by George Agassiz. Boston: Atlantic Monthly Press, 1922.

Maine at Gettysburg: Report of the Maine Commissioners. Portland: Lakeside Press, 1898.

Malone, Dumas, ed. *Dictionary of American Biography.* New York: Charles Scribner's, 1857.

Marsh, Henry C. *The Nineteenth Indiana at Gettysburg,* n. p., n. d. Copy GNMP Library, Original Indiana State Library.

Martin, David G. *Gettysburg July 1.* Rev. ed. Conshohocken, PA: Combined Books, 1995.

Matthews, Richard E. *The 149th Pennsylvania Volunteer Infantry Unit in the Civil War.* Jefferson, NC: McFarland, 1994.

Mattocks, Charles. *"Unspoiled Heart": The Journal of Charles Mattocks of the 17th Maine.* Edited by Philip N. Racine. Knoxville: University of Tennessee Press, 1994.

McCalmont, Alfred B. *Extracts from the Letters Written by A. B. McCalmont from the Front.* Edited by Robert McCalmont. Franklin, PA: Private printing, 1908. Venango County Historical Society.

McLean, James L. Jr. *Cutler's Brigade at Gettysburg.* Rev. 2nd ed. Baltimore: Butternut and Blue, 1994.

McPherson, James M. *Battle Cry of Freedom.* New York: Oxford Press, 1988.

Meade, George. *The Life and Letters of General George Gordon Meade.* 2 vols. Baltimore: Butternut and Blue, 1994.

Memoirs of Allegheny County, Pennsylvania. Vol. 1. Madison, WI: Northwestern Historical, 1904.

Miers, Earl S., editor in chief. *Lincoln Day by Day, A Chronology 1809–1865.* 3 vols. Dayton, OH: Morningside, 1991.

Miller, William J. *The Training of An Army, Camp Curtin and the North's Civil War.* Shippensburg, PA: White Mane, 1990.

MOLLUS War Papers, Commandery District of Columbia, Vol 1. Wilmington, NC: Broadfoot, 1993.

Nesbit, John W. *General History of Company D 149th Pennsylvania Volunteers.* Rev. ed., Pittsburgh: Oakdale, 1908.

Nevins, Allan. *War for the Union.* 5 vols. New York: Konecky & Konecky, 1971.

New York Monuments Commission for the Battlefields of Gettysburg, Chattanooga, and Antietam. *Final Report on the Battle of Gettysburg.* 3 vols. Albany, NY: J. B. Lyon, 1900.

_____. *In Memoriam, Alexander Stewart Webb 1835–1911.* Albany, NY: Lyon, 1916.

_____. *In Memoriam, James Samuel Wadsworth, 1807–1864,* Albany, NY: Lyon, 1916. Copy, D. Lorello, New York State Archives.

Nicholson, John P., ed. *Pennsylvania at Gettysburg.* 3 vols. Harrisburg, PA: State Printer, 1904.

Niebaum, John H. *History of the Pittsburgh Washington Infantry.* Pittsburgh: n.p., 1931.

Nolan, Alan T. *The Iron Brigade.* Indianapolis: Indiana University Press Edition, 1994.

O'Brien, Thomas M., and Oliver Diefendorf. General Orders of the War Department 1861, 1862 & 1863. New York: Darby & Miller, 1864.

Official Army Register of the Volunteer Force of the United Sates Army 1861–5. 8 vols. Gaithersburg, MD: Van Sickle Military Books, 1987. First published 1865 by Government Printing Office.

Onslow, James. "Sketch of Brigadier General Thomas A, Rowley," George McFarland Papers, J. Horace McFarland Collection, Pennsylvania State Archives. Copy, Michael Dreese.

Osborne, Seward R. *The Civil War Diaries of Col. Theodore B. Gates.* Hightstown, NJ: Longstreet House, 1991.

_____. *Holding the Left at Gettysburg,* Hightstown, NJ: Longstreet House, 1990.

Parke, John E. *Recollections of Seventy Years and Historical Gleanings of Allegheny, Pennsylvania.* Boston: Franklin Press, 1886.

Patrick, Marsena R. *Inside Lincoln's Army.* Edited by David S. Sparks. New York: Yoseloff, 1964.

Pearson, Henry Greenleaf. *James S. Wadsworth of Geneseo.* Ann Arbor, MI: UMI, 1997. First published 1913 by Scribner's.

Pennsylvania Department of Military Affairs. "Index of Civil War Soldiers, 1861–6." RG–19 Records, MHI Library.

Pennsylvania Executive Office, Military Department. *Roster of Commissions Issued to Officers of Penn. Vol's, Dec. 1, 1863 to Dec. 1, 1864.* 2 vols. Harrisburg: Singerly & Myers, 1865.

"Annual Report of the Adjutant General." *Reports of the Heads of Departments Transmitted to the Governor of Pennsylvania for the Financial Year Ending November 30, 1866.* Vol. 2. Harrisburg, PA: Singerly & Meyers, 1867.

Perret, Geoffrey. *Ulysses S. Grant: Soldier & President.* New York: Random House, 1997.

Pfanz, Henry W. *Gettysburg—The First Day.* Chapel Hill, NC: University of North Carolina Press, 2001.

Porter, Horace. *Campaigning with Grant.* New York: Century, 1897, Time–Life Reprint, 1981.

Rhea, Gordon C. *The Battle of the Wilderness, May 5–6, 1864.* Baton Rouge: Louisiana State University Press, 1994.

Rhodes, Elisha Hunt. *All for the Union.* New York: Random House, Vintage Civil War Library Ed., 1992.

Roe, William E. "A Memoir of Rufus R. Dawes" August 3, 1899 New York: De Vinne Press, 1900.

Rosengarten, Joseph G. "Address Delivered at the Meeting of the Philadelphia Bar, December 11, 1880, Upon the Occasion of the Death of Chapman Biddle." Philadelphia: J. M. Power Wallace, 1880. WRHS Archives/Library.

Roster of Wisconsin Volunteers, War of the Rebellion, 1862–1865, SHSW.

Sandow, Robert, ed. *"Remember Your Friend Until Death": A Collection of Civil War Letters from the West Overton Archives.* West Overton, PA: West Overton Museum, 1993.

Scott, James K. P. *The Story of the Battle of Gettysburg.* Harrisburg, PA: Telegraph Press, 1927.

Sears, Stephen W. *Chancellorsville.* Boston: Houghton Mifflin, 1996.

_____. *Landscape Turned Red.* New York: Ticknor and Fields, 1983.

_____. *To the Gates of Richmond.* New York: Houghton Mifflin, 1992.

Shue, Richard S. *Morning at Willoughby Run.* Gettysburg, PA: Thomas, 1995.

Snyder, Charles McCool. *Oswego County, New York in the Civil War.* Oswego, NY: OCHS and the Oswego County Civil War Centennial Commission, 1962.

Special Orders of the War Department and Headquarters of the Army, 1863. Washington: Printing Bureau, Adjutant General's Office, War Department, 1864, MHI.

Special Orders of the War Department and Headquarters of the Army, Washington: Printing Bureau, Adjutant General's Office, War Department, 1864, Parts 1, 2, and 3, MHI.

Speer, Lonnie R. *Portals to Hell.* Mechanicsburg, PA: Stackpole Books, 1997.

Spencer, James. *Civil War Generals.* New York: Greenwood Press, 1986.

Stackpole, Edward J. *From Cedar Mountain to Antietam.* Harrisburg, PA: Stackpole, 1959.

Stine, J. H. *History of the Army of the Potomac.* Washington: Gibson Bros., 1893.

Testimony of Brigadier General James S. Wadsworth, Washington, March 23, 1864, Joint Congressional Committee on the Conduct of the War. *Report of 1865.* Vol 1. p. 413, GNMP Library.

Tevis, C. V., and D. R. Marquis. *The History of the Fighting Fourteenth (Brooklyn Regiment)*. Baltimore: Butternut and Blue, 1994. First published 1911 by Brooklyn Eagle.

Thompson, Kenneth E. Jr. *Civil War Maine Hall of Fame, Political, Judicial, and Military Leaders 1861–1865*. Portland, ME: Thompson, 2000.

Thomson, Orville. *Narrative of the Service of the Seventh Indiana Infantry in the War for the Union*. Baltimore: Butternut and Blue, 1993. First published 1905 by the author.

Todd, Frederick P. *American Military Equipage 1851–1872*. New York: Scribner's, 1980.

Tompkins, D. A., and A. S. Tompkins. *Company K, Fourteenth South Carolina Volunteers*. Charlotte, NC: Observer, 1897. Copy, V7–SC14, GNMP Library.

Under the Maltese Cross, Antietam to Appomattox, Pittsburgh: 155th Regimental Association, 1910.

U. S. War Department, *The War of the Rebellion: A Compilation of the Official Records of the Union and Confederate Armies*. Washington, DC: Government Printing Office, 1880–1901.

Venango County Genealogical Club. "Alfred B. McCalmont Biography," Oil City, PA, 1997.

Wainwright, Charles S. *A Diary of Battle: The Personal Journals of Colonel Charles S. Wainwright*. Edited by Allan Nevins. Gettysburg, PA: Clark, 1962.

Warner, Ezra J. *Generals in Blue*. Baton Rouge: Louisiana State University Press, 1994.

_____. *Generals in Gray*. Baton Rouge: Louisiana State University Press, 1994.

Warren, Horatio N. *The Declaration of Independence and War History: Bull Run to the Appomattox*. Buffalo: Courier, 1894.

Webb, Alexander S. "An Address Delivered at Gettysburg, August 27, 1883 by General Alexander H. Webb." Philadelphia: Porter & Coates, 1883. Vertical file GNMP Library.

Weld, Stephen M. War *Diary and Letters of Stephen Minot Weld 1861–1865*. Boston: Riverside Press, 1912.

Wheeler, Richard. *On Fields of Fury*. New York: Harper Collins, 1991.

_____. *Witness to Gettysburg*. New York: Harper & Row, 1987.

White, J. G. *History of Mercer County, Pennsylvania*. Vol. 1. Chicago: Lewis, 1909.

Whitman, William E. S., and Charles H. True. *Maine in the War for the Union*. Lewiston, ME: Dingley, 1865.

Wilkinson, Warren. *Mother, May You Never See the Sights I Have Seen*. New York: William Morrow, 1991.

Zorn, Jacob J. *A Sergeant's Story*. Edited by Barbara M. Croner. Apollo, PA: Closson Press, 1999.

Manuscript Collections and Newspaper Sources

Allegheny Cemetery Interments, Allegheny Cemetery Historical Association.

Bowling Green State University, Center for Archival Collections
Henry A. Cornwell Correspondence

Charleston, SC, CWRT
Washington P. Shooter letter to George A. McIntyre, July 20, 1863.

University of Delaware
Letters of Chapman and Alexander Biddle.

Fredericksburg and Spotsylvania National Military Park Library
Papers Relative to the Mustering out of Brig. J. H. Hobart Ward.

Gettysburg College Library and Manuscript Collection.

Gettysburg National Military Park Library
  E. R. Gearhart Papers
  General Officers, First, Second, Fifth, and Sixth Corps, Army of the Potomac.
  Infantry Regiments and Artillery Batteries, 1st & 3rd Divisions, First Corps, Army of the Potomac.
  J. B. Bachelder Papers Transcripts.
  J. Horace McFarland Papers.

Historical Society of Pennsylvania
  Major General George Meade Papers,
  Official Army of the Potomac Corres., Letters, etc.,
  Diary of Captain George Meade.

Historical Society of Western Pennsylvania
  Washington Infantry Correspondence.
  The Pennsylvania Thirteenth, 102nd PA Infantry.

Library of Congress
  Journal of the Executive Proceedings of the Senate of the United States of America.
  Lincoln correspondence.

Joyner Library, Eastern Carolina Library
  Spencer G. Welch, letter to wife August 2, 1863, typed copy Gettysburg National Military Park.

National Archives
  Court martial file: Thomas A. Rowley, Box 1002.
  General's papers: James Wadsworth, Thomas Rowley.
  Military file: Thomas A. Rowley.
  Pension file: John Newton, Lysander Cutler, Thomas Rowley.
  Staff officer file: Lysander Cutler, John Newton, Thomas Rowley, and Alexander Hays;
  Box #448, W17 CB 1863; RG 94
  Part 1, 1st and 2nd Brigades, 1st Div., First Corps, and 4th Div., Fifth Corps AOP, RG 393,
  RG79, Box 32.
  Camp Berry Post Records September 1863 through March 1864.

New York State Library, Manuscripts, and Special Collections
  Major General Gouverneur K. Warren Papers, Box 26, SC10668.

Pennsylvania State Archives
  J. Horace McFarland Papers.
  John Porter, 102nd PA, Civil War Diary.
  Samuel P. Bates Papers.

Timothy Perkins Collection
  George W. Perkins Papers, 102nd PA.

Rutgers University Special Collections and Archives
  Frank J. Sterling, Letter to Father, July 10, 1863, Copy GNMP.

Slack Research Collections, Dawes Memorial Library, Marietta College
  Rufus Dawes Papers.

State Historical Society of Wisconsin
  Library and Archives
  Rufus Dawes Papers.

U. S. Army Military History Institute, Carlisle, PA
  Library, Manuscript and Photo Archives
  General Officers, First and Fifth Corps, AOP; Infantry Regiments and Artillery
    Batteries, 1st and 3rd Divisions, First Corps, AOP; Infantry Regiments, 4th
    Division, Fifth Corps, AOP.
  Civil War Miscellaneous Collection; Lewis Leigh Collection; "Save the Flags"
    Collection.

Western Reserve Historical Society Archives/Library
  "Civil War Reminiscences of William Acheson," n. p., Feb. 3, 1914, 102nd PA.

William Phillis Collection
  Colonel John W. Patterson Papers and Correspondence.

Wyoming Historical and Genealogical Society, Wilkes–Barre, PA
  Edmund L. Dana Papers:
    Personal diary, Personal notes Thomas A. Rowley Court–Martial Correspondence.

Magazine and Journal Articles

Anderson, Kevin. "Grant's Lifelong Struggle with Alcohol." *Columbiad* 2, no. 4: 16–26

Bonham, Milledge Louis. "A Little More Light on Gettysburg." *Mississippi Valley Historical Review* 24 (March 1938): 519–25, GNMP Library.

Dahlinger, Charles W. "Abraham Lincoln in Pittsburgh and the Birth of the Republican Party." *Western Pennsylvania Historical Magazine* 3 (1920): 145–177.

Elmore, Thomas L. "A Meteorological and Astronomical Chronology of the Gettysburg Campaign." *Gettysburg Magazine*, No. 13: 7–21.

Hancock, Winfield Scott. "Gettysburg, A Reply to General Howard." *Galaxy* (December 1876): 821–31.

Herdegen, Lance J. "The Lieutenant who Arrested a General." *Gettysburg Magazine* no. 4: 25–32.

Howard, Oliver O. "Campaign and Battle of Gettysburg, June and July, 1863." *Atlantic Monthly* (July 1876).

Krumwiede, John F. "A July Afternoon on McPherson's Ridge." *Gettysburg Magazine*, no. 21: 21–44.

Lord, Francis A. "Diary of Edward Lewis Hoon, 102 Pennsylvania Infantry." *North South Trader* 4, no. 1 (November–December 1976).

Matthews, Richard. "Colonel McCarter, the Fighting Parson." *Lebanon County Historical Society* 17, no. 1 (1987): 1–9.

Milledge, Louis Bonham. "A Little More Light on Gettysburg." *Mississippi Valley Historical Review* 24 (March 1938). GNMP Library.

Miller, J. Michael. "Perrin's Brigade on July 1, 1863." *Gettysburg Magazine*, no. 13: 22–32.

Ness, Charles H. "Excerpts from the Civil War Diary of George Randolph Snowden." *Western Pennsylvania Historical Magazine* 54 (April 1971): 158–166.

O'Brien, Kevin E. "'Give Them Another Volley, Boys': Biddle's Brigade Defends the Union Left on July 1, 1863.," *Gettysburg Magazine*, no. 19: 22–32.

Phillis, William. "John Williams Patterson, 102nd Pennsylvania Infantry Wilderness Victim." *Blue and Gray Magazine* (October 1999): pp. 40–1.

_____. "The Death of Colonel John Williams Patterson in the Wilderness." Submitted to *Friends of the Wilderness Newsletter*.

Staudt, Alfred D. "Diary of Alfred D. Staudt." *Historical Review of Berks County* 41, no. 1 (Winter 1975–6): 14–6, 32–3.
Sword, Wiley. "Capt. James Glenn's Sword and Pvt. J. Marshall Hill's Enfield in the Fight for the Lutheran Seminary." *Gettysburg Magazine*, no. 8 (January 1993): 9–15.

Newspapers

Army and Navy Journal, MHI.
Army and Navy Official Gazette, MHI.
Chippewa Herald, Chippewa Falls, WI.
The Daily Times, Stroudsburg, PA.
Meadville Evening Republican, CCHS.
Mercer Dispatch and Republican, Mercer County High School.
Milwaukee Sunday Telegraph, SHSW.
New York Times, Gettysburg College.
Philadelphia Inquirer, Gettysburg College.
Pittsburgh Commercial, Carnegie Library.
Pittsburgh Gazette, Carnegie Library.

Maps and Illustrations

1858 Map of Adams County, Adams County Historical Society, Drawn from Actual Survey by G. M. Hopkins, Traced by J. R. Hershey May 5, 1980.
Gallon, Dale. *Men of Iron*, Released summer 1994.
Warren, G. K. and J. B. Bachelder. "First Days Battle." *Maps of the Battle Field of Gettysburg*. New York: Endicott, 1876, Morningside reprint.

Index

Abercrombie, John J. 23; brigade 23, 27, 29, 31, 32; division 123
Acheson, William 17, 156
Alexander, E. Porter 28
Alexandria, MD 16, 34, 49
Allegheny Cemetery 173
Allegheny City, PA 4–5,
Allegheny County 1, 5, 9, 156–157, 160, 175, 186, 191
Allen, Harrison 49, 52, 54
Anderson, Richard 180; brigade 31; corps 181
Annapolis, MD 7
Antietam, battle of 35–39, 48
Antietam Creek 36–38
Archer's brigade 71, 76
Army and Navy Journal 106, 108, 152, 180
Army of Northern Virginia 26, 30, 34–35, 40, 53, 58–59, 61, 63–64, 83, 145
Army of the Potomac 9, 11, 15–16, 27, 32–33, 35, 37, 41, 43, 48, 51, 59–61, 63, 97–99, 103, 107–108, 111, 120, 123, 126, 140–143, 147–150, 152–153, 155, 175–176, 182
Army of the Shenandoah 164–165
Army of Virginia 33–35
Articles of War 95–96, 102, 110, 113, 134, 136, 199
Augusta, Georgia 203
Averell, William 157–159, 161, 164; division 158

Ballier, John F. 11
Baltimore, MD 61, 63
Baltimore Pike 72, 81
Baltimore Street, xi 72, 87–90, 92, 134
Banks, Nathaniel P. 150
Banks Ford 43
Barnesville, MD 36
Bartlett, Joseph J. 113, 115, 126

Baxter, Henry: brigade 74 81, 180
Bealeton Station, VA 59–60
Beauregard, P. G. T. 7, 9, 143–145
Belle Plain, VA 42, 47, 49, 52–53
Benedict, George 97
Berry, Hiram 104, 117
Biddle, Alexander 48, 53, 63, 65, 78–79, 85, 99, 112, 188, 190
Biddle, Chapman 48, 57, 63, 68, 71, 74–75, 78–80, 84–85, 87, 92, 96–97, 99–100, 112, 129, 186–187, 190; brigade xi, 87, 188
Biggs, H. S. 16; brigade 16
Birney, David B. 16, 140, 175, 177–178; division 122–123, 138, 174, 176
Boonsborough, MD 35–36
Bottom's Bridge 21–22
Bowling Green Road 42–43
Breck, George 74, 78, 87
Breckinridge, John C. 153, 163; division 143
Breck's battery 78–9, 83–84, 186, 188
Broad Run 60–62, 206
Broad Street 206–209
Brock Road 138, 140, 174–178, 181
Brockenbrough, J.M. 77–78; brigade 76, 80–81
Brooks, William 61, 152
Brown, Joseph 14, 85
Brownsville, MD 36
Buell, Don Carlos 10–11, 106, 160; division 11
Buford, John 68–69, 73, 83; division 64
Bull Frog Road 69
Bull Run, first battle of 10–1
Bull Run, second battle of 33, 48
Burnside, Ambrose E. 7, 37, 40–41, 64–65, 144–146; corps 37, 144
Butler, Benjamin 142–143

Cadwalader, George 48, 161–162, 167
Cameron, Simon 9, 14, 159, 161
Camp Berry 103–105, 107–108, 156, 185
Camp Curtin 6, 9, 48, 112, 137, 167
Camp Hamilton 19
Camp Spraque 9–10
Camp Tennallytown 10–11, 15
Cantonment Rowley 11, 14
Carlisle Road 88
Carr, Joseph B. 117
Casey, Silas 15, 19, 22, 26; division 20, 22–23
Cashtown, Pa. 64–65, 67
Cemetery Hill, xi, xii 72–73, 76, 85–87, 90, 92–94, 96, 98–99, 116, 118, 123, 125, 127–129, 131, 133–135, 138, 173–174, 199
Cemetery Ridge 176
Centreville, VA 60–61
Chain Bridge 10–11, 14–15, 34, 155
Chamberlin, Joshua 140, 146, 151, 184
Chamberlin, Thomas 53, 60; brigade 144
Chambersburg, PA 6, 40, 61, 63, 65, 150, 153–154, 156, 158–159, 161–163, 165, 182,
Chambersburg Pike 67, 71–73, 76, 78, 81, 83, 86–88, 92, 190
Chambersburg Street 88
Chancellorsville, battle of 25, 46, 51, 53, 56, 73, 100, 104, 117, 120, 181
Charles City Road 27
Charleston Mercury 205–206
Charleston, SC 166, 204–210
Charlestown, VA 9
Chesapeake Bay 16
Chickahominy River 21–22, 26
City Point, VA 143, 149–150, 155, 164
Coddington, Edwin B. 98, 186–187, 191
Cold Harbor, battle of 140, 142–143, 173, 176, 179
Cooper, J.H. 74, 87; battery 69, 71, 188
Cornwell, Henry A. 51
Couch, Darius N. 13–14, 19, 21–23, 26, 28–31, 33–34, 36–37, 39, 150, 152–156, 158–163, 165, 167, 185; brigade 10; division 15–16, 18–20, 23, 27, 31–32, 35, 37–39, 120
Crampton's Gap 36, 63
Crawford, Samuel W. 148, 151
Crook, George 157
Culpeper, VA, xii 16, 33, 35, 49, 59, 86, 96, 106, 108, 110–112, 119, 127, 130, 135–136, 166, 191–192, 201
Culp's Hill, xii 93–95, 174
Cummins, Robert P. 48, 63, 80, 87
Curtin, A. J. 153–154, 163–164, 201
Cutler, Lysander 42, 45–46, 64, 68, 89–91, 94, 99–100, 107, 111, 116, 118, 126, 128–130, 151, 181–183, 190; brigade 72, 74, 81, 88, 92, 94, 173, 188; division 121, 140, 145, 151, 173

Dahlgren, J.A. 209
Dain, Thomas 154
Dalgliesh, W. M. 92, 133, 184
Dana, Charles 143, 149, 176
Dana, Edmund L. 47, 49, 54, 56–57, 63, 92, 96, 98–100, 107, 110, 112, 114–115, 119, 126, 129–136, 165–167, 183, 192, 201–202, 204–210
Danville, VA 203
Davis, Jefferson 19, 26, 58
Dawes, Rufus R., xii 64, 71, 83, 93–95, 116, 130, 173–174, 190
Denniston, J.F. 104–106, 168
Department of Monongahela 61, 152
Department of Pennsylvania 6, 167
Department of the Susquehanna 150, 152–153, 165, 167, 185
Department of Virginia 16
De Trobriand, Regis 10, 20, 22, 121, 151, 178
Devins, Charles 21, 26; brigade 23, 67
District of Monongahela 154, 156, 165, 168
Doubleday, Abner, xii 6–7, 34, 46–47, 49, 51, 53, 55–57, 60–68, 72–74, 76, 78, 80, 85–86, 92–103, 105–106, 111, 116, 120–121, 128, 130, 134, 136, 156, 165, 184, 187–188, 190–192, 199; corps xi, 64, 76, 85–87, 90, 93–94, 96, 118, 120, 129; division 47, 52, 54, 60–61, 67–69, 71, 82, 97–98, 100, 123, 129–130, 136, 146, 151, 169–170
Dougherty, James 190, 191
Duff, Thomas 12

Early, Jubal 143, 152–157, 159–160, 163–166, 181–182; division 64, 143, 153, 164
Edward's Ferry 63, 66
Emmitsburg, MD 64, 67
Emmitsburg Road (Gettysburg Pike) 64–65, 68, 73, 97
Eustis, Henry L. 35, 37, 41, 108, 113, 120, 126, 166, 175–176; brigade 175
Ewell, Richard S. 34, 58, 63, 76, 96, 181; corps xi, 59–61, 65, 73–74, 81, 93, 143

Fair Oaks, battle of 21–26, 41–42, 122–123, 171, 193
Fair Oaks Station 22–23
Fairfax, VA 61
Fairfield, PA 67
Fairfield Road, xi 65, 69, 72, 75, 78, 81, 83, 85, 87–88

Falmouth, VA 42, 55–56
Finnicum, Mark 92–93, 127, 134, 183, 191, 200
Flagg, Charles H. 51, 62, 69, 98, 113
Fort Magruder 20–21
Fort Monroe 16, 34
Fort Stevens 155–156
Fortress Monroe 210
Foster, John G. 205–209
Fox's Gap 36
Franklin, William B. 36–37, 39, 41–42, 64; corps 26, 35–36, 39
Frazier's Farm 28
Frederick, MD 35, 48, 63
Fredericksburg, VA: 42–43 48, 53, 55–56, 58–59, 102, 154–155; battle of 49, 90, 120

Gamble, William 85, 87; brigade 67, 76, 81, 83, 85
Garland, Samuel 23; brigade 22
Gates, Theodore B. 65, 66, 72, 85, 87, 96, 99, 187, 190
Gearhart, Edwin 79–80
General court–martial 110–111, 113
Georgetown, MD 11, 15–16
Getty, George W. 138, 175, 178, 181; division 120, 155–156, 176, 178
Gettysburg 60 62, 64–66, 68–69, 72–73, 76, 78, 86–88, 90, 96–97, 99, 101–102, 110, 118, 132, 156, 166, 173, 176, 190–191, 193, 206; battle of xi, xii, 100, 103, 105, 112, 116, 119–120, 123, 128, 130–131, 134, 186
Gibbon, John 106, 118, 125; division 121, 125
Gilmor, Harry 158–159, 164
Glendale, VA 27–29
Glenn, James 56, 75, 131–132, 184, 192
Glenn, John 65, 72, 86–87
Gordonsville, VA 202
Grant, Ulysses S. 10, 20, 106, 110, 119, 123, 137, 141–142, 144–145, 147–150, 152, 157, 161, 164–165, 167, 170, 174–176, 178, 180–181, 183–184, 208
Great Falls 11, 14
Griffin, Charles 151, 184; brigade 29, 32; division 140
Grover, Ira G. 202
Grover, J. 94

Hagerstown, MD 35, 39, 61, 63, 154–158, 163–164
Hagerstown Road 69
Halleck, Henry 33–34, 61, 73, 157, 161, 164, 167, 180, 206, 208

Hamilton's Crossing 42
Hampton, VA 17
Hancock, Winfield Scott, xii 73, 93, 96, 101, 117, 123, 128, 142, 144–145, 174–175, 178; corps 98, 123, 125, 138, 143, 174–175
Harmon house/farm 69, 72, 74, 79, 96
Harney, George 94, 118, 126, 132, 191
Harper, Albert M. 164–165, 167–168
Harpers Ferry 6–7, 9, 35, 36–37, 39, 59, 120, 157, 165
Harrisburg, PA 6, 9, 11, 48, 65, 99, 112–113, 137, 138, 140, 154, 156, 159–163, 165–166–167
Harrison's Landing 27, 30, 32–34
Haxall's Landing 27–28, 30
Hays, Alexander 19, 97, 113–115, 119, 122–126, 135, 150, 166, 173, 175–177, 193; brigade 140; division 125
Heberton, George A. 46, 69, 104–106, 110, 155, 164, 167
Heffley, Albert 51–53
Heintzelman, Samuel P. 19, 22, 31, 106; corps 19, 26, 34, 121–122
Herbst woodlot/woods 74, 76
Herdegen, Lance 187, 190–191, 193
Herr's Ridge 69, 71, 74, 78, 81
Heth, Henry, xi 76, 138; division 67, 71, 81–82, 174
High Street, xi 88–90, 134
Hill, Ambrose P. 28, 36–37, 48–49, 58, 76, 81, 138, 173; corps xi, 59, 64–65, 67, 174
Hill, D. H. 31, 36; division 22, 31, 36–37
Hilton Head 206, 209–210
Holt, Joseph 136, 140
Hooker, Joseph 21, 26, 28, 34, 37, 43, 46, 51, 54, 59–61, 63, 117–118; corps 36; division 20, 22; Grand Division 43
Hoon, Edward 15, 35
Howard, Oliver O. 54, 64, 72–73, 76, 80, 85–86, 93, 96, 98, 101, 128; corps xi, 54–55, 63, 73, 76, 87, 96, 125
Howe, Albion 26, 31–32, 41, 154–155; brigade 26–27, 29–35; division 43
Huger, Benjamin 30; division 26
Humphrey, W. T. 67–68, 131–132, 184, 192
Humphreys, Andrew A. 144
Hunter, David 153, 155, 157–159, 164–165

Illinois cavalry regiments: 8th 69
Indiana infantry regiments: 7th 94; 19th, 80, 173
Iron Brigade *see* Meredith, Solomon, brigade

Jackson, Thomas J. 7, 14, 30, 33–36, 42–43, 58, 73, 157

Jackson Independent Blues 1–3
James City Road 27
James River 19, 28–29, 32–33, 142–146, 176
Jerusalem Plank Road 144–146
Johnson, Bradley T. 157–158; brigade 157, 159
Johnston, Joseph E. 7, 9, 15, 19–20, 22, 26, 170
Jones, George W. 132–133, 163, 184
Jones, Samuel 204–208
Judge advocate 111–116, 118, 126, 129, 131–133, 135

Kearny, Philip 20, 28, 34, 122; division 22, 31, 121–122
Kenly, John R. 98–99 104, 107, 121; division 99, 107
Kershaw, Joseph: division 145–146
Keyes, E. D. 11, 19–23, 26–27, 28, 30, 106; corps 15, 26, 120; division 15
Kinkead, Joseph M. 6, 9, 23, 25–26, 41, 43, 46, 56
Kirk, D. 26

Large, John 12, 17, 19, 21, 39, 44
Lee, Robert E., xi 26–29, 32–35, 39, 43, 52, 54, 58, 61, 63, 65, 73, 76, 78, 96, 138, 143–146, 153, 157, 174–175, 178, 181
Lee's Mill Road 19
Lee's Order 191 35–36
Leesburg, VA 61
Libby Prison 56
Licksville, MD 36
Lincoln, Abraham, xii 3–5, 10–11, 15, 22, 33–34, 39, 41, 45, 47, 51, 61, 63, 73, 103, 106, 114, 117–118, 136, 141, 153, 156–157, 159, 164–165, 167, 186, 206
Longstreet, James 20–21, 28, 34, 58, 65, 177–178, 180; corps 28, 43, 59, 64–65, 98, 145; division 28
Lutheran Theological Seminary 67, 69–71
Lynchburg, VA 202

Macon, GA 203–204, 209
Madaus, Howard 185
Magruder, John B. 19–20, 27, 30, 32
Malvern Hill 25, 27–33, 41, 56, 191; battle of 121, 123
Manassas, VA 7, 9, 15, 19–20, 34, 60
Marsh Creek 67, 69
Martin, Joseph B. 16, 21
Martinsburg, VA 7, 157
Maryland Heights 36–37
Massachusetts infantry regiments: 10th 35
McCalmont, A. B. 47, 49, 51, 53, 57, 62, 78–80, 87, 92, 99–100, 104, 111–113, 115, 133, 134, 137–138, 167, 183, 188, 190–192
McCarter, James M. 10, 21, 41–42
McCausland, John 157–159, 163–164; brigade 157–158, 161
McClellan, George B. 10–1, 14, 16, 20, 22, 26–29, 32–37, 39, 41, 65, 106, 117, 120, 160
McCoy, De Witt C. 111–115, 118, 126–131, 133, 135, 182
McDowell, Irvin 7, 9, 106
McFarland, George F. 45, 49, 51–55, 58, 61, 63–64, 69, 74–75, 80, 87, 99, 123, 140, 169–170, 190
McLaughlin, Thomas A. 26
McLean, Hancock T. 158
McPherson Farm 72–73, 92, 201
McPherson Ridge 69, 71, 74, 77, 83, 186–188
Meade, George G. 34, 48, 63, 65, 68, 73, 93, 97–98, 104, 106–108, 110–111, 114, 117, 123, 127, 136–137, 140–149, 151, 173–176, 178, 182, 184, 188; division 43
Mechanicsville, VA 30
Meredith, Solomon 64, 68, 74, 84, 93, 106; brigade xi, xii, 34, 65, 71–73, 78, 86–87, 93–94, 188
Meridian Hill 9, 11
Merrimack 17, 19
Michigan infantry regiments: 24th 53
Middle Creek 65
Middle Military Division 164–165, 180
Middle Railroad 71–72
Middle Ridge 71–74, 78–80, 83, 86, 188
Middle Street 88
Middletown, MD 63
Miller, J. Michael 187, 190
Miller, Thomas W. 90, 94, 118–119, 126, 183, 190
Miles, Dixon S. 6–7
Milroy, Robert 61
Monitor 17
Moore, Oliver K. 69, 88, 96, 103, 105, 113, 115, 130, 133–135, 137–138, 192
Moorhead, J. K. 11, 33, 41, 61–62, 138, 140, 156, 166–167
Morell's division 29, 30, 32
Moritz's Tavern 65, 68, 97
Morris, William H. 46, 100–101, 113, 121, 126, 166, 181
Morris Island 204, 206, 208
Morrison, M. P. 23–24, 171; brigade 181
Mott, Gershom: division 175 177
Mount St. Mary's College 64
Myers, Samuel 12

Negley, James S. 4
Neill, Thomas H. 16, 18, 21, 25, 35, 41–43, 45–46, 100, 113, 120, 126, 150, 166, 178, 179, 180–181; brigade 181
New Jersey infantry regiments: 6th 10
New Market Road 27
New York engineering: 50th 27
New York heavy artillery: 1st 74
New York infantry regiments: (14th Brooklyn; 84th) 53 71; (20th Militia; 80th) 66, 69, 72, 78–79, 87, 98–99; (23rd) 16; (55th) 10, 21–22; (62nd) 10–11, 14, 21, 35, 43; (95th) 71; (97th) 74; (147th) 94, 116, 118–119, 126, 132
New York Times 152, 163, 169, 173
Newport News, VA 19
Newton, John 39–42, 97–99, 101–102, 107, 117, 120, 142; corps 97, 100, 107; division 42
Nine Mile Road 23
North Carolina infantry regiments: (11th) 78–80; (26th) 78 80; (47th) 78–80; (52nd) 78, 79

Oak Grove, battle of 26
Oak Hill 72, 74, 78, 188
Oak Ridge 72–74, 76, 87–88
O'Brien, Kevin 187–188, 193
Offut's Crossroads 34–35
Old Mine Road 55
Orange and Alexandria Railroad 60, 202
Orange Plank Road 138, 140, 174–178, 181–182, 201
Osborne, Seward 187

Palmer, Innis N. 26; brigade 26, 29–32
Patterson, Almira 25, 41, 45, 56
Patterson, John W. 6, 8–9, 19–21, 25, 36, 39–41, 43, 45, 56, 108, 138–140
Patterson, Robert A. 6–7, 9
Paul, Gabriel 64, 106; brigade 74–75, 80, 86
Peck, John J. 9–10, 14–15, 21, 23, 25–26, 32, 101, 121; brigade 10–11, 15–17, 23, 25; division 27, 30
Pegram, William 81
Pender, Dorsey, xi; division 81–82
Peninsula Campaign 16, 29, 41, 101, 103, 117
Pennsylvania infantry regiments: (1st Volunteers) 1–2 47; (13th) 6–7, 10, 12–13, 44, 172; (11th) 74; (21st) 11, 88; (23rd) 21, 23, 25, 35, 120; (61st) 23; (63rd) 19, 122–123, 140, 175; (72nd) 176; (83rd) 111, 182; (93rd) 10, 21, 23, 35, 41, 43; (98th) 11, 21, 43; (102nd) 9–12, 14–15, 19–28, 31–36, 39–43, 45–46, 56, 100, 108, 138, 154–156,
171–172; (121st) 46, 48, 51, 57, 63, 65, 68–69, 78–79, 83, 85, 87, 96–99, 112, 186, 190; (135th) 46, 56, 188; (139th) 35, 43; (142nd) 46–48, 51, 60, 69, 78–80, 83, 87–88, 98–99, 108, 112–113, 115, 131, 134, 138, 183, 190; (143rd) 47, 49, 52, 54, 72, 92, 133–135, 166, 184, 201, 206; (149th) 52, 56, 65, 131–133; (150th) 48, 52, 72, 78, 132, 184; (151st) 46, 49, 51–52, 54, 63, 68–69, 74, 80, 83, 87, 96, 98–99, 123, 190; (208th) 167, 183
Pennsylvania Reserves 11, 15, 28, 46, 48–49
The Pennsylvania Thirteenth 7, 11
Perrin, Abner 83–84, 86–87; brigade 81, 83
Petersburg, VA 141–147, 151, 165–166, 182–183; battle of 142, 173
Pettigrew, James J. 77–78, 83, 190; brigade 67, 76, 78, 81
Philadelphia Inquirer 162, 181
Philadelphia, PA 1, 6, 9, 65, 154, 161–162, 165, 167
Pittsburgh Chronicle 2
Pittsburgh Commercial 147–148, 161, 164
Pittsburgh Gazette 153, 155, 161–162, 172–173, 194
Pittsburgh, PA 1, 4, 7, 9–10, 44–45, 47, 61, 99, 108–109, 122, 139, 152, 154–158, 160–163, 165–167, 169–173, 184
Pollock's Mill 55
Poolesville, MD 35
Pope, John 33–35
Port Royal, VA 52–53
Porter, Fitz–John 27–28, 30, 65, 101, 116
Porter, James R. 46–47; corps 26, 34, 123
Portland, Maine 103, 105, 108
Potomac River 7, 11, 16, 35, 37, 39–40, 61, 63, 153, 155–157
Powell, Frank M. 84, 88, 92, 131, 184, 192

Quaker Road 27–29, 31

Ramseur, Stephen 157
Rapidan River 34, 54, 106, 136, 138, 201
Rappahannock River 34, 42–43, 49, 52–56, 59–60, 64–65
Reilay, Charles W. 134, 184, 192
Reno, Jessie: corps 36
Revere, Joseph 117, 141
Reynolds, John F. 34, 46–48, 51–58, 60–61, 63–65, 67–69, 72–73, 76, 86, 97, 126, 129, 134, 188, 199, 201; corps 42, 48, 53, 60, 66, 121, 123
Rhode Island infantry regiments: 2nd 120
Rice, James C. 107–108, 115, 121–122, 126, 133, 135, 150, 166, 175, 181; brigade 181

Richmond, VA 6, 19, 21–22, 33, 86, 143, 153, 157
Ricketts, James: division 181
River Road 28, 30
River Road Bridge 30
Robinson, John C. 74–75, 90, 107, 113–115, 119, 121, 126–127, 130, 133, 135, 166, 173, 180–181
Robinson, William W. 74, 92–95, 116, 118, 127, 134, 183, 190, 199; brigade 122; division xi, 54–55, 64, 67–68, 74, 86, 88, 125, 180, 188
Rodes, Robert: brigade 23 31; division xi, 78, 81, 87
Rogers, Clayton E., xii 89, 93–95, 102, 116, 130, 173–174, 190
Rogers, Earl M. 183
Rhode Island infantry regiments: 2nd 16, 21, 25, 28, 35
Rohrersville, MD 36–37
Rowley, Henry (Harry) T. 9, 14, 31, 46
Rowley, Mary Ann 3
Rowley, Thomas A.: 13th PA Regt. 6–7 9–11; 102nd PA Regt. 12, 14–15; Antietam 35–39; Camp Berry 103–107; Chancellorsville 52–58; Civilian Life 169–173; Culpeper court martial 108–136; District of the Monogahela 152–164; First Corps Brigadier 45–51; Fredericksburg 42–44; Gettysburg xi–xii, 59–102; Mexican War 2–3; Peninsula Campaign 19–27, 29; Pittsburgh 1, 14; place in history 186–194 reaction to verdict 137–141; resignation 165–168; return to the Army of the Potomac 141–151

St. Francis Xavier Church 84, 88, 90
Savage's Station 23, 25–27
Savannah, GA 204–205
Scales, A. M.: brigade 81 84
Schurz, Carl 73
Scott, Winfield 2–3, 7, 11, 122
Sedgwick, John 56, 105, 142, 181; corps 56, 65, 110, 120, 138, 181
Seminary Ridge 71–72, 74, 76, 78–81, 85, 87, 118, 126, 131, 187–188, 191
Seven Days Campaign 26, 30, 32, 103, 122
Seven Pines, VA 26–27, 41, 56, 191; battle of 21–22, 25–26, 121
Seymour, Truman 202, 204
Shaler, Alexander 202
Sharpsburg, MD 36, 61
Shenandoah Valley 7, 59–60, 143, 152–153, 157, 164, 182
Sheridan, Phillip 151, 164, 165, 180

Sherwin, Gerald P. 192
Shooter, Washington 83–86
Shue, Richard 190–191
Sickles, Daniel E. 64, 73, 96, 106, 126, 209; corps 64, 73, 117
Sigel, Franz 153
Sisters of Charity 64
Slagle, Jacob F. 69, 71, 87, 90, 97, 188
Slocum, Henry W. 36, 73, 76, 81, 93, 95–96; corps 76; division 36, 37
Smith, William F. 15, 19, 41–42, 143–144, 147; corps 143; division 19, 36–37
Snowden, George 138
South Carolina infantry regiments: (1st) 83 85–87; (3rd) 89; (12th) 83, 85; (13th) 81, 83, 85; (14th) 83–85, 87
South Mountain 35–36, 48, 63, 81
Spotsylvania, VA 180–181; battle of 173–176, 178–179, 182
Stannard, George J. 97; brigade 99, 123
Stanton, Edward M., xii 14, 41, 45–47, 62, 73, 105, 127, 136, 141, 149, 152, 155, 161, 163, 165, 167–168, 175–176, 178, 180, 182, 186, 206
State of Maine 16
Stewart, A. M. 12
Stone, Roy 45–46, 52, 56, 62, 68, 71–72, 78, 84, 92, 99, 107, 112, 114, 133, 140; brigade xi, 47, 52, 55, 65, 78, 92, 107, 118, 140, 146, 151, 188, 190–191, 201
Stoneman, George 20
Stout, Charles B. 133, 184
Stuart, James E. B. 7, 39–40; cavalry 37, 59
Sumner, Edwin "Bull," 20–1 28, 31, 39; corps 22–23, 26; Grand Division 43
Sykes, George: division 27

Taneytown, MD 64, 68, 73
Tennallytown, MD 10–11, 15, 34
Theophilus Holmes 28
Thomas, Lorenzo 45, 56
Turkey Bridge 27
Turkey Run 28–30
Turner's Gap 36, 63
Two Taverns 73, 76

Ulster Guard, see 20th NYS Militia
unfinished railroad 71
Uniontown, PA 163–165
United States Ford 54–55

Vera Cruz, Mexico 2–3

Wadsworth, Craig W. 86, 88, 126–127, 182, 191

Wadsworth, James S, xii 46, 64, 68, 72, 76, 80, 86, 90, 93–94, 106, 111, 118, 126, 150, 175, 180, 182, 188–189, 201; division xi, 53–54, 56, 64–68, 71, 94, 107, 121, 130, 136, 140, 173, 181, 201
Wainwright, Charles S. 20, 71, 74, 79–80, 85, 87, 90, 186, 188
Wallace, Lew 155, 158
War Department 1, 6, 45, 47, 100, 103, 108, 116, 123, 138, 140–141, 152, 154, 167, 173, 180–181, 183
Ward, John H. H. 113–115, 121–122, 126, 166, 176–179; brigade 151, 177
Warren, G. K. 110, 112, 125, 140–142, 144–149, 166–167, 183, 185; corps 107, 121, 136, 138, 140–142, 144, 151, 174, 180, 201
Warren, Horatio N. 49, 79–80, 84, 100, 112, 131, 183–184, 192
Warwick Court House 19–20
Warwick, River 19
Washington DC: 7 10, 25, 33, 35–36, 38, 40, 42, 46, 60–61, 63, 98, 103, 106, 110, 117, 123, 127, 143, 149–150, 153–154, 157, 159, 164, 166, 176, 182
Washington Infantry 3–4, 6, 108–109, 170, 172
Webb, Alexander S. 108, 113, 123, 125–126, 175–177; brigade 175
Weld, Stephen M. 62, 95
Welsh, Spencer G. 81, 84
Western Run 29, 30, 31
Wheaton, Frank 16–17, 25, 28, 30, 35, 37, 41–43, 45–46, 56, 100, 113, 120, 126,

140, 155–156, 166, 174–175, 181–182; brigade 138, 155–156, 175, 181
White House Landing 26
White Oak Bridge 27
White Oak Church 60–61
White Oak Swamp 25–27, 28
Wilcox, Cadmus: brigade 20
Wilderness, battle of 136, 138–140, 142, 166, 173–176, 180–182, 184, 201
Williams, Seth 110, 112, 149–150
Williamsburg, VA 20, 41, 191; battle of 20, 22, 121–122
Williamsburg Stage Road 21–23
Williamsport, MD 7, 39–40, 61, 157
Willoughby Run 69, 71, 78, 82–83
Wilson, Henry 45–46, 115; Committee on Military Affairs 45, 47
Wilson, William L. T. 57, 59, 69, 88, 99, 105, 113, 133–135, 137, 166, 192
Winchester, VA 7, 61, 153, 157, 182
Wisconsin infantry regiments: (6th) xii; 42 90, 92–95, 171, 173–174; (7th) 74, 90, 92–93, 116, 118, 127, 134, 140, 173, 183, 199
Wister, Langhorne 48, 72, 78, 92, 201
Wool, John 16
Wright, Horatio 155, 157; corps 144, 155, 182

York, PA 6, 64
Yorktown, VA 19–20, 34

Zorn, Jacob J. 60, 88, 107–108, 110, 112, 115